Ballymoney Heroes
1914 - 1918

With Best Wishes

Robert Thompson

Compiled and Edited
by
ROBERT THOMPSON

Published by
Robert Thompson
9 Riverside Road, Bushmills,
Co. Antrim, N. Ireland, BT57 8TP

Telephone: 028 2073 2875

November 1999

Compiled and edited by
Robert Thompson

ISBN 0-9537583-0-3

Printed by
Coleraine Printing Company
117 Ballycastle Road, Coleraine, BT52 2DZ
Telephone 028 7035 4873 / 028 7035 8412

There are a number of people who need to be thanked for their help at various stages.

BALLYMONEY BOROUGH COUNCIL,
For staging two seperate exhibitions in the Heritage Centre in Ballymoney
in an attempt to put together as full a list of names as possible, and to encourage people
to come forward with a name if it was missing.

SAMUEL McLEAN,
Samuel McLean came originally from Finvoy, and had studied the soldiers
from that district who had died in the 1914-18 war.
When he discovered what I was trying to do he gave me all the information he had on them, including
photographs of some of them and of their graves in France and Belgium.
Not only that, when he was going on holiday to France and Belgium, he asked for my list of names and
returned with a vast collection of photographs of their graves or of their names on memorials.
This has made a vast difference to the book and is very much appreciated.

FERNAND VANROBAEYS
Fernand works in the Tourist Office in Ypres in Belgium and took a number of photographs for me of
graves in the Ypres district which it would otherwise have been almost impossible to have obtained.
Not content with the quality of the prints from the first attempt, he did
all of them again and it is dedication like this that means so much.

THE FAMILIES CONCERNED
Over the last two years I have sought out and visited many of the families from the Ballymoney district.
On each and every occasion I asked if there was a photograph available and when there was, it was
handed to me without a question being asked and I was allowed to copy it.
They have also helped with all the information they could give and this has been much appreciated.

JENNIFER BAMFORD
Jennifer Bamford has helped with details of the two Biggart boys and not only that, she found
an old hand written list of the names of Rasharkin men who had served in the 1914-18 war
with those who had been killed marked with a star. This was very useful and meant that as far as is
known all of the Rasharkin names are included.

ROBERT CONNOLLY
Robert is also from Rasharkin and has been a great help in tracing the Rasharkin families and finding
photographs for me and his help with this has been very much appreciated.

DENNIS CONNOLLY
Dennis has been a very close friend for many years and allowed me to use the photograph of the old gun
which was presented to Balnamore village after the end of the 1914-18 war as a memento of the village's
distinction of having the second highest number of casualties of any village of comparable size in Great
Britain. The gun was eventually broken up for scrap for the war effort of 1939-45.

SEAMUS McFERRAN
Saemus lives in Dunloy and was the means of identifying Michael Doherty. He also introduced me to a
Director of the Commonwealth War Graves Commission who was born near Dunloy, and who has since
been a very useful source of much information. I am very grateful to Saemus for his very thoughtful
action and appreciate this move deeply.

SAMUEL McCONAGHIE
Alderman Samuel McConaghie, of Ballymoney Borough Council, has on two seperate occasions
when he was sent on trips to Gallipoli, brought me back photographs of the graves of
Ballymoney boys who were killed in Gallipoli.
This has been a very big help to me and was the only way I was going to get pictures of them.
He is probably the only visitor from Ballymoney that these graves have ever seen.

Contents

Name	Page	Name	Page	Name	Page
James Adams	210	James Clarke	86	Hugh Hamill	181
Henry Adams	225	William Clements	221	John Hamilton	90
Charles Allen	15	Robert Coils	43	James Hanna	386
Joseph Allen	320	Robert Coleman	87	John Hanna	194
Samuel Anderson	202	Robert Colvin	119	William Hanna	364
Wm John Anderson	239	Thomas Conaghy	182	James Harte	374
John Armour	380	Arthur Corbett	18	Robert Hart	372
William Baird	349	John Craig	334	John Henry	50
Daniel Baird	55	Daniel Craig	122	Frank Heggarty	156
Samuel Balmer	315	Samuel Craig	271	Alex Hill	244
F.J. Bankhead	158	Thomas Craig	290	Daniel Hill	257
John Bellingham	19	Arthur Cramsie	33	S. Holmes	157
John Bellingham	41	Hugh Crawford	308	Alex Huey	245
William Beckett	34	Joseph Crenan	213	James Huey	57
John Biggart	240	John Culbertson	16	Wm W Huey	333
William Biggart	306	Peter Dallett	38	Samuel Jamison	121
Thomas Black	270	John Deane	139	J.W.C. Jack	175
Alex Blair	353	Joseph Dean	22	David Johnston	81
Herbert Blackmore	325	Isaac Dempsey	331	William J. Johnston	391
William Blackmore	83	Joseph Dempsey	178	Hugh Jordan	252
James A. Bleakley	185	John Devine	216	Thomas Kane	305
Samuel Boreland	321	John Dillon	79	Peter Kane	191
James Boorman	68	James Dickson	228	Samuel Kane	46
James Boyd	123	Thomas Dixon	356	Matthew Keers	82
Andrew Boyle	329	George Doherty	116	Archie Kennedy	265
James Boyle	363	Hugh Doherty	337	Frank Kennedy	91
William Bradshaw	168	Thomas Docherty	358	Samuel Kerr	269
Herbert Brangam	316	James Dougherty	52	George Killough	370
John Brangam	304	Arthur Donnelly	11	Les Kirkpatrick	360
Henry Brolly	285	Thomas Donnelly	74	Andrew Kinnaird	267
Wm J. Brolly	35	Charles Ellison	338	John Kirgan	54
Samuel Brolly	56	James Fenton	88	Alex Kirkpatrick	93
Samuel Buick	256	David Ferris	186	James Kyle	348
John Burns	84	Archie Forbes	124	John Laverty	273
Alex Cairns	242	Neil Forbes	40	James Laverty	390
John Caldwell	214	Samuel Fulton	89	Wm Laverty	94
Bryce Campbell	283	John Gamble	160	David Linton	95
Daniel Campbell	343	James Gaston	378	Thomas Logan	200
Edward Campbell	229	Thomas Gault	207	Samuel Logan	58
James J. Campbell	330	David Getty	389	Wm Logan	73
Robert Campbell	206	Alex Gibson	300	Wm Logue	144
Robert Campbell	140	Bryce Gilmour	65	James Lynn	149
Robert Campbell	117	John Gillen	170	Thomas Lynn	30
Thos. Campbell	67	Patrick Glass	319	Andrew Madden	59
Wm. S. Campbell	304	James Gow	145	R.H.C. Magenis	10
Thomas Carson	223	George L. Graham	251	John Magill	28
John Carson	391	George Graham	341	Robert Marshall	280
Robert Carson	86	William Graham	295	Samuel Meeke	384
Hugh Carton	143	John P. Gray	359	Patrick Mooney	176
James Cassidy	231	Samuel Gray	371	J.H. Moore	51
Robert Casey	36	J.K.M. Greer	150	George Moore	282
Samuel Casey	43	Neason Hale	234	Robert Moore	32

Name	Page	Name	Page	Name	Page
William Moore	77	John McKay	392	Wm. Shields	262
Alex Morrow	64	Patrick McKee	274	Wm. Shirlow	12
Alex Murdock	159	Archie McKee	355	Alex Simpson	219
Archie Murphy	78	J. McKeeman	103	V.J. Simpson	129
Charles Murphy	24	John McKinney	347	Alfred Smyth	172
Hugh Murphy	165	Geo. McLean	344	William Smyth	326
James G. Murphy	132	Dan McLernon	324	William Speers	340
Johnston Murphy	107	Sam McMillan	227	H. Stewart-Moore	138
Robert Murphy	362	Dan McMullan	146	Robert Stewart	236
John Murphy	105	John McMullen	104	Charles Stuart	382
William Murphy	166	Jos. McMullen	218	James Stuart	177
Lewis McAfee	48	R.J. McMullan	379	William Stuart	276
James McAleese	296	Robert McNaul	53	Alfred Taggart	13
Wm McAllister	21	Wm. McNaul	352	John Taggart	381
John McArdle	317	L. McNeill	388	David Taylor	232
John McAuley	142	Sam McNeill	136	Samuel Taylor	111
Wm. McAuley	224	Geo. McNocher	208	Homer Teaz	293
Dan McArthur	23	Wm. McNulty	130	E.J. Thompson	120
Andrew McBride	313	Wm. McToal	137	Hugh Thompson	45
Frank McBride	80	Dan Nevin	291	Jas. Thompson	27
Wm. McBride	76	Charles Newell	75	Jas. Thompson	37
James McCann	246	Archie Nicholl	72	John Thompson	27
Geo. McCaughan	346	Patrick Olphert	118	R. Thompson	112
R. McCaughan	71	Robert O'Brien	189	Wm. Thompson	286
R. McCaughan	327	Wm. O'Brien	63	J.L. Thompson	376
Wm. McCaughern	254	P. O'Donnell	171	Wm. J Thompson	302
Alex McClean	173	Luke O'Neill	153	Thomas Turner	209
James McClean	390	G. Patterson	266	Robert Turner	263
David McClelland	96	Samuel Patterson	148	Wm. Twaddle	31
Sam McClelland	97	James Pattison	387	Wm. Wade	198
John McConnell	212	John Pattison	247	George Wales	279
Wm. McConachie	134	James Patton	108	Alex Walker	125
Wm. McCormick	318	Hugh Patton	248	John Wallace	184
Geo. McCormick	152	Samuel Patton	192	James Watson	113
Jas. McCoubrey	196	Robert Paull	238	Joe Watson	47
David McCracken	60	John Porteus	161	Edward Weir	366
James McCrellis	383	Walter Quin	328	William White	249
Wm. McCurdy	307	Robert Ramsey	127	Patrick Wilson	391
Sam McDowell	135	Wm. Ramsey	154	Thomas Wilson	114
James McErlean	301	John Rankin	183	William Wilson	350
Malcolm McFadden	98	Hugh Reid	298	John Wisner	369
Edward McFall	99	John Reid	109	Wm. Workman	289
Michael McFerran	311	Robert Reid	163	Wm. Wright	260
Andrew McGahey	255	Thos. Robinson	179	Sam Young	299
Thomas McGhee	119	Hugh Rock	203	Thomas Young	131
Wm McKendry	100	Thomas Ross	155	Wm. Young	287
R. McIlhagga	258	Robert Scott	126	Pat Cumming	167
R. McIlhatton	101	Robert Shannon	190	John Hayes	188
Alex McIlreavey	367	C.F. Shaw	365	John Boyd	193
Wm. McIlvenna	336	E.W. Shields	110	Joseph Docherty	25
John McIntyre	70	Robert Shields	231	Introduction	6
Daniel McKay	102	Samuel Shields	115		

Introduction

In 1995, while I was preparing the Bushmills book for publication, I decided that I needed to compare my list of names with those on the Ballymoney war memorial, just to see what duplication there was.

I was just simply astounded to discover that after all those years there was not one name on the Ballymoney war memorial. This had a devastating effect on me and I went home determined to try to do something about it. After the Bushmills book was published and I had time to relax a little, I made up my mind to tackle the Ballymoney job. I approached Ballymoney Borough Council and explained the situation to their then Chief Executive, Mr. Alderdice. His immediate reaction was "Try it, and see if it can be done". To date I have over 300 names and a promise that these will be placed on the war memorial.

Right from the beginning it was obvious that certain battles were going to play a very big part in the past life of Ballymoney. The Retreat from Mons and the first battle of Ypres in late 1914 saw the start of what was going to be an appaling loss of life in the Ballymoney area. The campaign in Gallipoli, in early 1915, though far from home, cost the town dearly. At the same time the battles were still raging around Ypres, and in September the battle of Loos. At Loos it was mostly men who had been working in Scotland who lost their lives, but they were still Ballymoney boys at heart. Then in 1916, the battle of the Somme. On the opening day of this battle, 1st July 1916, twenty-eight young men from the district were killed, with many more deaths to follow before the battle finished in November. In 1917 the battles of Messines Ridge and Passchendaele were even worse and then the German Offensive of March 1918 and the subsequent British advance to victory. But of course the killing didn't stop between these battles and a steady stream of telegrams arrived in Ballymoney, bringing even more distressing news, in many cases to families who had already lost one son. The loss of a second was devastating. To Mrs Huey of Ballycraigagh, who lost two sons of her own, and a neighbour's son she had reared from childhood, this must have been hard to take.

The list of awards won by Ballymoney boys is astounding. Among those killed there were five Military Cross winners, and twelve winners of the Military Medal. Many more among those who survived.

Of the friends who have helped me, one in particular, stands out. Samuel McLean, of Ballymena, and originally from Finvoy, had been studying the Finvoy men previously and willingly gave me all the information he had on them, including photographs of them and of their graves in France and Belgium. Then, in 1998, when he was planning a trip to France and Belgium, he asked me for a copy of my list of graves and memorials. He returned with a huge selection of photographs taken all over France and Belgium of the graves of Ballymoney boys. This has been a terrific help and adds a great deal of interest to the book.

Not content with this, he asked for my list again, when he was going back in April of 1999. Again he returned with a selection of photographs of those he had been unable to do on the previous trip.

During my research many interesting facts have emerged, but one which has a direct link with Ballymoney has come to light. One of the most decorated Chaplains of the First World War, Rev James Gilbert Paton, M.C. and two bars, had married Margaret Patterson, of 5. High Street, Ballymoney in 1st Ballymoney Presbyterian Church on 15th September 1908.

In November 1998 I was invited to accompany Alderman Harry Connolly and Alderman Samuel McConaghy, both of Ballymoney Borough Council, on a trip to France and Belgium to commemorate the 80th anniversary of the signing of the Armistice. We visited the Ulster Tower at Thiepval for a service of Remembrance and then went to the opening of the Peace Park at Messines in Belgium, to be present at the ceremony attended by the Queen. This was a most enjoyable experience and I was highly honoured to be asked to be present. We stayed in a first class hotel in Lille and the weather, which had been wet previous to the trip, dried up and we had perfect, summer weather with continuous sunshine all the time we were there.

There can hardly have been a family in Britain which was not touched in some way by the tragedy of the First World War. Great Britain, alone among the major European nations, went to war with an army based on voluntary enlistment, numbering just over 247,000 at the outset, with 486,000 Reserves and Territorials. By November 1918 a further 5,000,000 had enlisted, over half of them volunteers.

The war developed into one of attrition as the Allies strove to break through the formidable German defences and by the end casualties on both sides were on a scale hitherto unparalleled.

Over 350 of these young volunteers, some of them from Ulster, eventually faced the firing squad. They had been Court Marshalled, many of them never given the chance to properly defend themselves. These young men, all of them far from home for the first time, and facing almost certain death, had for various reasons, left their post and been found guilty. Suffering from shattered nerves, caused by the noise and by the scenes of death and destruction all around them, these young men, many of them only in their late teens, had to pay the supreme sacrifice. The British Government has a lot to answer for and the least they can honourably do is to apologise for their wrong doing and clear the names of these young men. When they have that done Britain can once again hold her head high.

The Australian Government can hold their heads high. They refused point blank to impose the supreme sacrifice on their own men when they had done something wrong and no Australians had to face the firing squad. This was probably true of other countries as well.

Young Ballymoney men enlisted in all corners of the World. Many of them were serving in Scottish regiments, having gone there to find work. A few were in English regiments and a number of them had emigrated to New Zealand and Australia. Quite a few had emigrated to Canada. All of them, when the call came, enlisted to serve their country and as it turned out, to give their lives.

Those serving in Scottish Regiments were there for two reasons. A number of them had set up home in Scotland and were there permanently, the others were seasonal workers who went to Scotland every year for the harvest work on the large farms of Southern Scotland. It was August and harvest time and all of the talk was of the war. It was a chance they might never have again, and they used it to the full. Many of them, as soon as they enlisted, were taken for full time training, and almost before they knew it, were in France fighting for their lives. It was a shock for those at home to realise that what had originally been a parting for only a few weeks was now to be an indefinite period and very possibly for ever.

Another interesting fact has emerged. During the writing of the Bushmills book, it transpired that four of the Bushmills boys had been brought home from hospital for burial in Bushmills. It is interesting to note that not one of the Ballymoney boys was brought home, although, like the Bushmills soldiers, they had died in hospital in England.

It is sad to have to admit that for a small number of the Ballymoney soldiers there just does not appear to be any information available. A few of them have proved to be very difficult cases and deadlines eventually have to be met, so I hope you will understand that it was not for want of trying that there are a few with very little information.

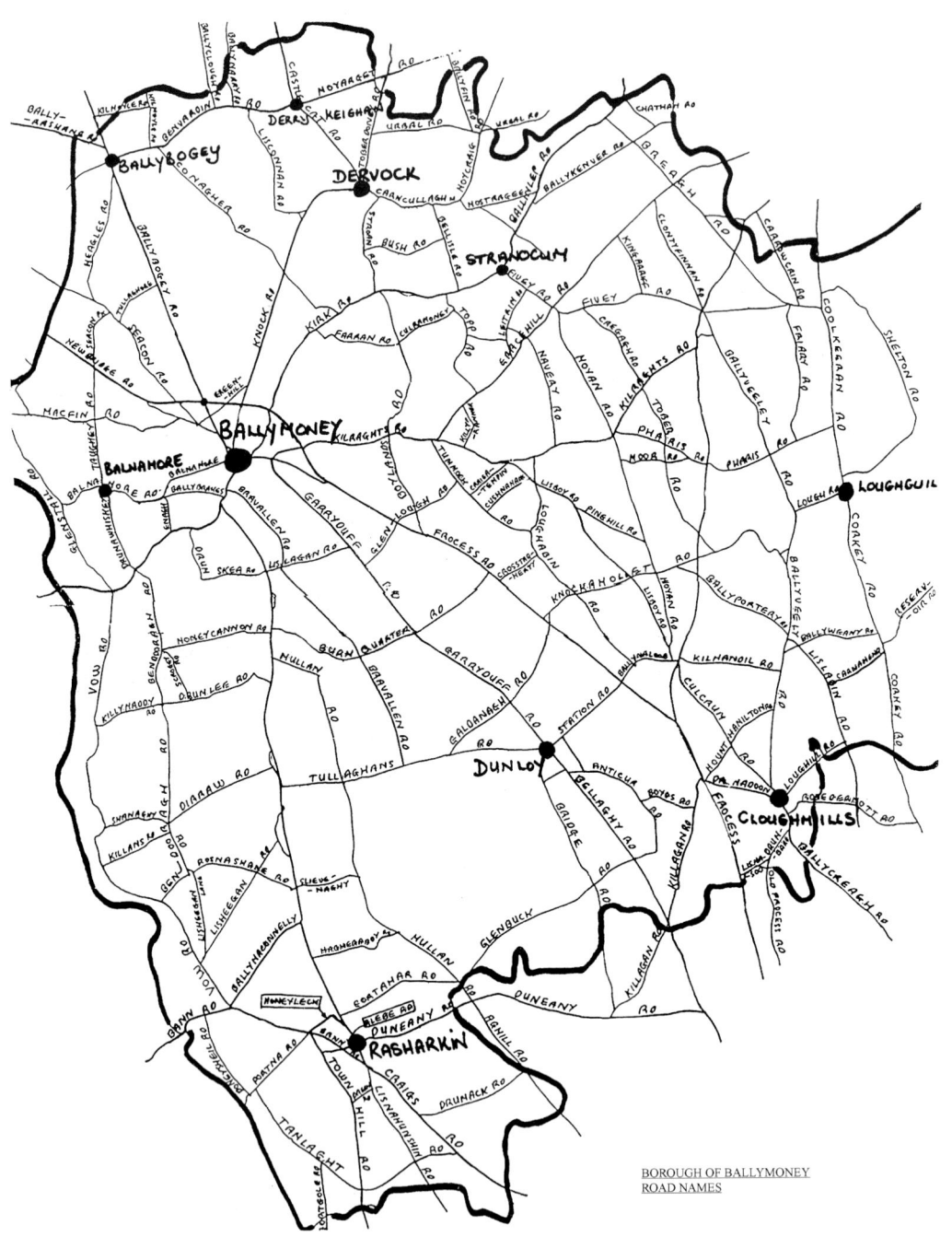

BOROUGH OF BALLYMONEY
ROAD NAMES

A Poignant reminder of the sacrifice of soldiers from throughout Ulster

At a field Hospital, 2nd July, 1916
Come close Bill old Comrade, I'm glad to have you here
It doesn't seem so hard to die when one we love is near
For as kids we played together, shot marbles on the wall
And a s youths on good old Brandywell we used to kick the ball
Just tell them in that dear Old Town old Derry on the Foyle
That the lads who drilled with wooden guns were worthy of their soil
You hardly need to tell them for now the world has heard
How the hardy sons of Ulster for King and Country dared.

When ordered from the trenches by just that one word 'Go'
Wit the war cry 'No Surrender' we quickly found the foe
And onward ever onward as streams the rushing tide
The Fountain, Dark Lane, Rosemount and the lads from Waterside
Pressed onward, ever onward, our progress none could stay
We weren't out goose stepping or singing Dolly's Brae
To rid the earth of him we hate, oh how those Germans ran
They hadn't time to wait and see at Omagh or Strabane.

It may have been someone blundered, the fault may have been our own
But when we reached trench number five we found ourselves alone
Alone and unsupported beneath a scathing fire
We held our winning gamely till the order came 'retire'
I cannot nor will any man the story ever tell
When caught in that triangle it seemed the mouth of Hell
With comrades falling, falling, we formed as on parade
We'll fight a rear guard action was all our Leader said.

And in that rear guard action I got the knock out blow
And now I'm going to travel the road we all must go
When lying faint from loss of blood I heard another call
I'll help you brother Ulsterman, I come from Donegal,
The Ulsters fought regardless with many a hearty cheer
The next thing I remember was being patched up here.

I know the effects are useless I fell I'm going fast
I see the new day breaking for me t'will be the last
I'll never again sit on the Wall on an evening calm and cool
And watch the youngsters playing tig around First Derry School.
I thought on Derry Walls away when joining in the fight
I said it is for Ulster we want it right left right
Just tell them in that dear old town, old Derry on the Foyle
That the lads who guarded old Ireland's shore
Sleep now in a foreign soil.

Contributed by Councillor Billy Larmour. Believed to be written by a soldier of the '10th Derries'

2nd LIEUT RICHARD HENRY COLE MAGENIS
3rd Bn Royal Irish Rifles
K.I.A. 15-9-14
Aged 27
No Known Grave. Commemorated on the La Ferte-sous-Jouarre Memorial.

Born   Drumdoe, Co. Roscommon.
*   on 20-4-1887*
Lived   Finvoy
Enlisted
Commemorated in Finvoy Parish Church.

Richard Henry Cole Magenis was born at Drumdoe, Co. Roscommon, on 20th April 1887, the son of Edward Cole Magenis of Drumdoe, Boyle, Co. Roscommon. and succeeded to the estates the year after the death of his father which occurred in 1908. There was a family residence at Finvoy and Lieut Magenis frequently stayed there during the shooting season. He was a nephew of the late General Magenis of Finvoy.

The draft, of which he was a part, left for France on 26th of August 1914 to reinforce his battalion, joining it on 7th September. He was killed in action eight days later near Vailly at the battle of the Aisne while advancing on the enemy's trenches and was included in the monthly casualty list for October 1914 as having been killed in action and no date mentioned. He had been educated at Radley College and was appointed 2nd Lieut in his battalion in February 1908. He was a very keen cricket and football player, while hunting, shooting, tennis and fishing were also among his recreations. He along with 2nd Lt H.P.Swaine were the first officer casualties sustained by the regiment in the Great War. He was unmarried and had two sisters who resided at Boyle, Co.Roscommon.

The Magennis's were landlords and owned the Craigs, Dirraw, the Knockans and the Mullans.

6450 GUARDSMAN ARTHUR DONNELLY
Scots Guards
K.I.A. 26-10-14
Aged 31
No Known Grave. Commemorated on the Menin Gate Memorial.

Born   Cloughmills.
Lived   Magherafelt
Enlisted Middlesborough.
Son of the late Arthur Donnelly

Ypres is a town in the province of West Flanders. The Memorial is situated at the eastern side of the town on the road to Menin and Courtrai, and bears the names of 55,000 men were lost without trace during the defence of the Ypres Salient in the First World War.

Arthur enlisted in the Scots Guards on the 2nd of March 1906 for a period of twelve years. On the next day he was examined by a doctor at Richmond in Yorkshire and passed fit for service. As his Mother and Father were dead and his next of kin was an uncle living in Magherafelt there probably wasn't much future for him at home and so he decided on a life in the Army. He was 22 years of age, six feet tall, with a fair complexion, brown hair and blue eyes. In March 1909, when he had three years of his time completed, he was transferred to the reserve. Then on 6th August 1914 he was mobilized. He embarked at Southampton on the 30th of August and disembarked in France on 2nd September. He was taken immediately to the area around Ypres in Belgium. His battalion was in action at Gheluvelt and were under desperate attack and it was here that he was killed on 26th October. He had been in the army for 8 years and 239 days. He has no known grave and is commemorated on the Menin Gate.

3995 RIFLEMAN WILLIAM SHIRLOW
2nd Bn Royal Irish Rifles
K.I.A. 27-10-14
Aged 37
No Known Grave. Commemorated on the Le Touret Memorial, France. Panels 42 and 43.

Born   Ballymoney.
Lived
Enlisted   Belfast.
Brother of Mrs. A. Magee, of 67 Grove St, Belfast.

On the outbreak of hostilities in August 1914 the 2nd battalion were stationed at Tidworth but landed at Rouen ten days later, on the 14th. They were at this time part of the 3rd Division and after some initial training they moved to the area around Festubert. It was close to here that William was killed. He has no known grave and is commemorated on the Le Touret Memorial. He had probably been a reservist called up on mobilisation. William was born in Ballymoney in 1877 and although any Shirlows' I have spoken to all claim to be related, no further information has come to light.

7275 RIFLEMAN ALFRED TAGGART
2nd Bn Royal Irish Rifles
K.I.A. 27-10-14
No Known Grave. Commemorated on the Le Touret Memorial. Panels 42 & 43.

Born   Friary, Armoy.
Lived   Friary, Armoy.
Enlisted Belfast.
Commemorated in Kilraughts Presbyterian Church.

When war was declared on 4th August 1914 the 2nd battalion were stationed at Tidworth. Ten days later they landed at Rouen. On 18th October they joined the 25th Division. This was one of the very early deaths and as a coincidence his brother, John, was one of the last, dying of wounds at a hospital in England on 23rd November 1918.

Alfred was a highly trained regular soldier and his loss at this time, along with thousands of others reduced the British fighting force to battalions of half trained militiamen, with a stiffening of regulars. His first major offensive was what was to become known as the battle of Mons. Here the 2nd Rifles were in well concealed positions on the Mons to Givry road and faced a very strong German attack. They allowed the Germans to come within 200 yards

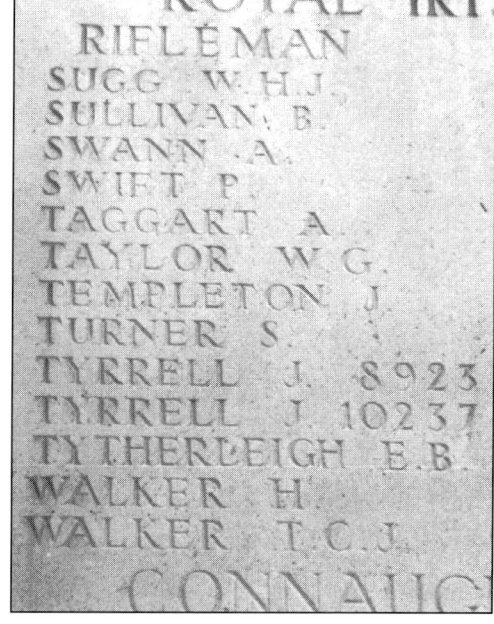

before opening fire. This, to the Germans, was devastating, and what was left of them had to hurriedly retire. This was on the 23rd of August. By now the British Army was being forced back by the attack of a huge German onslaught.

The retreat from Mons was now in full swing and during the last days of August the British were pushed steadily back. In early September the battle of the Marne took place, followed by the battle of the Aisne. During the advance to and the crossing of the Aisne the 2nd battalion had seen little fighting and had suffered only a few casualties in crossing by a footbridge. This was all to change and in the next few days they were heavily engaged, losing three officers and sixty-three men. The 2nd battalion was then moved north to the area around La Bassee and he was in action south of Neuve Chapelle in the attack on Le Pilly. This he survived, but the following week he was killed in very severe fighting on the 27th of October when the position his company held was overwhelmed. He has no known grave and is commemorated on the Le Touret Memorial. No contact has been made with the family and it would appear that they have died out. No one now living in the Friary district can remember the Taggart family living there. Three brothers served in the war and another of them was to lose his life just after the war ended in a hospital in England.

Le Touret Memorial, Pas de Calais, France

1535 PRIVATE CHARLES ALLEN
1st Bn Irish Guards
K.I.A. 18-11-14
Aged 29
No Known Grave. Commemorated on the Menin Gate, Ypres, Belgium. Panel 11.

Born   Belfast.
Lived   Liscolman
Enlisted   Ballymena.
Commemorated in Billy Parish Church

Charles Allen enlisted on 18th November 1902 at Ballymena, and was three years in the colours. He then spent nine years in reserve before being called up on 5th August 1914. He resided at Liscolman, with his wife and three children and was employed in Liscolman Spinning Mill. He was killed in the retreat from Mons, in the trenches near Klein Zillebeke, on 18th November 1914, exactly twelve years to the day after enlisting. Later on that evening the battalion moved to billets at Potijze. On the 4th of August the 1st Battalion received orders to mobilize for war against Germany. Then on the 12th, the Battalion entrained for Southampton in two trains at Nine Elms Station and by 4.00pm had embarked on S.S. Novara, sailing at 7.00pm. They reached Le Havre at 6.00am the following morning. On Friday, the 14th, they entrained at Havre station and after seventeen hours slow progress they halted at Wassigny. They then marched to Vadencourt, and their first billets. Here they rested for three days while innoculations were carried out. On 20th August the march towards Belgium began, via Etreux and Fesmy to Maroilles and billets. Then it was on to Pont-sur-Sambre and Hargnies, to La Longueville. In a few days they were in the suburbs of Mons. Here they were to meet the German Army in vastly superior numbers. They were immediately forced to retreat and by August 26th were back in the Wassigny area. They were forced back further still and in twelve days had been pushed back 140 miles from Mons.

They were then able to turn on the enemy and on September 8th were at Boitron Wood in preparation for the Battle of the Marne. Following this encounter and the crossing of the Marne and five days later they were at the Aisne and preparing for battle there. This was to last longer but after a successful battle they were ordered, on 11th October to be prepared to move at short notice. On 14th October they entrained at Fismes for Hazebrouck and the Ypres Salient. Their route is worth noting, Mareuil-sur-Ourcq, Ormoy, St. Denis outside Paris, Epluches, Creil, Amiens, Abbeville, Etaples, Boulogne, Calais and St. Omer. At 5.00pm on the 15th the battalion went into billets at Hazebrouck. They were then brought up through Ypres. Later they moved to Klein Zillebeke and were in the trenches here in early November. They were relieved on the 9th by the South Wales Borderers, but again relieved them in turn on the 14th. Snow had been falling fairly continuously and the cold and frost at night were numbing. The Germans were shelling regularly and there was never any rest for weary soldiers who had to keep alert at all times. These were the conditions the Irish Guards found themselves in in mid November 1914.

On 18th November, just as they were about to be relieved, Charles Allen was killed. He has no known grave and is commemorated on the Menin Gate.

The following Sunday morning at a service in Billy Parish Church, the Rev R. Moore Morrow. M.A. made a touching reference to Private Allen's death.

WALLACE J. F.	McCONNELL C.
WALSH H.	McDONNELL J.
WILSON T. W.	McGANN T.
WOODROFFE R.	McGINN J.
	McHALE M.
PRIVATE	McKENNA R.
ADAMS H.	McKEON J.
AHERN J.	McKERNIN F.
ALLEN C.	McMAHON D.
ARMSTRONG T.	McMILLAN R.
BARRY W.	McNICHOLAS
BIRMINGHAM P.	McPARTLAND
BIRNEY J.	McVEIGH W.
BLACK G. P.	MAHER D.
BOLGER W.	MAHER J.
BRACKEN S.	MAHER M.
BRENNAN M.	MASON J.
BRENNOCK W.	MASTERSON
BRESLIN A.	MEEHAN H.
BROGAN P.	MILLS A.

16120 RIFLEMAN JOHN CULBERTSON
6th Bn Royal Irish Rifles
DIED 18-11-14
Interred in Grangegorman Military Cemetery, Dublin. Pres 79.

Born   Finvoy
Lived   Ballyboyland, Ballymoney.
Enlisted Belfast
Commemorated in Trinity Presbyterian Church.

John Culbertson

The Grave in Grangegorman Cemetery

Grangegorman Cemetery, Dublin

The 6th battalion were formed at Dublin in August 1914 and trained at Fermoy with the 10th Division. In October they moved back to Dublin which probably meant Phoenix Park. At any rate it was during this time that John Culbertson died. John Culbertson was born in the Finvoy district, three or four miles south of Ballymoney but moved later with his family to live at Ballyboyland, a short distance away. He is commemorated in Trinity Presbyterian Church in Ballymoney, where the family worshipped. However, for some reason, John was not brought home to Ballymoney for burial, but was buried in Grangegorman Military Cemetery in Dublin close to where he died. He had not seen any military action other than training. The fact that he was buried in Dublin and not brought home was in direct contrast to what was happening a few miles away in Bushmills where four of the local soldiers were brought home for burial, three of them from hospitals in England.

Cemetery location information.

This Cemetery is on Blackhorse Avenue, Dublin, outside the north-east boundary of Phoenix Park. This cemetery was opened in 1876 and was used for the burial of British service personnell and their near relatives. It contains war graves from both world wars, but the large majority are 1914-18 war burials. In total there are nearly 800 war graves.

Within the cemetery are the Grangegorman Memorial and the Grangegorman (Cork) Memorial Headstones.

2nd Headstone on right Rifleman J. Culbertson

8939 RIFLEMAN ARTHUR CORBETT
1st Bn Royal Irish Rifles
K.I.A. 17-1-15
Interred in Royal Irish Rifles Graveyard, Laventie. Plot 1, Row A, Grave 7.

Born   Ballymoney
Lived
Enlisted   Belfast
Husband of M.Corbett of 19. Lesley St, Ligoniel,

The 1st Battalion were in Aden when war was declared and embarked for the U.K. on 27th September arriving at Liverpool on 22nd October. They then went to Hursley Park, Winchester, joining the 25th Brigade, 8th Div. They landed at Le Havre on 6th November 1914.

Arthur, a full time regular soldier, was married and his wife was living in Belfast. They were taken to the region to the south of Armentieres and it was here, a little over two months later that Arthur was killed.

Cemetery location information.

Laventie is a village about 11 kilometres south-west of Armentieres and the graveyard is three kilometres south-east of the village on a minor road from Fleurbaix to Couture.

Royal Irish Rifles Graveyard, Laventie

232 PRIVATE JOHN BELLINGHAM
1st Bn Argylle & Sutherland Highlanders "A" Coy.
D.O.W. 19-1-15.
Aged 28
Interred in Dickebusch Old Military Cemetery

Born   Kilraughts
Lived
Enlisted Co. Antrim
Commemorated in Kilraughts Presbyterian Church.
Son of Thomas and Anne Bellingham of Kilraughts

Dickebusch Old Military Cemetery, Belgium, middle row

John, like many of the young Ballymoney men had probably been working in Scotland before he enlisted. He was a regular soldier and had a number of years experience of life in the army.

The 1st battalion had been serving in India when war was declared and were immediately ordered home from Dinapore. The trip from Bombay was uneventful and they arrived at Plymouth on 19th November. They were sent to Winchester where they joined the 27th Div and landed at Le Havre on the 20th of December. This was a quick change from the temperatures in India to those of France or Belgium in mid winter. The wet and cold just had to be endured and they were put into shallow trenches at Kruistraat on 16th January 1915. This was their first taste of trench warfare in these shallow trenches which had to be built up in front with sandbags to give the soldiers any cover. Kruistraat is just to the south of Ypres and it was here that John was killed.only three days after arriving in the front line. A sniper had been waiting and as John raised his head he was hit. He was very seriously wounded but was immediately taken to a dressing station at Dikkebus. Here he was treated for his injuries, but in spite of all they could do, he died later that day. It was an unfortunate coincidence that John himself had been trained as a sniper. His sister, Elizabeth, married William Workman, who was later to win the Military Medal, and whose story is also included in the book. John is buried in Dikkebus Old Military Cemetery, Row A, Grave 3.

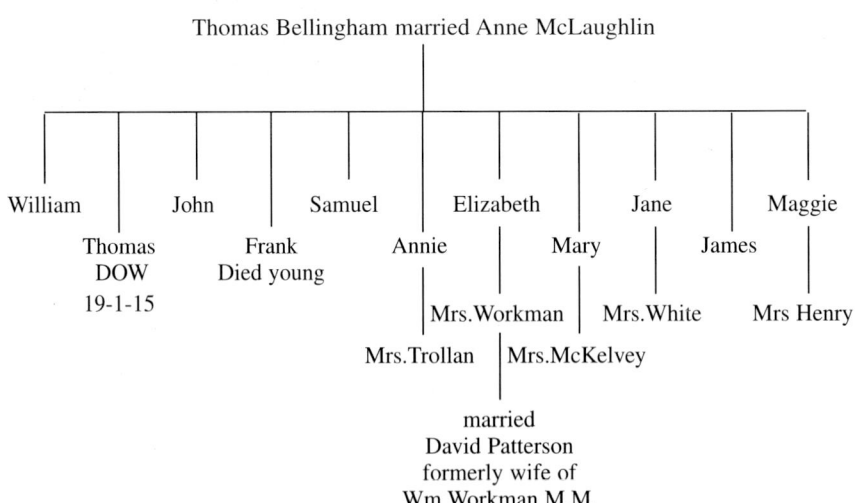

John's sister, Elizabeth married William Workman in Bushvale Presbyterian Church on 26th February 1913. Both of them lived in the Kilraughts district. William was killed in the Great German Spring Offensive of March 1918 and has no known grave.

10266 GUARDSMAN WILIAM McALLISTER
Scots Guards.
K.I.A. 25-1-15
Aged 27
Interred in Arras Road Cemetery. Plot 3, Row H, Grave 26.

Born   Knockanavery.
Lived   Ballymoney.
Enlisted   Edinburgh.
Son of Samuel McAllister, of Culduff, Ballymoney.

The McAllister family had been living at Knockanavery, a townland a short distance from Ballymoney. It was here that William was born. As a young boy he attended the local country school but there appears to be no record of him in any of the local churches.

William had been working in the Edinburgh area for some time as a coal miner. On the outbreak of hostilities he decided to join the war effort and enlisted at Edinburgh on the 8th of September 1914. He had a fresh complexion, with grey eyes and black hair and was about 5 feet 10 inches in height.

After just four months training they embarked at Southampton on 13th January 1915. Only twelve days later William was reported missing having served for just 140 days. He is buried in Arras Road Cemetery, just a short distance north of Arras. This is a mainly Canadian cemetery and one which I have visited to see the grave of Samuel J. Peden, of Macosquin, who is also buried there.

The Scots Guards were at this time fighting at Cuinchy Trenches on the La Bassee road, and this was where William was killed.

Also buried in this cemetery is another Ballymoney man, James Gaston, M.C. and during the summer of 1999 his family paid a visit to the grave.

3739 RIFLEMAN JOSEPH DEAN
11th Bn Royal Irish Rifles "C" Coy.
DIED 3-3-15
Aged 35
Interred in Belfast City Cemetery, H. 531.

Born   Ballynoney
Lived
Enlisted   Randalstown
Son of Joseph and Susan Dean of Balnamore.
Husband of Annie Dean of 15, Daisy Hill, Randalstown.
Died of pneumonia.

Joseph Dean was born in the Ballymoney district in 1880. His parents, Joseph and Susan Dean lived in Balnamore and Joseph went to school there. Later he married and moved to live in Randalstown. On the outbreak of hostilities he enlisted into the 11th battalion, Royal Irish Rifles at Randalstown. Much of his training took place at Clandeboye, but during training exercises in Co Down he became unwell. It was winter and most of their training was outdoors in all weathers, which meant their clothes were often wet, or not properly dried. He died of pneumonia on 3rd March 1915. No reason has been given for his burial in Belfast.

Cemetery visiting information.

Belfast city cemetery, in the Falls road, Shankill, belongs to the Corporation. It was opened in 1869, with the Glenalina Extension it now covers about 100 acres. It contains 287 war graves of which 133 are in the "Roll of Honour Ground" in plots H, H3 and 13 and a war cross is erected on an island site in plot 3. A screen wall, in plot H, records the names of those that are buried in that plot and of others whose graves are not marked by headstones. Belfast was a port of embarkation in August 1914, and an Auxiliary Patrol base later, and the Belfast war hospital with 500 beds, was in the Asylum.

Belfast City Council have confirmed in writing to me that the 1st World War headstones have been removed for safe keeping to the Sir Thomas and Lady Dixon Park. Some of them have already been damaged beyond repair but the War Graves Commission have indicated that these headstones may be replaced in the future. I think it is an absolute disgrace that we have to hide the headstones of our honoured soldiers in such a way.

The Ulster Tower at Thiepval

ASSISTANT STEWARD DANIEL McARTHUR
Mercantile Marine Reserve
K.I.A. 11-3-15
No Known Grave. Commemorated on the Plymouth Naval Memorial.

Born   Ballymoney
Lived   Castle St.
Enlisted
Commemorated in St.James's Presbyterian Church.

The family worshipped in St. James's Presbyterian Church, in Ballymoney and it is there that Daniel is commemorated. They lived in Castle Street and it is believed that Kennedy K. McArthur, who won the Marathon event at the Stockholm Olympic Games in 1912, was a brother.

Daniel's brother, Robert, was home on leave in January 1918 after eighteen months service in France. He survived the war.

Another brother, Albert, unfit for further service, was a Sergeant in the records office. He was also to survive the war.

Daniel was serving on H.M.S. "Bayano" when she was sunk in action with a submarine, U27, off Corsewall Point, Stranraer on 11th March 1915. She was an armed merchant cruiser with a displacement of 5,948 tons and was launched on 21st November 1914. She had a top speed of 13 knots. Daniel was lost at sea and has no known grave but is commemorated on the Plymouth Naval Memorial. This was the first of the Ballymoney boys to be lost at sea but unfortunately he was not to be the last.

John Devine of Townhead St was lost at sea when his ship blew up in Scapa Flow in July 1917.

Bayano as a commissioned escort vessel

18806 PRIVATE CHARLES MURPHY
3rd Bn Royal Inniskilling Fusiliers
DIED HOME 16-3-15
Aged 42
Interred in Londonderry City Cemetery, GA, Mil 14.

Born   Deffrick, Dervock.
Lived
Enlisted   Fauldhouse, Linlithgow.
Son of James and Matilda Mc.Allister Murphy
Husband of Janet Brown Murphy, of Den Row, Fauldhouse, West Lothian.

Charles Murphy was born at Deffrick, Dervock, in about 1873, probably the second son of James and Matilda Murphy who had been married in Billy Parish Church on 31st Oct 1870.

Charles had been working in Scotland for a number of years and on the outbreak of hostilities had enlisted in the Royal Inniskilling Fusiliers.

He had been training in County Londonderry when he contracted a fever from which he died in hospital in Londonderry. At the funeral, the remains were placed on a gun carriage and covered by the Union Jack. Lt Dickson was in charge of the firing party. Charles's wife, Janet, continued to live in Scotland. She kept in touch with Charles's brother James and his wife Margaret, in Townhead St, Ballymoney, and visited them on a regular basis for as long as she was able. On each of these visits she made a point of seeing Charles's grave in Londonderry City Cemetery.

The Singing Soldier

The machine-gun stood applauding, as the chorus fled his lips,
And paused when he lay sprawling, in the mire of his ditch.
He had sung his words of wisdom, sincerely from his heart,
And for reconciliation, from this world he did depart.
He was just one more statistic, in their catalogue of death,
But his family, friends and comrades, they never shall forget.
An infant in his cradle, the precious gift of life,
His parents proud and grateful, such joy should grace their lives,
A boy played in the schoolyard, a conker in his hand,
The pranks, the cane, the bullying of a generation damned.
A youth kissed Nancy Glover, 'neath a weeping willow tree,
then carved their names together, for everyone to see.
A man put on his uniform, then waved his home goodbye,
And marched off to those bloody fields, where Europe's sons would die.

A voice of peace is silenced, by the justice of a gun,
While generals drunk on cognac, prolong a war benumbed.

Paul Hutton   Coleraine

2825 PRIVATE JOSEPH DOCHERTY
1st Bn Gordon Highlanders
K.I.A. 17-4-15
Aged 21
Interred in La Laiterie Military Cemetery, Kemmel, Belgium. Plot 1, Row B, Grave 20.

Born   Ballymoney
Lived   Glasgow
Enlisted   Glasgow
Son of William and Elizabeth Docherty, of 190 Gourlay St, Springburn, Glasgow.

Joseph Docherty was born in the Ballymoney district but full time work was hard to find at the time and William and Elizabeth decided to take the family to Scotland in an attempt to find employment. They eventually settled in the Springburn district of Glasgow. The huge ship-building yards of the Clyde provided work for many of the local population and it was probably there that William found work. At any rate the family settled in Glasgow and it was there that Joseph eventually enlisted. The 1st battalion were involved in heavy fighting in the area to the north of Kemmel in April of 1915. Kemmel is the only hill of any commendable size in the area and was of immense strategical importance. Whoever held the summit could see for miles and had a good view in all directions. Joseph was involved in very heavy fighting about a mile to the north of this hill and it was here that he was killed. His battalion were very heavily shelled in the trenches at this time and many casualties were suffered during this bombardment.

La Laiterie Military Cemetery, Kemmel, Belgium.

Joseph is buried in La Laiterie Cemetery close to where he fell. This cemetery is situated on the roadside a short distance north of Kemmel on the road to Ypres. He was just twenty-one years of age. As one drives through this district it is still possible to pick out the signs of battles fought many years ago. German bunkers adorn the fields and hedgerows and many of them are used as shelter by the cattle of another age. Everything is quiet now and the fields have returned to pasture but it was not always a place of quiet tranquility. In 1915 this was a place of carnage. Bitter fighting for the city of Ypres, just a few miles to the north, was to be a constant drain on the young men of Ballymoney in the years immediately ahead.

La Laiterie Military Cemetery

10468 PRIVATE JOHN THOMPSON
1st Bn Royal Dublin Fusiliers
K.I.A. 25-4-15
Interred in V. Beach Cemetery, Gallipoli. Special Memorial, B 110.

Born   Ballymoney.
Lived   Londonderry.
Enlisted Belfast.
Son of Mr J. Thompson, of 57.Carnan St, Belfast.

John Thompson was born at Ballymoney, but it appears that the family first of all moved to Anrtim and then later settled in Belfast. He enlisted in Belfast into the Royal Dublin Fusiliers. After prolonged training, the Dublin Fusiliers sailed from Avonmouth on 16th March 1915, and arrived at Alexandria on the 30th. After a short rest they sailed to Mudros on the 9th of April. Much preparation then took place before the landing at V Beach on the 25th of April. At Sedd-el-Bahr (V Beach) a striking stage was set.

The shallow half-moon of the cove was crowned by low steep cliffs. On the right to one approaching from the sea, was a solid old castle, with the village behind and to the left, while trenches along and above the cliff prolonged the Turkish defences round the curve to another fort. About 3,000 men were approaching on tows and on the River Clyde, a converted collier, in whose sides sally ports had been cut. The Turks, with a deliberate and cool patience, reserved all fire until the boats had almost reached the shore, and then blasted whole boat-loads of the Dublin Fusiliers out of existance. The same hail met the Munsters as they rushed out of the stranded collier. The brave efforts of the survivers carried them to the beach and a bank under the cliff gave them some cover. Enemy fire kept them there and half of the 2,000 men in the collier's hold had to be kept back because of the withering fire. What courage it must have taken to row without hope towards the shore, with the sea turning red around them, through such a hail of lead. John Thompson was the only Ballymoney man killed in the landing on V Beach on the 25th of April 1915. Fierce fighting took place here, so fierce that it broke up the attack by the British and reinforcements had to be brought in next day. John's brother, Hugh, was among these reinforcements. When the cemetery at V Beach was being constructed many of the soldiers had to be put into a mass grave. Later, when the headstones were being put in place, these positions were lost, with the result that John now lies under a memorial headstone. The position of his grave is unknown and the inscription on the headstone reads "known to be buried in this cemetery".

In October 1997, Alderman Samuel McConaghie, of Ballymoney Borough Council visited his grave in V Beach Cemetery, one of the very few Ballymoney men to do so. The visit was repeated in 1999 when Samuel again went to Gallipoli and again visited the cemetery. He also went to some of the other cemeteries in the region, notably Skew Bridge cemetery where he got me a photograph of the grave of Niel Forbes, another Ballymoney man.

'V' Beach Cemetery, Gallipoli

PRIVATE JOHN MAGILL
"D" Coy, 1st Bn, Royal Irish Fusiliers
D.O.W. 27-4-15
Aged 23
Interred in Bailleul Communal Cemetery Extension, France. Plot 1, Row B, Grave 26.

Born   Dervock
Lived
Enlisted
Youngest son of the late James and Ellen Magill, of Lurgan, Co Armagh.

The 1st battalion were at Shorncliffe when war was declared, but moved a fortnight later to Harrow. On the 23rd of August 1914 they landed at Boulogne. They were taken almost at once to their new training area and shown as far as possible what to expect in the front lines. Soon afterwards they moved up to the front lines at Ypres and it was here that they saw their first action.

Although John was born at Dervock, about three miles from Ballymoney, and was the youngest son, the family seems to have moved from the district at a later date. John enlisted at an early age and had the intention of making the Army his life. He was a regular soldier. The first battalion were ordered, along with the 2nd Dublins, to attack St. Julien on Sunday the 25th of April 1915, the same day as the 1st Dublins were landing at Cape Helles.

This was a hurriedly planned attack and some

Bailleul Communal Cemetery, Centre Front

battalions had to march thirty miles to reach the area they were to attack from.

Under cover of a morning mist the 1st Irish Fusiliers, 2nd Dublins, 2nd Seaforth Highlanders and 1st Warwickshires advanced in the first line, supported by the 7th Argylls. They were met by a withering hail of machine-gun fire and casualties were catastrophic, 73 officers and 2826 other ranks, all highly trained regular soldiers, and at that stage of the war, irreplaceable. In spite of their losses the Irish Fusiliers and Dublins reached the outskirts of St. Julien.

It was in this attack that John Magill was seriously injured and was taken back to a hospital at Bailleul. He died from his injuries two days later and is buried in the local cemetery on the outskirts of the town.

This cemetery was used on three different occasions at a later date for the burial of men who faced the firing squad. W. Roberts, W. Moon and J Rogers were all found guilty of desertion and were executed at Bailleul. Roberts is buried in Plot 2, Row B, Grave 110. Moon, Plot 3, Row A, Grave 219. Rogers in Plot 3, Row A, Grave 3.

Part of Bailleul Cemetery

1810 PRIVATE THOMAS LYNN
2nd Bn King's Own Royal Lancaster Regt
K.I.A. 8-5-15
No Known Grave. Commemorated on the Menin Gate, Panel 12.

Born
Lived
Enlisted

On the outbreak of hostilities on 4th August 1914 the second battalion were at Lebong in India. On 19th November they sailed for Britain, landing at Plymouth on 12th December and joined the 28th Division at Winchester. They landed at Le Havre on 16th January 1915. They were taken to the Ypres Salient in what was by now mid-winter. Conditions in the trenches were primitive, with sacks filled with mud and piled up in front to give them any cover from the enemy. There was little or no cover from the elements and they were continually soaked to the skin. By early May conditions had improved dramatically. The weather had dried up and they were beginning to enjoy bright sunshine. They were involved in a very heavy attack on the morning of the 8th of May and the position Thomas held was over-run. He has no known grave and is commemorated on the Menin Gate in Ypres. Unfortunately this is one of the families I have been unable to contact and so very little information has come to light concerning Thomas.

2719 PRIVATE WILLIAM TWADDLE
2nd Bn King's Own Royal Lancaster Regt.
K.I.A. 8-5-15
Aged 37
No Known Grave. Commemorated on the Menin Gate Memorial, Belgium.

Born Benvarden.
Lived Benvarden.
Enlisted
Son of Liz Twaddle of Benvarden
Commemorated in Derrykeighan Parish Church.

William was born at Benvarden, about five miles north of Ballymoney. He probably attended Kilmoyle old Primary school. The family worshipped in Derrykeighan Parish Church and it is there that William is commemorated. It appears that for a number of years he was living in England and that he eventually enlisted there.

At thirty-seven years of age he was a lot older than most of the soldiers at the time and was probably either a reservist or a serving soldier. I have been unable to find any family details but it would appear that he was not married. In spite of many appeals in the newspapers no information has come to light and one can only assume that the family has died out.

The 2nd battalion were stationed at Lebong in India when war was declared. On 19th November 1914 they sailed for England, arriving at Plymouth on 22nd December and joined the 28th Division at Winchester. After training and re-organisation they sailed for France, arriving at Le Havre on 16th Jan 1915. They were immediately taken to the area around Ypres and it was here that William was killed on the 8th of May. There is no known grave and he is commemorated on the Menin Gate Memorial.

1708 RIFLEMAN ROBERT MOORE
1ST BN ROYAL IRISH RIFLES
K.I.A. 9-5-15
Aged 24
No Known Grave. Commemorated on the Ploegsteert Memorial, Belgium.

Born Mosside.
Lived Port Glasgow.
Enlisted Greenock, Renfrewshire.
Son of George and Annie Moore, of Liscolman.
Husband of Agnes Laverty McPherson of 117, Bouverie St, Port Glasgow.
Commemorated in Billy Parish Church.
Brother of William Moore, killed in action 27th April, 1916.

Robert had spent much of his early life around Liscolman where he had gone to school. He was a son of George and Annie Moore of Liscolman. After he got married he went to live in Port Glasgow with his wife, Agnes. He had probably gone to Scotland in search of work. Farms in Scotland were much bigger than those in N. Ireland and could employ many more workers. When the seasonal work was over there was always the coal mines or the ship-building yards of the Clyde. When war was declared Robert couldn't wait and enlisted immediately. Training was soon taking place and early in 1915 he was taken to France where he was at once transferred to the front lines and the area around Bailleul. Much heavy fighting was taking place in this region. At this time the German Armies were attacking in great strength and the British were finding it difficult to defend their own lines and not be pushed back. It was during these attacks in May 1915 that Robert was killed. He has no known grave and is commemorated on the Plugsteert Memorial. This memorial commemorates 11,447 soldiers who have no known grave. Less than a year later his brother William was killed a few miles to the south at St. Eloi. Two other brothers, George and Tommy, also served, but survived.

LIEUT ARTHUR BUTLER CRAMSIE
2nd Bn Northumberland Fusiliers
K.I.A. 8-5-15
Aged 21
No Known Grave. Commemorated on the Menin Gate Memorial, Ypres

Born   O'Harabrook.
Lived
Enlisted
Commemorated in Ballymoney Parish Church.

Arthur Cramsie was an Uncle of Colonel Cramsie, of O'Harabrook who for many years and up until his death in 1987 had been President of Ballymoney Agricultural Show. Arthur was born at O'Harabrook in about 1894 and spent some of his early years there. Later moving to Cumberland, he joined the School House at St. Bees in 1906 and although he went to Wellington he spent the greater part of his school life at St. Bees. He joined the Northumberland Fusiliers at the age of nineteen and shortly after this went with his regiment to India, spending the best part of two years there. On the outbreak of hostilities he was recalled and arrived back home in December 1914. A few weeks later, in January 1915, he was sent with his unit to France and from there moved into the front lines at Ypres in Belgium. On the morning of the 8th of May the enemy guns opened fire at 3.30am with high explosive and schrapnel which increased in volume about 7.00am and continued all day until the enemy attacked on the right of the line held by the 84th Infantry Brigade at about 3.30 pm. The line of trenches extended from the St Julian road to the Zonnebeke road, north of Verlorenhoek which were held by the following units commencing from the right. 2nd Bn Cheshire Regt, 1st Bn Suffolk Regt, 1st Monmouthshire Regt and 2nd Northumberland Fus.

The line of the Cheshires was broken and the enemy got through to the rear and enveloped the Suffolk Regt. The Monmouths fell back and made a counter attack which failed, and the enemy outflanked the headquarters of D,C and B Coys. No 1,2, and 3 platoons of A coy, under 2nd Lieut W.Watson and Sergeants Lane and Hague

A.B. Cramsie, 1910 held on to their trenches and fought gallantly. Their devotion to duty saved the situation. These platoons were relieved at 4.00am on the 9th by a detachment of the East Lancashire Regt. It was in this action that Arthur was killed at Ypres on 8th May 1915 when his regiment was practically annihilated.

He was at the time of his death, Regimental Machine-Gun Officer. He has no known grave and is commemorated on the Menin Gate Memorial. His name is recorded on the family headstone in the Lamb's Fold at O'Harabrook.

Cemetery location information.

Ypres is a town in the province of west Flanders. The memorial is situated at the eastern side

of the town on the road to Menin and Courtrai, and bears the names of 55,000 men who were

lost without trace during the defence of the Ypres salient in the First World War.

ST. BEES SCHOOL, CUMBERLAND

THE

ROLL OF HONOUR

AND THE RECORD OF

OLD ST. BEGHIANS

WHO SERVED THEIR KING AND COUNTRY
IN THE GREAT WAR
1914-1919

COMPILED BY J. W. ALDOUS, M.A.

EDINBURGH
PRINTED BY T. AND A. CONSTABLE LTD.
AT THE UNIVERSITY PRESS
1921

10341 PRIVATE WILLIAM BECKETT
2nd Bn Scots Guards
K.I.A. 16-5-15
No known grave. Commemorated on Le Touret Memorial. Panels 3 and 4.

Born   Balnamore
Lived   Whiteinch, Glasgow.
Enlisted   Glasgow.
Son of Mr John Beckett, of Balnamore.

The 2nd battalion were stationed at the Tower of London when war was declared. In September they joined the 7th Div at Lyndhurst and on 7th October 1914 landed at Zeebrugge.

William was born at Balnamore, the son of John Beckett. He was a keen footballer and played regularly for Balnamore. John Beckett had four sons on active service during the 1914-18 war. John, the eldest, in Nairobi, British East Africa. William in the Scots Guards, Samuel in the Scots Territorials and Robert in the Seaforth Highlanders.

William Beckett enlisted on the same day as William McAllister, 8th September 1914, having passed his medical examination at Glasgow the previous day. He was described as being 5 feet 10 inches tall, fresh complexion, with grey eyes and black hair. He was married to Ellen McLelland, of Ballymoney, on 7th August 1911, and there were two children, David and John, who were born at Balnamore. Sometime during 1914 the family moved to Scotland and were living in Glasgow. William was a labourer and had probably gone there in search of work. Having enlisted and completed his training, he embarked at Southampton on 16th March 1915. He was killed at Festubert on 16th May, and was first reported as wounded and missing, and then, killed in action. A letter written by a comrade, James Dyer, who saw him killed, confirms this.

James Dyer appears to have survived the war as no record appears in Soldiers Died. During battlefield clearance operations in July, William's body was found by "A" Company, 2nd Bn, Yorkshire Regiment, and buried. This was on 15th July 1915. The grave was probably destroyed in later fighting, as there is now no known grave and he is commemorated on the Le Touret Memorial.

In October 1917, Samuel Beckett was wounded and admitted to hospital. L.Sergeant John Beckett was still in East Africa and Robert was with the Seaforth Highlanders. Robert had been through the Battle of the Somme and the Battle of Arras and had been shell-shocked at Arras. All three were to survive the war.

A cousin, Alex Beckett, also of Balnamore, was, in August 1917, on leave at Balnamore. He was the son of James Beckett. Alex had been wounded on 1st July 1916 at the Battle of the Somme and invalided home. On recovering from his wounds he transferred to an English regiment and since then had been transferred to the Military Police.

Cemetery location information.

Le Touret memorial is located at the east end of Le Touret military cemetery, on the south side of the Bethune - Armentieres main road. From Bethune follow the signs for Armentieres until you are on the D171. Continue on this road through Essars and Le Touret village. Approximately 1 kilometre after Le Touret village and about 5 kilometres before you reach the intersection with the D947, Estaires to La Basse road, the cemetery lies on the right hand side of the road. The memorial takes the form of a loggia surrounding an open rectangular court. The court is enclosed by three solid walls and on the eastern side by a collonade. East of the collonade is a wall and the collonade and wall are prolonged northwards to the road and southwards forming a long gallery. Small pavillions mark the ends of the gallery and the western corners of the court. The names of those commemorated are listed on panels set into the walls of the court and the gallery, arranged by Regiment, Rank and alphabetically by surname within the rank. Over 13,000 names are listed on the memorial of men who fell in this area before 25th Sept 1915 and who have no known grave.

7679 A. CPL, WILLIAM JOHN BROLLY
2nd Bn Royal Inniskilling Fusiliers
K.I.A. 16-5-15
No known grave. Commemorated on Le Touret Memorial. Panels 16 and 17.

Born   Ballymoney
Lived   Drumahiskey
Enlisted Belfast

It is believed that William, after spending much of his early life at home at Drumahiskey, had enlisted into the Army in about 1907 and been placed on the Reserve List. He was a very promising young footballer and after playing for the local team at Balnamore had gone on to play for Brantwood and Distillery. By the time war broke out he was married and living in Belfast. He lived in Pittsburg St, off the Shore Road.

On the outbreak of hostilities the 2nd Battalion were stationed at Dover and William joined them soon afterwards to commence his training. William Brolly was seriously wounded and was being carried out of the firing line when a shell exploded near him, killing him outright. He was probably blown to pieces as there is no grave. He had been through the Battle of Mons where a bullet struck a button on his tunic, another went through his greatcoat and a third took away part of one of his toes.

In a letter home to his Father he wonders why his two brothers, Clarke and Samuel didn't join his regiment when they enlisted.

The 2nd battalion were at Richebourg in a brigade advance with the 2nd div. Richebourg is about half way between Arras and Armentierres and was the scene of much very heavy fighting in the early months of 1915. It was during this advance that William was wounded and then killed. His brother James was injured at Mons and was afterwards discharged as medically unfit. Three other brothers were also serving. Samuel and Clarke with the Ulster contingent, and Thomas with the Seaforth Highlanders.

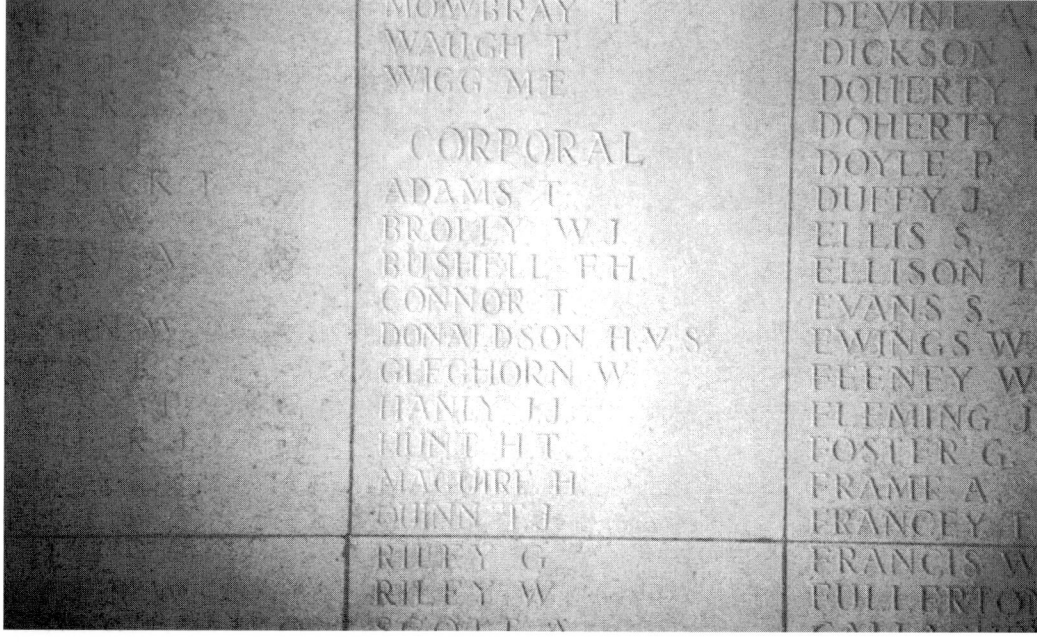

9906 PRIVATE ROBERT CASEY
1st Bn Royal Inniskilling Fusiliers
K.I.A. 26-5-15
Interred in Pink Farm Cemetery, at Helles in Gallipoli. Plot 3, Row A, Grave 15.

Born   Ballymoney
Lived
Enlisted   Hamilton, Lanarkshire.

In October 1997, Alderman Sam McConaghie of Ballymoney paid a visit to Gallipoli. Whilst there he visited Pink Farm Cemetery and the grave of Robert Casey, one of the very few Ballymoney men to do so.

On the 26th of May 1915 the 1st battalion were in reserve at Gurkha Bluff with the 29th Division. Further forward, fighting was extremely heavy but in the back areas it was mostly shell-fire which they had to contend with, dangerous as it was.

It was during this continual shelling that Robert was killed. The heavy guns had a range of anything up to 6 miles and could stay far back where it was easy to bring up ammunition. A month later Robert's brother Samuel, was also to die in Gallipoli.

8295   PRIVATE JAMES THOMPSON
1st Bn Royal Inniskilling Fusiliers
K.I.A. 7-6-15
No Known Grave. Commemorated on the Helles Memorial, Gallipoli. Panels 97 - 101

Born   Carnaff, Dervock.
Lived   Ballywattick, Ballymoney.
Enlisted Coleraine.

James's Mother was born at the Strone, between Dervock and Stranocum, and lived there until she was married.

The family lived in a house at Carnaff, part of which can still be seen down the lane behind Willie Peden's farm yard. There were three of the first family, Margaret, James, and Annie.

James, along with his sisters Margaret and Annie went to school at Derrykeighan, and worshipped in Carnaff Reformed Presbyterian Church, where James is commemorated. By the time James's half brothers and half sister, Robert, Matt and Mary McAlister were born, the family had moved to Culduff. At some stage prior to 1912 the family moved to live at Ballywattick and it was from here that James went to enlist. It is possible that he was a serving soldier when war was declared. At any rate he survived the landing at Gallipoli. The Royal Inniskillings were at Ghurka Bluff when a fierce engagement of the enemy was ordered. The attack started on Friday afternoon. At first everything went well and the enemy were being pushed back. Through Saturday the British advanced still further but by Sunday the Turks had brought up more troops and were in a position now to hold up the British attack and to drive it back. On Monday the Turks attacked and in a ferocious engagement drove the British back almost to where they had started. It was during this attack that James Thompson was killed. He has no known grave and is commemorated on the Helles Memorial

His sister Margaret married James Murphy of Deffrick and they lived all their lives in Townhead Street. James was a breadserver, and his daughter, Mrs McLester, can clearly recall being taken in the van around the countryside on his daily deliveries and being shown the old family home at Carnaff.

Annie married Charles Ralph and emigrated to America. Robert lived in Dunloy. Matt emigrated to Canada where he spent the rest of his life and Mary married and settled in Kilkeel, Co Down.

James Murphy's brother Charles had been married and was living in Scotland. He enlisted into the Royal Inniskillings and was training in County Londonderry when he contracted a fever and died on 16th March 1915. He is buried in Londonderry City Cemetery. His daughter, who continued to live in Scotland, regularly visited James and Margaret in Townhead Street and on every occasion went to see Charles's grave in Londonderry.

The Helles Memorial, Gallipoli

16389 PRIVATE PETER DALLETT
2nd Bn Royal Irish Fusiliers
K.I.A. 9-6-15
No Known Grave. Commemorated on the Ploegsteert Memorial, Belgium.

Born   Ballymoney
Lived   Ballymoney
Enlisted Ballymoney on 12th November 1914.
Son of Michael Dallett

A report tells of Peter emigrating to Canada to find work, but returning on the outbreak of hostilities to enlist at Ballymoney.

Peter was a son of Michael Dallett and was born in Townhead St. Michael and Mary, Peter's father and mother, had a shop in Townhead Street, beside the toilets where the entrance to the Council car park now stands. This was where they lived. The boys were all joiners and built the two houses that are now vacant on the upper side of the entrance to the car park. He was also a tallented footballer and played for the Coronation Blues.

Peter and his brothers all attended the Chapel School in Castle street. As a young man he emigrated to Canada, but on the outbreak of hostilities he returned home and enlisted at Ballymoney on 12th November 1914. In August 1914 the 2nd battalion were at Quetta, but arrived at Winchester on 20th November, joining the 82nd Brigade, 27th Division, and arrived in France on 19th December 1914. Reinforcement drafts for Irishbattalions at the Front simply poured over to France. Peter joined them in a draft during the early Spring of 1915 and was present at the bitter fighting at Mouse Trap Farm near St. Julien, to the north-east of Ypres. No Man's Land was only about thirty yards wide at this point and when the Germans released gas on the morning of 24th May there was no warning whatever. The position was lost and at a high cost. Almost four hundred men were casualties, either gassed, wounded or taken prisoner. Peter survived this attack but was killed in action a few weeks later. He has no known grave and is commemorated on the Plugsteert Memorial. In June and July the battalion had a quiet time, mostly spent in the trenches north of Houplines close to Armentieres. In June the battalion lost eight men killed in what the official history describes as normal trench duties. Peter, apparently, was one of those eight. On that date there wasn't a major battle in progress and a close study of "Soldiers Died" reveals only two other soldiers from his battalion killed on this day. This would suggest that he was probably killed by a sniper, but then there was usually time to properly bury these casualties.

The other possibility that they were all out on patrol together at night in No Man's Land and were spotted by the enemy is the more likely one, and would account for the fact that there is no known grave. This type of manouvre was common practice at the time and was used by both sides as a useful way of gathering information.

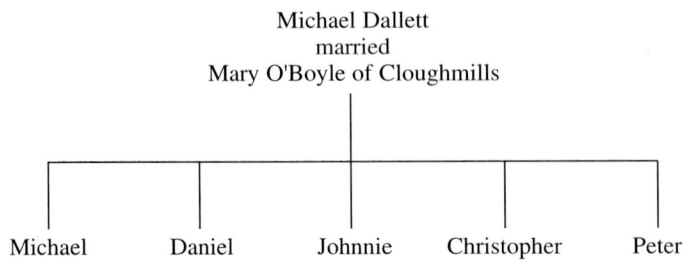

Peter's Mother could not accept the fact that he had been killed and would not be coming home. She died soon afterwards suffering mainly from the stress of Peter's death.

Cemetery location information.

The Ploegsteert Memorial stands in Berks Cemetery Extension, which is located 12.5 kilometres south of Ypres town centre, on the N 365 leading from Ypres to Messines, Ploegsteert and on to Armentieres

From Ypres town centre the Rijselsestraat runs from the market square, through the Lille Gate and directly over the cross roads with the Ypres ring road. The road name then changes to the Rijselseweg (N336).

3.5 kilometres along the N336 lies a fork junction with the N365. The N365 which forms the right hand fork, leads to the town of Messines. The cemetery lies 3 kilometres beyond Messines on the right hand side of the road and opposite Hyde Park Corner Royal Berks Cemetery.

ABLE SEAMAN NEIL FORBES
Royal Naval VolunteerReserve. Nelson Battalion, R. Naval Div.
DIED 15-6-15
Aged 30
Interred in Skew Bridge Cemetery. Plot 2, Row F, Grave 6.

Born   John St, Ballymoney.
Lived   Greenock, Scotland.
Enlisted
Son of John Forbes of Greenock.

It is now believed that the Archie Forbes, whose story appears elsewhere in the book, was a brother of Neil Forbes. Research shows that the family moved to Greenock in the early years of this century. They had lived in John Street, in Ballymoney, for many years and were a long established family in the town. Neil was ten years younger than his brother Archie and was on the reserve and was called up on the outbreak of hostilities. The Nelson battalion was sent to Gallipoli but it is believed that Neil became ill after being ashore for some time. The illness was probably Dysentry as this affected a great number of the men and he died in hospital on Tuesday the 15th of June 1915. His brother, Archie, had just left home after being on leave, to go back to the front, three hours before the news of Neil's death arrived. Neil is buried in Skew Bridge Cemetery on the Gallipoli Peninsula. This must have been a harrowing time for the parents but worse was to come when Archie was killed at the Somme on 31st July 1916. Skew Bridge Cemetery was named after the wooden bridge that stood behind it across the Achi Baba Nullah and was first established at the end of the Second Battle of Krithia. After the war a number of smaller cemeteries were moved into it from places like Orchard Gully, where the Royal Naval Division's 3rd Field Ambulance was situated, from Backhouse Post and Romano's Well further up towards the front.

Across to the left of the cemetery's gate, a few yards up the side of Observation Hill, is the start of a long communication trench that runs parallel to the road. It is generally about four feet deep and very broad and the usual scrub lines it's course. After about a hundred yards a large pit on the side of the trench contains the remains of an old rusted mortar set on a concrete base. Further up the side of the hill and working round to the right one comes to the entrance to a deep gully which leads into a broad valley. It was in this valley that the Royal Naval Division had it's divisional headquarters.

An advertisement placed in the Greenock Telegraph asking for information about the Forbes family has been very successful, and a relative, Mr David Magill, has been in touch. He lives in Greenock, and has been extremely helpful.

In May of 1999 Alderman Samuel McConaghie, of Ballymoney Borough Council paid a visit to Gallipoli. During this visit he saw the grave of Neil Forbes in Skew Bridge Cemetery and brought me back a photograph. He also visited the Helles Memorial where a number of Ballymoney men are commemorated.

The grave of Neil Forbes in Skew Bridge Cemetery, Gallipoli

7451 PRIVATE JOHN BELLINGHAM
8th Bn Highland Light Infantry
K.I.A. 28-6-15
No known grave. Commemorated on the Helles Memorial, Gallipoli.

Born   Ballymoney
Lived   West Calder. Midlothian.
Enlisted Wood Muir. Midlothian.

It would appear that John Bellingham's Father had taken the whole family away from Ballymoney to live in Scotland. At any rate they settled in a little village called Tarbrax, south of West Calder and it was here that the family grew up. John's father was a farm labourer. Much of the work was seasonal, like harvest time, or gathering potatoes, and then there were the coal mines. There was always plenty of work for willing young men to do and with the outbreak of hostilities in August 1914 there was now a new adventure to be followed up. John and his brother David enlisted together and both fought at Gallipoli.

He enlisted at Wood Muir and went with his unit to start what was going to be a very intensive and short training period. By the time his training was considered to be complete men were desperately needed in Gallipoli, and he was transported there as quickly as possible. It was not to last long. Sixteen days later he was dead, killed in a desperate attempt to take Gully Ravine.

Although John Bellingham is commemorated on the Helles Memorial as belonging to the 8th battalion of the Highland Light Infantry, this is not strictly correct. The 8th H.L.I. did not go overseas as a unit, and very little is known about them. It would appear that John Bellingham was

attached to another unit and was serving overseas with them. This other unit was more likely to have been a battalion of the Royal Scots Fus as it is this regiment which is mentioned after his name on the local war memorial in Scotland. He landed with his unit on the 12th of June 1915 in Gallipoli at Cape Helles. This was wild and difficult country. Attacks by the Turks were taking a heavy toll of the British Forces who were finding it very hard going. They were pinned down in most cases on the beach or very close to it and the Turks were there in such numbers that it was extremely difficult to get a good attack under way and get away from the sea. They did eventually work their way into the rugged hills and by 25th June were involved in an attack on Gully Ravine. This attack was supported by a heavy bombardment from the British ships out at sea, but much of this fell short, and indeed some of it helped the Turks by falling on our own men. By Monday the 28th another fierce attack was in progress, again supported by the ships, and at 11.00am our troops attacked. It took five waggons working all out to take the wounded down to the beach and the relative safety of the hospital ships. As usual the heat was unbearable and the flies, in black hordes, were simply awful. Most of the wounds were caused by shrapnel from the exploding shells and this caused a steady stream of casualties. Later that afternoon when the Turks attacked with rifle fire our troops were forced to dig in and try to hold the line. It was during this fighting that John Bellingham was killed. He has no known grave and is commemorated on the Helles Memorial.

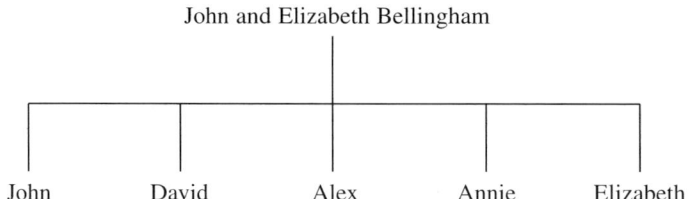

17465 PRIVATE SAMUEL CASEY
1st Bn Royal Dublin Fusiliers
K.I.A. 29-6-15
No known grave. Commemorated on the Helles Memorial, Gallipoli. Panels 190-196.

Born
Lived
Enlisted

The Dublin Fusiliers had been in India and sailed from Bombay on 19th November 1914, arriving at Plymouth on 21st December.

In January 1915, they went to Nuneaton, where they joined the 86th Brigade, 29th Div. and were brought up to full strength with new recruits. On 16th March they sailed again, this time from Avonmouth for Alexandria, arriving on 30th March. On 9th April they sailed for Mudros, and then the landing at Helles on the 25th April 1915. It was here that they were cut to pieces as they tried to reach the beach. Half of the men on the "River Clyde" had to be held back, so fierce was the enemy fire, their only shelter, a hollow at the top of the beach, which was almost impossible to reach, and a target which cost many of them their lives.

Letter in the Chronicle dated 9th Oct 1915.

BALLYMONEY MAN'S EXPERIENCES.

L.Cpl John Casey, 6th Bn Leinster Regt. at the Dardanelles, writing to his brother in Townhead St, says, --

> When we sailed from England we were about 7,000 strong, so you can have an idea what a crush it was. The heat was very hard to stand at night, and we buried a few at sea. We used to be on deck with our lifebelts on in case of emergency, as one never knows the minute, but thank goodness, after twelve days, we got landed safely. A short tine after this my regiment was sent to the firing line and I can tell you I have come through something since. God knows I would like to forget all that I have seen, but that is one thing that will never leave my memory. On the night of the 11th August we landed on a hill with very little covering, when we gave the Turks a bit of touch and go. At the same time the Turks did not spare us. My own company lost it's four officers --- all we had here. When we got the order to charge I cannot tell you how I felt, but, thank God I came through it safe along with a few others, and we managed to dig ourselves in, and hold on to the ground we had taken. The Turks did not give us much peace, and were soon at us again, but reinforcements arrived in our support, and this enabled us to repel the enemy. This is an awful country, all big hills, and as the Turks are concealed, they are hard to get at. The fighting goes on day and night. At present we are in the trenches with the Australians, who are very brave fellows, and seem to know no fear. I am after getting a spell now, and am writing this in the trenches, having to go on duty again at six o'clock, where I will stay until the morning. The heat and the flies would drive you mad but when one has got a job on like this it is good to keep up heart and say " I will see this

Suvla Bay and Salt Lake Chocolate Hill in the distance. Taken from Nex Cemetery on Gallipoli.

thing through ". So long as my health keeps good I am always cheerful, and this war can't last for ever. I could not tell you how long it is since I had my boots or clothes off, but I could do with a change any time. I often wonder how I am able to stick it when I see hardened men falling down beside me every day completely worn out. There is no one knows what war is like unless those who have been in it. I could not describe it to you, as words would not express what I want to convey. We all would like to get the Turks beaten before the winter sets in. I may say I was in the same battle as Mr Clarke Murphy's son was wounded. You know he is an officer, and seems a very nice chap, and I knew him the first time I saw him. There is a big battle coming off very soon. I expect it will be before this beach, as we are all getting prepared for it. If I go under I shall not be any worse than some of the best of the brave chaps that have gone before me. As I am tired and require an hour's sleep, I will now close, hoping you will write soon.

John Casey.

In July 1917, another brother, William, was injured, with a bullet wound in the arm.

The officer referred to above was Johnston Murphy of Main Street.

2846 PRIVATE HUGH JAMES THOMPSON
1st Bn Royal Inniskilling Fus
D.O.W. 11-7-15
Buried at Sea

Born Antrim.
Lived
Enlisted Belfast
Son of Mr J.Thompson of 57 Carnan St, Belfast.

This family had at one time lived in the Ballymoney district and at least one of the family was born there, Hugh's brother, John. The family seems to have left the Ballymoney district in the early years of this century and moved to Antrim, followed by a subsequent move to Belfast. It was there that Hugh enlisted.

Hugh was a son of Mr J. Thompson of Carnan St, Belfast and was the second son of the family to die in the war. His brother John had been killed in Gallipoli at the landings of 25th April 1915. Hugh died of wounds on a hospital ship and is buried at sea.

It is interesting to note that Hugh was also at Gallipoli and was in the reinforcements that landed at Cape Helles the following day, when they were sent in to help the desperately depleted forces to establish a base from which to attack at Cape Helles. He was not to know that his brother had just been killed at the landings the day before. A base was eventuall established that evening from which the troops were subsequently able to attack and drive the Turks back slowly towards Krithia. This was desperate fighting in unfamiliar territory with cliffs and steep sided gullies everywhere.

As well as this the whole country was covered in thick prickly scrub, which when it burned, filled the air with an acrid smoke. Scrub fires were very easily started in the dry landscape, it only took an exploding shell to start one, and depending on the direction of the wind, could either act for the troops or against them. Hugh was injured in heavy fighting at the beginning of July and was evacuated to a hospital ship out in the bay for urgent treatment. His injuries were very serious and he died soon after arriving on board. As was common practice in these cases, after a short committal service, he was buried at sea. This meant that in the space of less than three months the family at home suffered the loss of two of their sons.

Close to Devonshire Cemetery, Fricourt, France

1139 PRIVATE SAMUEL KANE
1/5 Bn Argylle & Sutherland Highlanders
K.I.A. 12-7-15
No Known Grave. Commemorated on the Helles Memorial, Gallipoli.

Born   Bushmills,
Lived   Seneirl, Bushmills.
Enlisted   Coleraine
Commemorated in Derrykeighan Parish Church.

Samuel is described as being born at Bushmills although this does not necessarily mean in Bushmills itself. The family lived at Seneirl, a townland about three miles south of Bushmills and it was more than likely that it was here that Samuel was born. He attended the old school at Seneirl. The family worshipped in Derrykeighan Parish Church and Samuel is commemorated on the Roll of Honour inside the church. He enlisted at Coleraine but there was probably a very good reason for joining the Argylle and Sutherland Highlanders which is not now apparent.

This is probably a name that should have appeared on the Bushmills War Memorial since Scncirl was well within the Bushmills district but now appears on the memorial in Dervock. Samuel had most likely gone to Scotland in search of work. This was common practice at that time. There were more opportunities across the water for young men who were willing to work. The farms were bigger and much seasonal work had to be done.

There was also the ship building yards of the Clyde and the coal mines. The 1/5th battalion were based in Greenock on the outbreak of hostilities in August 1914, and were attached to the Black Watch Brigade on Scottish Coast Defences. On 24th April they went to the Lowland Division at Dunfermline. Then on 11th May the formation became the 157th Brigade of the 52nd Div. On 1st June 1915 they embarked at Devonport, reaching Alexandria on 12th June, and arrived at Mudros on 1st July. On the 3rd of July they landed at Cape Helles. It was here that Samuel was killed, nine days later. He has no known grave and is commemorated on the Helles Memorial, panels 183 and 184.

19896 PRIVATE JOSEPH WATSON
11th Bn Highland Light Infantry
K.I.A. 19-7-15
Aged 22
Commemorated in Finvoy Presbyterian Church. Interred in Le Touret Military Cemetery.

Born   Unchinagh,
Lived   Ballymaconnelly,
Enlisted Hamilton, Lanarkshire.
Member of Ballymaconnelly L.O.L. 360 .

The 11th Battalion of the Highland Light Infantry was formed at Hamilton, Lanarkshire in August 1914, and it was here, in September, that Joseph Watson enlisted. They were taken immediately to Bordon Camp in Hants for training and placed in the 28th Brigade, 9th Div. In March 1915 they were taken the short distance to Bramshott where they completed their training and in May they landed at Boulogne. On 26th June orders were recieved to relieve the 7th Division in the line near Festubert, and accordingly the 26th and 27th Brigades took over the front line on the nights of the 1st and 2nd July.

The 28th , in which Joseph served, was in reserve. This was the first occasion in which the Division was responsible for a section of the front line, which it held east of Festubert until 18th August, and during this period all ranks became used to the trials of trench warfare. It was during this period, on the morning of 19th July, as he was washing and shaving, that Joseph Watson was shot by a sniper. He was just 22 years of age and is buried in Le Touret Military Cemetery.

Le Touret Cemetery

CAPTAIN LEWIS ALEXANDER McAFEE.
"A" Coy, 8th Bn Rifle Brigade.
K.I.A. 30-7-15 AT HOOGE
Aged 26
No Known Grave. Commemorated on the Menin Gate Memorial. Panels 46-48 and 50.

Born   Ballymoney
Lived   West.Kirby.
Enlisted Son of William McAfee, M.D. J.P. of Cooleen, West Kirby, Cheshire.

Lewis Alexander McAfee was a son of Dr William and Mrs McAfee who lived for a time in Ballymoney. Lewis was born in Ballymoney on 10th September 1888. The family seems to have moved to Edinburgh while Lewis was still a young boy. He was educated at Merchiston Castle School, in Edinburgh, where he was a prefect and Pembroke College, Cambridge, and was studying at the London Hospital in 1914. At some time during this period the family appears to have moved to Cheshire. He enlisted into the 8th Service Battalion of the Rifle Brigade and was commissioned 2nd Lt on 9th September 1914 and Lieut on 7th December of the same year.

He was in "A" Coy which arrived in France on 20th May 1915 and when the Officer Commanding "A" Coy , Capt C.F.Ballentine, was killed on 2nd July 1915 (his head was blown off by a gas shell direct hit) McAfee became Company Commander and was promoted Captain in July 1915.

At 10.00pm on 29th July 1915 the 8th Rifle Brigade moved out of Ypres to relieve the 7th Rifle Brigade in the trenches at Hooge and by 2.00am on the 30th the takeover was complete.

The opposing trenches here were sometimes as little as fifteen yards apart so sentries had to be very alert all the time. At 3.15am the Germans attacked and parts of the British front line were engulfed in flame and smoke. The new horror weapon had apparently been placed in position during the British changeover. The position was over-run by swarms of enemy bombers, most of whom had broken through at Hooge Crater, and were seen spreading out in both directions in an effort to take as much ground as possible. Both "A" and "B" Companies sustained heavy losses whilst "C" was completely anhiliated. Next day a counter attack in daylight failed. The 8th was relieved at 2.00am on the 31st. It had lost 342 men killed and injured, and 132 missing. The battalion's officers fared even worse, losing 19 out of 24, six killed, three missing and ten wounded. Lewis McAfee was one of the three missing. Missing in this case being synonymous with burned to death. He was never found and is commemorated on the Menin Gate Memorial, Ypres.

At Hooge, Captain Lewis A. McAfee on right

Only the extreme right and left hand Rifle Brigade platoons in the firing line, who had not been touched by the fire, were able to repulse attempts to bomb them out. In particular, 2nd Lieut Sydney Clayton Woodroffe and his platoon, cut off from the battalion and surrounded by German troops, held off all attacks until their supply of bombs ran out. Woodroffe then extricated his men in good order and turned about, intending to take the enemy in the flank, but while cutting our own wire he was shot and killed. His bravery earned him a posthumous V.C.

The news of the death of Lt Lewis Alexander McAfee, B.A. son of Dr McAfee, a native of Ballymoney, caused much regret in the town. His brother, John Duncan McAfee, was also a very brave young man. When two attempts to remove a wounded man from a regimental aid post had failed owing to the stretcher bearers being killed, he at once led forward a third party, and succeeded in getting all the wounded back to a place of safety under very heavy shell-fire. He showed splendid courage and self sacrifice.

McGEE J.	BUTTERWORTH H. M.	LAWRENCE
McGINLEY J.	CARMICHAEL D.	LIPSCOMBE
McGLYNN J, M. M.	DIMSDALE E. C.	McLEAR J
McGRATH J.	DRUMMOND S. H.	MANSELL
McGUINNESS C.	EDWARDS B. W.	MARSHAL
McGUINNESS J. 5725	HARDY R. M.	MASON C
McGUINNESS J. 7732	IRVINE C. K.	MILLER
McGUINNESS J. 10208	McAFEE L. A.	MOBERLY
McGUINNESS T.	MARTIN W.	MOWBRAY
McGUIRE M.	PARKER W. M.	O'BRAN
McKERNAN H.	PATEY E.	OFFEN G
MACKEY R.	PAWLE B.	PATERSO
McLOUGHLIN L.	PURVIS J R.	PERRIN
McMAHON P.	SCHOLEY C. H. N.	PERRY F
McMANUS T.	TURNER B. A., D. S. O.	PLUMPT
McMILLAN D.	WILLOUGHBY	PORTT
McNALLY J.	HON. F. G. G.	RASMUS
McNALLY T.		RAY W
MAGUIRE M.	LIEUTENANT	REYNO
MAHONEY M.	BENSON H. C.	RICHAR

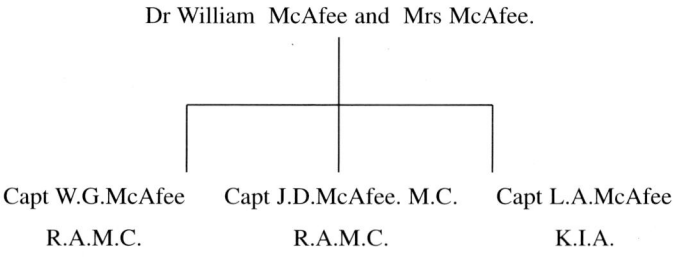

Dr William McAfee and Mrs McAfee.

Capt W.G.McAfee   Capt J.D.McAfee. M.C.   Capt L.A.McAfee

R.A.M.C.   R.A.M.C.   K.I.A.

5222 PRIVATE JOHN HENRY
7th Bn Royal Munster Fusiliers formerly 12948 R. Inniskilling Fus.
K.I.A. 15-8-15
No Known Grave. Commemorated on the Helles Memorial, Gallipoli. Panels 185-190

Born   Finvoy
Lived   Eden, Finvoy.
Enlisted   Ballymoney
Son of George Henry, of Maddykeel.
Commemorated in Finvoy Presbyterian Church.

.John Henry was born at the Eden, a townland in the Finvoy district and worshipped in Finvoy Presbyterian Church, where he is commemorated. He was a son of George Henry of Maddykeel and he enlisted at Ballymoney soon after war was declared. John's unit was part of the 29th Division which sailed for Gallipoli on the 26th of March 1915.

This is a family which appears to have died out and no-one from the Finvoy district that I have spoken to seems to have any memory of them. It is sad when something like this turns up but it appears there is nothing that can be done about it. John Henry seems to have been on very good terms with James Dougherty from Balnamore and they seem to have spent much of their time together. The attack in which John was killed took place along the Kiretch Tepe Ridge on the morning of the 15th of August. It was a highly dangerous attack on the enemy's main ammunition dump in the area and the Irish, poorly equipped with ammunition, were gradually forced back after the initial attack. It was during the fierce fighting of this retreat that John was killed.

The careers of John Henry and James Dougherty had followed a very similar pattern. Both had been in the Royal Inniskilling Fusiliers to start with and both had transferred to the Munsters. They were both at Gallipoli together and in a letter home James Dougherty tells of seeing John being killed beside him. Fifteen days later James would be dead too. John Henry has no known grave and is commemorated on the Helles Memorial.

Suvla is perhaps the lovliest part of Gallipoli. From Chunuk Bair there is a sparkling view north across the whole area with the Salt Lake, when it is dry, shimmering diamond white in the sun. Around it yellow fields and green trees are scattered across the low lying plain, while beyond, a harsh, black line of hills scars the horizon. To the west, the violet blue waters of the bay are kept deathly still by the ring of land that reaches out into the Aegean Sea. Along the margin of the bay a long hot beach of powdery sand runs for several miles in absolute solitude and it is hard to imagine a more beautiful place.

In 1915 this beach was a very different place, littered with the dead and dying and with men seeking shelter from the hail of lead being poured upon them from the relative safety of the surrounding cliffs. It was a very hostile environment.

Cemetery location information.

The Helles Memorial bears over 20,000 names whose graves are unknown or who were lost or buried at sea in Gallipoli waters. The Memorial stands on the tip of the Peninsula and is in the form of an obelisk over 30 metres high that can be seen by ships passing through the Dardanelles.

3222 PRIVATE JAMES HENRY MOORE
1st Bn Royal Inniskilling Fusiliers
K.I.A. 21-8-15
Aged 21
No Known Grave. Commemorated on the Helles Memorial, Gallipoli. Panels 97-101.

Born
Enlisted
Son of Robert and Catherine Moore, of 57 Ashmore St, Belfast.

James Henry Moore lived at Balnamore, the son of Robert and Catherine Moore of Belfast. He enlisted into the Royal Inniskilling Fusiliers and very soon afterwards was on his way to Gallipoli. He survived all of the fierce early fighting and on 21st August 1915 was involved in one of the biggest battles on the Peninsula. A major assault on Scimitor Hill and Hill 60 to the south-east of the Suvla Plain was planned for this date and the 29th Division was brought round from Cape Helles to lead it.

The soldiers fought in an unseasonable fog which obscured the hills from the British artillery at the beginning of the battle and as the day wore on scrub fires broke out, filling the air with acrid smoke. These fires spread rapidly and engulfed many of the British positions forcing the attacking soldiers to change direction.

The countryside here is rugged and covered in dense scrub which burns fiercely and it was a case of having to fight around the fires. In terms of numbers of men engaged this was the greatest battle fought in the Gallipoli campaign. It was during this battle that James Henry Moore was killed. He has no known grave and is commemorated on the Helles Memorial. This memorial, built at the tip of the peninsula, and visible for many miles out to sea, commemorates the names of 20,752 men who went missing without trace and who have no known grave.

5261 PRIVATE JAMES DOUGHERTY
7th Bn Royal Munster Fusiliers formerly 13024 R. Inniskilling Fus.
K.I.A. 30-8-15
Aged 20
No Known Grave. Commemorated on the Helles Memorial, Gallipoli. Panels 185-190.

Born   Balnamore
Lived   Balnamore
Enlisted Coleraine
Son of George Dougherty, of Balnamore, and the late Mary Dougherty.

The 7th battalion were formed at Tralee in August 1914 and trained at the Curragh with the 10th Division. In May 1915 they went to England to train at Basingstoke and on 9th July sailed from Liverpool, arriving at Mudros at the end of the month.

They took part in the landing at Suvla Bay on the 7th of August.

James Dougherty's father was a stone mason and had lost an eye, probably as a result of his work. James enlisted into the Royal Inniskilling Fusiliers in August 1914 and was engaged in the Army Signals Corps but later transferred to the Munsters. He sailed for the Dardanelles on 9th July 1915. He was an only son.

Soon after arriving he was very seriously injured and was evacuated to one of the hospital ships moored out at sea. A letter from one of the Chaplains tells us more. The Rev V.L.Keelan wrote, " I deeply regret to tell you that Private Dougherty (5261) Royal Munster Fusiliers died of wounds on our ship on 30th August, and I buried him at sea. He was very seriously wounded in the head and was unconcious. May God help you in this great sorrow. You may well be proud of this brave soldier and his noble sacrifice".

As James was buried at sea there is obviously no known grave and he is commemorated on the Helles Memorial, the huge memorial at the tip of the Gallipoli Peninsula.

James, writing from Gallipoli, in his last letter home to his Father says,

"I expected to write to you sooner to tell you something of what is going on, only I could not get any paper. The Munsters have been in the thick of it now for almost a month, and so far I have escaped.

The battalion has made a name for itself, but a good number of the brave fellows are gone. I had a chum here called Henry, who came from Eden. Whether you know him or not, I don't know, but on Sunday last we were making an attack on the enemy trenches. We hadn't gone ten yards when Henry was killed. It will be almost two months now since I had a letter from you. Private Tom Chambers is out here somewhere but it's not easy to locate anyone out here as you will understand. I have had some narrow shaves since I came out here. One day I took cover behind a rock, and after waiting some time, put out my head to see what was in front when a sniper put a bullet through my helmet. I have the helmet yet.

Tell all my friends I was asking for them."

Cemetery location information.

The Helles Memorial bears over 20,000 names and is both the memorial to the Gallipoli campaign and to men who fell in that campaign and whose graves are unknown or who were lost or buried at sea in Gallipoli waters (other than Australian or New Zealanders who are named on other memorials) Inscribed on it are the names of all the ships that took part in the campaign and the titles of the army formations and units which served on the Peninsula. The Memorial stands on the tip of the Peninsula and is in the form of an obelisk over 30 metres high that can be seen by ships passing through the Dardanelles.

13/1406A TPR ROBERT McNAUL
Auckland Mounted Rifles New Zealand Exp Force
D.O.W. 1-9-15
Aged 23
Interred in Cairo War Memorial Cemetery. Row D, Grave 79.

Born   Ballygan.
Lived
Enlisted
Commemorated in St. James's Presbyterian Church.

Robert McNaul was born at Ballygan, a townland close to Balnamore. The family worshipped in St. James's Presbyterian Church in Ballymoney and it is there that Robert is commemorated. He was a son of James and Louisa Agnes McNaul. Robert had been living in New Zealand for some time before he enlisted and had served for a time in Gallipoli. After arriving in Egypt he was seriously wounded and died in hospital in Cairo. He is buried in the cemetery nearby.

Tank Corps Memorial at Pozieres

5790 RIFLEMAN JOHN KIRGAN
2nd Bn Royal Irish Rifles
K.I.A. 11-9-15 AT HOOGE
Aged 25
No Known Grave. Commemorated on the Menin Gate Memorial, Ypres. Panel 40.

Born   Ballymoney
Lived   Milltown, Ballymoney.
Enlisted   Belfast.
*Son of Mr and Mrs Eliza Kirgan, of 1, Brand St, Lome Sq, Ibrox, Glasgow.
Commemorated in Ballymoney Parish Church.*

On the outbreak of hostilities the 2nd battalion were stationed at Tidworth. They joined the 7th Brigade, 3rd Division and landed in France on 14th August. This part of the line at Hooge was fought over continuously and was taken and re-taken on many occasions and it is no surprise to discover that John has no known grave.

The family lived at the Milltown in Ballymoney in the early years of this century but seems to have moved to Scotland at some stage although there are still connections here. John was born at the Milltown in 1890 and spent the early years of his life there. He enlisted in Belfast and this partly explains why he was serving in the 2nd battalion of the Rifles.

A comrade writing home tells of John being hit by a stray bullet which killed him instantly and then wounded another soldier in the chest. It would seem more likely that he was killed by a sniper who had lain in wait for just such a chance. He has no known grave and is commemorated on the Menin Gate.

Menin Gate Memorial

Menin Gate Memorial side view

3312 PRIVATE DANIEL BAIRD
11th Bn Highland Light Infantry.
K.I.A. 25-9-15
Aged 30
Interred in Cambrin Churchyard Extension, France. Row J, Grave 35

Born   Mosside, Co Antrim.
Lived   Mosside, Co Antrim.
Enlisted Hamilton, Lanarkshire.
Killed in action at Loos.
Son of Stewart and Martha Baird.

The 11th battalion were formed at Hamilton in August 1914 and did much of their training at Bordon. From here, in March they moved to Bramshott and in May 1915 landed at Boulogne.

In September 1915 the 11th battalion were east of Vermelles and attacking the German positions on the Lens- La Bassee road. On the morning of the 25th September our artillery opened at 5.50am and gas and smoke were discharged along the whole front. The wind was light and changeable and in many areas the gas and smoke drifted back over the British lines causing havoc among the troops. This is flat country and the smoke had been meant to give the troops some cover but they had to attack as best they could without it. At 6.30am the attack began with the 6th KOSB leading and the 11th HLI in support and it was in this attack that Daniel Baird was killed. A short distance away, another Ballymoney man, William O'Brien, was to die of his wounds at an advanced dressing station near Haisnes on this same day. Altogether five more Ballymoney men would be killed on this day.

Cambrin is a village about 24 kilometres north of Arras, on the road to La Bassee. Cambrin Churchyard Ext is on the south side of the main road, 200metres from the Mairie. The Commonwealth plot will be found behind the church.

Cambrin Churchyard Extension, Pas de Calais, France. Grave of Daniel Baird

17216 L. CPL. SAMUEL BROLLY
2nd Bn Royal Irish Rifles.
K.I.A. 25-9-15
Aged 23
No known grave. Commemorated on the Menin Gate Memorial, Ypres. Panel 40

Born   Ballymoney
Lived   Drumahiskey
Enlisted   Ballymoney on 10th October 1914.
Son of Robert G. and Ellen Sophia Brolly, of Balnamore.
Commemorated in Drumreagh Presbyterian Church.

Ypres is a town in the province of West Flanders. The memorial is situated at the eastern side of the town on the road to Menin and Courtrai, and bears the names of 55,000 men who were lost without trace during the defence of the Ypres salient in the First World War.

Samuel Brolly as a young lad had played football for Balnamore. Following on from that he had played for Derry Celtic and Distillery and was making quite a name for himself on the football field. But on 10th October 1914 he enlisted at Ballymoney into the 2nd Battalion Royal Irish Rifles. The 2nd battalion had been at Tidworth on the outbreak of hostilities and landed at Rouen ten days later, on the 14th of August. By the time Samuel enlisted the battalion were already in action. They had been sent to the area around Ypres in Belgium and it was here that Samuel joined them. He was killed somewhere in the vicinity of Hooge. There is no known grave and he is commemorated on the Menin Gate Memorial in Ypres.

3190 RIFLEMAN JAMES HUEY
2nd Bn Royal Irish Rifles
K.I.A. 25-9-15
No Known Grave. Commemorated on the Menin Gate Memorial, Ypres, Panel 40.

Born   Ballynagashel.
Lived   Ballycraigagh. Stranocum.
Enlisted   West Calder, Midlothian.
Son of William and Rose Huey, of Ballycraigagh, Stranocum.
Commemorated in Bushvale Presbyterian Church.

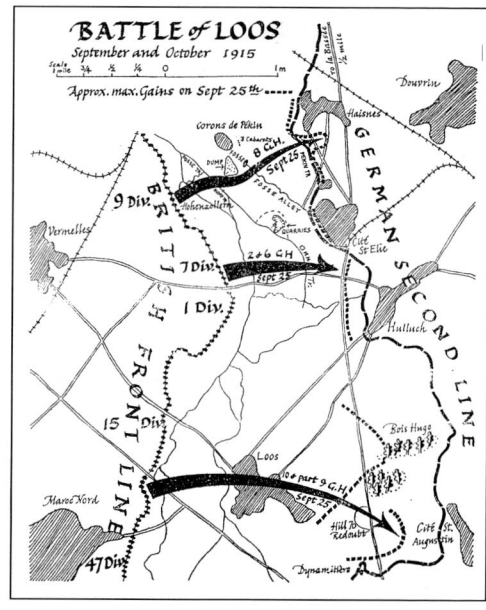

The family headstone in the graveyard of Bushvale Presbyterian Church records the death of William Huey on 28th December 1911 at the comparatively young age of 46. His wife Rose lived to be 80 years of age and died on 13th June 1950. James was working in Scotland when war was declared. He enlisted in West Calder and came home to train. There are many letters from both boys who wrote regularly to their Mother from wherever they were. There was also a very close relationship with the Laverty family and William Laverty is mentioned in many of the letters. In fact it turned out that Mrs. Huey had reared William Laverty after both his Mother and Father had died. A letter from James in Belfast in December 1914 confirms that he will be training there for some time. Letters follow at regular intervals and one in March 1915 is from Victoria Barracks in Belfast.

There is one from France on 13th June 1915 mentioning Alex Huey and Willie Laverty being home on leave. On 26th July there is another letter from James stating that he is well and asking about all at home. In November there is an anxious letter from Alex saying that he has not heard from James for seven weeks and wondering if he has been killed. On 14th October Mrs. Huey wrote to James asking if he was alright, but the letter was returned with a note to say that as far as could be ascertained, he was still with his unit. Then on 2nd November there is an official note to say that James is missing since 25th September 1915. And then from the record office in a letter dated 7th September 1916 official confirmation that James was killed on 25-9-15 at the Battle of Loos.

3104 PRIVATE SAMUEL JAMES LOGAN
9th Bn Gordon Highlanders
K.I.A. 25-9-15
No Known Grave. Commemorated on the Loos Memorial

Born   Castle St, Ballymoney
Lived
Enlisted   Uddingston, Lanarkshire.
Son of Mary Logan of Castle St.
Commemorated in Trinity Presbyterian Church

The 9th battalion was formed at Aberdeen in September 1914 and went to train with the 15th Division at Aldershot. In November they moved to Haslemere, and then in January 1915 became the Pioneer Battalion for the 15th Division. In February they moved to Perham Down and then in May to Andover, and landed in France in July 1915.

Samuel Logan and his brother William had both gone to Scotland in search of work. This was common practice at that time and many young men from North Antrim went to Scotland to find work. Their mother was by now, living on her own, in Castle Street, Ballymoney. She had been a widow for some time. When war broke out both boys enlisted with Samuel going to the Gordon Highlanders. By early 1915 his training, or what he was to get of it, was complete, and he was taken to France. The battles around Ypres were at their height, the weather had been wet, and there was mud and stench everywhere. As the Summer wore on, the fighting continued, and

Samuel and his mates were moved further south to the area around Loos. The 9th was a pioneer battalion, responsible for erecting barbed wire, trench digging, and other work in the front line. It was attached in platoon strength to the 9th Black Watch, 8th Seaforths, 7th Camerons, and 10th Gordons, all part of the 44th Brigade. The rest billets for the men here was in the village of Mazingarbe, where, at the local abbatoir, many British soldiers had been executed by firing squad.

On Friday, the 24th September, as the troops were being moved up for the big attack next morning, the rain came down in sheets, and the men had to stand in the trenches all night. They were soaked to the skin. They were to attack the German positions on the Lens-La Bassee road just south of the village of Haisnes. Early next morning the battle commenced and it was during this action that Samuel was killed. He has no known grave and is commemorated on the Loos Memorial.

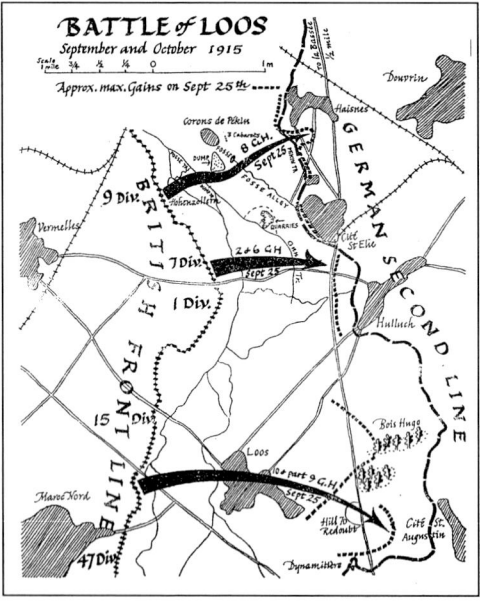

12327 PRIVATE ANDREW MADDEN
9th Bn Cameronians (Scottish Rifles)
K.I.A. 25-9-15
Aged 31
No Known Grave. Commemorated on the Loos Memorial.

Born   Finvoy
Lived   Killymaddy, Bendooragh.
Enlisted   Glasgow
Son of Thomas and Jane Madden, of Bendooragh.
Commemorated in Finvoy Presbyterian Church.
Memorial -- Dud Corner Cemetery.

The 9th battalion were formed at Hamilton in August 1914 and trained with the 9th Division at Bordon. On 12th May 1915 they landed at Boulogne. Andrew Madden was with the 9th battalion just east of Vermelles and the plan was to attack the enemy line on the south edge of the village of Haisnes, on the Lens to La Bassee road, cross over this and go on to Douvrin.

The preliminary bombardment opened according to plan on the 21st of September and the 9th battalion was ordered to make a number of feint attacks during the period before Zero Day. This was done with such vigour as to provoke heavy artillery retaliation. Each night patrols were ordered out to inspect the enemy wire. At 10.00am on the 24th the 9th Scottish Rifles was relieved by the 10th Highland Light Infantry and marched back to Cambrin to prepare for the battle next day. At 5.50am on the 25th of September an intense bombardment began and gas was released from the British front line. But the light breeze changed direction and much of the gas drifted over the waiting battalions and they were seriously affected. By 6.30am it had actually drifted behind the British trenches so that the attack was begun under very adverse conditions. To add to this, the German artillery placed a barrage on the British trenches and some of the gas cylinders were hit, causing them to explode, killing anyone waiting near them for the signal to assault.

The ground in front was level and without cover and it was over this that the 9th battalion had to advance. It was during this attack that Andrew Madden was killed. William O'Brien, from Dervock, was serving with the 10th Highland Light Infantry here, and was killed on the same day as Andrew.

9035 L. CPL. DAVID McCRACKEN
2nd Bn Highland Light Infantry
K.I.A. 25-9-15
No Known Grave. Commemorated on the Loos Memorial. Panels 108-112.

Born   Dunloy.
Lived   Uddingston, Lanarkshire.
Enlisted Hamilton, Lanarkshire.

As a youngster David attended school at Galdanagh, Dunloy, with his brothers and sisters. When he left school he went to Scotland and found work in the coal mines of Lanarkshire. Later he joined the Navy but when his mother found out about this she bought him out. He was a very fit young man and interested in sport and had taken up boxing. By the time he enlisted at Hamilton he had become a very competent boxer and at one time sparred with the British Champion, Billy Wells.

When war was declared on 4th August 1914 the 2nd battalion were in Maida barracks in Aldershot. They joined the 2nd Division and landed at Boulogne ten days later, on the 14th of August.

In September 1915 the 2nd Battalion H.L.I. were at Givenchy, north of Arras. During the night of 24-25th orders were recieved that an attack would commence at 5.30am on the 25th with an emmision of gas and smoke. The wind was not quite in the required direction and very light but it was decided to go ahead anyway. At 5.45am the artillery commenced to bombard the enemy trenches and at 5.50am the gas cylinders were discharged. The gas slowly drifted towards the German trenches and at 6.00am the brigade advanced to the assault.

After severe hand to hand fighting in an elaborate trench system the second line trench was reached. The bomb with which the British troops were armed was of the ball pattern of which much was expected. The ignition of this bomb was achieved by striking the fuse on a match-striker worn on the wrist. But the day was wet and the bombs failed to ignite and the Germans were able to regain their lost ground. It was during this action that David McCracken was killed. He has no known grave and is commemorated on the Loos Memorial. Two of his brothers also served, Robert for much of the war, and Samuel enlisted late in the war but didn't get to France.

Cemetery location information.

Loos-en-Gohelle is a village about 5 kilometres north-west of Lens. The Loos Memorial forms the side and back of Dud Corner cemetery where over 1,700 officers and men, the great majority of whom fell in the battle of Loos, are buried. Dud Corner Cemetery, which stands almost on the site of a German strong point, the Lens Road Redoubt, captured by the 15th Scottish Division on the first day of the battle, is located about one kilometre west of the village, to the north-east of the N43, the main Lens to Bethune road.

The Loos Memorial commemorates over 20,000 officers and men who fell in the area from the River Lys to the old southern boundary of the First Army, east and west of Grenay, and who have no known grave. It covers the period from the first day of the Battle of Loos to the date of the Armistice.

Sarah McCracken married Dick McKendry, a postman in Dunloy and a brother of William McKendry who was killed at Hamel on the first day of ths Somme.

I am very much indebted to Roy McCombe of Ballymoney for his story of the McCracken family which is as follows. The Warrant for LOL 536 was issued, on the 18th of Nov 1829, to John McCracken. The McCracken farm was adjacent to where the Garryduff Orange Hall now stands, and prior to 1920, when the hall was opened, the Lodge (536) met in McCracken's barn. 37 years after the issue of the Garryduff Warrant in 1866, Archibald McCracken was Worshipful District Master of Ballymoney District, and served a second term in the Office from 1870 to1873. James McCracken was born in 1842 being initiated into Garryduff LOL 536 in 1859, he was most probably a relation of the above mentioned John and Archibald. James was later to purchase a farm at nearby Dunloy, where he would raise a large family of nine boys and five girls. James McCracken was a very enthusiastic worker for the Orange Order and decided that Dunloy should have it's own Orange Lodge. When James's plan got abroad he recieved several threatening letters, one of which said he would be kicked to death if he started an Orange Lodge in Dunloy. The letters had the opposite effect on McCracken than that desired by the letter writers, and he pressed ahead with his plan. The inaugural meeting of the Lodge being held on the 7th of April 1893. The Lodge took the title of Dunloy Union Defenders and was issued Warrant number 496. Eventually all his nine sons would follow him into the ranks of the Lodge, and on one memorable occasion on the 12th of July he walked with all his nine sons either in the Lodge or the band.

The story of how his eldest son, also named James, joined his father's lodge is interesting. Apparently James jun shared his father's interest in the Orange Order, but had not attained the required age, so on the 2nd of July 1896 he secreted himself in the old fashioned chimney, (presumably of the Orange Hall which was opened the following month of August) to hear for himself what went on. Halfway through the meeting, which was chaired by his father, he made a noise and was discovered. His father, the Worshipful Master of the Lodge from it's inception until 1921, a total of 28 years, took the only course of action open to him, and James jun became the newest and youngest member of Dunloy 496. As already mentioned, the hall was opened in August 1896 and was built by voluntary labour.

During the early years of it's existance, the Dunloy Lodge, like the majority of other lodges in those days, was headed on parade by Lambeg drums. With the McCracken boys being keen on flutes and drums, a flute band was formed in connection with the Lodge, being known as Dunloy Union Defenders Flute Band. On the eleventh of July evening 1908 when the band was out for their usual march, they were attacked by a mob, who had gathered into Dunloy for this purpose, their intentions being to finish the band once and for all. When the attack was made the attackers had to flee, having bitten off more than they could chew. During this period Dunloy 496 belonged to the Rasharkin District, James McCracken representing his Lodge at District meetings, and walking eight miles over the mountain to do so, summer and winter. His enemies were also aware of this, but they also knew that he carried a revolver and would not hesitate to use it should the need arise. In 1909 Dunloy transferred to the Ballymoney District, but there is no record of why they transferred, but permission to do so was granted by the Grand Orange Lodge of Ireland at it's half yearly meeting in Dungannon Orange Hall on the 9th of June 1909. John had been initiated into the Lodge in December 1899 and recieved the Royal Arch Purple degree on 16th July 1900. William was initiated into 496 in July 1902, gaining the Royal Arch Purple degree in 1903 he went to Scotland, and was involved in having a Lodge started in Plains near Airdrie, he became the first Worshipful Master of the Lodge which had the title Park Guff Union Defenders LOL 261, echoing the title of his father's Lodge back home in Dunloy. On the 4th of July 1914 Warrant no 261 was exchanged for no 70. William served as Worshipful Master until his death in a pit accident in 1924. He was succeeded as W.M. by his younger brother, Joseph. This Scottish connection has been maintained to the present day with Bro Chapman from LOL 70 travelling to parade with the Dunloy brethren and Ballymoney District at the Bi Centenary Parade at Loughgall on Saturday 23rd September 1995.

Archie was initiated into Dunloy Lodge with his brother William in July 1902. David followed in 1906 but was killed in 1917 at the Battle of Loos. Tom was initiated in 1910.

Two years later, in 1912, Robert was initiated. After the end of the 1st World War, Robert emigrated, first to Australia, where he stayed for just one year before moving to New Zealand, where he joined New Zealand LOL no 89 becoming W.M. and in keeping with tradition was succeeded by his son. He came home for the first time in 37 years to walk on Derry's Walls on the 12th of August with his nephews.

After William's death in the pit accident in 1924 his younger brother, Joseph became W.M. and held this office until 1942, when the Lodge went dormant due to the 2nd Wold War. Joseph's son, James, the third generation to bear the name, got the Lodge restarted on 4th March 1948, with a change of name and location, being now situated in the village of Caldercruix, and entitled Caldercruix Truth Defenders LOL 70. James was elected W.M. In 1955 the Lodge had Dunloy Union Defenders Flute Band to lead them at their demonstration at Armdale. In 1960 James McCracken was still the W.M. and was Deputy District Master of Airdrie District with LOL 70 being the largest Lodge in the District. Leslie McCracken was initiated in 1919 and died in the service of his country as a "B" Special.

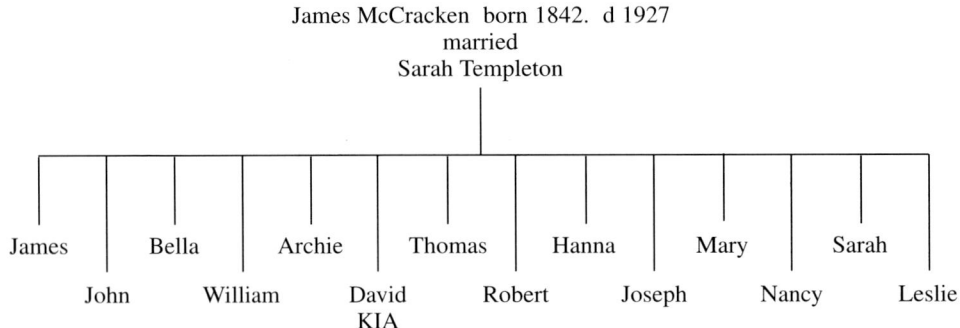

16875 CORPORAL WILLIAM JOSEPH O'BRIEN
10th Bn Highland Light Infantry
D.O.W. 25-9-15
Interred in St. Mary's A.D.S. Cemetery, Haisnes, France.

Born   Dervock
Lived   Dervock
Enlisted Glasgow
Son of Thomas and Sarah Ann O'Brien, of Dervock.
Commemorated in Derrykeighan Parish Church.

William was a son of Thomas and Sarah Ann O'Brien of Church Street, Dervock. There was four of a family, three boys and a girl and they all attended school in Dervock. The family worshipped in Derrykeighan Parish Church and it is there that the two boys who were killed are commemorated.

The 10th Battalion of the Highland Light Infantry was formed at Hamilton in August 1914 William O'Brien had been working in Scotland for a short time just before the outbreak of hostilities and enlisted in Glasgow into the 10th Battalion. They were taken to Bordon Camp in Hants where they joined the 28th Brigade, 9th Div, for initial training. In March 1915 they were moved the short distance to Bramshott to finish their training, and in May they landed at Boulogne. By September of 1915 they were between Loos-en-Gohelle and Haisnes. William was very seriously injured there and died of his wounds at a dressing station. He is buried close by in St Mary's A.D.S. Cemetery, near Haisnes.

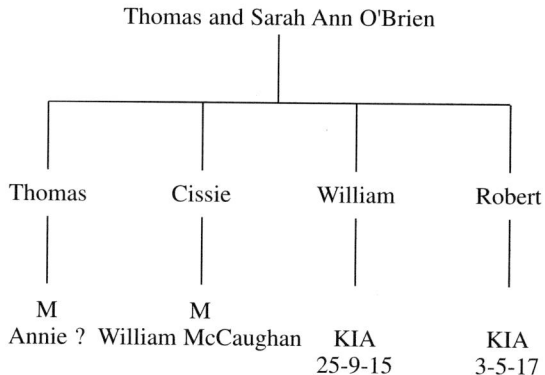

3035 PRIVATE ALEXANDER MORROW
2nd Bn Irish Guards
K.I.A. 27-9-15
No Known Grave. Commemorated on the Loos Memorial, France.

Born   Ballymoney
Lived
Enlisted   Belfast.

Alex Morrow enlisted in Belfast into the 2nd Battalion of the Irish Guards which was formed on 15th July 1915. He had actually completed much of his training previous to this and had been in the 2nd reserve battalion. On the 16th of August the battalion left Brentwood station for Southampton and that evening boarded the "Anglo-Canadian" and the "Viper" and escorted by destroyers, tied up at Le Havre at midnight. It was their first taste of France. They were taken by train to Lumbres and then marched to billets at Acquin, a small village a few miles from St. Omer.

Here they trained and it was during this training that they met up for the first time with their own 1st battalion. At this time plans were being laid for the Battle of Loos and training was intensified. From here they were taken via Noux-les-Mines, Noyelles and Vermelles to trenches in front of the small village of Le Rutoire in readiness for the battle. By now the battalion had been on the move for 48 hours, most of the time without food, and certainly all of it without sleep. They were both tired and hungry but the attack was due to begin and they had to go into the line. At 2.30am the attack started. The 2nd Irish Guards were to advance into Chalk-Pit Wood and to establish themselves on the north-east and south-east faces of it. By this time they were under intense German heavy artillery attack and it was almost impossible to get forward. They eventually did advance and reached tha village of Haisnes with heavy losses. It was during the battle in Chalk-Pit Wood that Alex was killed. He has no known grave and is commemorated on the Loos Memorial. He had been less than six weeks in France.

6770 CORPORAL BRYCE GILMOUR
2nd Bn, Irish Guards
K.I.A. 30-9-15
No Known Grave. Commemorated on the Loos Memorial, France. Panels 9 and 10.

Born   Roscommon, Co.Roscommon.
Lived   Londonderry
Enlisted   Dublin

It is believed that Bryce was a son of a Mr Bryce Gilmour who was in charge of the Ballymoney Workhouse and who lived in Charlotte Street in the town. The family appears to have come to live in Ballymoney at some stage and that Bryce enlisted in Dublin. He had been a policeman in the Royal Irish Constabulary and was based in Cookstown. He was the third son of the family and before leaving for the front was allowed to spend a short leave with his Mother and Father in Ballymoney.

Another son of the family who had previously emigrated to Canada, was serving with the Canadians.

The 2nd battalion of the Irish Guards was formed on 15th July 1915 and was to be made up out of men already enlisted in the reserve battalion. One of these was Bryce Gilmour. They were trained in the old Warley Barracks. They did their first route march on the 6th of August, a distance of sixteen miles, in the flat countryside around Warley. On the 16th of August they left Brentwood station and that evening were packed tightly on two ships, the "Anglo-Canadian" and the "Viper", at Southampton. They had to be escorted by destroyers because there were too many German submarines about and at midnight were safely tied up at Le Havre. They were immediately marched to camp on the outskirts of the city where they spent the next two days and on the 18th entrained for Lumbres and from there marched to billets at Acquin, a little village on a hillside a few miles from St. Omer. It was here that their final training took place and by the end of the month they were considered ready for an advance to the front line. On 1st September they joined up with their Brigade, the 2nd Guards Brigade, and shared a wet day at practice in coming up into the line. Wet days were now becoming more common and by the middle of the month it rained almost every day. They billeted at Haquin, very wet and tired, at one in the morning of the 26th of September and had breakfast at half past four, as there was a chance of an early

Loos Memorial, France.

move. However no orders came and shortly after noon, they moved via Noeux-les-Mines, Sailly-Labourse, Noyelles and Vermelles to trenches in front of La Rutoire. At 2.30am they were instructed to advance and to take possession of a captured German trench and by the time this was complete it was almost broad daylight. The plan was for the 2nd battalion to advance and take Chalk Pit Wood. At half past two that afternoon a heavy bombardment, lasting one and a half hours would be delivered on that sector. At 4.00pm the 2nd battalion Irish Guards would advance on Chalk Pit Wood and establish themselves on the north-east and south-east faces of it, supported by the 1st Coldstreams, and were to hold it at all costs. By the 29th their ranks had been seriously depleted and the German heavy guns had the range to an inch. They had been under continuous strain since the 25th, and from the 27th to the 30th in a punishing action which had cost them 324 casualties. Bryce Gilmour was one of those killed on the 30th and that night they were taken out of the line and sent to billets for rest. He has no known grave and is commemorated on the Loos Memorial.

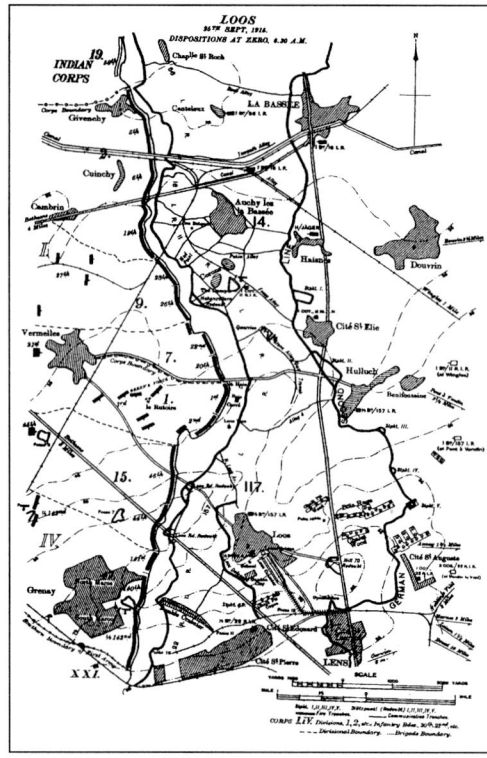

Loos Memorial, France.

LIEUT THOMAS CALLENDER CAMPBELL
11th Div. Royal Engineers
D.O.W. 8-10-15
No Known Grave. Commemorated on the Helles Memorial, Gallipoli. Panels 23 to 25, and 325 to 328.

Born
Lived
Enlisted
Commemorated in 1st Ballymoney Presbyterian Church.
Son of the late Rev. William Howard Campbell and Mrs Campbell, of Wellington Park, Belfast.

Thomas Campbell was a son of the late Rev. William Howard Campbell and Mrs Campbell of Wellington Park, Belfast. He had emigrated to Canada some years before and was working there as an engineer on the outbreak of hostilities. He immediately came home and enlisted into the Royal Engineers. He had been educated at Foyle College in Londonderry before emigrating and was a nephew of Mr S.B.Boyd of Ballymoney. Soon after joining the Army he was granted a commission, but before proceeding with the Expeditionary Force he married Miss Georgina McGugan, a daughter of Mr Alexander McGugan, of the Ulster Bank in Ballymoney. Soon after this he went with his unit to Gallipoli. It was while serving there that he was very seriously wounded on the 5th of October. He died of his wounds three days later.

It is unusual for a soldier who deid of wounds not to have a known grave, but heavy fighting over the same ground at a later period would most likely have obliterated any signs of a grave. Thomas is commemorated on the Helles Memorial and in 1st Ballymoney Presbyterian Church, where the family worshipped. In 1998 and again this year, 1999, Alderman Samuel McConaghy, of Ballymoney Borough Council, visited the scene of these battles in Gallipoli. He brought me back many photographs of their graves and of their names on memorials. He is probably the only Ballymoney man ever to visit these graves.

The Helles Memorial, built at the tip of the Gallipoli Peninsula, commemorates men from Western Europe, from Australia and New Zealand, from Asia and Africa, who fought under the British flag. On the four outer faces of the walls which surround this memorial the names of 20,752 men, the missing of the Gallipoli campaign, are recorded. In all, seven Ballymoney men are commemorated here.

8364 PRIVATE JAMES BOORMAN
2nd Bn, Cameronians (Scottish Rifles)
D.O.W. 20-11-15
Aged 41
Interred in Sailly-sur-la-Lys Canadian Cemetery, France. Plot 2, Row E, Grave 116.

Born   Dunloy.
Lived   Belfast
Enlisted   Dunfermline
Brother of Mrs Maggie McCartney, of 57 Melrose St, Belfast.

James Boorman was born in the village of Dunloy, about four miles south of Ballymoney. The family may have moved to live in Belfast as this is the place of residence given in "Soldiers Died". But as James enlisted in Dunfermline he may very well have been working in Scotland. His age is also something to be taken into account. At 41 he was a bit older than the average and so may have been a regular soldier. If this is the case, when war was declared on 4th August 1914, he was serving in Malta. On 15th September 1914 the battalion sailed for England and arrived at Southampton on the 22nd. They were taken to Hursley Park, where they joined the 23rd Brigade, 8th Division, and on 5th November 1914, landed at Le Havre.

By the time of the Battle of Loos in September 1915 the 2nd battalion were in operations north of the La Bassee Canal in a diversional attack to hold enemy reserves in that area and to keep

Sailly-sur-la-Lys Canadian Cemetery, centre front row

them from moving south to help in the main battle. They remained in the Fleurbaix, Laventie area for the next few months and withstood much heavy fighting in this time. In an attack at Laventie in mid November James was very seriously injured and was taken by stretcher-bearers to the field hospital at Sailly-sur-la-Lys. He died there on the 20th of November 1915 and is buried in the cemetery nearby. His battalion remained in this area to March 1916, when they moved south in preparation for the Battle of the Somme.

Cemetery Information

The village of Sailly-sur-la-Lys lies seven kilometres west of Armentieres. From Armentieres follow the road to Estaires. Follow the D 945 for five kilometres until reaching the village of Sailly-sur-la-Lys. Continue through the village for two kilometres and the Cemetery is on the left opposite the Anzac Cemetery.

Sailly-sur-la-lys cemetery was used for the burial of two men who went in front of the firing squad on 3rd October 1915. They were George Lee and W. Smith, both on a charge of desertion. Lee was aged 30 and had already served twelve years in another regiment. Smith was 37 and had served in the Boer War.

2924 L.CPL JOHN McINTYRE
5th Bn, Argylle & Sutherland Highlanders
DIED 6-12-15 OF APPENDICITIS
Aged 21
Interred in Greenock Cemetery Scotland. Plot HHH, Grave 180.

Born   Aghadowey
Lived   Mosside
Enlisted
Commemorared in Drumtullagh Parish Church.
Son of James and Martha McIntyre, of Mosside, Stranocum.

James and Martha McIntyre worshipped in Drumtullagh Parish Church, about a mile outside Mosside village. Their son, John had been born at Aghadowey, but as the family appears to have later moved to Mosside, he is commemorated in Drumtullagh, where he regularly attended church.

This battalion was based in Greenock at the beginning of the first World War, and was involved in Scottish coast defences. John McIntyre had probably gone to Scotland in search of work, like many of the young men of the time, and then ended up enlisting into the Army to see a bit of the world. John died in the local hospital from a very severe bout of Appendicitis and was buried in Greenock Cemetery. The photograph of the grave was taken for me by a relative of one of these soldiers, Miss Alexandra Kirkpatrick, who now lives in Greenock. John was only twenty-one years of age when he died.

The grave of John McIntyre in Greenock Cemetery

5143 PRIVATE ROBERT McCAUGHAN
5th Bn Connaught Rangers
K.I.A. 7-12-15
Aged 46
No Known Grave. Commemorated on the Doiran Memorial, Greece.

Born   Mosside, Dervock.
Lived   Johnstone.
Enlisted Paisley, Renfrewshire.
Son of John McCaughan of Moycraig.
Husband of Mary Jane Clyde McCaughan, of 65, Garriochmill Rd, Glasgow.

Robert McCaughan was born at Moycraig in about 1869, the son of John McCaughan.

No other family details are known. He had been living in Scotland . At the time he enlisted he was listed as living in Johnstone but later his wife is stated to be living in Glasgow. At 46 years of age he was one of the oldest of the men from Ballymoney. Robert enlisted into the Connaught Rangers and saw much action on the Gallipoli peninsula in the summer of 1915. In August of that year very heavy fighting took place in Gallipoli and Robert was through all of this. When this battle was over the 5th battalion were moved to Salonika and the fighting there. They arrived in time for a very severe winter. A blizzard on 23rd November saw temperatures of 30 degrees below zero. In these conditions it was impossible to dig trenches and shelters had to be constructed as best they could.   By early December they were in the north of Greece, close to the Yugoslav frontier near the south-east shore of Lake Doiran.

It was in this region during the heavy fighting that took place on the 7th of December that Robert was killed. He has no known grave and is commemorated on the Doiran Memorial. This memorial stands on what was known as Colonial Hill, and can be seen from a distance and is a landmark.in the area. It is the Battle Memorial of the British Salonika Force, for which a large sum of money was subscribed by the officers and men of that force and is also the Commonwealth War Graves Commission's Memorial to over 2,000 British dead in Macedonia whose graves are not known.

The Memorial takes the form of an obelisk, 12 metres high, guarded by two recumbent stone lions. It stands on a square platform, the sides of which are marked by shorter piers, and the names of the dead are inscribed on marble panels sunk in these piers. This Memorial is close to Doiran Military Cemetery, which is about two kilometres from Doiran village and is reached by a farm track after turning left in the village at a large tavern.

Thistle Dump Cemetery at the Somme

22112 PRIVATE ARCHIBALD NICHOLL
1st Bn Royal Dublin Fusiliers. Formerly 3108 R.G.A.
K.I.A. 22-12-15
Interred in Twelve Tree Copse Cemetery, Gallipoli. Plot 2, Row E, Grave 4.

Born   Mosside,
Lived   Liscolman, Dervock.
Enlisted   Ballymoney.
Commemorated in Mosside Presbyterian Church.

On 4th August 1914 the 1st battalion were at Madras, in India and sailed from Bombay on 19th November, arriving at Plymouth on 21st December 1914 and were stationed at Torquay in billets. In January they moved to Nuneaton, where they joined the 29th Division and on 16th March sailed from Avonmouth for Alexandria, where they arrived on 30th March 1915. On 9th April they arrived at Mudros and then on 25th April they took part in the landing at Cape Helles. Here they suffered extremely heavy casualties in what as a desperately difficult landing and the battalion was almost wiped out. They were for a time amalgamated with the 1st Royal Munster Fusiliers.

According to records, the evacuation of the 1st Dublin Fusiliers took place on the 20th December 1915, two days before the death of Archie Nicholl.

One report states, Sunday 19th December 1915, Gallipoli. The firing line of trenches from Karakol Dagh, North of Suvla, to Lone Pine Plateau, South of Anzac Cove, was held by picked Riflemen, one every seven yards. These were known as " The Last Ditchers". Their job was to hold off the enemy until the evacuation was complete. Archie Nicholl was probably a "Last Ditcher" which would explain why his death occurred two days after the evacuation.

The Cemetery where Archie Nicholl is buried is also the Cemetery where one of those men shot at dawn is buried. Sergeant John Robins, an Englishman serving with the 5th Wiltshires, disobeyed an order, claiming to be sick. He had medical evidence to back up his claims, but a court martial did not accept this and he was sentenced to death. He was shot at 8.00am on 2nd January 1916 on the beach at Cape Helles.

7679 WILLIAM LOGAN
10th Bn Scottish Rifles
K.I.A. 27-1-16
Aged 19
No Known Grave. Commemorated on the Loos Memorial, Panels 57 to 59

Born   Castle St. Ballymoney
Lived   Ballymoney
Enlisted Glasgow
Son of Mrs. Mary Anne Logan of Castle St. and the late James Logan.

The 10th battalion was formed at Hamilton in September 1914 and went immediately to train with the 15th Division at Bordon. Then in February they moved to billets in Winchester and in April to Salisbury Plain, Park House and Chisledon. On 10th July 1915 they landed at Boulogne. William Logan, as was common practice at the time, had gone to Scotland in search of work along with his brother Samuel. He was working in Glasgow when war broke out and enlisted there. His mother was by now living by herself at her home in Castle Street. She had been a widow for some time. When William first went to France in July of 1915 it was fairly quiet, but this was not to last. The battle of Loos was about to begin and on 25th September 1915, the first day of the battle, William was wounded. He had been hit in the head by machine-gun fire and was lucky to survive. By November he had recovered well enough to pay a visit home. He returned to his regiment when they were in rest billets at Noeux-les-Mines. Life in the 15th Division now meant moves in and out of the line at the Quarries, Hohenzollern Redoubt and Hulluch, each sector with it's own peculiar disadvantages. The wire had to be repaired, defences strengthened, and trenches made habitable. The least exposure of a head brought an almost instantaneous crack of a rifle bullet. On the 27th of January, the Kaiser's birthday, it was expected that the German artillery would celebrate the occasion with a heavy bombardment. As it turned out this was correct and at 4.00pm the bombardment opened. It lasted for an hour. It was during this bombardment that William was killed. He has no known grave and is commemorated on the Loos Memorial. His brother, Samuel, was reported wounded and missing on the 25th of September, the same day as William was so lucky to escape with his life. As it turned out, Samuel was killed on this day. They were both sons of Mrs Mary Logan, of Castle Street. William was just nineteen years of age.

5884 RIFLEMAN THOMAS DONNELLY
2nd Bn Royal Irish Rifles
D.O.W. 28-1-16
Aged 18
Interred in Boulogne Eastern Cemetery. Plot 8, Row C, Grave 84

Born   Ballymoney
Lived   Bendooragh, Ballymoney.
Enlisted Belfast
Son of John and Mary Donnelly, of Maddydoo, Bendooragh.

The 2nd battalion had been at Tidworh on the outbreak of hostilities,and landed at Rouen ten days later, on the 14th of August 1914.

Thomas enlisted at Belfast and joined the battalion in a later draft when he had undergone some initial training. This would have been early in 1915, when the battalion was still in the region around Ypres. Like the 1st battalion, the 2nd recruited heavily from Belfast and Dublin and at the Battle of La Bassee the battalion had been decimated. It was probably at this time that Thomas joined them. If it was, and it is the most likely time, then he was through much of the fighting of 1915. Much of this was in the Ypres sector around Heronthage Chateau. There is nothing definate to tell us when Thomas was injured, but it is assumed to have been around the middle of January 1916. Neither is there anything to tell us whether it was the work of a sniper or of a high explosive shell or shrapnel. All we know is that he was very seriously injured and was taken by ambulance to Boulogne where everything possible was done for him. The intention was to take him to hospital in England but he quickly became too ill to travel and a few days later died from his injuries.

The news that Thomas had been seriously injured came to his sister, Kate, at Maddydoo, in January 1916. Then the following week, another letter, this time to say that he had died of his wounds in Boulogne hospital.

Before enlisting he was employed by John Henry, a contractor, and later by James Wright, of Drumaheglis, close to his home.

The Donnelly name appears to have died out in the Maddydoo district. No one that I have spoken to now remembers them and it would seem that there is now no-one left to contact. This is one of the sad things about doing research of this kind that the death of one son in the war can wipe a family out completely.

Boulogne Eastern Cemetery is one of the town cemeteries and stands on high ground on the eastern side of Boulogne, on the road to St. Omer.

Opening times:
This Cemetery is open 7 days a week, all year round.
From 1st October to 15th March 08.00 - 18.00
From 16th March to 30th September 08.00 - 19.00

Bazentin Cemetery at the Somme

18559 RIFLEMAN CHARLES NEWELL
13th Bn Royal Irish Rifles "B" Coy
K.I.A. 7-2-16
Aged 19
Interred in Mesnil Ridge Cemetery, France. Row G Grave 6

Born   Ballymoney
Enlisted   Newtownards.
Son of Mrs. Eliza Newell, of 54 South St, Newtownards

Charles Newell was born in Ballymoney in 1897. He must have been a particularly well built young man to have got past the recruiting officer at his age and to be allowed to enlist although some of the recruiting officers were not too caring what age the boys were.

Charles Newell enlisted at Newtownards on the 17th of September 1914 and left England for France on the 6th of October the following year.

They were based in the Martinsart, Mesnil, Mailly-Maillet area of Northern France, close to where the battle of the Somme was to be fought, but Charles would not live long enough to take part in this battle. The 36th Division took over a section of the line for the first time at noon on the 7th of February 1916 and later that afternoon Charles was killed. He is buried in Mesnil Ridge Cemetery close by.

He was only four months in France when he was killed in action on 7th February 1916, aged only nineteen. He had been a member of "B" company of the U.V.F. and had been a stretcher-bearer with the 13th Rifles.

21406 PRIVATE WILLIAM McBRIDE
2nd Bn Royal Inniskilling Fusiliers formerly 16698 Royal Irish Rifles
K.I.A. 10-2-16
Interred in Authuille Military Cemetery, Row A, Grave 36

Born   Dervock
Lived   Dervock
Enlisted Belfast
Commemorated in Derrykeighan Parish Church.

William McBride was born at Dervock, a village about four miles north-east of Ballymoney. He enlisted into the Royal Irish Rifles in 1902 and served for eight years, seeing service in Malta, Cyprus and Egypt. At the end of his time in the army he came home and spent the next four years on the reserve. On the outbreak of hostilities he was called up and afterwards transferred to the Royal Inniskilling Fusiliers, going out to France with a draft of this Regiment. His battalion were serving in the area around Authuille about a mile south-west of Thiepval with the 32nd Division. Although they were a mile back they were still well within range of the heavy German artillery and were repeatedly shelled.

It was still winter and the weather had been very cold with a severe frost at night. William was killed on one of his stints in the front line and is buried in Authuille Cemetery. This cemetery is constructed on very steep ground and William's grave is on the front row at the bottom of the slope.

Cemetery location information
Authuille is a village 5 kilometres north of Albert. Authuille Military Cemetery is on the south side of the village. The Cemetery is   signposted on the main road (D159) through the village.

Authuille Military Cementary

3216 RIFLEMAN WILLIAM MOORE
2nd Bn Royal Irish Rifles
K.I.A. 27-4-16
Aged 32
Interred in Ecoivres Military Cemetery, Mont-St-Eloi. Plot 1, Row F, Grave 25

Born   Liscolman.
Lived   Port Glasgow.
Enlisted   Greenock, Renfrewshire
Son of George and Annie Moore of Liscolman.
Husband of Mary Ann Moore.
Commemorated in Billy Parish Church.
Brother of Robert Moore, Killed in Action on 9th May 1915.

William was born in Liscolman around 1884 and spent much of his early life there. He was eight years older than his brother Robert but both boys went to live in Port Glasgow, in Scotland. As was common practice at the time, William probably went to Scotland in search of work. The shipbuilding yards of the Clyde could provide steady employment most of the time and if that was slack then the farms of Southern Scotland could provide seasonal work. As a last resort there was always the coal mines. When war was declared William immediately enlisted. On being taken to France he was moved to the area around St. Eloi and it was here that he was killed in April 1916. Two other brothers, George and Tommy, also served, but survived.

Ecoivres Military Cemetery. Grave of W. Moore, front centre

9866 L. CPL. ARCHIBALD MURPHY
1st Bn Royal Inniskilling Fusiliers
D.O.W. 7-5-16
Aged 24
Interred in Auchonvillers Military Cemetery, France. Plot 2, Row D, Grave 20

Born   Ballymoney.
Enlisted Belfast.
Son of John and Elizabeth Murphy.

It is more than likely that Archie Murphy had already served a few years in the Army before war was declared. At any rate his battalion were assigned to the 29th Division and after initial training sailed for Gallipoli.

The strange territory was difficult to get used to, hot and humid by day, cold at night. They had been under extremely heavy fire during the landing and had suffered many casualties, but Archie was lucky enough to survive this. After a successful evacuation in January they arrived back in France for the long train journey up to the Western Front.

The 29th Division had by now been back from Gallipoli long enough to be back up to strength and get their training completed. They were now at Mailly-Maillet preparing for action in the Battle of the Somme. Shelling had been heavy and the 1st battalion were out repairing trenches. It was during these repairs that Archie Murphy was injured. He was transferred to the nearest dressing station but died soon afterwards from very serious injuries. He is buried nearby at Auchonvillers Military Cemetery.

A. Murphy 8th from right, 2nd row

23042 JOHN PATRICK DILLON
8th Bn Royal Irish Fusiliers
D.O.W. 28-5-16
Aged 19
Interred in Bethune Town Cemetery, Plot 5, Row D, Grave 53

Born   Ballinaloob
Lived   Dunloy
Enlisted Ballymoney
Son of John and Annie Dillon, (Nee Heron), of Ballymacaldrick, Dunloy.

Annie Heron, John's mother came from near Letterkenny. They had probably met through John being hired in the Letterkenny area. There were eventually four of a family with John Patrick being the oldest. They all attended the old school on what is now known as Presbytery Lane. John had been working in the Kilraughts district at the outbreak of war and enlisted along with some of his mates at Ballymoney.

Like many of the young men at the time he was under age when he enlisted. At that time John's father worked on the nearby railway and another son, Charles worked in the local Post Office. When the telegram arrived to break the news of the death of John Patrick, it was the younger brother, Charles who had the heartbreaking job of delivering it to his mother and father.

John lived with his parents, John and Annie Dillon, in the townland of Ballymacaldrick, just outside the village of Dunloy. In 1914 Dunloy was only a small village but over the last twenty years the building of new housing estates has more than doubled it in size.

The 8th battalion were formed at Armagh in September 1914. Much of their training took place at Pirbright in Surrey. They landed in France in February 1916. They moved to the Hulluch area almost at once and it was here on the 27th of April that the 8th battalion came under very severe attack. The morning of the 27th was dry and warm with a light easterly breeze, ideal conditions for a gas attack. At 5.10am huge clouds of gas could be seen rolling towards the British front line, released from nearly 4,000 cylinders. The gas helmets used by the British forces at this time were of inferior quality and many of the soldiers were badly affected. The Germans attacked behind this cloud of gas and casualties among the British were very high. Eventually the Germans were driven back and the position restored but it had been very costly, over half of the men were casualties.

Two days later another gas attack took place here against the same troops but half way through the wind changed and blew the gas back over the waiting Germans. This allowed the British to open fire on the fleeing enemy and cause heavy casualties. The trenches in this area were in a poor condition and due to the soggy nature of the ground couldn't be dug any deeper. German snipers were constantly on the look-out for unwary soldiers and took any opportunity which presented itself. Over eighty years after the conflict it is almost impossible to tell what happened to John Dillon but two possibilities arise.

He may have been a victim of the gas attacks of the 27th and 29th of April or he could at any time have been hit by a sniper. At any rate he was removed to hospital at Bethune and died there on the 28th of May. The Rev George L. Craven administered the last rites and he is buried in the nearby cemetery.

It is nice to know that the grave has been visited by members of John's family and that he is not forgotten.

Cemetery location information
Bethune is located 29 kilometres north of Arras. Bethune Town Cemetery is on the northern outskirts of Bethune near the junction of the river Lawe and the Aire la Bassee Canal. From the town centre turn right in front of the Tribunal and second right at the bottom of the road down to the cul-de-sac where the cemetery will be found.

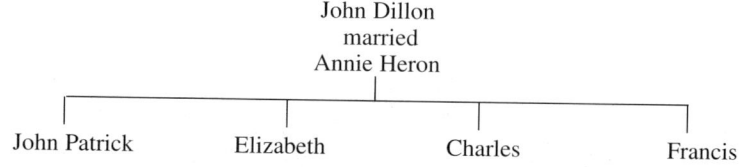

3414 PRIVATE FRANK McBRIDE
11th Bn Australian Infantry
K.I.A. 30-5-16
Interred in Rue-Petillon Military Cemetery, Fleurbaix. Plot 1, Row H, Grave 53

Born   *Ballycastle.*
Lived   *Perth, Western Australia,*
Enlisted *Perth, Western Australia, on 19th July 1915.*
Son of John McBride, of Market St, Ballymoney.

Frank McBride was a labourer, and had emigrated to Australia in 1911. He was six feet seven inches tall, with a fresh complexion, blue eyes and light coloured hair.

He enlisted at Perth in July 1915 and went with the Australian troops to Egypt, landing there on 1st November. On 27th November he was detained in barracks and admitted to hospital for treatment at Abbassia. Later he was moved to hospital at Ghezireh and released on 12th January re-joining his battalion at Habieta on 2nd March 1916. He then embarked with his battalion on H.M.T. "Corsican" at Alexandria on 29th March and landed at Marseilles on 5th April. His brother James served in the North Irish Horse and survived the war. His sister, Gretta, was a nurse in France during the war and it was to her that his Commanding Officer, Lt. J.T.Forbes, wrote, telling of Frank's death, in a night attack on the Australian lines, on the night of 30th-31st May, 1916, between Laventie and Fleurbaix.

Frank's father, John McBride, was the owner of a public house in Market Street.

Rue-Petillon Military Cemetery

21527 PRIVATE DAVID JOHNSTON
8th Bn Royal Irish Fusiliers
K.I.A. 2-6-16
Aged 18
Interred in St. Patrick's Cemetery, Loos. Plot 1, Row N, Grave 1

Born   Broughshane
Lived   Mounthamilton, Cloughmills.
Enlisted Larne
Commemorated in Ballyweaney Presbyterian Church.
Son of the late Hugh Johnston of Cloughmills.

David Johnston was born at Broughshane in 1898. He was a son of Hugh Johnston, who later moved to live at Mounthamilton, Cloughmills.

The family worshipped in Ballyweaney Presbyterian Church and it is there that David is commemorated. By the time he enlisted his father had been dead for a number of years. Unusually for a Ballymoney boy he enlisted at Larne possible the only one to do so. At the time he was very much under age and this is probably one of the reasons why he had to go there. He would have been completely unknown and probably a well built young man and if he added a year or two to his age the Recruiting Officer usually didn't ask too many questions. By the time he was killed at Loos he was still too young to be in the Army. He is buried in St.Patrick's Cemetery at Loos and at eighteen years of age is one of the youngest of the Ballymoney boys to be killed in action.

The village of Loos-en-Gohelle is just north of Lens on the N43, Lens to Bethune road.

Turn right off the N43 onto the D165, signposted for Wingles and La Bassee, and continue along this road for 0.5 kilometres. Turn left at the village square and left again. Continue along this road and the cemetery is on the right after approximately 200 metres.

German Machine Gun Post close to the Ulster Toner at Thiepval

757516 RIFLEMAN MATTHEW KEERS
15th Bn Royal Irish Rifles
D.O.W. 12-6-16
Aged 30
Interred in Warloy-Baillon Communal Cemetery, France. Row A, Grave 16

Born   Ballymoney
Lived   Linenhall St, Ballymoney.
Commemorated in Ballymoney Parish Church.
Son of Matthew and Ellen Keers

The Keers family worshipped in St.Patrick's Parish Church in the town and it is there that Matthew is commemorated on the Roll of Honour in the church.

The 15th battalion were raised from the North Belfast Volunteers and did their training at Ballykinlar. Matthew Keers had been born in Ballymoney and the family lived in Linenhall Street in the town. When their preliminary training was finished they moved across to Seaford on the south coast of England for final instruction and then went to France in October of 1915. On 9th October the 107th brigade moved up to a quiet sector of the line for instruction in trench warfare with the 4th Division. This was supposed to last for only a few days but the weather was bad and many of the trenches had to be cleared of mud so the time here was extended. On the 10th of June the Germans attacked a little salient in the British lines known as William Redan, on that night held by the 15th Rifles. It was during this raid that Matthew Keers was injured. There was an advanced operating centre at Warloy and it was here that Matthew was treated for his injuries. He died here two days later and is buried in the cemetery nearby. Another Ballymoney man is buried in this cemetery, Samuel Holmes of Liscolman, killed on the 23rd of October 1916, lies in Plot 6, Row C, Grave 4. And an Uncle of Mrs Stewart-Moore, of Ballydivity, Dervock, Captain Oswald Brooke-Webb, is buried here as well.

Cemetery visiting information
Warloy-Baillon is a village in the dept of the West Somme, about 13 miles from Amiens and six from Albert. The nearest railway station is at Contay, about 3 miles away. The Communal cemetery is on the east of the village, and the extension is to the east of the cemetery. The first British burial took place in the communal cemetery in October 1915 and the last on 1st July 1916. By that date Field Ambulances had come to the village in readiness for the attack on the German front line, five miles away, and the extension was begun. The fighting from July to November, 1916, on the northern part of the Somme Front accounts for the majority of the burials; but a certain number are due to the German attack in the Spring of 1918, which reached the former British front line. There are now buried in the extension 857 soldiers from the United Kingdom, 318 from Australia, 152 from Canada, and three unknown. and in addition 17 German Prisoners of War. The extension is reached by a flight of steps from the road. at the south-east corner. The register of the Communal Cemetery records the details of 46 British burials, and the register for the extension those of 1330 British and Dominion burials.

17272 RIFLEMAN WILLIAM BLACKMORE
12th Bn Royal Irish Rifles
K.I.A. 1-7-16
No Known Grave. Commemorated on the Thiepval Memorial.

Born   Ballycastle
Lived   Chatham, Armoy.
Enlisted   Ballymoney.
Commemorated in Armoy Parish Church.

For various reasons the men from Ballymoney enlisted in many different regiments, but the most common of them was the Royal Irish Rifles.

Most of the local men went into the 12th Battalion. This battalion suffered extremely at the Somme. The area to the north of the Ancre gave an easy target to the enemy and machine-gunners at Thiepval had a clear line of sight on them. The enemy directly in front of them and from the high ground where the Ulster Tower now stands just simply mowed them down. Seventeen Ballymoney men, serving with the 12th battalion, were killed that day. It shows the ferocity of the fighting that of these seventeen, only three have a known grave.

The two Blackmore boys enlisted together at Ballymoney and did their training at Clandeboye. From there they moved to Seaford on the south coast of England and from there to France in time for the Battle of the Somme. Camp at Martinsart was crowded. Thousands of men were here in preparation for the battle. The weather had been wet and there was mud everywhere. The 1st of

July dawned sunny and bright and at 7.30am everyone was ready for the attack to begin.

As the whistles sounded, men everywhere climbed out of their trenches and set off, the Blackmore boys among them. It was the last time they were to be together. Later that morning William was killed as he tried to cross No Man's Land in his attempt to reach the German trenches.

This attack left the battalion decimated and they were withdrawn for reorganisation. We can only guess at Herbert's feelings as he searched the rows of faces for the brother that meant so much to him. William has no known grave and is commemorated on the Thiepval Memorial.

Ancre Valley Cemetery

1707 RIFLEMAN JOHN BURNS
12th Bn Royal Irish Rifles
K.I.A. 1-7-16
Aged 25
Commemorated on Thiepval Memorial, pier and face 15A and 15B

Born   Ballymoney
Lived   Balnamore
Enlisted   Ballymoney
Commemorated in Drumreagh Presbyterian Church.
Only son of Joseph and Annie Burns of Balnamore.

The 12th battalion were on the right bank of the River Ancre at Hamel.

They were to advance in conjunction with the 29th Div. on their left to Beaucourt station and north of it. They left their trenches two minutes before zero and were already under fire going through their own wire.

At this point the German lines were 600 yards away and as the 12th battalion crossed No Man's Land they fell continually, machine-guns at St Pierre Divion just simply mowed them down. Machine-gunners to the north of the Ancre also had a clear line of sight on them and only a very few of them reached the German front line trenches. When Germany declared war on France on 3rd August 1914, the German army had more than 1,600 machine-guns, Maxim (MG08's). No other combatant army could match this firepower, and the effect on the massed infantry and cavalry assaults of the early months of the war was massive. The machine-gun was the king of the last few hundred yards of No Man's Land, and the most deadly and efficient of them all were Maxims. This was the situation in which John Burns found himself in the swampy ground close to the river. There was no cover what-so-ever and he was left with no alternative but to try to keep going. He has no known grave and is commemorated on the Thiepval Memorial. His brother Joseph also served, returning to his home after the war. He was employed for the rest of his life as a postman. He had a son, John, but it is believed that this son is also dead, and so the family seems to have died out.

ORANGEMEN AND THE WAR
The monthly meeting of Bendooragh L.O.L. 804. (O'Hara's True Blues) was held in the lodge room on Friday. Br. Robert J. Boyd, deputy master, in the absence of the W.M. in the chair, and Br. Thomas McDowell in the vice-chair. The following resolutions were passed unanimously on the motion of Mr. D. McNabb. (sec). 1. That we, the members of Bendooragh LOL No 804 hereby place on record our heartfelt sorrow at the loss of Br. John Burns, one of our most popular and highly respected members, who like so many Ulster heroes, nobly laid down his life on the battlefield in the cause of civilisation and Christianity. 2. That we desire to convey our sincere sympathy to the parents and relatives of those of our brethern who have been wounded in the recent great battle on the Western Front, and we are proud and thankful to know that our brethern and friends in this district have like the rest of their fellow Ulstermen, acquitted themselves so gallantly in the fiercest conflict that the world has ever witnessed.

Cemetery location information
The Thiepval Memorial will be found on the D73, off the main Bapaume to Albert road (D929).

108 RIFLEMAN ROBERT CARSON
12th Bn Royal Irish Rifles
K.I.A. 1-7-16
Aged 21
No Known Grave. Commemorated on the Thiepval Memorial

Born   Kilraughts.
Lived   Bushfoot.
Enlisted Ballymena

Robert Carson was born at Lavin, Knockahollet, in 1895, the son of James and Ellen Carson of Lavin. At some time after this they moved from Lavin to live at Bushfoot, Portballintrae and attended Dunluce Presbyterian Church, where Robert is commemorated and many of Robert's relatives still live in the Bushmills area. When Robert enlisted at Ballymena he was one of the very first to volunteer. His early training took place at Clandeboye where he was placed in "D" Company of the 12th battalion. He went with the others to Seaford on the south coast of England for final training in July of 1915 and then in October sailed for France. He eventually arrived at the vast camp at St. Omer and had his first look at trenches in this area. From here he was taken into the area that was to become known as the Western Front. He was based at Martinsart, a village close to the front line.

On the morning of the 1st of July 1916, Robert attacked on the north side of the River Ancre at Hamel. Here machine-guns at St.Pierre-Divion, a hamlet to the south of the river, had a clear line of sight on the 12th battalion and they were just mowed down. Some of them made it to the first German trench and it is thought that Robert was one of these as his parents at home had to wait until November 1917 before the Army was forced to conclude that he had been killed on the 1st of July 1916.

He is commemorated on the family headstone at 1st Kilraughts Presbyterian Church along with other details of the family. Robert's Aunt Maud later married Tom Magee of Bushmills and their only child, Thomas, was accidentally drowned in the River Bush at Bushmills in January 1931. He is also mentioned on the family headstone at Kilraughts.

William Carson, James's father, died on Christmas eve 1886 at the age of 75, his wife, Jane having died the previous February. James himself died on 14th May 1931, just four months after the death of his Grandson, Thomas Magee, at Bushmills. Ellen, his wife died on 11th August 1935.

James Carson married Ellen McCarrol
in Ballyweaney Presbyterian Church on 25th Jan 1878

	Jane	William	Maria	Maud	
	B 1881	B 1885	B 1888	B 1899	
	D 1945	D 1948	D 1943	D 1971	
Elizabeth	Annie	Nellie	Robert	James
B 1879	B 1883	B 1887	B 1895	B 1902
D 1944	D 1962 married Hugh Glass Hugh, William, Neill, Nellie	D 1961 married Tom Magee	K.I.A. 1-7-16	D 1908

17441 RIFLEMAN JAMES CLARKE
12th Bn Royal Irish Rifles
K.I.A. 1-7-16
No known grave. Commemorated on the Thiepval Memorial. 15A & 15B.

Born   Ballynacree
Lived   Ballynacree
Enlisted   Ballymoney
Commemorated in Ballymoney Parish Church.
Son of Robert Clarke of Meetinghouse St.

The Clarke family worshipped in St.Patrick's Parish Church in Ballymoney and it is there that James is commemorated on the Roll of Honour.

James was born at Ballynacree, Ballymoney, in June 1899. He enlisted on the outbreak of hostilities, aged just fifteen. The 12th battalion was formed in County Antrim, from the Antrim Volunteers, in September 1914. Much of their early training took place at Clandeboye, in County Down, and when this was completed in July of 1915 they were moved to Seaford on the south coast of England, for final training. In October of that year they crossed to Boulogne and to more training in France. Here they went into trenches for the first time, trenches that were made deliberately to match those at the Somme, so that the soldiers would know what to expect when they went into battle, and the kind of terrain they would be expected to attack. Nothing could have prepared them for what they had to face when they left the shelter of their trenches on the morning of the 1st of July. A virtual hail of machine-gun fire met them as they tried to cross No Man's Land on that bright, sunny morning. The 12th battalion were on the north bank of the River Ancre, attacking where Ancre Valley Cemetery now stands.

St. Pierre-Divion, a small French hamlet, on rising ground to the south of the river, was a German strong point at this time, with a nest of machine-guns. This had not been attacked by the troops south of the river and so the Germans were free to attack the Ulstermen to the north. The heights around St.Pierre-Divion gave the enemy a perfect target and the Ulstermen were just simply mowed down. Many years before, when James was just a baby, an old gypsy had predicted that he would die young, and on a battlefield. This was forgotten for many years until his death, when Jane Clarke, his older sister, remembered it. James has no known grave and is commemorated on the Thiepval Memorial. His Father, Robert Clarke was working in Rosyth Naval Dockyard in Scotland when James was killed at the Somme.

The Thiepval Memorial is on the D73, off the main Bapaume to Albert road (D 929).9

The family was as follows - Jane, Margaret, Agnes, John (died in infancy), Robert, Samuel, John, Sarah Elizabeth (died in infancy), Sarah Ann (died young), James (killed at the Battle of the Somme), Christina.

Their Father was a gardener by profession, having served his time in Belfast.

The family lived in a house at Ballynacree belonging to the retired Army doctor to whom Robert worked. When this old man died the family moved back to Ballymoney. By the time James was killed their father was working in Rosyth Naval Dockyard and it was here that the news reached him.

761 RIFLEMAN ROBERT JOHN COLEMAN
12th Bn Royal Irish Rifles
K.I.A. 1-7-16
Aged 21
No Known Grave. Commemorated on the Thiepval Memorial. Pier 15a & 15b

Born   Ballymaconnelly
Lived   Ballymaconnelly
Enlisted Belfast on 12-10-14
Son of John and Mary Coleman.
Member of Ballymaconnelly L.O.L. 360
Commemorated in Finvoy Presbyterian Church.

Robert John Coleman was a son of John and Mary Coleman, of Ballymaconnelly.

He was a quiet lad with dark hair and blue eyes and about five feet eight inches tall.

They had four of a family, two boys and two girls. Just after the outbreak of war, when he was only nineteen years old, on 12th October 1914, he went to Belfast and enlisted. His early training was done at Clandeboye camp and then they were taken across to England and the camp at Seaford on the south coast.

Intensive training took place here during the Summer of 1915 and then in August of that year they were moved to Bordon, in Hants, for final training. When their training was finished they were allowed home on leave for a few days.

Robert Ramsey, Matt Brown, Stanley Connolly and Robert John were all home at the same time.

In October the move to France took place and at the same time the weather, which in England, had been fairly good, changed. Steady rain took the place of warm summer sunshine and turned everything to mud. Martinsart village was their base, and the action of thousands of pairs of boots on the soft French chalk turned the ground into a sticky morass. It was impossible to stay clean and mud stuck to everything. They were housed wherever shelter could be found, in cellars, in attics, in cattle houses, or in tents.

As the winter wore on, the weather became colder and in January the conditions of rain, snow, sleet and frost made life in the trenches almost unbearable. On days away from the trenches more training took place or if new trenches were needed then they dug them. It was never rest.

As the weather improved and the days got longer, the amount of stores and ammunition being moved up to the front increased. Fresh battalions were being brought up and men were everywhere. It was obvious that something was afoot. By the end of June everything was ready for a big attack, but the weather changed and heavy rain forced a postponement for two days. The Battle of the Somme was about to begin. By the 30th of June the rain had stopped and the weather had improved dramatically.

Men were moved up for an early attack next morning and at 7.30am the attack began. The position of the 12th Bn, in the valley of the River Ancre, meant that machine-guns from the high ground on both sides of the river had a clear line of sight on them, and as they came out of their trenches, they were just simply mown down. It was in this early attack that Robert John Coleman was killed. He has no known grave and is commemorated on the Thiepval Memorial.

In January 1915, when Robert John Coleman and Robert Ramsey were home on leave, a presentation of gold medals was made to them in Rasharkin Orange Hall, in appreciation of their service to their country.

John and Mary Coleman

Robert John	Elizabeth	William	Martha
KIA	M		
1-7-16	Stanley Connolly		
	on 14th March 1918	*Stanley Connolly also served and had been a prisoner of war in Germany.*	

17629 L. CPL JAMES FENTON
12th Bn Royal Irish Rifles
K.I.A. 1-7-16
Aged 25
No Known Grave. Commemorated on the Thiepval Memorial

Born   Dunloy in 1891
Lived   Dunloy
Enlisted   Ballymoney
Commemorated in Dunloy Presbyterian Church.

Samuel Fenton married Margaret Caves and there were six of a family, four boys and two girls. All of them attended Galdanagh school and worshipped in Dunloy Presbyterian Church. William John farmed all his life at Dunloy. Alexander had been in Australia for a time but eventually came home and bought a farm at Anticur. In January 1919, Maggie married Richard McKendry, a brother of William McKendry who was killed at the Somme on the same day as James Fenton. Maggie died a few years later and Dick as he was known, married Sarah McCracken, a sister of David McCracken, who had been killed at the Battle of Loos in September 1915. Richard had been a prisoner of war in Germany and spent a lot of the time in railway carriages being moved from one place to another. It was something that he didn't talk much about.

James Fenton enlisted at Ballymoney in September 1914 into the 12th Battalion of the Royal Irish Rifles. He went with the battalion almost immediately to train at Clandeboye.

After this initial training he was taken to Seaford on the south coast of England for more intensive training. By this time plans were being made for the Battle of the Somme and the 12th battalion were moved across the Channel to Martinsart in Northern France in preparation for that battle. In June of 1916 the weather had been warm and dry but towards the end of the month it changed and the rain came down in torrents. The battle, planned for the 28th of June, had to be postponed. The chalky French soil quickly turned to a glutinous mud and boots became twice and even three times their normal weight. It was impossible to keep clean.

Over the next two days the weather gradually improved and the 1st of July was agreed for the start of the battle. The day dawned fine and clear and the soldiers were told to walk across No Man's Land as no Germans could have survived the preliminary bombardment. This was proved totally wrong as thousands of perfectly healthy Germans came up from their deep bunkers with rifles and machine-guns and opened fire on the unsuspecting British forces.

The 12th battalion were at Hamel, on the north bank of the River Ancre and German machine-gunners on the high ground on both sides of the river had a clear line of sight on them.

Ballymoney had 28 young men killed on that day, although not all of them had been with the 12th Rifles, some of them had been with other regiments in the Thiepval area. James Fenton's body was never found, so we can assume that he managed to get well into No Man's Land before he was killed. So many of the battalion were either killed or injured that the battalion had to be withdrawn next day for re-organisation and later moved to Belgium.

We can only imagine the thoughts of the people of Ballymoney and the surrounding district as news began to filter back of the slaughter on the Somme. The distraught mothers waiting at the door as the telegram boy came up the street and the relief when he went past. Today that valley is quiet, with cows grazing peacefully in the silent meadows. Time has made changes but the line of trenches can still be followed, a reminder that this valley was not always the quiet haven that it is today.

Samuel Fenton married Margaret Caves					
William John m. Annie Calderwood on 7th Feb 1912	Alexander	James KIA 1-7-16	Samuel	Bella	Maggie

7239 PRIVATE SAMUEL FULTON
10th Bn Royal Irish Rifles
K.I.A. 1-7-16
Aged 18
No known grave. Commemorated on the Thiepval Memorial

Born   Seacon, Ballymoney
Enlisted   Belfast,
Commemorated in St. James's Presbyterian Church, Ballymoney.
Son of the late John Fulton, of 16 Maralin St, Belfast.

Samuel Fulton was definately under age when he enlisted into the 10th Battalion of the Royal Irish Rifles. He was born at Seacon, on the outskirts of Ballymoney, in about 1898. The family worshipped in St. James's Presbyterian Church in the town and it is there that Samuel is commemorated on their Roll of Honour. The family appears to have lived at Seacon for some con-siderable time but probably moved to Belfast as the family were growing up.

Samuel enlisted in Belfast into the 10th Battalion of the Royal Irish Rifles, the South Belfast Volunteers, and did his initial training at Ballykinlar, in County Down. When this was complete he was taken to Seaford, on the south coast of England for final training and then moved to France in October of 1915. The huge training camp at St.Omer was his first stop and after more training there and an introduction to trenches similar to those they would see at the Somme, they were moved to the Martinsart area. This was very close to the Thiepval area where they would see their first action. For many of them this would be their only action. On the morning of the 1st of July they attacked across the face of a steep hill south of the River Ancre in full view of the enemy machine-gun positions on the high ground north of the river. There was no cover whatsoever. They were also faced with machine-gun and rifle fire from the Schwaben Redoubt at the top of the hill and from St.Pierre-Divion almost directly in front. They never had a chance.

Samuel was killed as he crossed No Man's Land on what had turned out to be a lovely bright Saturday morning. He has no known grave and is commemorated on the Thiepval Memorial.

2ND LIEUT JOHN HAMILTON
11th Bn Royal Inniskilling Fusiliers
K.I.A. 1-7-16

Lived Ballyrobin, Stranocum. Commemorated in Carncullagh Presbyterian Church.

John had been a leading sportsman in the years before the 1st World War and was prominent in athletics as well as being a member of Bann Rowing Club. He rowed number two in Jack Lowry's senior four in 1913. He was a son of Mr John Hamilton, of Woodview, Stranocum, and before enlisting worked in the Belfast Bank in Coleraine. He enlisted on the outbreak of hostilities, joining the Royal Inniskilling Fusilieers. At first, training took place at Finner Camp, in County Donegall, starting on 20th September 1914.

Finner Camp had originally been used to provide training facilities for soldiers during the Boer War and was known locally as the Boer War Camp. Much progress was made in the early stages as the men had already been in training for other reasons. In early January the battalion marched to the hutted camp at Shanes Castle, near Randalstown, and remained there. In February John Hamilton was sent on a course of instruction to Chelsea Barracks and received his commission on 19th April. On the evening of Wednesday 7th July 1915 they embarked at Dublin on their way to Bramshott, in Surrey. Much intensive training now took place and on 5th October they sailed for France. At Folkestone they embarked on the St. Oriel transport vessel and arrived at Boulogne at 3.00am. They immediately marched to Ostrohove rest camp and remained there all next day. Soon after this they were moved up to the area close to the front to help with trench digging and for more training. On the 1st of July, as the attack began at 7.30am and the 11th battalion left their trenches, they were immediately hit by machine-gun fire and rifle fire. John was with Captain Myles as they crossed No Man's Land and it was after they had left the sunken road and were approaching the Crucifix that Capt Myles was injured. John then took command of the Company and led them on towards the German positions. It was as they approached the German wire and were searching for a way through that John was hit in the neck by machine-gun fire. He was reported missing. Much later, and long after the news that he was missing had reached home, his sister Margaret applied for a court order presuming his death in action.

A letter from the Chaplain, the Rev J.J.Wright of Ballyshannon, told how 2nd Lieut Hamilton had been struck by a bullet in the left side of the neck and killed. The Judge granted the application.

Three other young Ballymoney men serving with the 11th battalion were killed on this day. Samuel McClelland is buried in the nearby Mill Road Cemetery. John Reid of Finvoy, and Alex Kirkpatrick, both killed as they attacked the Schwaben Redoubt, were never seen again.

7578 RIFLEMAN FRANK KENNEDY
12th Bn Royal Irish Rifles
K.I.A. 1-7-16
Aged 33
No Known Grave. Commemorated on the Thiepval Memorial

Born   Armoy
Lived   Armoy
Enlisted   Ballycastle
Commemorated in Armoy Parish Church.

Survived by his mother, Ruth, of the Park, Armoy.
Sisters, Ruth, Sadie and Maggie.
Maggie married Robert Baillie, of Church St, Bangor.

William Kennedy married Ruth Thompson

William born 1874 died 1889
Frank Dawson born 1884 died 1916
Charles born 1887 died 1935

Maggie married Robert Baillie of Church St, Bangor.
Georgina emigrated to America
Mary married Mooney
Sally went to Belfast.
Ruth married McLernon
Elizabeth married Reed and lived in Scotland but later moved to Stranocum.

William Kennedy was a journeyman blacksmith in the Armoy area. Later, when he set up his own smithy at Bellaney, Ruth Thompson became his striker. They married in about 1873. Their son, Frank, attended school in Armoy and later, on the outbreak of hostilities, enlisted at Ballycastle. He went almost immediately to train at Clandeboye and Newtownards. Much of this time was spent on route marches in the hilly Co Down countryside to bring the men up to peak fitness. When this was complete they were sent to Seaford on the south coast of England for further training, and then moved across to France. The French Commanders had been clamouring for the British to do something to draw the German Armies away from Verdun. The result was the Battle of the Somme. Frank was taken to the small French village of Martinsart, and there they were housed in tents, the only accomodation available.

Every house and shed in the area was packed with troops. Up to now the weather had been good but it suddenly changed and the rain came down in torrents. What had been dry, chalky soil, quickly turned to glutinous mud. Thousands of soldiers were on the move and we can only imagine what it was like living outdoors under those conditions. It was so bad that the date of the battle had to be postponed for two days. By the end of June it had shown signs of improving. The forecast was good and the decision was taken to go ahead on the 1st of July. The troops were moved up to the front lines on the night of the 30th of June. The barrage, which had been going on for a week, now reached a new height.

The mine which created Hawthorn Ridge Crater was blown ten minutes early, thus warning every German in the area that an attack was imminent and they were ready. As the whistles blew and our troops came out of the trenches the German machine-guns opened fire. The 12th Battalion, on the low ground at the edge of the River Ancre, were under severe attack. Machine-gunners at St. Pierre Divion could see them easily and had a clear line of sight on them. There were also machine-guns on the heights on the north side of the river and they were caught in a deadly crossfire. They were just simply mowed down.

Frank has no known grave and the reason for that was explained to me by his nephew, Councillor Bill Kennedy. While the children were still young William and Ruth had moved to live at the Park, but in 1910 William died. This left Ruth to bring up a young family on her own. Frank's brother, Charles, took over the tennancy and Ruth moved to a cottage in Ballykenver. She died there on Christmas eve 1931.

On the morning of the 1st of July 1916 Frank left the shelter of the trenches to take his chance in No Man's Land. His Uncle, Samuel Thompson, also from Armoy, was at his side as they crossed the open ground. When Frank was killed Samuel was there with him and stopped to see what he could do to help. Knowing that Frank was dead, Samuel went through his pockets and took his blood stained paybook and other personal belongings, which included the "dog tags", and took them home to his mother at the Park. It was only afterwards when it was too late that he realised his mistake. There was now no identification left on Frank and when the time came to gather up the bodies for burial after the battle he couldn't be identified and so he is buried in an unknown grave. He is commemorated on the Thiepval Memorial. Samuel Thompson survived the war and returned home to Armoy. He finished his life in the Lisburn area. Frank was killed by a single bullet wound through the neck.

Samuel Thompson, brother of Ruth Kennedy who was along with Frank Kennedy when he was killed and who took Frank's possessions with him and return them to Armoy.

14882 L.CPL ALEXANDER KIRKPATRICK
11th Bn Royal Inniskilling Fusiliers
K.I.A. 1-7-16
Aged 24
No Known Grave. Commemorated on the Thiepval Memorial. Pier 4D & 5B

Born Ballymoney on 10th February 1892
Lived Polentamney, Ballymoney
Enlisted Belfast
Son of George Kirkpatrick.

The battalion was raised in September 1914 from the Donegal and Fermanagh Volunteers and they began training at Finner Camp on the 20th of that month. Finner Camp was originally used to provide training facilities for soldiers during the Boer War and was known locally as the Boer War Camp.

In early January they marched to the hutted camp at Shane's Castle, near Antrim. Here they recieved regular drafts of new recruits and it is possible that this was the time when Alex Kirkpatrick joined them. On the evening of Wednesday the 7th of July they embarked at Dublin for the journey to Seaford, a town on the south coast of England. A few weeks later they moved to Bramshott, in Surrey and then on the 5th of October they embarked at Folkestone on the St.Oriel transport vessel and arrived at Boulogne at 3.00am. They then marched to Ostrohove rest camp where they stayed for two days before being taken to the area around Martinsart in preparation for the Battle of the Somme.

On the morning of the 1st of July 1916 bright sunshine greeted the troops. As the 11th set out at 7.30am they were at first shielded from the incessant machine-gun fire from Thiepval, but as they crested a slope in the ground they took the full force of the fire and machine-guns trained on the gaps in the German wire mowed them down. It was in this situation that Alexander was killed as he tried to advance to attack the German positions. He has no known grave and is commemorated on the Thiepval Memorial. Three other Ballymoney men, John Reid of Finvoy, John Hamilton of Stranocum, and Samuel McClelland of Drumahiskey, serving with the 11th battalion, were killed on this day. Of the four, only Samuel McClelland has a known grave.

Alex was born on 10th February 1892, the youngest child of George and Jane Kirkpatrick,

*Seated centre: Alex Kirkpatrick,
born 10 February 1892, died 1 July 1916.
Standing Centre: John Kirkpatrick,
born 14 March 1882, died 15 December, 1956.
At right: believed to be Samuel McClelland of
Balnamore K.I.A. 1-7-16 (27741)*

of Polentamney, near Ballymoney. Sadly Jane died six months after Alex was born and the children were cared for by their Grandmother and Aunt. All of them attended Polentamney school. At the outbreak of the Great War John and Alex enlisted into the Royal Inniskilling Fusiliers. Alex was killed at the Battle of the Somme, on 1st July 1916. John, too, fought at the Somme, but survived. He was wounded, gassed and later taken prisoner but survived. He was awarded the Belgian Croix de Guerre and the citation appeared in the London Gazette.

George Kirkpatrick married Jane Cuthbertson Adams in 1878

| George | John | Nancy | Mary | Martha | Alex |

642 RIFLEMAN WILLIAM LAVERTY
12th Bn Royal Irish Rifles
K.I.A. 1-7-16
Interred in Ancre British Cemetery, France. Plot 7, Row C, Grave 2

Born   Ballymoney
Lived   Dervock
Enlisted Belfast

William Laverty as far as I can make out was an only child. In 1908 a very severe Flu epidemic swept N. Ireland and both of William's parents died as a result. He was left to fend for himself and Mrs Huey, his next door neighbour, at Ballycraigagh, took him in and reared him as one of her own. Three years later Mrs Huey's husband died and she was left on her own to bring up her family.

When war broke out in 1914 her son James enlisted in Scotland. He was immediately followed by her son Alex and by William Laverty. Alex and William did much of their training together at Clandeboye.and went together to Seaford for final training and eventually arrived in France together. Alex was in the habit of writing home regularly and letters from both boys still exist. On the 1st of July 1916 Alex and William attacked from the trenches in front of Hamel village together and there is a letter from Alex to his mother telling of William being killed. Mrs Huey wrote on two different occasions to the records office to ask about William, only to be put off by an evasive answer, saying that as far as they knew he was still serving with his unit.

Her only confirmation of the truth was the letter from Alex. Seventeen Ballymoney men serving with the 12th battalion were killed within an hour and a half of leaving their trenches on this morning. Of those seventeen, only three have a known grave. William is one of these three. He is buried in Ancre Valley Cemetery, now built on ground over which they had attacked on the morning of the 1st of July. A very interesting and moving sequel to events happened in early 1999 after I had advertised for relatives to come forward with any help they could give me. I had a phone call from Mr Patrick of Derrykeighan to say that he had a plaque in his possession with the name of William Laverty on it. Could I throw any light on the subject. It had been found behind a shutter during renovations to the Glebe House at Derrykeighan and he wanted to return it to the family.

I was able to tell him about the Huey family and what they had done for William Laverty. It has now been presented to the Huey family. What a lovely gesture.

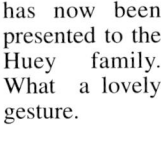

Ancre Valley Cemetery, Grave of Wm. Laverty

6186 RIFLEMAN DAVID LINTON
12th Bn Royal Irish Rifles
K.I.A. 1-7-16
Aged 19
No Known Grave. Commemorated on the Thiepval Memorial, France

Born   Cloughmills
Lived   Clough
Enlisted Ballymena
Son of Robert John and Mary Linton, of Artnacrea, Clough.

Robert John Linton married Mary Gregg. There were eventually eight of a family, six boys and two girls. Three of the Linton boys enlisted and served in the 1st World War. All of them attended the old Carnbeg school and as young men all of them worked on the family farm at Artnacrea Samuel was a Corporal serving in the Royal Field Artillery and was awarded the Military Medal and Distinguished Conduct Medal, both being awarded at a special parade in Victoria Barracks in Belfast. Robert John served in the Royal Garrison Artillery, and when he enlisted the officer in charge asked him if he had learned to shave yet. He was only sixteen years of age. In spite of this he was allowed to enlist and served throughout the war. David enlisted at Ballymena into the 12th Battalion of the Royal Irish Rifles and did his training at Clandeboye. Following this initial training they moved to Seaford on the south coast of England for more intensive training before going to France in October of 1915. They were taken straight away to the huge camp at St.Omer where they had an introduction to the type of trenches they would encounter at the Somme. This was to be their first taste of battle and had been arranged at the insistance of the French to draw fresh German troops away from Verdun. By late June the British plans for the Somme were almost complete and men were being drafted into the area in their thousands. The 12th battalion were stationed at the small French village of Martinsart on what we now know as the Western Front and about half a mile away from their intended jumping off point at Hamel. At 7.30am on a lovely bright Saturday morning, the 1st of July 1916, they left their trenches at the sound of the whistles and moved into No Man's Land. They had been warned there would be no need to run, nothing could have survived the bombardment which the British had laid on the German trenches in the previous week. How wrong this proved to be as the men, laiden with bombs, ammunition, rolls of wire, guns and all the other things that they were supposed to need, tried to cross this difficult terrain, which had been continuously churned up with exploding shells. They attacked from the edge of Hamel village on the north bank of the River Ancre. High ground to their immediate north hid a nest of machine-guns and the same on the slopes rising around St.Pierre-Divion on the south side of the river. They were caught in this murderous cross-fire as they tried to take the German trenches close to Beaucourt and the attack was a failure.

David was killed as he tried to cross No Man's Land in this first attack. The family tell me that he was killed by a German shell exploding very close to him. He was never found and as a result there is no known grave and he is commemorated on the Thiepval Memorial. He was only nineteen years of age.

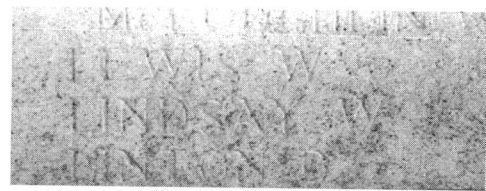

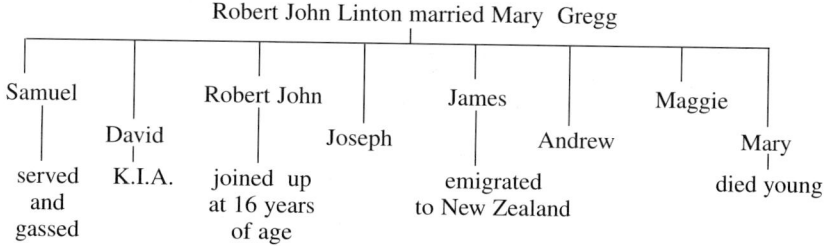

18136 RIFLEMAN DAVID McCLELLAND
12th Bn Royal Irish Rifles
K.I.A. 1-7-16
No Known Grave. Commemorated on the Thiepval Memorial

Born   Ballymoney
Lived   Tullaghgore
Enlisted   Ballymoney,
Son of David and Maggie McClelland.

David, a son of David and Maggie McClelland, was one of a family of ten.

He enlisted on the outbreak of hostilities and went immediately to train at Clandeboye. When this part of his training was complete he was taken to Seaford on the south coast of England. Here he was also trained as a machine-gunner. While at Seaford the men could hear the noise of battle quite plainly but once they reached their destination in France they seemed to be further from the front as the noise of the guns didn't carry so well.

Soon they were on their way to the front. Most of it was done on foot with stops in billets along the way. After arrival at Martinsart more training took place. The weather had been wet and the chalky ground had turned to mud and French mud sticks to everything. It was difficult for the men to keep clean and tidy but still they had to train.

Men and supplies were being brought up continually and it was evident that a big attack was being planned. At the end of June everything was ready, but the weather turned wet again and the attack was postponed for two days in the hope that it would improve.

Saturday, 1st July, dawned bright and sunny. The Battle of the Somme was about to begin. At 7.30am the attack started. The 12th battalion at Hamel village, on the north bank of the River Ancre were on low lying ground and machine-guns at Thiepval and St. Pierre Divion had a clear line of sight on them. They were targets as soon as they left the trench.

It was in this early attack that David was killed. He has no known grave and is commemorated on the Thiepval Memorial. He left a wife and two children. They lived in Charlotte St.

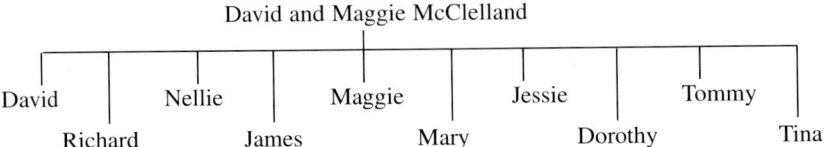

David and Maggie McClelland

David | Nellie | Maggie | Jessie | Tommy
Richard | James | Mary | Dorothy | Tina

27741 PRIVATE SAMUEL McCLELLAND
11th Bn Royal Inniskilling Fusiliers
K.I.A. 1-7-16
Aged 20
Interred in Mill Road Cemetery, Somme, France. Plot 19, Row D, Grave 6

Born   Ballymoney
Lived   Balnamore
Enlisted   Ballymoney.
Son of Thomas and Ellen McClelland, of Balnamore.
Commemorated in Drumreagh Presbyterian Church.

The Battalion was raised from the Donegal and Fermanagh Volunteers in September 1914. They began training at Finner Camp in County Donegal on the 20th of September. Finner Camp was originally used to provide training facilities for soldiers during the Boer War and was known locally as the Boer War Camp. In early January the battalion marched to the hutted camp at Shane's Castle, near Randalstown. Drafts of new reinforcements arrived on a regular basis and it may have been about this time that Samuel joined them. On the evening of Wednesday the 7th of July the battalion embarked at Dublin for the journey to Seaford, a town on the south coast of England. After a few weeks intensive training they moved to Bramshott in Surrey. On the evening of the 5th of October they embarked at Folkestone and landed at Boulogne at 3.00am and marched to Ostrovone rest camp.

Two days later they were taken to the area around Martinsart in preparation for the Battle of the Somme.

On the 1st of July 1916 at 7.30am Samuel set off with his battalion to attack the Schwaben Redoubt. It was one of the strongest positions in the entire German front line. As they crested a rise in the ground they were hit by murderous machine-gun fire, and it was probably here that Samuel was killed. He is one of the very few to have a grave and is buried in Mill Road Cemetery, which was made on top of part of the Schwaben Redoubt at Thiepval. Three other Ballymoney men serving with the 11th battalion were killed on this day. They were John Hamilton of Stranocum, John Reid of Finvoy and Alex Kirkpatrick of Ballymoney, neither of them with a known grave. Samuel's brother, Edward, was also serving and was in hospital in Edinburgh in August 1916 with an injury to his foot. He survived the war.

The grave of Sam McClelland in Mill Road Cemetery, Somme, France

Cemetery location information
Thiepval is a village on the D151 road about 8 kilometres north of Albert. The cemetery, signposted at Thiepval, is about 1 kilometre northwest of the village on the north side of the D73 road to Hamel. Access to the cemetery, 500 metres from the road, is by a track.

2493 RIFLEMAN MALCOLM McFADDEN
12th Bn Royal Irish Rifles
K.I.A. 1-7-16
Aged 23
No Known Grave. Commemorated on the Thiepval Memorial

Born   Grange of Drumhillagh
Lived   Dervock
Enlisted Ballymoney
Son of Mrs. Jane McFadden
Commemorated in Mosside Presbyterian Church.

Malcolm McFadden enlisted at Ballymoney on the outbreak of hostilities and did most of his training at Clandeboye. He was allowed home on leave on a number of occasions while he was at Clandeboye but once he went to Seaford it was a different matter and leave wasn't so easy to come by. There they had to settle and get on with their training. When this was finished they were taken to France and the area around Mesnil and Martinsart. The French had been taking a battering at Verdun and the French Commanders were clamouring for the British to do something to take the pressure off and to force the Germans to send troops to another area. It was agreed that the British would engage the Germans further north to draw troops away from Verdun. The area north of the River Somme was chosen and so plans were drawn up for what was to become known as the Battle of the Somme. By June 1916 plans were almost complete and the date of 28th of June set for the battle, but bad weather at the end of June forced a change of plan and the battle was postponed for three days. On the morning of the 1st of July the troops went over the top for the first time and into a maelstrom of rifle and machine-gun fire. Highly trained machine-gunners at St.Pierre-Divion could see them clearly and they were just mowed down. A heavy load of equipment didn't help matters, a load that many of them would never need. Malcolm was killed in this advance across No Man's Land and was never seen again. He has no known grave and is commemorated on the Thiepval Memorial.

4871 RIFLEMAN EDWARD McFALL
12th Bn Royal Irish Rifles
K.I.A. 1-7-16
No Known Grave. Commemorated on the Thiepval Memorial. Pier 15a & 15b

Born   Ramoan, Co Antrim
Lived   Stranocum
Enlisted Newtownards

Edward McFall was born in the Ballycastle area and the family later moved to Stranocum.

As well as being remembered on the Stranocum war memorial, he is also named on the one in Ballycastle. He enlisted at Newtownards and started his training almost immediately. After a few months training and route marches in the hilly Co Down countryside the battalion was considered well enough advanced to be taken to England. They were moved over to Seaford on the south coast for very intensive training. Here they spent the winter months on the open countryside of the South Downs. By May of 1916 plans were being made for a huge offensive by the British to take the pressure off the French army trying to hold back the Germans around Verdun. It was to take place at the Somme. The 12th battalion were sent to France in May and taken to the small French village of Martinsart, close to the Somme. The weather at this time was dry and warm and although the Germans were only a few hundred yards away, many of the men bathed in the River Ancre in the evenings after training was over for the day. Towards the end of June the weather changed from sunshine to a steady downpour. The soft French chalk turned to mud and there was water everywhere.

It didn't take time to run round the tents, it ran through them. Conditions were just unbelievable and the men had to stay there. The date for commencement of the battle, 28th June, was put back to 1st July, and by then the weather had improved. That Saturday morning dawned bright and sunny and at 7.30am the attack commenced. The 12th battalion were at Hamel, on the north bank of the River Ancre. The ground rises fairly steeply from the river on both sides and the enemy had a clear line of sight on them. Machine-guns opened on them right away from the high ground at St. Pierre-Divion and the battalion was decimated. It was in this attack that Edward was killed. He has no known grave and is commemorated on the Thiepval Memorial.

1777 RIFLEMAN WILLIAM McKENDRY
12th Bn Royal Irish Rifles
K.I.A. 1-7-16
No Known Grave. Commemorated on the Thiepval Memorial

Born   Ballymoney
Lived   Dunaverney
Enlisted   Ballymoney
Son of George McKendry, of Dunaverney.

William McKendry married Jane Lamont of Seacon in St Patrick's Parish Church, Ballymoney on 17th April 1915. He was a serving soldier at the time and was still training in Newtownards.

Three of the McKendry brothers served in the war, John, who served in Serbia and Salonika before being promoted to Brigade Quarter Master Sergeant in April 1917. George, who served throughout the war but survived, and William, who was killed at the Battle of the Somme. When William enlisted he was taken almost immediately to the training base at Newtownards. He was one of the first of the local men to enlist and did his early training there. Long route marches in the hilly County Down countryside soon had the men in good condition. When their training at Newtownards was finished they were moved to Seaford on the South coast of England. Again, route marches took up a fair bit of their time over the rolling farmland of the South Downs. But soon they were to be on their way to France and the continuous thunder of the guns. When they arrived at Martinsart village the weather, which had been good, turned showery. They were living in tents and the ground around them soon turned to mud. Nothing sticks to boots like the chalky mud of the Somme countryside and it was to get worse. By the end of June it was so wet that the planned attack had to be postponed for two days. Saturday, the first of July dawned bright and sunny, and as whistles sounded all along the line, young men leapt to their feet, climbed out of the trenches and set off over No Man's Land towards the enemy. The low lying ground beside the River Ancre is swampy and the ground had already been ploughed up by shells. There was mud everywhere. They had been ordered to walk, (with the weight of ammunition and all the other things they were supposed to need, it was almost impossible to do anything else), but they were only walking into a death trap. The machine-guns at St Pierre Divion made certain of that. William was killed by machine-gun fire as he tried to cross No Man's Land in this now quiet valley. He has no known grave and is commemorated on the Thiepval Memorial.

Commemorated in Ballymoney Parish Church.

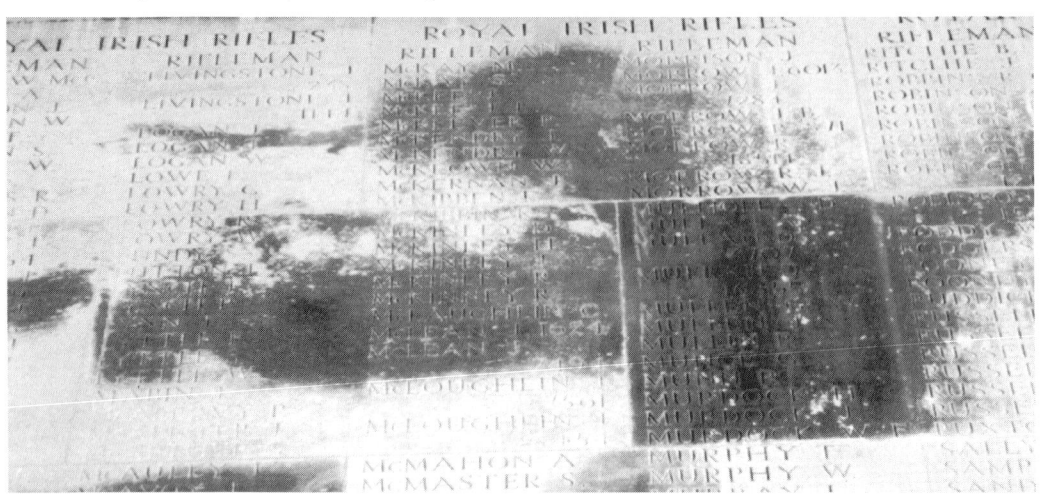

1016 RIFLEMAN ROBERT McILHATTON
11th Bn Royal Irish Rifles
K.I.A. 1-7-16
No Known Grave. Commemorated on the Thiepval Memorial, pier 15A

Born   Rasharkin
Lived   Kingarve, Stranocum
Enlisted   Ballymoney.
Commemorated in Bushvale Presbyterian Church.
Son of the late William John McIlhatton and Margaret McIlhatton

The family had a flax mill and it was there that Robert worked. As a young boy he attended Ballycraigagh school. Trained at Clandeboye. While the family were still quite young, their father, William John, died. This left Mrs McIlhatton to bring up the children on her own. One day during work at the flax mill, Fanny, the only girl in the family, got caught in the rollers and was killed.

On the outbreak of hostilities William James and Robert both enlisted. It is more than likely that the brothers both enlisted into the same Regiment and that both of them trained at Clandeboye. We know for a fact that Robert did train at Clandeboye and that when his training was completed he was moved to Seaford on the south coast of England. From here he was taken to France and the area around Mesnil and Martinsart at the Somme.

The battle, planned to take place at the end of June, had to be postponed because of the weather, and was re-scheduled for the 1st of July. That day dawned bright and clear and at 7.30am the British troops left their trenches for the attack across No Man's Land. Robert was in the valley beside the River Ancre, on low lying ground which easily flooded, and had to make his way through this as he tried to reach the German lines. Machine-guns were strategically placed on the high ground at St. Pierre-Division and the troops were just mowed down as they struggled with their load of equipment across No Man's Land. It was during this attack that Robert was killed.

He has no known grave and is commemorated on the Thiepval Memorial.

William James was seriously injured in this same attack but after a time spent in hospital, he re-joined his unit. He survived the war and returned to spend the rest of his life in the Stranocum area. Their cousin, Hugh Patton, survived this attack, to be killed at Passchendaele in August 1917.

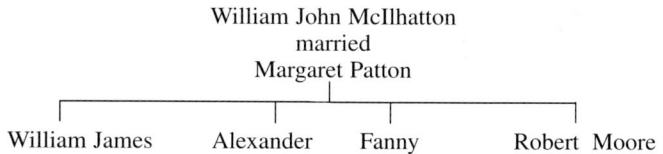

William John McIlhatton married Margaret Patton

William James | Alexander | Fanny | Robert Moore

18311 RIFLEMAN DANIEL McKAY
12th Bn Royal Irish Rifles
K.I.A. 1-7-16
No Known Grave. Commemorated on the Thiepval Memorial

Born   Armoy
Lived   Armoy
Enlisted   Ballymoney

Daniel McKay enlisted in Ballymoney in September 1914 and was almost immediately taken to Newtownards for training. After a few months he was sent to Seaford on the south coast of England and then as the planning for the Battle of the Somme was now in full swing, the move across the Channel to the small French village of Martinsart.

Here, close to the front line, a lot more training took place, and as the planned date for the battle approached, more and more troops arrived until the place was literally swarming with men. They were mostly housed in tents. During early June 1916 the weather had been fine but as the month wore on it began to change and by the 25th and 26th the rain was coming down in sheets. The chalky French soil turned to mud and thousands of men training on it kept it that way. The attack, planned for 28th June, had to be postponed to 1st July.

By then the weather had improved and it was decided to go ahead with the battle. Saturday, the 1st of July, dawned bright and sunny. The exploding of the Hawthorn Ridge mine ten minutes before Zore Hour was a disaster, warning every German for miles around that an attack was imminent. The 12th battalion were at Hamel village on the north bank of the Ancre with high ground on both sides of the river. They were literally mowed down as they crossed No Man's Land by machine-guns on this high ground. This was one of the worst days of the war for Ballymoney losing 28 of it's young men on this one day alone.

They were not all with the Rifles, some of them were Inniskillings, and a few were with other regiments, but they were all at Thiepval. Daniel McKay was killed as he crossed No Man's Land early on that Saturday morning. He has no known grave and is commemorated on the Thiepval Memorial.

25105 PRIVATE JAMES McKEEMAN
9th Bn Royal Inniskilling Fusiliers
K.I.A. 1-7-16
Aged 20

Born Benvarden
Lived Benvarden
Enlisted Coleraine
Son of Nancy Mc.Keeman,
of Kilmoyle, Dervock.
Commemorated in Carnaff Reformed Presbyterian Church.

Nancy's family lived at Kilmoyle, a townland about five miles north of Ballymoney, and a short distance from the village of Ballybogey.

James McKeeman was born at Benvarden, about a mile from Ballybogey, in 1896. He was an only child. He had dark brown hair, blue eyes and a fair complexion. After he was killed his mother could not settle. She had no-one to turn to and her grief at the loss of her only child was too much to bear. She moved to live at Moycraig for a number of years and then to Bushmills.

Eventually she went into an old peoples home in Portrush and it was there that she died at an advanced age. All through her life she talked of her son being killed at the Somme. This was the only real topic she could think of and it dominated her life. James enlisted at Coleraine towards the end of 1914 when he was just eighteen years of age. He did his early training at Finner Camp before moving to Randalstown in January 1915. Then in July of that year they moved to Ballycastle, before going in early September to the Bordon area of England. In October 1915 they landed in France. From there they went eventually to the area around Martinsart, close to where they would be in action at the Somme.

The 9th battalion were with the 36th Ulster Division in Thiepval Wood on the first day of the Battle of the Somme. Amazingly James was the only Ballymoney man with the 9th battalion to be killed on this day. Others were killed, certainly, but they were with other battalions. At first the 9th were sheltered from the machine-guns at Thiepval by a hollow in the ground, but as the ground rose as they advanced they soon became exposed and it was here that they had so many casualties. Machine-guns at Thiepval just mowed them down as they came into view. This was in the region to the south of the Ulster Tower at Thiepval and is just as exposed to-day as it was then. It is good farming country with very few hedges and is cropped continually. Much can still be picked from the chalky French soil, schrapnel is everywhere, bullets that have been fired, pieces of shell, brass buckles, some with the leather still attached, eighty years after the conflict. What it must have been like at the time one can only guess.

James McKeeman and his mother Nancy

22400 PRIVATE JOHN McMULLEN
1st Bn Royal Dublin Fusiliers
K.I.A. 1-7-16
No Known Grave. Commemorated on the Thiepval Memorial, France. Pier 16C

Born   Dunloy
Lived   Swatragh
Enlisted Coatbridge

On the outbreak of hostilities the 1st battalion were in Madras and sailed for England from Bombay on 19th November 1914. They arrived at Plymouth on 21st December and moved to Torquay.

Then in January they went to Nuneaton, where they joined the 29th Division and sailed from Avonmouth on 16th March arriving at Alexandria on the 30th. On 9th April they sailed for Mudros.

They took part in the landing at Cape Helles on 25th April 1915, suffering heavy casualties. It was here that the battalion was almost wiped out and on 30th April were amalgamated with the 1st Royal Munster Fusiliers. On 1st January 1916 they left Gallipoli for Mudros and on 8th January sailed for Egypt. They left Alexandria on 13th March bound for Marseilles and arrived six days later.

John McMullen had been with the Royal Dublin Fusiliers in Gallipoli serving in the 29th Division. When they were brought back to France for the Battle of the Somme they were sent to the area north of the River Ancre to attack Beaumont Hamel. On the morning of the 1st July they were in the support trenches but when it came to their turn to attack they were delayed by returning wounded. They left their trenches, however, shortly before 8am but found the German wire mostly uncut and the few gaps choked with dead and wounded men.

Machine-gun fire from the Beaucourt Ridge immediately cut them down as they tried to find a way through. It was here that John McMullen was killed as he tried to advance. He has no known grave and is commemorated on the Thiepval Memorial.

18536 RIFLEMAN JOHN MURPHY
12th Bn Royal Irish Rifles
K.I.A. 1-7-16
Aged 20
Interred in Knightsbridge British Cemetery, Mesnil-Martinsart. Row D, Grave 47

Born Ballymoney
Lived Greenville, Ballymoney
Enlisted Ballymoney.
Son of James and Jeannie Murphy, of Greenville, Ballymoney.
Commemorated in St. James's Presbyterian Church.

As youngsters the children all attended Landhead school. They lived at Greenville, which is opposite what is now the Rugby Club. The farm at that time was owned by the Best family, and the Murphy's lived up the same lane. The Best family had two sons in the army, one of them winning the Military Medal. The Murphys worshipped in St.James's Presbyterian Church in the town and it is there that John is commemorated.

After leaving school John Murphy was in the employment of Mr. John Baxter, J.P. During his spare time he was interested in the Orange Order and became the foundation Treasurer of one of the local Lodges, Ballymoney Rising Star L.O.L. 954. His father, James became the foundation Worshipful Master of the same lodge. At the time he enlisted John was working in the Milltown Mill, on the outskirts of Ballymoney. At that time it was a flour mill. John, like many of the young men at the time was in the U.V.F. and had done some initial training in that organisation. This stood him in good stead when he was sent to Clandeboye because he already had a good knowledge of firearms.

John enlisted at Ballymoney soon after war was declared and his first training was at Newtownards.

After a few months spent at Newtownards they were moved to Seaford, on the south coast of England.

This was the first time that John had been away from home but he had met a lot of new friends and time passed quickly. It didn't pass so quickly for his mother and father, left at home, who realised full well just what the risks would be. Seaford was a busy camp and training and route marches were taking place every day. In May 1916 they were moved across to France and marched to the little French village of Martinsart. This was close to what we now know as the Western Front. The quiet country roads were narrow and dusty and water was a big problem, for both men and horses. The men were housed in tents and soldiers were being brought into the area at an ever increasing rate.

The Battle of the Somme was about to begin. The weather had been dry and warm during most of June and the soldiers were in the habit of bathing in the River Ancre when they were off duty, but this all had to stop as preparations for the battle increased. The date had been set for 28th June but the weather deteriorated with such heavy rain that the date just had to be changed. The soft French chalk turned to mud very quickly and moving around was almost impossible. The horses couldn't pull guns which just sunk to their axles as soon as they were moved. Conditions were awful and the battle was postponed until 1st July. Water was now a problem of a different kind. Saturday, the 1st of July, dawned bright and clear. John was with the rest of the battalion at Hamel on the north bank of the Ancre and as soon as the whistles blew at 7.30am he set off on the attack. He had only just started to cross No Mans Land when he was killed by machine-gun fire from the heights around St. Pierre-Divion. After darkness his body was found and taken back for burial in Knightsbridge Cemetery.

His mother and father were notified almost at once and were one of the first families in Ballymoney to get news from the Somme.

John's brother, James, also served but at some stage he was gassed and in hospital. After being released from hospital he was allowed home on leave and after a period of rest at home was ordered back to the Front.

Later he was taken prisoner and served the last nine months of the war in a German prison camp. He was in the same prison as another Ballymoney man, Tommy Owens.

John's father, James, had a milk run after the war, and his youngest son, Ronnie, used to help on the run.

This had to be done twice a day, morning and evening, in all weathers, and Ronnie still has very vivid memories of his time in that job. Because of the close connections with the Best family, Ronnie was christened Ronald Best Murphy. He was the youngest of the family and is the only surviving member.

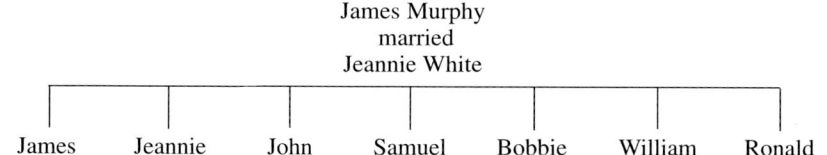

James Murphy
married
Jeannie White

| James | Jeannie | John | Samuel | Bobbie | William | Ronald |

LIEUT JOHNSTON MURPHY
6th Bn Royal Irish Rifles
K.I.A. 1-7-16
No Known Grave. Commemorated on the Thiepval Memorial

Born   Ballymoney
Lived   Main St, Ballymoney
Son of Clarke and Lizzie Murphy, of Main St, Ballymoney.
Commemorated in St. James's Presbyterian Church.

The 6th battalion were formed at Dublin in August 1914 and in September they went to train at Fermoy with the 10th Division. They then moved to Dublin in October, where they stayed until February 1915, when they moved to The Curragh. In May they moved to Hackwood Park, near Basingstoke in England. On 7th July 1915 they sailed from Liverpool, bound for Mudros, via Alexandria, and arrived on 26th July. They landed at Anzac Cove, on the Gallipoli Peninsula on 5th August 1915 and this appears to have been a very quiet landing as the battalion seems to have suffered no casualties on this day. The battalion sailed again for Mudros on 29th September, and then in early October arrived in Salonika. It was soon after this landing at Anzac Cove that Johnston was severely injured. He was at first treated in a Red Cross hospital but eventually had to face the long journey home to a hospital in London. He had been injured in the shoulder and the bullet had lodged in his lung. Although he was treated for his wounds in hospital in London, according to the newspapers the bullet was not removed, at that stage at any rate. After a few weeks in hospital he was showing good signs of improving and was allowed home on leave. He arrived in Ballymoney on Saturday 11th September on a months leave and left to join his unit in October with the bullet still in his lung. Six Months later, in April 1916 he was home on leave again, this time just for a few days. He had been born and brought up in Ballymoney and as a young man had attended Trinity College in Dublin. It was here that he passed his Officer Training Corps exams. He re-joined his unit in time for the build up for the Battle of the Somme. It was here that Johnston was killed on the morning of the 1st of July as he led his men to the attack. He was at first reported missing and the family at home spent anxious months waiting for news of him, but were eventually forced to accept that he had been killed. He has no known grave and is commemorated on the Thiepval Memorial.

His sister, Martha, died on 31st December 1876 aged just sixteen months.

Fourteen years later, on 6th September 1890, another sister, Mary, died, at the age of 13. The following year Johnston's mother, Lizzie, died while he was still a young boy, on 12th October 1891 and then his brother, Clarke on 3rd April 1897 at the age of ten.

On the 12th of January 1915 Johnston's father married Matilda McMicheal in St. James's Presbyterian Church. Clarke had a coopering business in Main Street, about half way down on the right hand side, ie Town clock side.

He was very interested in the well being of the town and was on the Urban District Council. He became a J.P. in September 1917 and adjudicated at the local Petty Sessions Court. He died the following year, on 3rd July 1918 at the age of 65. His son Robert, who was on active service, was allowed home for the funeral and soon after he went back, on 2nd October 1918, he was killed in action.

According to the newspapers at the time, Clarke was one of the practical jokers of the town, and when one looks at the number of deaths in his family it must have stood him in good stead on many occasions.

9243 L. CPL. JAMES PATTON
15th Bn Royal Irish Rifles formerly 1186 Army Cyclists Corps
K.I.A. 1-7-16
No Known Grave. Commemorated on the Thiepval Memorial, France Pier 15 A

Born   Finvoy
Enlisted   Ballymoney
Commemorated in Finvoy Presbyterian Church.
It was May 1917 before the family were told officially that he was dead.

James Patton enlisted at Ballymoney and started training almost immediately at Ballykinlar. By the end of September 1914 training there was in full swing but the weather changed to usher in a very cold, wet winter. These were the conditions under which training had to take place. It took time to house the troops properly and in the meantime they just had to put up with it. By the time training was considered complete the French Commanders were clamouring for the British to start an offensive to draw the German troops away from Verdun. This was to be to the north and the area chosen was at the Somme. British troops were brought in by the thousand and billeted in the rear areas. The build up to the Battle of the Somme was stupendous. For miles around every building was crammed with troops and supplies and tents were erected for those not lucky enough to have better accomodation. On the first of July James attacked on the low ground to the South of the River Ancre and towards the village of St. Pierre Divion. The village is situated on rising ground to the north of the Schwaben Redoubt and it was close to here that James was killed as he attacked with his unit. Machine-gun fire from St. Pierre Divion was poured into the men as they came up the valley. They were also in full view of machine-gunners to the north of the river and the cross-fire was deadly. James's body was not found and he was reported missing. It was May of the following year before the family at home were told that he had definately been killed. He has no known grave and is commemorated on the Thiepval Memorial.

27147 PRIVATE JOHN REID
11th Bn Royal Inniskilling Fusiliers
K.I.A. 1-7-16
No Known Grave. Commemorated on the Thiepval Memorial

Born   Knockans, Finvoy
Lived   Knockans, Finvoy
Enlisted Ballymoney
Commemorated in Finvoy Parish Church

The battalion was raised in September 1914 from the Donegal and Fermanagh Volunteers. They started training at Finner Camp in Donegal on 20th September.

Finner Camp was originally used to provide training facilities for soldiers during the Boer War and was known locally as the Boer War Camp. In January the battalion marched to the hutted camp at Shane's Castle near Randalstown. New drafts continued to arrive for the battalion on a regular basis and it is more than likely that John Reid joined them at this time. On the evening of the 7th of July they embarked at Dublin for the journey to Seaford, a town on the Sussex coast. Here they trained for a few weeks before moving to Bramshott in Surrey. On the 5th of October they embarked at Folkestone and arrived at Boulogne at 3.00am and marched to Ostrohove rest camp. From here they were taken to the area around Martinsart to prepare for the start of the Battle of the Somme.

On the morning of the 1st of July 1916 John Reid advanced with his battalion to attack the Schwaben Redoubt. It was one of the strongest positions on the whole German front line. Most of the men who reached the Schwaben Redoubt were never seen again. Almost all of them were either killed or taken prisoner. Four Ballymoney men serving in this battalion were killed on this day, John Hamilton, Alex Kirkpatrick, Samuel McClelland and John Reid.

Of the four, only Samuel McClelland has a known grave, and he is buried within a few yards of where he fell, in Mill Road Cemetery, just across the field from the Ulster Tower at Thiepval. John Reid attacked up a slight dip in the ground at first out of sight of the machine-guns at Thiepval.

Here it was relatively safe until they reached higher ground and appeared on the skyline. Once on the higher level they were mowed down by fire from Thiepval and from the heights north of the River Ancre. We will never know just how far John Reid got on this day. All we know is that he didn't come back. He has no known grave and is commemorated on the Thiepval Memorial.

John's granddaughter, who is just home from a trip to France to see her grandfathers name on the Thiepval Memorial, tells me that he also served throughout the Boer War. At 36 years of age when he was killed in 1916 he was much older than the normal solder and this would tie in with the dates of the Boer War. The loss at this particular time of thousands of experienced solders like John Reid meant that the British Army was reduced to Battalion of half trained militiamen most of them away from home for the first time. It was to prove costly.

18757 L. CPL. ERNEST WALTER SHIELDS
Bn Royal Irish Rifles
K.I.A. 1-7-16
Aged 18
No Known Grave. Commemorated on the Thiepval Memorial, France, Pier 15 A & 15 B

Born   Bushmills
Lived   Kirkfield House, Dervock
Enlisted   Ballymoney
Commemorated in Derrykeighan Parish Church.

The family had probably lived in Bushmills in the late 1890's as Ernest was born there in 1898. By the time he enlisted they were living at Kirkfield House, Dervock. When he enlisted at Ballymoney he probably lied about his age in order to be allowed to enlist.

This was common practice among the young men of the time as they all thought that the war would be over by Christmas and they would miss the chance to see a bit of the world. Ernest trained at Clandeboye and his story is much the same as the others who were serving with the 12th battalion. There is no need to go

into details about the preparations for the Battle of the Somme but Ernest would have been well across No Man's Land at Hamel before he was killed as he waited his turn to go through the gaps in the German wire. The fighting was so severe that many of these bodies lay unburied for months. It was just impossible to get near them. Ernest has no known grave and is commemorated on the Thiepval Memorial.

Sam McConaghy at the Ulster Tower at the Somme, 11th November 1998

7537 RIFLEMAN SAMUEL TAYLOR
12th Bn Royal Irish Rifles
K.I.A. 1-7-16
Aged 18
Interred in Ancre British Cemetery, Beaumont Hamel, France. Plot 8, Row A, Grave 83

Born   Meetinghouse St, Ballymoney on 31-8-1897
Lived   Castle St, Ballymoney
Enlisted   Ballymoney
Son of David John and Jane Taylor of Castle St, Ballymoney.
Commemorated in 1st Ballymoney Presbyterian Church.

The Taylor family lived in Castle Street in Ballymoney. They worshipped in 1st Ballymoney Presbyterian Church where Samuel and his brother David are both commemorated on the Roll of Honour. Samuel enlisted in Ballymoney at the age of sixteen and this greatly upset his parents who immediately set about buying him off. This worked at first but as soon as he got their backs turned he went back and enlisted all over again. They eventually, much against their will, relented and allowed him to go. The 12th battalion trained at Clandeboye with long route marches through the hilly County Down countryside which brought the men up to a very high state of physical fitness in a short time.

Following this they moved to Seaford on the south coast of England for final training before going to France in October 1915. Their first major engagement was to be the Battle of the Somme, planned to take the pressure off the French at Verdun and to draw German troops north and away from Verdun. The 12th battalion was based at Martinsart, a small French village near what we now know as the Western Front. At the end of June the weather, which had been dry and warm up to now, suddenly turned very wet. As anyone who has visited the Western Front knows, the chalky French soil quickly turns to glutinous mud. The weather was so bad that the attack had to be postponed until it would dry up. By the 1st of July the weather had improved and it was decided to press on with the attack. A huge mine had been constructed under a German strong point at Hawthorn Ridge and it was eventually decided to blow this mine ten minutes before zero on the first of July. The noise as it erupted warned every German for miles around that an attack was imminent. When the whistles blew and the men left their trenches at 7.30am every German was ready.

The 12th battalion suffered very heavy casualties both from machine-guns on the heights ahead of them and from St. Pierre-Divion across the river. Altogether Ballymoney lost thirty young men on this one morning. Samuel was killed in this first advance, hit by a hail of machine-gun fire as he tried to cross No Man's Land. He is buried in Ancre Valley Cemetery on the north bank of the river, close to where he fell. He was just eighteen years of age.

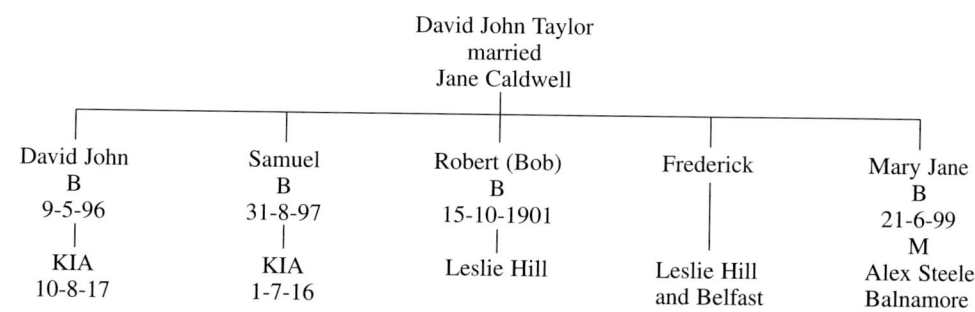

6512 L. CPL ROBERT THOMPSON
1st Bn Royal Irish Rifles
K.I.A. 1-7-16
No Known Grave. Commemorated on the Thiepval Memorial, France. Pier 15 A

Born   Ballymoney
Enlisted Belfast

On the otbreak of hostilities the 1st battalion were in Aden and on 27th September embarked for the U.K. arriving at Liverpool on 22nd October. They then went to Hursley Park, Winchester, joining the 25th Brigade, 8th Div. They landed at Le Havre on 6th November 1914.

This was a battalion of seasoned troops and very little training in this type of warfare was needed. I have been unable to trace any relative of this soldier in the Ballymoney district and as far as I can make out he is not commemorated in any of the local churches.

It is possible that the family moved away from the Ballymoney district while Robert was still a youngster and by the time churches began to put up Rolls of Honour the family had been forgotten.

If this is the case it is extremely sad that anyone could be as easily and as completely forgotten. It would appear that he was a regular soldier and had made the army his life.

He was killed in action after leaving the shelter of the trench on the morning of the 1st of July 1916. There is no known grave and he is commemorated on the Thiepval Memorial.

19297 CORPORAL JAMES WATSON
12th Bn Royal Irish Rifles
K.I.A. 1-7-16
No Known Grave. Commemorated on the Thiepval Memorial

Born   Ballymaconnelly
Lived   Ballymaconnelly
Commemorated in Finvoy Presbyterian Church

It is believed that James and Joseph Watson were brothers. Both of them belonged to Finvoy Presbyterian Church and both lived at Ballymaconnelly.

Joseph was killed at Festubert in July 1915 and James a year later at the Somme.

James did his early training at Clandeboye and then went to England to complete his training at Seaford. From there they went to France and the little French village of Martinsart. This was close to the area of the Somme.

For most of June 1916 the weather had been good but two days before the battle the rain came down in torrents. The chalky French ground quickly turned to mud and the date of the battle had to be postponed. The new date, 1st July 1916, dawned bright and sunny and at 7.30am the whistles blew. Men climbed out of their trenches all along the line and set off across No Man's Land towards the German wire. The few gaps that had been cut in the wire were crammed with soldiers waiting to get through when the German machine-guns opened up. They never had a chance. Months later, the bodies were still lying where they had fallen and many were never found. James has no known grave and is commemorated on the Thiepval Memorial.

604 RIFLEMAN THOMAS WILSON
11th Bn Royal Irish Rifles
K.I.A. 1-7-16
No Known Grave. Commemorated on the Thiepval Memorial. Pier 15 A

Born   Rasharkin
Lived   Duneaney, Rasharkin
Enlisted Ballymena

Thomas Wilson lived at Duneaney, Rasharkin. He enlisted at Ballymena soon after war was declared and went immediately to train at Clandeboye.

They were then moved across to England to complete their training, and from there to France and the small French village of Martinsart. After some weeks training and digging trenches in preparation for an attack on the Germans word began to filter through that the Battle of the Somme was about to begin. The 11th Battalion were in the 108th Brigade and would be in the area around the village of Hamel. The village lies in the valley of the River Ancre and it was to the low lying ground of this valley that the battalion were sent. Wet weather postponed the battle for two days, but Saturday, the 1st of July dawned bright and sunny, and at 7.30am the attack began.

As the men left their trenches they were told to walk across to the German wire, there would be nobody there to stop them, the bombardment had been too heavy. This proved to be totally wrong, and the Germans came out in droves. The British were caught in the open as they tried to get through the few gaps that had been cut in the German wire and were simply mowed down. Thomas was killed by machine-gun fire as he tried to get through the wire. He has no known grave and is commemorated on the Thiepval Memorial. What was then a killing field is now a quiet French valley where cattle graze peacefully in the meadows beside the river.

13588 SERGEANT SAMUEL SHIELDS M.M.
8th Bn Royal Irish Rifles
K.I.A. 2-7-16
Aged 23
No Known Grave. Commemorated on the Thiepval Memorial, France. Pier 15 A & 15 B

Born   Stranocum
Enlisted   Belfast
Son of Samuel and Sarah Shields, of 33, Upper Frank St, Belfast.

Samuel's parents appear to have moved from Stranocum at some time previous to the start of the war and were living in Belfast. Samuel enlisted there and did his training at Ballykinlar. When this was completed he was taken to France in preparation for the Battle of the Somme, which had been planned to take some of the pressure off the French Armies at Verdun.

Although the emphasis has always been on the first day of the Somme, the fighting did not stop then. I think it would be reasonably safe to assume that Samuel was one of those who got into the Schwaben Redoubt and subsequently were forced, through lack of ammunition, to try to get back to their own lines. This would certainly explain why there is no known grave.

He was also the only Ballymoney man to be killed on this day and it would appear very likely that he was killed in the act of trying to get safely back. Although by the next day the British Army were, to some extent, licking their wounds, the fighting still had to go on, or be over-run. It was during this second day that Samuel was killed. He has no known grave and is commemorated on the Thiepval Memorial.

7876 RIFLEMAN GEORGE DOHERTY
2nd Bn Royal Irish Rifles
K.I.A. 8-7-16
Aged 19
No Known Grave. Commemorated on the Thiepval Memorial, France. Pier 15A and 15B

Born   Ballymoney
Enlisted   Belfast
Son of George and Margaret Doherty, of 9. Cromac Square, Belfast.

The Thiepval Memorial will be found on the D73 off the main Bapaume to Albert road (D929).

The 2nd batalion were at Tidworth when war was declared and landed at Rouen ten days later. They joined the 25th Division on 26th October 1915.

By the time plans had been formulated for the battle of the Somme they were with the 7th Division in the Fricourt, Mametz area and it was here that George was killed on the 8th of July 1916 aged only nineteen. There is no known grave and he is commemorated on the Thiepval Memorial.

8176 RIFLEMAN ROBERT CAMPBELL
7th Bn Seaforth Highlanders
K.I.A. 10-7-16
Aged 20
No Known Grave. Commemorated on the Thiepval Memorial, pier 15c

Born   Fermagh, Rasharkin
Lived   Mossend, Glasgow.
Enlisted Glasgow.
Commemorated in Rasharkin Presbyterian Church.
Worked in the Scottish coal mines.

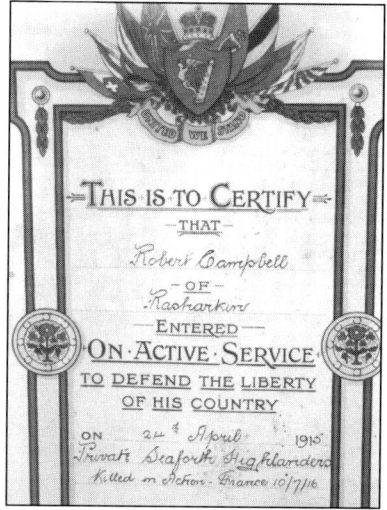

The family lived at Fermagh, Rasharkin. Before enlisting, Robert worked in the coal mines outside Glasgow, as a miner. He enlisted at Glasgow on 24th April 1915, and after intensive and hurried training he was taken to France with his unit. He was killed at the Battle of the Somme on 10th July 1916. There is no known grave and he is commemorated on the Thiepval Memorial, pier 15c.

The 7th Seaforth were formed at Fort George in August 1914 as part of Kitchener's First New Army, K1. They joined the 26th (Highland) Brigade of the 9th (Scottish) Division at Aldershot. During the winter of 1914-15, the battalion trained in the South of England and on Salisbury Plain. The 9th Division was the first of the New Army Divisions to reach France. In May 1915 the 7th Seaforth landed at Boulogne, and on 1st/2nd July 1915 the 9th Division took over the trenches near Festubert. The first major battle for the 7th Seaforth was the attack at Loos on 25th September 1915. It was the first occasion on which the British used poison gas.

The 7th Seaforth and 5th Camerons attacked the strong German position of the Hohenzollern Redoubt. In a series of attacks over three days, the battalion took it's objective at a cost of over 500 casualties.

The 7th spent October to December 1915 in the Salient at Ypres, in the particularly bleak period of cold, muddy trench warfare where the British Corps clung grimly to the gains it had made in the battle of Ypres.

From January to May they were at Ploegsteert where the trenches and billets were much better. After a gruelling time at Ploegsteert they were moved south in preparation for the battle of the Somme. Their destination was the area around Longueval and the attack on Delville Wood and it was in preparation for this attack that Robert was killed. He was only twenty years of age.

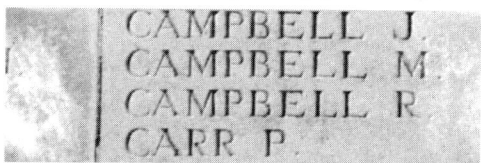

		Alexander Campbell	married	Liza Bailey	
Alex b. 1874	Bessie b. 1878	Agnes b. 1883	Wm John b. 1891		Robert b. 1895
Annie McIlroy b. 1876	Maggie b. 1881	Thomas b. 1884	James b. 1892 KIA 10-7-16		Jennie b. 1897 Died young aged 6

28648 PRIVATE PATRICK OLPHERT
2nd Bn Royal Inniskilling Fusiliers
K.I.A. 10-7-16
Aged 20
No Known Grave. Commemorated on the Thiepval Memorial, France

Born   Union St, Ballymoney
Lived   Union St, Ballymoney
Enlisted Ballymoney
Son of Patrick and Jane Olphert.

Born in 1896 at his home in Union St, Patrick spent all of his early life in Ballymoney. He was employed, after leaving school, by Mr. W. Hill, Church St, as a saddler, an occupation which at that time, was a very popular and successful one. At the outbreak of war, Patrick enlisted in the Royal Inniskilling Fusiliers, was trained and taken with his Battalion to France. The weather in the winter of 1915-16 was severe, with long periods of snow and frost. Patrick, after many nights spent in the open, had to go to hospital with frostbite. This was in March 1916. When he was showing good signs of recovery he was allowed home on leave.

In late April of that year he was at his home in Union St for the first time since enlisting. In early May he returned to his unit in France. He was killed at the Battle of the Somme on 10th July 1916 at the age of only twenty. He was at first reported missing, then, a few months later, missing, presumed killed, and finally, after more weeks of waiting, he was reported killed in action. At home the waiting was the worst bit, and then when the news came, no more hope.

It was a devastating time for many Ballymoney families, some of whom lost two sons, and many of them never really recovered from the shock.

The 2nd battalion had been in the front line at Ovillers with the 2nd Div, when Patrick was killed. His brother, Michael, a Trooper in the North Irish Horse, also served but survived the war, and was home on leave in September 1917, and in September 1918 he was again home on leave. On 5th August 1919, Michael married Margaret Oakman of Balnamore.

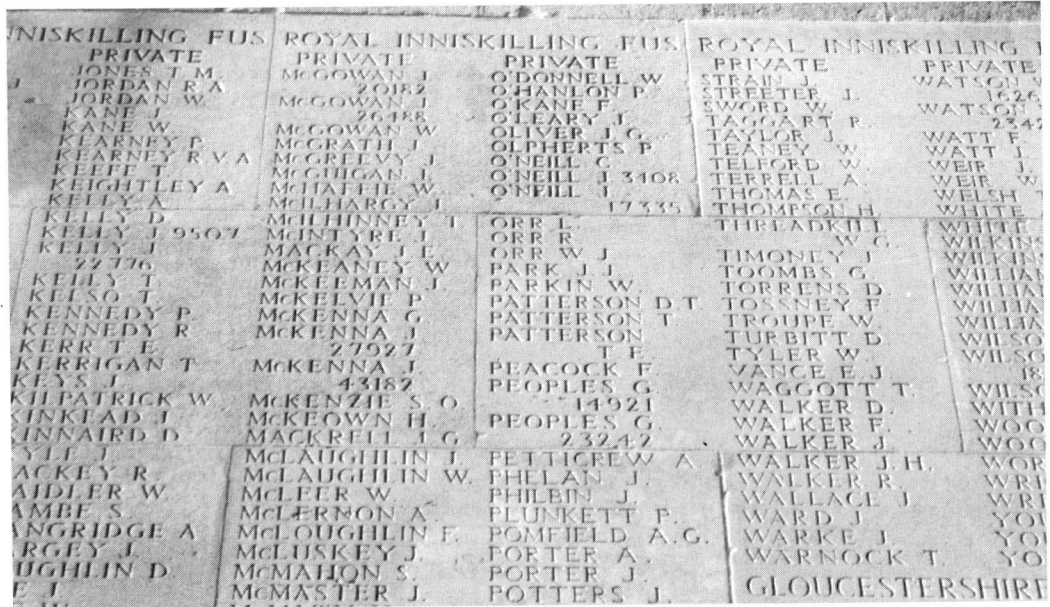

12680 THOMAS McGHEE
1st Bn Royal Scots Fusiliers
K.I.A. 14-7-16
Aged 24
No Known Grave. Commemorated on the Thiepval Memorial. 3c

Born   Mosside
Enlisted   Port Glasgow
Son of James and Mary Ann McGhee of 1/33, Bouverie St, Port Glasgow.

Thomas McGhee was born in the village of Mosside. This village lies on the main Ballycastle-Coleraine road about five miles from Ballycastle. The family appears to have moved to Scotland at around the turn of the century as no trace of them now remains in this area. Thomas is not commemorated in any of the local churches nor is he named on the Dervock War Memorial. These ommissions probably mean that the family had been gone for some considerable time. James and Mary McGhee had an address in Port Glasgow but an appeal for information in the Greenock Telegraph produced nothing and we can only assume that the Scottish connection has died out and is gone for ever. Thomas enlisted at Port Glasgow soon after war was declared and joined the 1st battalion of the Royal Scots Fusiliers. His first major battle was the Battle of the Somme

in July of 1916. Thomas was killed in the bitter fighting at the Battle of the Somme and has no known grave. He is commemorated on the Thiepval Memorial. He was just twenty-four years of age and as far as I know was still single. This is one of the names that I found when I went to Londonderry to study Ireland's Memorial Records in St. Columb's Cathedral. Had I not done so we would never have known about him, and the fact that he gave his life would have gone un-noticed.

3638 PRIVATE EDWARD JAMES THOMPSON
60th Bn, Australian Inf
K.I.A. 19-7-16
Commemorated at V.C.Corner Australian Cemetery Memorial, Fromelles

Born   Ballywattick, Ballymoney
Son of Mr James Thompson of Ballywattick, Ballymoney.

Fromelles is a village 16 kilometres west of Lille and V.C.Corner Australian Cemetery is 2 kilometres north-west of Fromelles on the road to Sailly.

V.C.Corner Cemetery was made after the Armistice and contains the graves of 410 Australian soldiers who fell in the attack at Fromelles and whose bodies were found on the battlefield, but the identification of even a single body proved to be impossible.

It was therefore decided not to mark the individual graves, but to record on a screen wall the names of all the 1,298 Australian soldiers who fell in the engagement and whose graves were not known. Of these 314 belonged to the 60th battalion, 241 to the 59th, 190 to the 53rd, 163 to the 32nd, 373 to other infantry battalions, eleven to the Australian Machine-Gun Corps, and six to the Engineers.

The Cemetery consists of a grass lawn on which the burial is outlined, a rubble wall and a hedge. On the further side of the road is a stone terrace, on which the Cross of Sacrifice stands, flanked by two buildings, and behind the Cross is the screen wall bearing the names with the inscription, "In honour of 410 unknown Australian soldiers here buried, who were among the following 1,298 Officers, Non Commissioned Officers and Men of the Australian Imperial Force, killed in the attack at Fromelles, July 19th and 20th 1916."

It would appear that the family may have emigrated to Australia many years ago. No-one can now remember them living at Ballywattick and two of the sons were serving in the Australian Forces, Edward James, who was killed, and his brother, S. Thompson, who survived.

Edward James enlisted at Broadmeadows, which is to the north of Melbourne, when he was just over nineteen years of age, on the 4th of October 1915. His mother, now a widow, was living at nearby Collingwood. He was five feet, six inches tall with blue eyes, light brown hair and a fair complexion. The family was Roman Catholic, which accounts for him not being commemorated in any of the local churches, and one of the reasons his name was hard to find. He formally signed up on the 3rd of January 1916 and two days later embarked at Melbourne on the H.M.A.T."Afric". On 23rd February he was taken on strength of the 58th battalion direct from training camp at Tel-el-Kebir and then on 15th March was transferred to the 60th battalion, still at Tel-el-Kebir.

On 17th June 1916 he was up on a charge at Moascar for using "insulting words to an N.C.O.". This cost him seven days forfeiture of pay but no other explanation is given. The following day he embarked at Alexandria on the "Kinfaune Castle" and disembarked at Marseilles eleven days later on the 29th of June 1916. They now faced a long train journey up to the Western Front and the next report on his record is being reported missing on the 19th of July at Fromelles. He has no known grave and is commemorated at V.C.Corner Australian Cemetery Memorial. The Australian Authorities made every effort to find and identify as many of the Australian bodies as possible. The base records office at Melbourne wrote to Mrs Thompson on 18th July 1921 asking for any information which might help to identify his remains if they were found. She replied immediately that there was nothing she could do to help as his last letter home had been from Egypt and she had not heard from him since.

3769 RIFLEMAN SAMUEL JAMIESON
12th Bn Royal Irish Rifles
D.O.W. 26-7-16
Interred in St. Sever Cemetery, Rouen, France. Plot A, Row 30, Grave 2

Born   Coleraine
Lived   Dervock
Enlisted Newtownards
Commemorated in Carncullagh Presbyterian Church.

In the first attack on the 1st of July at the Battle of the Somme, Samuel Jamieson was seriously wounded. Found by stretcher-bearers, he was evacuated to the nearest dressing station but was found to be too ill to be treated there and was immediately sent to hospital at Rouen.

Word was sent to his mother at her home at Ballynagor, Dervock, that if she wished she could visit him at the hospital as he was not expected to recover. She immediately set out on this long, tiring journey, eventually arriving at Rouen in time to spend a few days with her son.

An operation was the only hope but he did not survive the effects of the operation and he is interred in St. Sever Cemetery.

He was the first of five Ballymoney men to be buried here. Rouen was a busy embarkation point for the wounded being taken by sea to hospital in England. William McConachie of Dervock died here on the 7th of September 1916. J.K.M. Greer, of the well known firm of solicitors, Greer, Hamilton and Gailey, died here on 3rd October 1916, from injuries received at the Battle

of the Somme. William Murphy, of Leslie Hill, died here of pneumonia on 12th February 1917 and James McCrellis, of Stranocum died on the 4th of January 1919.

La Plus Douve Cemetery

3/6483 PRIVATE DANIEL CRAIG
8th / 10th Bn   Gordon Highlanders
K.I.A. 30-7-16
No Known Grave. Commemorated on the Thiepval Memorial. Pier 15b and 15c

Born   Ballymoney
Lived   Townhead St.
Enlisted Leith, Scotland in January 1915.

Daniel Craig was born in Ballymoney but enlisted at Leith in January 1915.

He is listed as being killed in action on 30th July 1916 among the dead of the 8th / 10th battalion, Gordon Highlanders. There is something of an anomaly here, as the 8th / 10th battalion war diary shows it did not engage the enemy on that date, and there is no report of shelling, nor of any casualties at all.

The 30th July 1916 was the date of a major attack by the 51st Highland Division around High Wood. It is possible that Daniel Craig was attached to one of the Gordon battalions involved.

The 153rd Infantry Brigade, 51st Highland Division, attacked at 6.10pm on that date. The objective was Wood Lane and High Wood, where very high losses were suffered. High Wood was fiercely defended and from the cover of the wood the German machine-gunners had a clear view of anything that moved. The British, trying to attack over the open, rolling countryside of the Somme, were just simply mowed down, as the huge cemeteries in the area testify.

Daniel was at first reported missing but was later confirmed killed in action. He had served for one and a half years. His sister, Mrs Annie Grant, lived in Broomhill Street in Glasgow.

2953 L. CPL JAMES SMYTH BOYD
6th Bn Black Watch
K.I.A. 30-7-16
Aged 25
No Known Grave. Commemorated on the Thiepval Memorial, Face 10a.

Born   Knockans, Finvoy.
Lived
Enlisted
Son of John and Margaret Boyd of the Knockans, Finvoy.

John Boyd was born at the Knockans in 1834 and later married Margaret Smyth.

They lived for some time at the Knockans but John eventually died in Belfast in 1912. I only have details of two of the family but there were probably more.

James was probably working in Scotland before he enlisted into the 6th battalion of the Black Watch. He is commemorated on the family headstone in the graveyard of Finvoy Presbyterian Church. James was killed in the Battle for Pozieres Ridge close to the small French village of Bazentin le Petit. This was an area that saw a great deal of very heavy fighting and the many cemeteries in the region testify to this. There was an Advanced Dressing Station here at one time and Bazentin-le-Petit Cemetery is evidence of this. There is no known grave and he is commemorated on the Thiepval Memorial. The 6th battalion were stationed at Perth on the outbreak of hostilities and were engaged in defence of the Forth at Queensferry. In April 1915 they moved to Bedford and in May landed at Boulogne. They joined the 51st Highland Division and saw a great deal of action at the Somme. In spite of a lot of enquiries made locally, no-one can remember the Boyd family living at the Knockans and certainly he is not commemorated in Finvoy Presbyterian Church, so the family must have been gone for a long time. He had celebrated his twenty-fifth birthday at the Somme only ten days before he was killed.

This was one of the ones that was very nearly missed. I had gone to Finvoy Presbyterian Church burying ground to study the headstones in case there was some information there that I could use. I did find some useful facts but went home discontented with the feeling that I had missed something. I went back the next day just to check and the first headstone that I went to was the one with James Boyd on it.

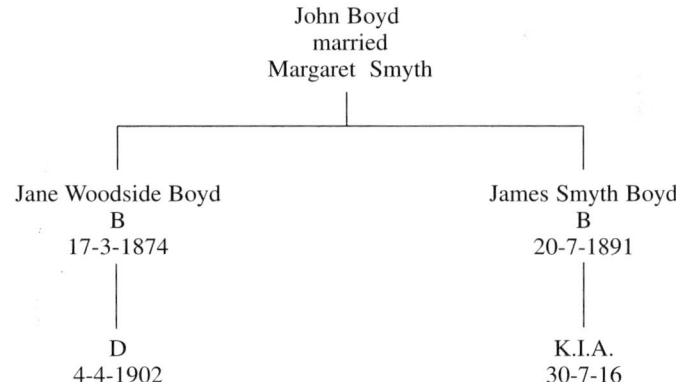

23293 PRIVATE ARCHIBALD FORBES
2nd Bn King's Own Scottish Borderers
K.I.A. 31-7-16
Aged 40
No Known Grave. Commemorated on the Thiepval Memorial, Pier 4a and 4d

Born   John St, Ballymoney
Lived   Greenock, Renfrewshire
Enlisted Greenock, Renfrewshire
Son of James and Elizabeth Forbes of John St.

Archie Forbes was a son of James and Elizabeth Forbes of John Street in Ballymoney.

The family appears to have moved at some stage to live in Scotland as reference is made to them as living at No 7, Bruce St, Greenock. At any rate Archie enlisted into the 2nd battalion of the King's Own Scottish Borderers and after a lengthy period spent training, they moved to France. They were to be at the Somme for two and a half months. On 19th July they marched from Fricourt across country towards High Wood. After dark the battalion was guided to the old German second line between Bazentin-le-Grand and Guillemont, and took up position. Their first objective was Wood Lane, a sunken road on the other side of a slight rise about 400 yards away.

350 yards up a gentle slope, over the top and then 50 yards in full view of the enemy.

The attack started at 3.30am and they took their objective, which they held all day, being relieved by the Royal Warwickshire Regt that night.

Their ultimate objective, the German third line, "Switch Trench", ran east from the north of High Wood. Heavy fighting took place here in an attempt to take High Wood and after a few days the 2nd battalion were taken back for rest.

On the evening of the 29th the battalion left their rest area at Pommiers Redoubt to relieve the 95th Infantry Brigade at Longueval, on the west side of Delville Wood.

It was a perilous post, spattered all day with gun and machine-gun fire, and casualties came thick and fast. They managed to hold on and although not much was achieved, they had done what they had been sent to do. After a long drawn out, difficult relief by the 15th I.B. the battered K.O.S.B. crawled back in small parties, in the small hours of the 31st, to Pommiers Redoubt. They had lost 244 men. It was in the process of this relief that Archie was killed on the west side of Delville Wood. He has no known grave and is commemorated on the Thiepval Memorial.

An advertisement placed in the Greenock Telegraph in April 1999 asking the family to get in touch has produced a lot of information and in this case has been well worth while.

Before he enlisted Archie was a shipping clerk with a local provisions company in Greenock. He was a superb artist and had a number of works published in the Greenock Telegraph and did all the art work for the Company Magazine of the Greenock Boys Brigade. He also played cricket at Greenock as an opening batsman and it is believed that he represented Scotland.

2938 PRIVATE ALEXANDER WALKER
48th Bn Australian Infantry
K.I.A. 6-8-16
Aged 29
No Known Grave. Commemorated on the Villers-Bretonneux Memorial.

Born   Gladhill, Stranocum.
Lived   Bridgetown, Western Australia
Enlisted   Blackboy Hill, Western Australia.
Son of David Walker, of Gladhill, Stranocum.
Commemorated in Bushvale Presbyterian Church.

The Walker family lived at Gladhill, close to Stranocum, a village about four miles east of Ballymoney. The family worshipped at the nearby Bushvale Presbyterian Church and it is there that Alex is commemorated on the Roll of Honour. As children, they all attended the old Ballycraigagh school. Relatives of the family still live in the same area and Alex's name is engraved on the Stranocum War Memorial.

As a young man Alex emigrated to Western Australia a few years before the start of the 1st World War and was a timber worker there. On the outbreak of hostilities he decided to enlist and presented himself for a medical examination at Bridgetown on 20th July 1915, with the intention of enlisting and enlisted at Blackboy Hill on 29th September. He was five feet seven inches tall with a fair complexion, grey eyes and light brown hair. He was a son of Mr David Walker, of Gladhill, Stranocum.

They embarked at Freemantle on 1st October 1915 on A30 "Hororata."

The troops were taken to Egypt and at Abbassia Alex was admitted to hospital where he remained for three weeks, being discharged on 20th November 1915. On 8th January he re-joined his unit at Ismalia but on 25th January he was again taken to hospital, this time at Cairo with Laryngitis. On recovery he was transferred to the 48th battalion on the 3rd of March at Tel-el-Kabir. Three weeks later, on the 24th of March, he was again admitted to hospital, this time with tonsilitis. Five days later he was discharged from hospital and on the 31st re-joined his unit at Serapeum. On the 2nd of June 1916 they embarked on H.M.T. "Caledonia" at Alexandria and reached Marseilles on the 9th.

There followed a very long train journey up to the Western Front but they arrived in time for the Battle of the Somme.

Alex was killed in heavy fighting at the Battle of the Somme on 6th August 1916. He has no known grave and is commemorated on the Villers-Brettoneux Memorial. Along with his military records there is a note listing personal possessions removed from his pockets at the time of his death. It follows that he must have been buried close to where he fell a short time after being killed. Subsequent searches of the battlefield after the cessation of hostilities failed to find his body and he was declared missing. He will be there still. His brother, John, also served throughout the war, but survived. The Australians were at this time embroiled in desperate fighting close to the village of Pozieres and it is believed to have been here that Alex was killed. Pozieres village sits astride the main Albert, Bapaume road and at the start of the Battle of the Somme was in German hands. The higher ground where Pozieres windmill was situated was a very useful vantage point and it was this higher ground that the British Armies were so anxious to capture. Thousands of Australian soldiers were lost in the fierce fighting which took place in the battles for Pozieres village as the many cemeteries in the region testify. One only has to visit the region and study the layout of the trenches to realise something of the harsh realities of life in the front line. Most of these young men were away from home for the first time, many of them never to see home again, and it must have been a daunting task to come out of the comparative shelter of their trenches and attack an army that they knew was lying in wait for just such an opportunity. They eventually took Pozieres Ridge after huge loss of life. This is why we want the names of men like Alex Walker inscribed on the Ballymoney War Memorial. They have earned it.

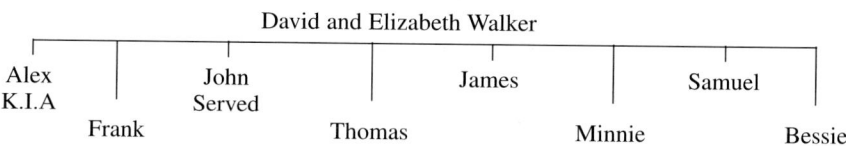

David and Elizabeth Walker

Alex K.I.A | Frank | John Served | Thomas | James | Minnie | Samuel | Bessie

735 TROOPER ROBERT WILLIAM SCOTT
Royal Horse Guards
K.I.A. 10-8-16
Aged 37
Interred in Bouzincourt Communal Cem Ext. Plot 2, Row F, Grave 13

Born Meetinghouse St, Ballymoney. Enlisted about 1904 Commemorated in Trinity Presbyterian Church. Husband of Mrs W.V.Scott, of 64 Tontine St, Folkestone. Eldest son of Mr. John Scott, by now living in Glasgow.

Robert William Scott was for fourteen years valet to Captain Fitzgerald and had served seventeen months in the South African war. He was the eldest son of Mr. John Scott of Meetinghouse St. Later the family moved to Manister, Mosside and later still to Glasgow. Robert William was killed by shell-fire on 10th August 1916, at the age of 37. Bouzincourt is a village just a short distance north of Albert and the cemetery lies on the outskirts and is very easily found. This region would have been well within range of the large German artillery and it was probably very close to here that he was killed. The cemetery was also used for the burial of one of the men who faced the firing squad. This happened on 22nd July 1916 while the Battle of the Somme was raging and the soldier had been recommended for mercy at his trial. Arthur Earp is buried in Plot 1, Row C, Grave 25.

18672 SERGEANT ROBERT RAMSEY
12th Bn Royal Irish Rifles
K.I.A. 23-8-16
Aged 21
Interred in Ration Farm Cemetery, (La Plus Douve Annexe). Belgium. Plot 3, Row C, Grave 2.

Born   Culmore, Kilrea
Lived   Culmore, Kilrea
Enlisted   Ballymoney
Son of Daniel and Ellen Ramsey.
Commemorated in Rasharkin Parish Church.

Robert's father, Daniel, had been coachman to Captain Armstrong, of Culmore, for many years. The family worshipped in Rasharkin Parish Church and it is there that Robert is commemorated.

Before the war Robert worked in the linen trade and was a linen lapper at Clarke's of Upperlands. After enlisting in September 1914 he went to Clandeboye Camp for initial training. He was a very conscientious young man and wrote to his father and mother at least twice a week. He was very ambitious and by mid October had already been promoted to Lance Corporal and in a letter home says he won't be content until he gets the other two stripes. On 21st October a letter from him tells of 'D' Company marching from Portrush through Bushmills and Ballycastle to Larne in two days and staying at McNeill's hotel, Main St, Larne, and going on through Whiteabbey and back to Clandeboye. On being promoted to Lance Corporal, Robert was warned by his superior officers to keep his former mates at a distance and not to associate with them as closely as previously, but his answer to them was that they had always been his pals and nothing was going to change that, not even three stripes.

By early summer 1915, they were at South Camp, at Seaford, on the Sussex coast.

It was here that he was made Orderly Sergeant. The extra work meant that during his time at Seaford he was only out of camp on three occasions. Once to London, and twice to Newhaven. From here they were moved in August to Borden Camp in Hants, and by September the weather had turned very wet. Then in a letter from home he is told about his friend, Joseph Watson, of Rasharkin, being killed at Le Touret.

In October 1915, they were taken to France, and two weeks later a letter tells of conditions there. Rain has turned the ground into a quagmire and it is mud everywhere.

By the third week in October he is in the trenches and still the rain pours down.

November brings snow and frost and Bobbie, as he is known at home, has a painful knee, and Matt Brown has to help carry his kit for him. Matt Brown survived the war, and after returning

home he married Bobbie's sister Mary. They later emigrated to Canada.

In January 1916, he is sent to Army Training School for four weeks, but after returning to his unit the weather deteriorates and conditions in the trenches of rain, snow, frost and mud are atrocious.

He was home on leave from 3rd May to 11th May 1916, and the actual ticket still survives.

In early June he was again at 4th Army Infantry Training school, for more instruction.

At this stage there is mention of Robert John Coleman getting home on leave. He was in the same unit as Bobbie Ramsey and lived just up the road from Ramsey's.

Bobbie was back with his unit in time for the Battle of the Somme and took part in the attack of 1st July. It was on this day that Robert John Coleman was killed, and a letter tells of him being reported missing, and of only three other men from the district, surviving, Wallace, Carson, and Ramsey.

The Battalion had been decimated and was withdrawn for re-organisation.

A few days later it was moved to the Messines area of Belgium, and it was here, close to Ration Farm Cemetery, on the evening of 22nd August 1916, that he wrote his last letter home.

Robert Ramsey was killed at 10.30 a.m. the next morning, the 23rd of August.

He had just fired five rounds and inadvertently stood up straight to re-load his rifle, when he was hit in the head.

A sniper had been waiting for just such a chance. He had been on trench duty, and was himself watching for snipers. He was a member of Ballymaconnelly L.O.L. 360.

William John McCaughern, of Rasharkin is also buried in this cemetery, as is Alex Taylor, of Bushmills.

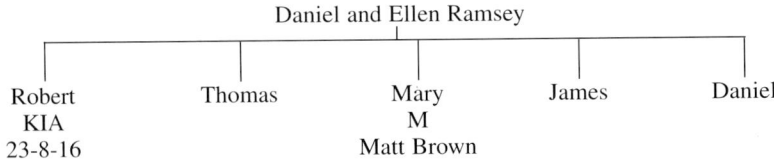

Daniel and Ellen Ramsey

Robert KIA 23-8-16 | Thomas | Mary M Matt Brown | James | Daniel

2ND LIEUT VICTOR JAMES SIMPSON
5th Bn King's Shropshire Light Infantry
K.I.A. 24-8-16
No Known Grave. Commemorated on the Thiepval Memorial. Pier 12a and 12d

Only Son of David and Mrs. Simpson, of Birkdale.
Nephew of Mr. and Mrs. Megaw, of Ballymoney.
Grandson of the late Archie Moore.

Victor James Simpson was educated at Birkdale House School. He enlisted in 1914 and gained his Commission on 15th June 1916 in the King's Shropshire Light Infantry. He was sent to France immediately and had only been at the front two months when he was killed.

On 15th July 1916, the Commanding Officer of the 5th Battalion KSLI, Lt Col. O.C.Borrett, was transferred to the command of the 1st Bn of his own regiment, the King's Own Royal Lancashire Regiment. His place was taken by Major Delme-Murray. Early in July it became known that the 5th Bn would take part in the Battle of the Somme. When, therefore, the battalion was relieved on the 27th of July by the 9th Lancashire Fusiliers, and marched to Agnez-Les-Duisans, no one was surprised to hear that the march to the battle had commenced.

The battalion was certainly not lucky in the weather for it's marches, it was now extremely hot, even for July, and after a prolonged period of comparative inactivity the strain of marching fully equipped was very great. Fortunately the marches were short and the billets at Grand-Rullecourt, Barly and Candas, where halts were made, were comfortable. From Candas a long train journey was made to Mericourt, and then a two mile march to Buire-sur-L'Ancre which they reached on 7th August.

During July Victor James Simpson joined the 5th battalion after a number of other officers had been wounded. On the 12th August the battalion marched to bivouac near Fricourt, and six days later, on the 18th, a portion of the battalion was lent to the 43rd Brigade, who were making an attack on the enemy, as reserve, and five other ranks were wounded.

On the 21st the battalion had taken up a line of trenches on the edge of Delville Wood and a continuous bombardment was kept up on the enemy's lines on the 22nd and 23rd. The 5th KSLI was in the centre with 9th Kings Royal Rifles on the right and the 5th Ox and Bucks on the left.

At 5.45am on the 24th the attack began. At first it was successful and they gained ground, with the enemy being cleared from the edge of the wood.

But a heavy German attack followed and they were pushed back. It was during this attack that Victor James Simpson was killed.

They had captured 2 machine guns, 2 officers and 115 other ranks.

He qualified for two medals, the British War Medal, and the Victory Medal and these were forwarded to his parents on 20th December 1922.

There is no known grave and he is commemorated on the Thiepval Memorial.

His Uncle, W.J.Megaw, was Chairman of Ballymoney Urban District Council from 1888 to 1920, and had a big wholesale and retail grocery business in Main Street where Taggart's is today. Megaw Park was named after him.

21255 PRIVATE WILLIAM McNULTY
1st Bn, Royal Irish Fusiliers
K.I.A. 26-8-16
Interred in Railway Dugouts Burial Ground
Valley Cottages Cemetery, Zillebeke. Mem, Row F, Grave 3

Born   Ballybofey, Co Donegal
Lived
Enlisted   Belfast

Before he enlisted William was employed by Mr Robert Black in Church Street, Ballymoney.

The 1st battalion were with the 4th Division at the Somme just to the north of Beaumont Hamel in June 1916 and gas was discharged by this Division on the 26th causing havoc among the German forces opposite. On the 1st of July the blowing of the Hawthorn Ridge mine ten minutes before zero hour warned every German for miles around that an attack was imminent, and they were ready. The Division, now directly across from Hawthorn Ridge, lost heavily on the morning of the 1st of July and William was very lucky to escape injury on this day.

Prior to the attack of 1st July the battalion had dug two tunnels under No Man's Land to within a few yards of the German wire, opened the ends and placed a trench mortar in each but within ten minutes of the start of the attack these had been put out of action. They are probably still there.

A short time after this they were moved to the south of Ypres and the area around Zillebeke. It was here that William was killed on the 26th of August. He is buried in Railway Dugouts Burial Ground, Valley Cottages Cemetery, Zillebeke.

2674 L SGT THOMAS YOUNG
6th Bn Royal Irish Regt
K.I.A. 3-9-16
Aged 43
No Known Grave. Commemorated on the Thiepval Memorial.

Born   Cloughmills
Commemorated in Killagan Parish Church.
Son of John And Elizabeth Young

Although Thomas is listed in "Soldiers Died" as being born at Templemore, Co.Derry, this would appear to be a mistake. Other sources claim him to be born at Cloughmills. He certainly had some close connection with the district when he is commemorated in Killagan Parish Church. His rank would suggest that he had been in the Army for some time and that he had probably been in the Army before war was declared. His age would also suggest this.

The battalion was formed at Clonmel in September 1914. They trained at Fermoy until September 1915 and then moved to Aldershot. In December they landed at Le Havre and from there went into trenches in preparation for the Battle of the Somme. These trenches were a near replica of what they could expect at the Somme but nothing could have prepared them for the hail of lead that met them as they left their trenches. Thomas was killed at the Somme on 3rd September 1916 and has no known grave. He is commemorated on the Thiepval Memorial.

Tyne Cot Cemetery, Belgium

427452 PRIVATE JAMES GILMORE MURPHY
13th Bn Canadian Infantry 13th Bn Royal Highlanders of Canada
K.I.A. 5-9-16
Aged 24
Interred in Serre Road Cemetery, No 2. Plot 26, Row A, Grave 8

Born   Killymaddy, Bendooragh
Lived   Weyburn, Saskatchewan
Enlisted   Weyburn, Saskatchewan

2nd son of William Murphy, of Killymaddy. Commemorated in Drumreagh Presbyterian Church.

James Gilmore Murphy was born at Killymaddy on 9th January 1892, the second son of William Murphy. Some time after leaving school he emigrated to Canada, settling in Weyburn, Saskatchewan, where he worked as a farmer. On 29th December 1914, he enlisted at Weyburn. He was a tall young man at five feet eleven and a half inches, with a fair complexion, grey eyes and brown hair.

After initial training in Canada he embarked at Halifax on 21st October 1915 on S.S. Lapland, and arrived in England on the 2nd of November. From here they went to Aldershot for more training. He was admitted to Connaught Hospital, in Aldershot on 11th March suffering from illness and was released on the 29th of March. Then on the 16th of June 1916 he was sent with the 13th battalion to France and taken on strength in the field next day. This was in time for the start of the Battle of the Somme and he was in it from the beginning. He was killed in action on the 5th of September and is buried in Serre Road Cemetery No 2. at the Somme.

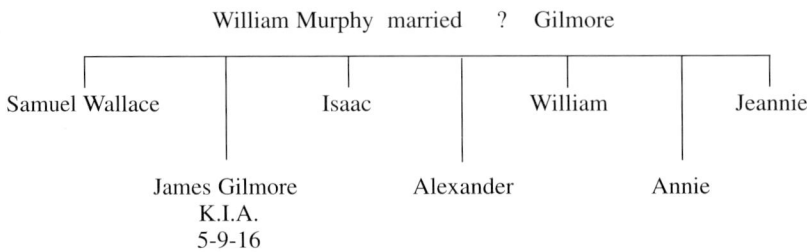

James Gilmour Murphy is buried in the front row, 3rd left

Serre Road Cemetery

132253 PRIVATE WILLIAM McCONACHIE
73rd Bn Canadian Infantry Royal Highlanders of Canada
K.I.A. 7-9-16
Aged 28
Interred in St. Sever Cemetery, Rouen. Plot 1, Row J Grave 2

Born Dervock.
Lived Montreal, Canada
Enlisted Montreal, Canada

William McConachie was born at Dervock on 2nd April 1888, the son of Alexander McConachie. At some stage after he left school he emigrated to Canada to live with his sister Grace in Montreal. Another brother, David, had also emigrated to Canada and was living in Montreal.

William worked as a labourer and was five feet four and three quarter inches tall, with a fair complexion, fair hair and blue eyes. He enlisted at Montreal on 6th September 1915, and after training, sailed from Halifax on the S.S. Adriatic on 31st March 1916, arriving at Liverpool on the 9th of April. While in England, very intensive training took place. This was the period just prior to the start of the Battle of the Somme and although men were needed in their thousands, the real urgency to replace men had not begun. It was only after the losses of the 1st of July that the pace was really stepped up and these Canadians were still not ready. They eventually embarked for France on the 12th of August arriving at Le Havre the next day. They were sent to join their unit immediately in the desperate fighting at the Somme. Although the weather had been good in the August-September period, it quickly deteriorated during October, turning the French chalk into glutinous mud. The wet weather and cold nights made conditions almost unbearable for the troops in the front line where shelter at night was minimal and food and ammunition difficult to get forward. It was in these conditions that William was very seriously wounded on the 7th of November.

He was taken back for medical attention but his condition was so serious that he was immediately sent to hospital at Rouen. He was suffering from gunshot wounds to the shoulder and the cold coupled with loss of blood had left him dangerously ill. He died from his injuries later that day and is buried in St. Sever Cemetery at Rouen.

Hamel Village where 12th RIR attack started on 1-7--16. The first day of the Somme

16255 SERGEANT SAMUEL McDOWELL M.M.
7th Bn Canadian Infantry British Columbia Regiment
K.I.A. 8-9-16
Aged 30
No Known Grave. Commemorated on the Vimy Memorial

Born   Finvoy on 24th May 1886
Lived   Rectory Lodge
Enlisted Valcartier, Quebec
Son of Mr. Matthew McDowell of Rectory Lodge, Finvoy.
Commemorated in Drumreagh Presbyterian Church.

Samuel McDowell was a son of Mr. Matthew McDowell, of Rectory Lodge, Finvoy, and had emigrated to Canada in 1906. He enlisted at Valcartier Camp, Quebec on 23rd September 1914, where, two days later, William Hill Chambers, of Bushmills, would enlist.

This was a huge camp a few miles North-West of Quebec where they could start training almost as soon as they enlisted.

At the time Samuel enlisted the family were living at the Enagh and then a few years later they were living at 21 Charlotte St. He was six feet one and a half inches tall, with a fair complexion, grey eyes and thick, light hair. His unit sailed for England on 3rd Oct 1914.

Before going to Canada he was in the employment of the late Captain Cramsie, of O'Harabrook, as coachman, and later with Colonel Macausland, of Garvagh. On 3rd May 1915, he was wounded at Ypres, a bullet through his right lung and arm, and was sent to hospital in England. He was first reported missing, but then it was discovered that he had been evacuated quickly to Huddersfield Royal Infirmary. By 15th June he was well enough to be transferred the Canadian Convalescent Hospital at Bromley, and then on 3rd July he was discharged. He was home at the Enagh on sick leave at this time. After he returned to England he was immediately sent to rejoin his unit in France and did so on 28th August.

On 2nd February 1916 he was granted nine days leave of absence, probably for family reasons. Anyhow, after he returned he was admitted to No 18 General hospital with sickness followed by a forfeiture of pay. By the end of May he was well enough to rejoin his unit and then on 17th June was appointed Lance Corporal followed by Corporal on 27th July. He was awarded the Military Medal for bravery on 1st Sept 1916 and was killed in action just seven days later at Vimy Ridge.

The facts concerning the death of Sergeant McDowell are contained in a letter from Sergeant H.H.Weeks and show the indomitable spirit of the deceased soldier. The letter is as follows.

" It is with the deepest regret that I write this letter to tell you of Sam's death, and yet I feel it is my duty, for he was my best pal. He was killed on the 9th inst, whilst performing his duty, and more than his duty. We were in the front line and Sam was in charge of a Lewis machine-gun. You may have heard that he was promoted sergeant recently.

The enemy was attacking, and Sam, to obtain a better field of fire, went out in front of the trench with his gun. The enemy saw him, and he, and three of his men were killed.

It was a very brave deed , but then Sam was always doing brave things. His body was recovered and buried just to the rear of our lines. I was machine-gun sergeant for some months and have known your son since the outbreak of war. He was on my gun crew for over a year and during that time there was no better or braver man than he. Since I left the section Sam had lost his pal, Private McArthur, and now, I am sorry to say, the whole of the old gun crew, called "the Irish Brigade", are either killed or wounded. Sam's death is deeply regretted by the whole of the Battalion, for he was universally liked by all. It was only quite recently that he and I recieved the Military Medal. I had no opportunity of securing his personal effects, but no doubt they will be forwarded on to you. All his friends and myself offer our deepest sympathy to you in your sad bereavement, and I sincerely trust that the thoughts of his brave deeds may be a little consolation to you in your great loss".

25444 PRIVATE SAMUEL McNEILL
8th Bn Royal Inniskilling Fusiliers
K.I.A. 9-9-16
Aged 28
No Known Grave. Commemorated on the Thiepval Memorial, France

Born   Drumcon, Rasharkin.
Enlisted   Londonderry.
Son of James and Mary McNeill, of Drumcon. Commemorated in Rasharkin Presbyterian Church.

The battalion was raised at Omagh in September 1914 and were with the 16th Div at Tipperary. In August of the folowing year they were training at Finner Camp. By September they had been moved to England and the camp at Woking.

They went to France in February 1916.

The 8th battalion were with the 16th Division in France at this time. The Battle of the Somme was still raging and the 16th Div were attacking Guillemont. The 8th were in the front line and German shelling was extremely heavy. It was during this heavy bombardment that Samuel was killed as he went forward to the attack.

Drumcon is just a short distance outside Rasharkin village and the family worshipped in Rasharkin Presbyterian Church. The village is about eight miles south of Ballymoney.

Two other Ballymoney men were to be killed on this day, Samuel McMillan and William McToal.

2079 PRIVATE WILLIAM JOHN McTOAL
6th Bn Royal Irish Regiment
K.I.A. 9-9-16
Aged 30
No Known Grave. Commemorated on the Thiepval Memorial, France. Pier and face, 3A

Born   Ballymoney
Lived   Loughguile
Enlisted Ballymoney
William John McToal married Fanny Workman in Trinity Presbyterian Church on 28th Oct 1904.

William John McToal was living in the Kilraughts area when he married Fanny Workman, of Crosstagherty, in 1904. He was a son of John McToal and Fanny was a daughter of Andrew Workman. They were married in Trinity Presbyterian Church, Ballymoney. It is believed that Fanny was a sister of William Workman, M.M. whose story is also told in this book. The 6th battalion was formed at Fermoy in October 1914 and shared new barracks with 6th Connaught Rangers. By the spring of 1915 each battalion had about 1600 men. After their training was completed they went to France landing at Boulogne and Le Havre and reached Bethune just before Christmas 1915. At the end of January their training under artillery fire began in earnest. The battalion entered the line for the first time at Puits 14 bis, just to the north east of Loos. This was a time of desperately heavy fighting in difficult weather conditions. Severe cold at night hampered them when everything tended to freeze solid. Night time was when wiring parties were at work or raiding took place on the enemy trenches and the cold made this difficult in the extreme. During the gas attack at Hulluch on 27th to 29th April 1916 the men saw plenty of action and William was lucky to come through this safely.

Their next major battle was to be the Somme and here they were to be at Guillemont and Ginchy. In early September the weather was warm and humid and the battalion rested at Carnoy on the night previous to the battle. Next day they had to attack across a bare valley with no shelter against a bombardment of high explosive and shrapnel shells. They went through it. Casualties were high but the attack had to go on. William again got through safely. In the attack on Ginchy on 9th September he was not so lucky. Ginchy was one of the strongest of all the fortified villages in the German line and it's capture was one of the most important achievements since the taking of Pozieres. It was also one of the most difficult. William was killed in this attack. He has no known grave and is commemorated on the Thiepval Memorial.

LIEUT HENRY STEWART - MOORE
5th Bn Royal Inniskilling Fusiliers
K.I.A. 10-9-16
Aged 30
Interred in Struma Military Cemetery, Greece. Plot 5, Row C, Grave 13

Born   Ballydivity on 26-11-1885.
Son of James and Elizabeth F. Stewart-Moore,
of Ballydivity.

The 5th and 6th battalions of the Royal Inniskillings had been serving in Gallipoli but were withdrawn in October 1915 and transferred to Salonika. They moved in November to the section of the Allied Front east of Dorian Lake and met the full rigours of the winter in this area. During a blizzard on November 23 the temperature was 30 degrees below zero. To dig trenches was impossible, and shelter had to be found by the construction of stone sangers faced with earth. Fierce fighting was taking place all along the line and in December 1915, in the face of heavy Bulgarian attacks, our line was withdrawn a little. In this section the Inniskillings, holding Kevis crest, showed great gallantry in fighting a rearguard action, thus delaying the Bulgarians and allowing our line to be withdrawn. There then followed a quiet time when very little fighting took place and the troops were mainly engaged in road making and in strengthening the defensive works of the Salonika base. In July 1916 they moved up to the advance line on the Struma River and had to cope with intense heat, the temperature ranging up to 108 degrees. In September 1916, the Inniskillings took part in the advance across the Struma River. This was a fierce attack, and having fulfilled it's purpose our troops were withdrawn across the Struma. It was in this attack that Harry was killed. The family owned vast estates in Australia and it was here that the news of Harry's death reached them.

He is buried in Struma Military Cemetery close to where he fell about 65 kilometres north east of Salonika. Access is by a signposted track on the north side of the village.

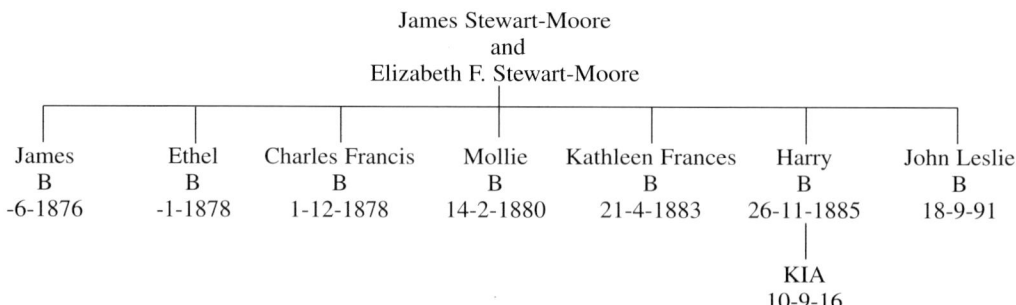

15288 RIFLEMAN JOHN DEANE
2nd Bn Royal Irish Rifles
K.I.A. 13-9-16
Interred in Vermelles British Cemetery, France. Plot 2, Row D, Grave 24

Born   Loughan
Lived   Balnamore
Enlisted Ballymoney

On the 1st of July 1916 the 2nd battalion were with the 7th Division and were to attack between Carnoy and Mametz at the Battle of the Somme. Here the Division suffered heavily from many German counter attacks and from machine-gun nests around Fricourt.

John Deane was lucky to survive the attacks of this terrible day. He was later moved north to the area around Vermelles and it was here that he was killed on 13th September.

Cemetery location information
Vermelles is a village midway between Bethune and Lens and north of the main road connecting these two towns. The Brirish Cemetery is on the south-western outskirts of the village and on the north side of the road to Mazingarbe. Take the N43, Lens to Bethune road, to it's junction with the D75 in Mazingarbe. Turn right at this junction and travel for about 900 metres. The cemetery lies on the left side of this road.

Vermelles British Cemetery

13976 L. CPL. ROBERT CAMPBELL
2nd Bn Scots Guards
K.I.A. 15-9-16
Aged 23
No known grave. Commemorated on the Thiepval Memorial

Born   Balnamore
Lived   Balnamore
Enlisted   Hamilton, Scotland.
Son of Robert Campbell, of Troy, New York.
Commemorated in Drumreagh Presbyterian Church.

Robert was born at Balnamore in about 1893 and lived most of his life in the village.

It is believed that a short time before he enlisted he had gone to Scotland in connection with his work. He had been a policeman. The family worshipped in Drumreagh Presbyterian Church and it is here that Robert is commemorated

When war was declared on 4th August 1914 the 2nd battalion were stationed at the Tower of London. In September 1914 they joined the 7th Div at Lyndhurst.

Robert Campbell enlisted at Hamilton on 24th May 1915.

He commenced training at Caterham the following day and was promoted to L.Cpl on 24th January 1916. On 23rd July, he was one of a fresh batch of troops sent to make up numbers

and to bring battalions back to strength after the disastrous start to the Battle of the Somme. S.S. Copenhagen was the ship used, sailing from Southampton and arriving early next morning. They were moved from the Depot to join the battalion on the 10th of August 1916 after they had been given more training.

On 15th September 1916 he was reported missing, presumed killed. It was not until 10th November that he was confirmed killed in action. His relatives were informed of his death on 14th November 1916. The 2nd Battalion were at this time fighting at Ginchy, and it was here that Robert was killed. This was over very open country with very little cover for attacking troops and casualties were heavy. He has no known grave and is commemorated on the Thiepval Memorial.

For reasons not now apparent his Father was living at 514, Eighth St, Troy, New York.

We don't know whether his Mother was still alive or not.

3132 SERGEANT HUGH CARTON M M.
1st Bn Irish Guards
K.I.A. 15-9-16
Aged 29
No known grave. Commemorated on the Thiepval Memorial, Pier and Face 7D

Born   Ballymoney
Lived   Kirkhills
Enlisted   Coleraine
Commemorated in Carncullagh Presbyterian Church.
Son of Robert Carton of Kirkhills, Ballymoney.

In mid February 1915 Hugh had a very near call when he got a bullet through the ear.

Then in June a report tells of him being mentioned in despatches. A few weeks later at the end of July, he was home on six days leave.

Chronicle 28-4-17
Private Joseph Doherty, Irish Guards, son of Mr Robert Doherty, Seacon, has an interesting story to tell of his experiences in France. Enlisting in Ballymoney on the 13th of May 1915, after receiving his training he was sent to France and served under the late Lieut J.K.M.Greer from Ballymoney.

> "On the morning of the 15th September last we were at Ginchy and our objective was a small village called Flers. The Coldstreams led the attack and we followed and the supports were the Scots Guards and the Grenadiers. When we got to the first line of the enemy trenches we stopped a few minutes. Lieut Greer then led us to the second line of trenches. He had a revolver in one hand and a stick in the other, and rushed in front pointing his stick towards the enemy, and shouting to us to come on. It was between the trenches he got hit on the head, and fell. He gave his revolver to Sergeant Hugh Carton and told him to 'carry on'. Carton then told us to follow him, and that we did, right into the German third line. It was pretty hot here I may tell you. Our N.C.O. then called ten volunteers to go out and make a barricade in order to bomb the Germans in case of a counter attack. As a Ballymoney man, when there were so many there, I did not hesitate. It was during the erection of the barricade that Sergeant Carton got knocked out with shrapnel in the head. Three of us bandaged him as well as we could, but he died about three minutes after he got it. There was only four of us left now out of the ten so we had to retire into the old German third line trench.
>
> Another officer was coming out at the time we were building the barricade and got wounded.
>
> I tried to pull him in, and that was the time I got it with shrapnel, a bullet going right through my leg above the ankle and shrapnel in my thigh and stomach. I knew nothing after that. It was six in the evening when I got to the dressing station, and was sent to Rouen, and then right away to England. I am now home on 28 days leave."

Sally worked to Gage of Rathlin and came from Limavady. Hugh was district secretary of Ballymoney district independent L.O.L. No1 in 1906.

In December 1917, Ross Carton was injured by shrapnel in France.

Robert Carton married Sally Doherty

- Robert & James
- Ross
- Hugh K.I.A.
- Sarah (Died Young)
- Twins

7411 PRIVATE JOHN McAULEY
2nd Bn Irish Guards
K.I.A. 15-9-16
Aged 22
No Known Grave. Commemorated on the Thiepval Memorial.

Born   Balnamore.
Lived   Balnamore.
Enlisted Coleraine.
Only son of Margaret McAuley, of Balnamore.

John McAuley was born at Balnamore, the only son in a family of six. His five sisters were Nellie, Lizzie, Rosie, Kathleen and Maggie. After leaving school he served his time as a tailor with Mr Thomas Henderson of High Street, thought to be where the Gift shop or Kerr's Drapery now stands.

The 2nd battalion were formed on 15th July 1915 and John probably enlisted about May 1915 and then placed in the 2nd Reserve battalion. His training was intensive and on 16th August they left Brentwood Station for Southampton, and that evening boarded the "Anglo-Canadian" and the "Viper" and escorted by destroyers, arrived at Le Havre at midnight. On 18th August they were taken by train to Lumbres, and marched next day to Acquin, a small village on a hillside a few miles from St. Omer. Their first test was to be the Battle of Loos. After training at Acquin and a meeting with the 1st battalion, they set off to march through Neux-les-Mines, Noyelles and Vermelles, reaching the trenches at Le Rutoire on 26th September. The attack started at 2.30am next morning which meant that for 48 hours they hadn't seen food nor sleep. At 2.30am a heavy bombardment lasting an hour and a half was to take place and at 4.00am the 2nd battalion would advance upon the Chalk-Pit. They took the Chalk-Pit and held it. They were relieved by the Norfolk regt on 30th September. After a short rest, they moved, on 3rd October, the short distance to Vermelles, and more trenches. They were now opposite another German stronghold, the Hohenzollern Redoubt. This was one of the strongest positions in the whole German line. On 21st October they were relieved and sent back for rest and were taken away from that sector altogether two days later. They then marched to

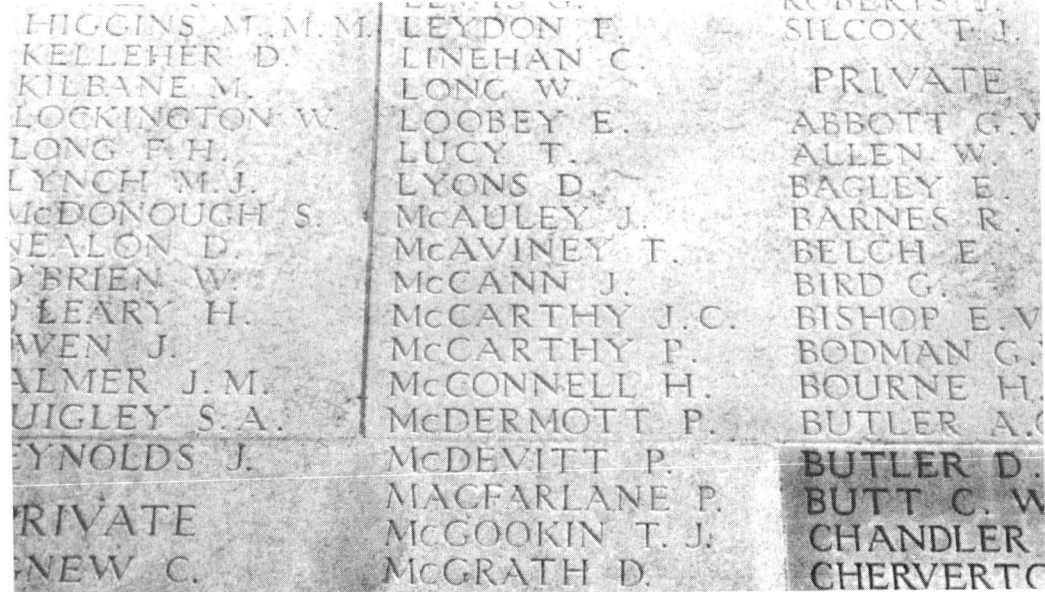

Bethune where they were put on to a train for Lillers and billets at Bourecq. Here they stayed for some considerable time, spending Christmas in the Laventie region. Afterwards they moved to La Gorgue for rest and then further back to Merville. Soon they were back, this time to the Ypres Salient. April saw them at Poperinghe and then at Wieltje, Brandhoek, and Hell Fire Corner. On 1st June they were moved out to Wormhout, fourteen miles away. Then, after a short break, they were back at the Salient and the area around Hooge where they relieved the 1st Coldstreams on the night of 18th June. On the 30th of July they marched out to Esquelbecq where they entrained together and moved via Hazebrouck, Berguette, and St. Pol to Petit Houvain. Now they were on their way to the Somme. The area south of Fricourt was where they were to go. They were to attack between Combles and Martinpuich on 15th September. At 6.00am our heavy guns started and this brought on the German barrage exactly where it was expected but our troops were lying out in front of that and so they survived only to run into a fierce hail of machine-gun fire. It was in this attack that John McAuley was killed. He was reported missing but never found and the following June was presumed killed in action. Joe Shiels was with him at the time and saw him killed. His mother could never accept that he had been killed and fed all the beggars who came to her door, thinking that John might be wandering about looking for food. Agnes has the last Woodbine cigarette he

smoked before he went away. He has no known grave and is commemorated on the Thiepval Memorial. In December 1917 Joe Shiels was seriously injured and lost his right leg below the knee. We can't be sure where this happened but it was most probably at the heavy fighting at Bourlon Wood. Joe survived the war.

The scroll presented to John's family after he was killed

440526 PRIVATE WILLIAM LOGUE
Royal Canadian Regiment
K.I.A. 16-9-16
Aged 24
Interred in Courcellette British Cemetery, France. Plot 8, Row E, Grave 16.

Born   Coleraine
Lived   Seacon
Enlisted Prince Albert early 1915.
Emigrated to Canada in 1912.
Son of James and Lizzie Logue, of Seacon, Ballymoney.
The family maintains that he was shot by a sniper

William Logue was born on 24th February 1892 at Coleraine, and later the family moved to Secon. In 1912 when he was just twenty years of age, he emigrated to Canada where he worked as a farmer. Three years later, on 1st April 1915 he enlisted into the Royal Canadian Regiment at Prince Albert. He was five feet ten inches tall with a fair complexion, blue eyes and brown hair. He embarked at Halifax on 29th March 1916, a year almost to the day after enlisting, and landed at Liverpool, from the Empress of Britain on the 9th of April. After more training he embarked for France on the 8th of June 1916 in time for the start of the Battle of the Somme.

It was during the later stages of the Battle of the Somme, on 16th Sept, that he was at first reported missing. The Canadians were by this time attacking the village of Courcellette and it is in the Cemetery just outside the village that William is buried. William Hill Chambers of Bushmills is buried in the same cemetery. William Logue was first reported missing, then killed in action. We don't know exactly what happened, but the family tell me that he was shot by a sniper. This was a time of very intense fighting as the Canadians advanced on the village of Courcellette. All day on the 15th heavy fighting took place west of the village and it was here that most of the Canadians buried in Courcelette Cemetery were killed. William was killed the following morning in the attack on Hesian Trench very close to where the cemetery now stands. There are 783 Canadians buried here.

Courcelette British Cemetery at the Somme

19522 RIFLEMAN JAMES GOW
11th Bn Royal Irish Rifles
D.O.W. 27-9-16
Interred in Aveluy Wood Cemetery, France. Plot 1, Row A, Grave 10.

Born   Ballymoney
Lived   Ballymoney
Enlisted   Belfast
Only son of William and Anne Gow

The fact that James enlisted in Belfast probably has a lot to do with him being in the 11th battalion, the South Antrim Volunteers.

The battalion was formed from the Antrim Volunteers and trained at Clandeboye.

When their training was considered complete they moved across to Seaford, on the south coast of England in July of 1915 and landed at Boulogne the following October.

From there they went to the huge training camp at St. Omer. By this time the French were clamouring for the British to make an attack in an attempt to draw off German reinforcements from Verdun and an attack was planned for the Somme. James was taken to the small French village of Martinsart, close to the Somme. Here they were housed in tents until better accommodation could be made available. As the date of the attack drew near the weather changed from dry to very wet indeed.

A dressing station was sited in Aveluy Wood beside where the cemetery now stands.

It was here that James was brought, seriously wounded, in September 1916, from the nearby fighting at the Somme. The cemetery is not a large one, which would suggest that the dressing station was only there for a short time and was mainly a means of getting injured troops moved quickly to the bigger hospitals further away from the fighting.

The Gow family lived in a small house in Charlotte St, next to where the road turns up into Eastermeade. There were three houses in the row and in one of the other two lived the family of Alex McIlreavey who was killed at Harlebeke, in Belgium, in October 1918.

James was the son of William Gow, a labourer. There was a sister, Ellen, who was born on 10th January 1894, whilst James himself was born on

6th September 1896. He had spent his twentieth birthday at the Somme. The family now seems to have left the Ballymoney district and a phone call from Group Captain Tuft in Cambridgeshire in January 1999 confirmed this, and whilst he lives in England, his sister lives in Downpatrick. These would appear to be the closest living relatives.

Cenetery location information
The cemetery is about 5 kilometres north of the town of Albert and situated in woodland on the eastern side of the road from Albert to Hamel (D50). The cemetery is signposted in the village of Aveluy (D50) which you pass through on the way to the cemetery.

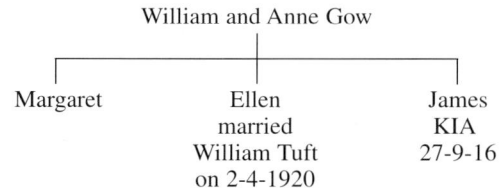

William and Anne Gow

| Margaret | Ellen married William Tuft on 2-4-1920 | James KIA 27-9-16 |

8444 PRIVATE DANIEL McMULLAN
2nd Bn Irish Guards
D.O.W. 29-9-16
Aged about 25
Interred in Etaples Military Cemetery. Plot 11, Row C, Grave 1.

Born   Rasharkin.
Lived   Rosnashane.
Enlisted   Belfast.
Son of Mr. Daniel McMullan, Killans,
Ballymoney.

Corporal McAleese, who was killed on 24th March 1918, and is buried in Grand-Seraucourt British Cemetery, was a cousin of Daniel McMullan.

Daniel was the elder son of Daniel and Sarah McMullan, of Killans, about five miles south of Ballymoney. There were two boys and seven girls in the family. Unfortunately two of the girls, Sarah and Ethel, died young, both of them having contracted Scarletina. Daniel, as a young boy, attended St. Columba's school at the Killans and later when he had left school, he worked as a farm labourer wherever work could be had. He enlisted in Belfast into the Irish Guards and was eventually placed in the newly formed 2nd battalion.

The 2nd battalion was formed at Warley Barracks on 18th July 1915, and landed at Le Havre on the 17th of August of that year. These were men who were surplus to requirements of the 1st battalion and who had already gone through much of their training programme. On the 16th of August they left Brentwood station and that evening at Southampton were packed into two ships, the "Anglo-Canadian" and the "Viper". After they arrived in France they immediately set out to meet up with the 2nd Guards Division and boarded their train at Lumbres on the 18th. Next day they marched to billets at Acquin, a small village close to St. Omer. Their first experience of action was to be the Battle of Loos. They were taken to a position just to the north of Loos, known as Chalk Pit Wood and it was here that they first went into battle. They were to be in the region around Vermelles for almost a month. They were then taken back for a rest and moved a few miles north to the area around Neuve Chapelle and Laventie in November and December. In March of 1916 they were moved into the Salient to the north of Ypres and the fighting around St.Jean and then in July, when the fighting at the Somme was devouring men by the thousand they were moved south to play a large part in that battle. On the 15th of

September the 2nd battalion attacked Lesboeufs, a small French village.

Much bitter fighting took place here and casualties were high. Over the next few days the battalion were in and out of the line but on the 25th of September a major attack was to take place at Guillemont and Ginchy, just to the south of Lesboeufs.

We don't know the date on which Daniel was injured but it was the result of an accident while Daniel was making the tea. He had lit a fire and was waiting for the water to boil when the fire exploded. It is thought that the heat of the fire must have set off an unexploded shell, and Daniel, who was nearest to the fire took the worst of it. He was rushed immediately to the nearest dressing station and then despatched to the hospital.

Daniel was taken to hospital at Etaples, with the intention of having him transferred to hospital in England, but by the time a ship was available he

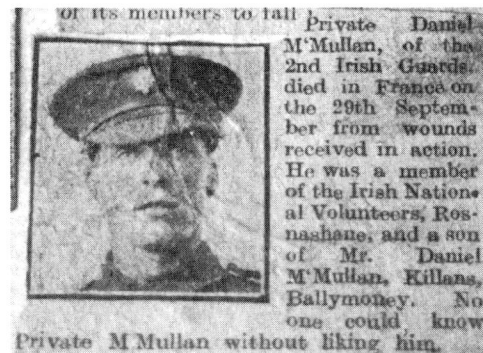

was too ill to be moved and he died at Etaples on the 29th of September.

By this time the battalion were resting in bivouacs in Trones Wood, near Lesboeufs just to the North-east of Ginchy. Daniel is buried in the huge cemetery beside where the hospital was at Etaples.

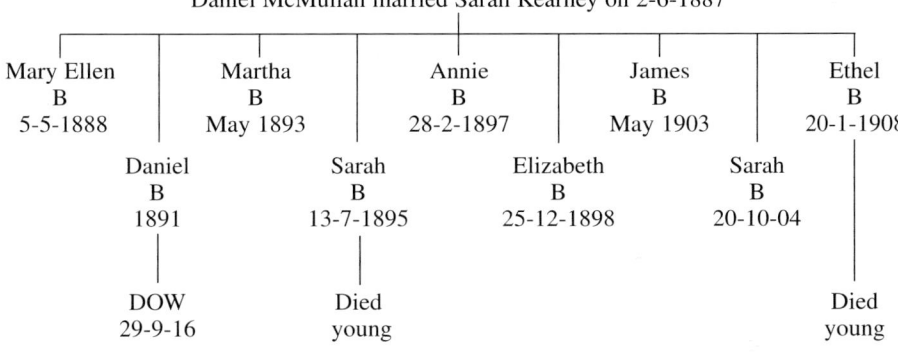

440195 PRIVATE SAMUEL PATTERSON
2nd Bn Canadian Mounted Rifles (1st Central Ontario Regiment)
DIED 29-9-16
Aged 27
Interred in Villers-Bretonneux Military Cemetery, Plot 16a, Row E, Grave 5

Born   Drumabest, Kilraughts.
Lived
Enlisted

Samuel Patterson was born at Drumabest on 21st April 1889. After leaving school he and his twin brother, William, emigrated to Canada, where Samuel took up farming. He was five feet eleven inches tall, with a fair complexion, brown eyes and light brown hair. He enlisted at Sewell, on 28th March 1915.

Sewell is a town south of the city of Winnipeg in the state of Manitoba. It was in this good farming region that Samuel had settled. After exactly a year spent in training he sailed from Halifax on 29th March 1916, on the S.S. Empress of Britain. Only three weeks prior to sailing he had been in hospital in Winnipeg suffering from Mumps but had quickly recovered. He arrived in England on the 9th of April and embarked for France eight weeks later, on the 8th of June 1916. The following day he was taken on strength of the 2nd battalion Canadian Mounted Rifles and joined his unit for action next day. On the 16th of September he was wounded for the first time, but a week later he was back with his unit. Then on 29th September, after a fierce action, he was reported wounded, and then wounded and missing.

There is nothing in his record to indicate just where this action took place but it was during the time of the Battle of the Somme and many Canadian units were in action around Courcelette at this time. It is possible that he was killed somewhere in this region and taken back to a quiet area for burial at Villers-Brettoneux. His brother William was killed four years later in an accident in Spokane, Washington.

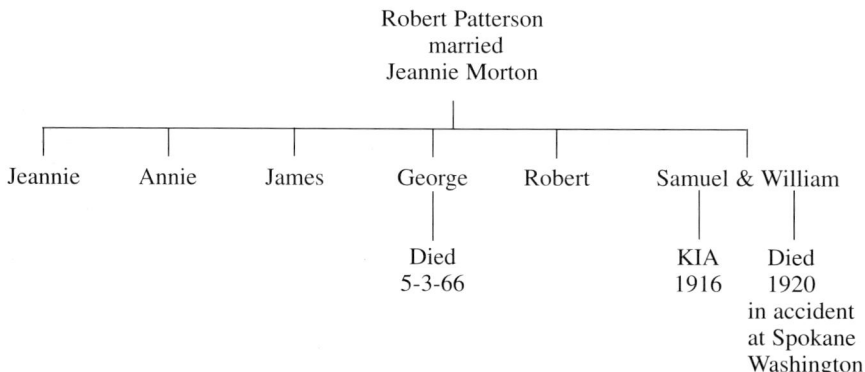

9645 RIFLEMAN JAMES LYNN
2nd Bn Royal Irish Rifles
K.I.A. 30-9-16
No Known Grave. Commemorated on the Thiepval Memorial

Born   Ballymoney
Enlisted   Ballymoney
Commemorated in Ballymoney Parish Church.

The Lynn family worshipped in St.Patrick's Parish Church in Ballymoney and it is there that James is commemorated. A few years after he left school in Ballymoney he enlisted into the 2nd battalion of the Royal Irish Rifles. It is believed that he did not see action at the start of the Battle of the Somme but joined the Regiment in a draft at a later date.

The 2nd battalion were stationed at Tidworth when war was declared on 4th August 1914. Ten days later, after joining the 3rd Division, they landed at Rouen. On 18th October 1915 the 7th Brigade joined the 25th Div. Fighting at the end of September had become a battle of survival. The weather had deteriorated to such an extent that it was a case of fighting the mud as well as the enemy. Most of the villages in the area were by this time a pile of rubble, battered to pieces by the heavy German artillery. Any trees growing in the area were by now just splintered stumps and the ground a mass of shell holes. It was in conditions like these that the men had to fight. Is it any wonder that some of them were never seen again.

James was killed in bitter fighting at the Somme when the position he and his comrades held with such courage was obliterated and they were overwhelmed. He has no known grave and is commemorated on the Thiepval Memorial.

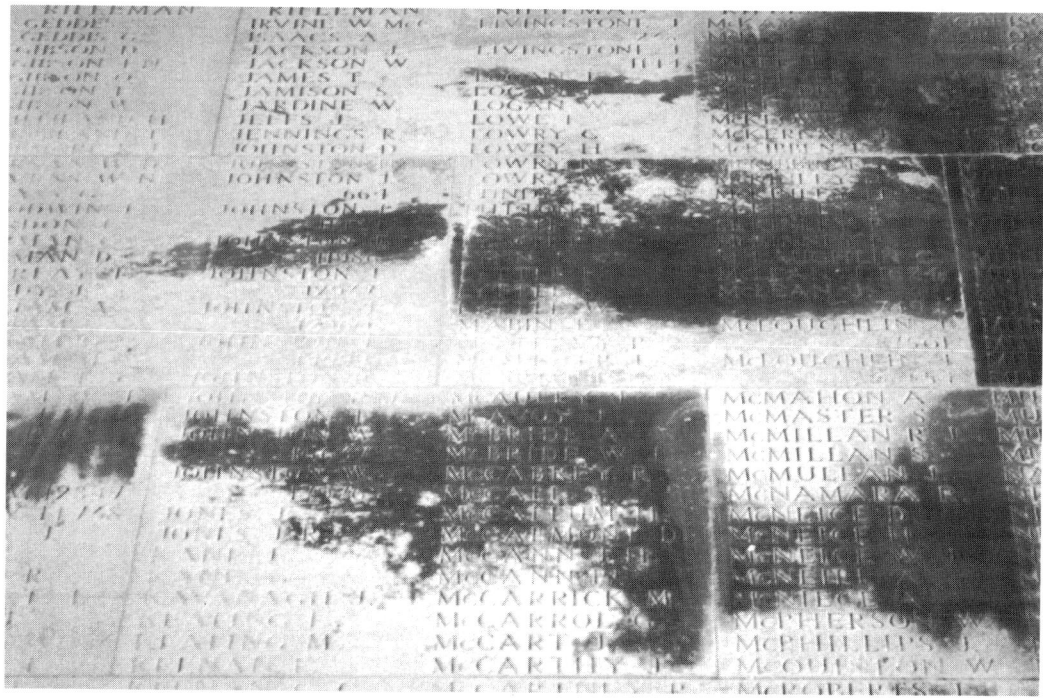

LIEUT. JAMES KENNETH MACGREGOR GREER. M.C.
1st Bn Irish Guards
D.O.W. 3-10-16
Aged 31
Interred in St. Sever Cemetery, Rouen. Plot A, Row 11, Grave 2

Born   Ballymoney.
Lived   Ballymoney.
Son of Thomas Macgregor Greer and Margaret Baines Greer of Ballymoney.
Commemorated in 1st Ballymoney Presbyterian Church.

James Kenneth Macgregor Greer was the only son of the well known Ballymoney solicitor, Thomas Macgregor Greer, of Westoncrofts, Charlotte Street, Ballymoney.

Although James was the only son there were also two daughters, Eileen and Constance, all of them born in Ballymoney. A short time after James enlisted he was home to see his parents at Westoncrofts. This was in January 1915. In early March a bullet struck the scoop of his cap, passed through his hair, and came out through the back of his cap without injuring him. Lieut McNeill, from Gardenvale, Stranocum, was with him at the time and they decided to keep the cap as a souvenir. On 18th May 1915, at the battle of Festubert, Lieut Greer sustained a number of bullet wounds, the worst being damage to his right hand, for which he was transferred to a London hospital. This soon healed and in a short time he was back with the troops. Then the following January he was awarded the Military Cross for gallant and distinguished service rendered in conjunction with military operations in the field. In June 1916 he was again home on leave, a break before the start of the Battle of the Somme.

During the early weeks of the battle he had a number of near misses but was eventually very seriously injured on 15th September in the attack on the small village of Flers, situated to the south of the main road from Bapaume to Albert.

The Coldstream Guards led the attack and the Irish Guards were supporting them. After the attack on the first line of enemy trenches the Irish stopped for a few minutes to re-group. Then Lieut Greer led them on towards the second line of German trenches. In spite of fierce enemy fire they had almost reached the second line of trenches when Lieut Greer fell. They had gone on too fast and a group of Germans hiding in a trench they had just captured, sprang up and attacked them from behind. While still consious Lieut Greer gave his revolver to another Ballymoney man, Sgt Hugh Carton, who had stopped to try to help his Officer. He ordered Carton to take command of the men and to go on with the attack. A short time later, during this same attack, Carton was killed. Lieut Greer was later picked up by stretcher bearers and taken to the nearest dressing station but owing to the seriousness of his wounds he was ordered to be taken immediately to hospital. He eventually arrived at Rouen but in spite of all that could be done he died there on 3rd October 1916. He was mentioned in despatches by Sir John French for his bravery in this attack. By this time the 1st battalion were in rest camp at Hornoy.

Lieut Greer was the only son of Mr Thomas Greer, (of Greer and Hamilton) solicitors, Ballymoney.

A lovely brass plaque to his memory was erected in Ballymoney Courthouse by the North Antrim Solicitors Association, and reads,

> This tablet is erected by the North Antrim Solicitors Association to the memory of J. Kenneth M. Greer, B.A.T.C.D. M.C. solicitors apprentice and Lieutenant 1st battalion Irish Guards who volunteered as a trooper in the North Irish Horse at the outbreak of the war, was given his commission for services in the field. Afterwards received the Military Cross and died at Rouen on 3rd October 1916 of wounds recieved in the advance of the Guards at the Somme.

The plaque was unveiled in November 1917 by Mr R.C.Martin.

That plaque has now been removed from a very dilapidated old courthouse and in April 1998 was brought to the offices of Greer, Hamilton and Gailey to be mounted there and cared for by Mr Hugh Clarke.

The name of J.K.M.Greer appears on many memorials. He is commemorated in the High Court buildings in Belfast. In 1st Ballymoney Presbyterian Church. On the Ballycastle War Memorial and, I think, in Ballycastle Presbyterian Church as well. His cousin, Captain Talbot Reed, of the Dorset Regiment, had been killed in action on Saturday, the 13th of March 1915. His father had been a brother of Mrs Greer, of Westoncrofts and Talbot Reed is commemorated on the war memorial in Ballycastle.

Arthur Gowers, who married Constance was from Cavendish Square, London, the son of Dr William Gowers.

This same Mrs Gowers, in early 1918, inaugurated a scheme in which Commonwealth soldiers on leave could stay in homes in the Ballymoney district, so that for a time, at least, they could have peace and quiet. This was a very successful scheme and resulted in many Australian, New Zealand and Canadian staying and making new friends in the Ballymoney district.

The organ in 1st Ballymoney Church was presented by Thomas and Mrs Greer, in memory of their son and of the other members of the Congregation who fell in the war and the inside of the church was completely re-designed at that time to accommodate the organ. The inscription on the organ reads,

> To the glory of God and in memory of their son, James Kenneth McGregor Greer, M.C. Lieut Irish Guards, and of the other members of the church who fell in the Great War, 1914-1919, this organ is given by Thomas McGregor and Margaret Greer, December 1919.

It is interesting to note that the Lieut McNeill mentioned above survived the war, but died in South London after a lengthy period of ill health, thought to have been the after effects of gas, and is buried in Sanderstead Churchyard.

Although Lieut Greer was awarded the M.C. for some reason it was awarded without a citation and was announced in the Gazette on 14th January 1916 with name only.

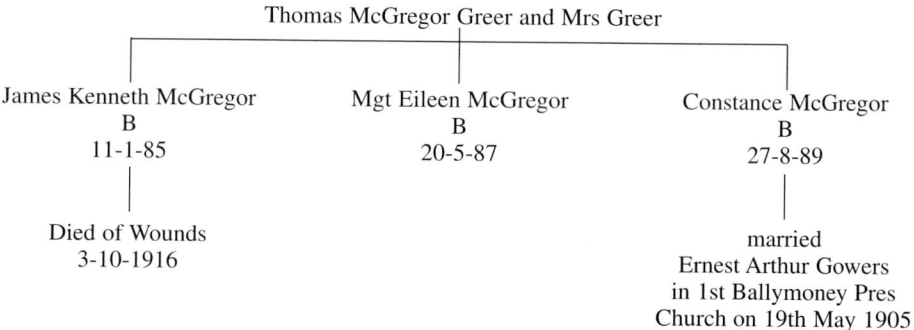

Thomas McGregor Greer and Mrs Greer

James Kenneth McGregor
B
11-1-85

Died of Wounds
3-10-1916

Mgt Eileen McGregor
B
20-5-87

Constance McGregor
B
27-8-89

married
Ernest Arthur Gowers
in 1st Ballymoney Pres
Church on 19th May 1905

A/ 20092 PRIVATE GEORGE McCORMICK
16th Bn, Canadian Infantry Manitoba Regt.
K.I.A. 9-10-16
Aged 24
No Known Grave. Commemorated on the Vimy Memorial.

Born   Monaclough, Armoy.
Lived   Carrowlaverty
Enlisted   Winnipeg, Canada.
Commemorated in Armoy Presbyterian Church.
Son of the late Thomas and Catherine McCormick, formerly of Ballycastle.

George had emigrated to Canada and had settled in Winnipeg. His sister, Cassie, was also in Winnipeg and it is more than likely that they shared the same house. His brother, John, had emigrated to Canada as well but was living in Govan, Saskatchewan. George was born on 23rd March 1892, at Monaclough, near Armoy and was not married. He enlisted at Winnipeg on 18th December 1914. He was five feet ten inches tall, with a fresh complexion, blue eyes and dark hair. It would appear that the Cassie McCormick mentioned above later became Mrs Joseph Morgan, of 617 Atlantic Ave, Winnipeg as the new name is written in and she is still described as his sister.

There is no record of which port he sailed from in Canada but his unit left Canada on 1st June 1915. He was taken on strength of the 16th Bn on the 17th July 1915 in France.

On 2nd October he was admitted to No2, Field Ambulance, suffering from influenza but four days later was back at his post. Then on 12th February he was sent on a machine- gun course at Wisques for six days. Towards the end of April he was appointed Lance Corporal and on 4th May he was given seven days leave. On tenth July 1916 he was appointed Acting Corporal and then Corporal. A short time later, in early August he sustained schrapnel wounds to his back. This needed hospital treatment and he was sent to Boulogne. By mid September he was well enough to be discharged to rest camp.

On the night of 8th-9th October 1916 he was reported wounded, and then wounded and missing. He was never seen again. He has no known grave and is commemorated on the Vimy Memorial.

22128 PRIVATE LUKE O'NEILL
1st Bn Royal Irish Fusiliers
K.I.A. 12-10-16
Aged 22
No Known Grave. Commemorated on the Thiepval Memorial, France

Born   Portglenone.
Lived   Rasharkin.
Enlisted   Coatbridge, Lanarkshire.
Son of Roderick and Mary Ann O'Neill, of Portglenone.

On the outbreak of hostilities the 1st battalion were stationed at Shorncliffe with the 4th Division and moved to York on the 18th of August 1914. Five days later they landed at Boulogne. Although Luke O'Neill had been born at Portglenone, he had lived most of his life at Rasharkin, but was at the time he enlisted, working in Scotland. Luke joined the 1st battalion in a later draft to make up for men lost in earlier battles, but was with them in time for the Battle of the Somme. It was in this battle that he was killed on 12th October 1916. He has no known grave and is commemorated on the Thiepval Memorial.

64 PRIVATE WILLIAM RAMSEY
1st Bn Royal Irish Fusiliers
DIED 12-10-16
No known grave. Commemorated on the Kirkee 1914-1918 Memorial, India.

Born   Getty's Close.
Lived
Enlisted.

In May of 1999 a very good friend from Dunloy contacted me and invited me to come to Dunloy to meet someone.

This turned out to be a Director of the War Graves Commission, Mr Liam J. Hanna, home on a holiday to visit relatives in Dunloy, and he promised to help me with the identification of some of the soldiers who were giving me problems. This turned out to be a massive stroke of good fortune and he has already positively identified a number of men who were proving difficult to locate.

I believe that I have now been able to identify William Ramsey.

William was born in what at the time was known as Getty's Close in the town. It appears that Getty's Close was in Charles St opposite Riada House. William was a regular soldier and at the outbreak of hostilities was serving in India. In the stifling heat of India disease was a common problem and it is believed that William died from one of these Tropical diseases. In spite of a number of appeals in the local papers nothing has come to light concerning him and it would appear that the family has just simply died out. This is one of the sad things about writing a book like this that you can suddenly come across someone who has been just completely and utterly forgotten. William is not commemorated in any of the local churches and the only place where his name can be seen on a memorial is thousands of miles away in India.

If we get the names engraved on the Ballymoney War Memorial it will be a very fitting tribute to these brave men.

Kirkee, also known as Khadki, is a Military Cantonment adjoining the large university town of Poona on the plateau above Bombay.

It can be reached by train from Bombay to Poona or by long distance taxi service from Dada Taxi Stand, Bombay. There are direct flights from Bombay, Madras and Dehli but these tend to be irregular.

Kemmel Chateau Cemetery

109576 PRIVATE THOMAS ROSS
4th Canadian Mounted Rifles
D.O.W. 14-10-16
Aged 20

Born   Glencar, Sligo,
Lived   Dervock
Enlisted Toronto

Thomas Ross was born in Glencar, Co Sligo on the 10th of October 1895. It would appear that soon after this his mother and father died. All through his records there is never any mention of his parents and his Aunt is named as his next of kin. So he was an only child.

At some stage he came to live in Dervock, probably because of work after leaving school, and is commemorated on the Dervock War Memorial. He then emigrated to Canada, settling in the small town of Brantford, close to Toronto, and worked as a farmer. Thomas enlisted at Toronto on 27th November 1914 into the 4th Canadian Mounted Rifles. He was five feet eight and a half inches tall, with a fair complexion, blue eyes and fair hair.

By the summer of 1915 he had arrived in France and after serving a short time with his unit was taken to hospital at Etaples on 13th December with gunshot wounds to his right eye and leg. He recovered quickly and a fortnight later was back in action. Then on 3rd June 1916 he was injured again and was taken to hospital in Boulogne. The first injury to his face had not healed properly and was still giving him a great deal of pain. After a few days treatment he was returned to his unit to carry on with the war effort.

In early October he was again in hospital, this time at Rouen, and on 12th October was reported dangerously ill from gunshot wounds to the leg, foot and hand. The first injury to his eye was still giving trouble and the combination of all the injuries was to prove too much for him and he died of his wounds at Rouen on the 14th of October 1916.

Bouzincourt

10203 PRIVATE FRANK HEGGARTY
25th Co. M.G.C. Royal Irish Rifles
K.I.A. 23-10-16
Aged 18
No known grave. Commemorated on the Thiepval Memorial.

Born   The Park, Armoy.
Lived   The Park, Armoy.
Commemorated in Armoy Presbyterian Church
Interred at Le Transloy
Son of Francis and Isabella Heggarty, of Park Mills, Armoy.

The family lived just outside the village of Armoy, at Park Mills.

They worshipped in Armoy Presbyterian Church in the village and Frank is commemorated on a lovely plaque just inside the door of the church. This plaque is unusual in that it gives the date of death beside the name of the soldier which is very useful. Usually these plaques only give the name and in some cases the regiment. When Frank enlisted he gave a false age in order to get away with his mates and was still only eighteen when he was killed.

In June 1916 Frank Heggarty was chosen as part of a machine-gun team but remained in the same battalion. There is a report that Frank was buried at Le Transloy. This would infer that he had been wounded and taken for treatment and probably buried close by. The grave, it would appear, has been lost as he is commemorated on the Thiepval Memorial.

3/10463 SERGEANT SAMUEL JAMES HOLMES
8th Bn Norfolk Regt
D.O.W. 23-10-16
Aged 38
Interred in Warloy-Baillon Comm Cemetery. Plot 6, Row C, Grave 4.

Born   Billy, Bushmills.
Lived   Liscolman
Enlisted
Commemorated in Bushvale Presbyterian Church.
Son of Fanny and the late Samuel Holmes of Liscolman.

The 8th battalion was formed at Norwich in September 1914. They went immediately to Shorncliffe to join the 18th Div. In October they moved to Colchester. After a few months training here they moved, in April 1915 to Codford. Then on 25th July 1915 they landed at Boulogne.

Their first major battle was the Battle of the Somme and here Samuel attacked with his comrades near Carnoy on the 1st of July 1916. They were in the front line and attacking towards Pommiers Redoubt but the trenches in front of the Redoubt were strongly held and a fierce battle ensued. Here the Norfolks suffered many casualties and were held up when one end of the trench they were in could not be taken immediately.

By night-time they had taken Pommiers Redoubt and other units fighting with them had taken the whole of Montauban Ridge. Samuel came safely through this first day of the battle and remained with his unit until he was seriously injured in October. He was taken to a field hospital at Warloy-Baillon. Here he was well cared for but in spite of all that could be done he died of his injuries. He is buried in the nearby cemetery where another Ballymoney man, Matthew Keers, is buried. It is interesting to note that another soldier buried in this cemetery, Capt Oswald Brooke Webb, is an uncle of Mrs Stewart-Moore of Ballydivity, Dervock. He lies in Plot 3, Row B, Grave 2, and died of wounds on 4th July 1916.

424544   PRIVATE FRANK JOHN BANKHEAD
1st Canadian Mounted Rifles Saskatchewan Regiment
D.O.W. 29-10-16
Aged 25
Interred in St. Catherine British Cemetery, France. Row M, Grave 2

Born   Pretoria, South Africa.
Lived   Ballymoney
Enlisted Canada
Son of Samuel and Elizabeth Anne Bankhead, of Victoria St, Ballymoney.

Frank John Bankhead was born in South Africa on 25th June 1890. At some time after this the family moved to live in Victoria St, Ballymoney. Frank later emigrated to Canada, where he worked as a Moving Picture Operator in a cinema. He enlisted at Brandon on 19th May 1915. He was five feet seven and a half inches tall, with a dark complexion, blue eyes and dark brown hair.

While still at training camp he was admitted to hospital on 9th December 1915 suffering from Influenza but was discharged five days later. He sailed from Halifax on the S.S. Baltic on 13th March 1916 and arrived in England on the 25th. He arrived in France on the 8th of June 1916 and joined his unit in the field the next day. He was killed in action on 29th October 1916 and is buried in St. Catherine Cemetery on the northern outskirts of Arras. His Mother had by this time left Ballymoney and was living in Ballymena.

Queens Cemetery on the Serre Road

9140 SERGEANT ALEXANDER MURDOCK
2nd Bn Highland Light Infantry
K.I.A. 13-11-16
No Known Grave. Commemorated on the Thiepval Memorial, France. Pier 15C

Born   Ballymoney.
Lived   Glasgow.
Enlisted Hamilton, Lanarkshire.

In January 1916 Alex was in hospital suffering from injuries but was improving and looking forward to ten days leave. I have been unable to trace the family of Alex Murdock but he was with his battalion north of the River Ancre in October 1916.

The first week of November saw a change in the weather, with some prospects of a lasting improvement. The weather had been very wet and the terrible condition of the water-logged trenches, many of which, including important communication ways, were little better than treacherous quagmires, while others were filled with water to a depth of three or four feet. The attack, however, was set for the 13th, zero hour being 5.45am.

On the 11th the battalion occupied their trenches for the last time and after the huge amount of repair work which had been done on them they were so deep that it was almost impossible to get out of them and a great number of ladders had to be used to overcome the difficulty. So impetuous were the leading waves of the attack that they entered the enemy front line at the same time as the British barrage, and undoubtedly suffered many casualties from their own shell fire. Within six minutes the line was captured and many German prisoners taken. It was during this attack that Alex Murdock was killed. He has no known grave and is commemorated on the Thiepval Memorial.

17890 L.CPL JOHN GAMBLE
2nd Bn, Royal Inniskilling Fusiliers
K.I.A. 23-11-16
Interred in Waggon Road Cemetery, France. Row C, Grave 33

Born   Craigs, Finvoy.
Enlisted   Glasgow

When war was declared on 4th August 1914 the second battalion were stationed at Dover. From here they moved into Norfolk and landed at Le Havre on the 22nd of August. By early December they were at G.H.Q. and saw a lot of action with the 32nd Division.

John Gamble enlisted in Glasgow and was probably working in the shipyards there.

Although he was born in Finvoy, five or six miles south of Ballymoney, and Gamble is a very common name in the district, I have been unable to find any family connections.

The Cemetery is situated on the Redan Ridge, between the villages of Beaumont Hamel and Serre. This was a region which saw desperate fighting at the Battle of the Somme and the land on which the cemetery is sited was in German hands at that time. Although the Battle of the Somme officially ended on 13th November 1916, this does not mean to say that the fighting stopped, far from it. But as far as the Ballymoney men were concerned, deaths for a time did ease off. John Gamble was killed just after the battles here finished and it was more than likely that he was shot by a sniper.

Waggon Road Cemetery

28977 PRIVATE JOHN PORTEOUS
7th Bn Royal Inniskilling Fusiliers.
D.O.W. 17-1-17
Aged 33
Interred in Bailleul Communal Cemetery Extension, France. Plot 3, Row A, Grave 121.

Born   Killosnet, Co. Leitrim.
Lived
Enlisted   Ballymoney, in February 1916.
Son of Charles and Elizabeth Porteous, of Clooneen, Manorhamilton, Co. Leitrim.

John Porteous had been born in County Leitrim but had been living in Ballymoney for a number of years and had been in the employment of Mr. W. M. Renison, of Main St for some time. He also took a very active part in the work of the Salvation Army and had been attending their meetings in and around Ballymoney for a considerable time. In February 1916, he decided to enlist, and joined the Royal Inniskilling Fusiliers.

Training at the time was intensive as troops were urgently needed and very soon he was on his way to the Front. Much of his early fighting took place in the area south of Ypres in Belgium. He had only been in Belgium a short time when he was wounded and he sent a card to Mr. Renison with this news. This would give the impression that he did not have any close relatives living in Ballymoney and that possibly the wounds were not life threatening at this time. The 7th battalion were with the 16th Division in trenches at Kemmel Shelters when he was wounded in

Middle front row, Bailleul Cemetery

December 1916. He was taken to a dressing station at first and then on to a field hospital close to Bailleul. He died of his injuries on 17th Januay 1917, still at this same hospital. Conditions being as primitive as they were at the time it is possible that some other complications set in which ended his life so prematurely. Mr Renison had a large grocery business on the corner of Seymour St and Meetinghouse St. Now no more.

Bailleul is a large town in France, near the Belgian border, 14.5 kilometres south-west of Ypres and on the main road from St.Omer to Lille. The Communal Cemetery is on the eastern outskirts of the town.

Connaught Cemetery at the Somme with Thiepval Wood in the background

CLYDE 211969 ROBERT ANDERSON REID
Royal Naval Volunteer Reserve, H.M.S. Laurentic.
Killed at sea, 25-1-17
Aged 22
Commemorated on Portsmouth Naval Memorial, Hampshire. No. 28.

Born   Balnamore
Lived   Balnamore
Enlisted
Son of Robert and Mary Anderson Reid, of 79, Earlspark Ave, Newlands, Glasgow.

Robert Anderson Reid was born in Balnamore in 1895, the son of Robert and Mary Anderson Reid. They lived for a time at Balnamore before eventually settling in Glasgow.

H.M.S. Laurentic was built in Belfast by Harland & Wolff Ltd in 1909, and formerly belonged to the Oceanic Steam Navigation Company of Liverpool. She had a net tonnage of 9,255 and a gross of 14,892, was driven by screws and her engines developed 1,492 HP giving her a speed of 19 knots. She carried a crew of 475. Commander Mathias was in command of Laurentic during the first 27 months of the war and spent most of this time on patrol duty in the Indian Ocean. She was ordered home in the Autumn of 1916 and was due at Liverpool just before Christmas. Mrs Mathias and her two little children were informed and proceeded to the port of arrival to await the homecoming. But it was the dead body of her Commander the Laurentic

brought into port -- killed in a brave endeavour to save some of his men from an awful fate.

Two days run from port a serious fire was discovered in No2 hold. A squad of men with the Chief Officer at their head, plunged in to fight the fire but it gained such headway that it swept round them towards one of the magazines and cut off their escape. Word of their plight was sent to Commander Mathias, who was on the bridge, and he immediately headed a relief party himself. They fought their way into the smoke filled hold and succeeded in dragging out some of the imprisoned men. Commander Mathias went back for the rest. As he made his way into the furnace-like hold to rescue the last man, an iron beam, warped out of it's place by the intense heat, fell on him and the men who were pluckily following him. Commander Mathias was instantly killed and several of the men injured. Another rescue squad extricated them and succeeded in recovering the body of the Commander. He was succeeded as Commander by Captain R.A. Norton, R.N.

H.M.S. Laurentic was an armed merchant cruiser and was hired by the Royal Navy on 31st October 1914. She carried eight 6 inch guns and two 6 pounder guns, and had a displacement of 14,892 tons.

A short time after this as she started out on her next voyage around the North coast of Ireland on her way to the Atlantic she struck a mine and went down very quickly.

This accident happened two miles 070 degrees off Fanad Point, Lough Swilly on 25th January 1917. Twelve Officers and 109 men were saved. At that time of the year even if Robert Reid did survive the mine explosion the water would have been too cold and he would only have survived for a very short time. He is commemorated on the Portsmouth Naval Memorial.

Laurentic as an AMC

Harry Connolly, Ballymoney Borough Council at the 16th Irish Div. Memorial at Guillemont France, 11th November, 1998

10913 PRIVATE HUGH MURPHY
1st Bn Royal Inniskilling Fusiliers
K.I.A. 30-1-17
Aged 20
No Known Grave. Commemorated on the Thiepval Memorial, France. Pier 4d and 5b.

Born   Ballymoney.
Lived
Enlisted   Coleraine.
Son of John Murphy, of Stone Row, Coleraine.

Hugh Murphy was born at Ballymoney in 1897. The family appears to have moved to live in Coleraine at a later date as his father is mentioned as living in Stone Row. By February of 1916 the 1st battalion were back from Gallipoli and were in billets at Mailly- Maillet and it is thought that it was here that Hugh joined them. Preparations were by now in full swing for the Battle of the Somme and everywhere was a hive of activity.

New troops were arriving daily by this time and in great secrecy but it was difficult to keep this number of men hidden and it soon became obvious that something was brewing. The 29th Division were to attack north of the River Ancre in the region around Beaumont Hamel on the morning of the 1st of July 1916. The blowing of the Hawthorn Ridge mine ten minutes before zero hour had warned every German for miles around that an attack was imminent and they were ready. The battle dragged on until it slowly ground to a halt in November. By this time the Division had been moved south and were close to Guillemont.

On the 30th of January 1917 the 1st battalion, still with the 29th Division, were in reserve at Guillemont. It was here that Hugh Murphy was killed. He has no known grave and is commemorated on the Thiepval Memorial.

The village of Guillemont is the site of one of the monuments to the Irish Guards and it was to this village that we paid a visit when we were in France and Belgium for the opening of the Peace Park at Messines in November 1998.

2073 TROOPER WILLIAM McKEE MURPHY
North Irish Horse
DIED 12-2-17
Aged 23 of pneumonia.
Interred in St. Sever Cemetery Extension, Rouen. Plot O 5, Row C, Grave 7

Born
Lived   Leslie Hill.
Enlisted   January 1916.
Commemorated in St. James's Presbyterian Church.
Son of Thomas Murphy, of Leslie Hill.

William was a son of Thomas Murphy of Leslie Hill, an estate on the edge of Ballymoney. Some of the local families found work here and many of them lived in houses on the estate. The family worshipped in St. James's Presbyterian Church in the town and William is named on a lovely plaque inside the church. He enlisted in January 1916 and after his training was finished he was taken to France, arriving there in early January 1917. It was mid winter and the weather was cold and very wet. Freezing temperatures at night kept the troops in a state of near exhaustion. It was difficult to keep the men fed and even more difficult for the men to keep dry and they had to sleep in wet clothes. It was during this time that William contracted pneumonia. He was taken to hospital at Rouen but the illness had taken too much of a hold and he died a few days later. He had only been in France for a month. He is buried in the local cemetery at Rouen along with four other Ballymoney boys. A report in the local papers at the time stated that another brother, James, was in hospital, dangerously ill, in France but he seems to have recovered and survived the war.

La Neuville at Corbie

27777 PRIVATE PATRICK CUMMING
1st Bn, Cameronians (Scottish Rifles)
K.I.A. 17-2-17
No Known Grave. Commemorated on the Thiepval Memorial, 4d.

Born   Ballymoney
Lived
Enlisted   Glasgow.

The 1st battalion were stationed in Glasgow on the outbreak of hostilities and landed at Le Havre eleven days later. On the 22nd of August they joined the 19th Brigade at Valenciennes and by 12th October were attached to the 6th Division. On 31st May 1915 they joined the 27th Division and then in August were sent to the 2nd Division. By November of 1915 they were with the 33rd Div and stayed in this Division until the end of the war. Patrick was a later recruit, enlisting in Glasgow, where he had gone in search of work. He has no known grave and is commemorated on the Thiepval Memorial.

LIEUT WILLIAM ROBERT BRADSHAW
6th Bn Connaught Rangers
K.I.A. 19 -2-17
Aged 34
Interred in Kemmel Chateau Military Cemetery. Row G, Grave 11.

Born
Lived   Charlotte St, Ballymoney
Enlisted
Son of George T.M. and Annie Bradshaw, of 33, Charlotte St.

G.T.M. Bradshaw was a Locomotive Superintendant and lived in Charlotte Street in the house which is now the museum.

Kemmel Chateau Military Cemetery is located 8 kilometres south of Ypres on the edge of Kemmel village. This is one of the cemeteries used for the burial of troops shot at dawn. Private S Stewart of the 2nd R. Scots Fus, had been suffering from shell shock and in hospital and was returned to action too soon. Whilst under arrest he escaped when a shell burst close to where he was held. He was shot at Kemmel on 29th August 1917. Another soldier, 26 year old James Smith, from Bolton, faced charges of desertion and disobedience and was executed at Kemmel on 5th September 1917. Although these facts do not in any way reflect on the story of William Bradshaw it is interesting to note that these two soldiers are buried in the same cemetery.

The 6th battalion was formed at Kilworth in September 1914 and went immediately to train at Fermoy joining the 16th Div. In September 1915, having completed their training here, they crossed to England and were stationed at Blackdown. Then on 18th December 1915 they landed at Le Havre. On Sunday 17th January 1916, William surprised his parents when he unexpectedly turned up at his home in Charlotte St on leave from the trenches. His brother, John, had been working in Germany before the outbreak of hostilities and was interned for 18 weeks before being released and making his way home. Soon after this John got a job teaching languages in Ballycastle High School, and worked there until he died of pneumonia on 29th March 1919. Apparently there were two other brothers in the family, James and M.H.F. Bradshaw.

Kemmel Chateau Military Cemetery.

Entry in the Chronicle for 3-3-17.

Official intimation was recieved on Friday last by Mr G.T.M.Bradshaw M.I.M.E. Charlotte St, that his son Lieut William R, Bradshaw had been killed in action. Prior to enlisting deceased was employed in the Midland Railway Company's office here and was transferred to Londonderry. After some time he secured a better position with a steamship company at Limerick, a position which he relinquished to join as a private in the Royal Munster Fusiliers. He was promoted to the rank of Sergeant and after being over a year on active service was just a year ago granted a commission in the Connaught Rangers. After undergoing training at Galway, the late Lieut Bradshaw returned to France when after six months active service he was granted leave and visited home. He returned to his regiment from here at the beginning of February, and had only been in the trenches about a week. Up to this time he had not been injured.

Kemmel Chateau Military Cemetery.

504742 SAPPER JOHN GILLEN
2nd Field Coy. Canadian Engineers
K.I.A. 1-3-17
Aged 22.
Interred in Givenchy-en-Gohelle Canadian Cemetery. Row E, Grave 5.

Born   Clintyfinnan, Armoy.
Lived   Emigrated to Canada.
Enlisted   Vancouver, Canada.
Commemorated in Armoy Presbyterian Church.
Son of William John and Charlotte Gillen of Abbotsford, British Colombia.
John had won the Bronze Medal for Military Valour (Italy).

William John Gillen lived at Clintyfinnan and married Charlotte McMullan. There were at least two sons of the marriage, John and Robert Daniel.

After the two boys were born the family emigrated to British Colombia. John was born at Clintyfinnan on 7th July 1894 and was a surveyor in Canada. He enlisted at Vancouver on 11th February 1916. He was five feet seven inches tall, with a fresh complexion, blue eyes and brown hair and embarked for England on board SS. Baltic on 15th May 1916, arriving on 29th May. Immediately they were taken to Bramshott where they arived on 1st June. Intense training then took place and they were moved across to France on the 12th of August 1916. Towards the end of November he was granted ten days leave but there is no indication of where he spent his leave. He re-joined his unit on 10th December. There is no further entry on his record until he is mentioned as killed in action on 1st March 1917.

On 26th May 1917 he was posthumously awarded the Bronze Medal for Military Valour. LG 30096. He is buried in Givenchy-en-Gohelle Canadian Cemetery which stands on the western slopes of Vimy Ridge above the village of Souchez. The Abbotsford War Memorial was constructed and dedicated on 7th April 1929. It is composed of grey British Colombia granite and stands nine feet high. On it are the names of the dead from the 1st World War, the 2nd World War and the Korean War.

London Cemetery

9328 PRIVATE PETER O'DONNELL
2nd Bn Irish Guards
K.I.A. 15-3-17
Interred in Sailly-Saillisel British Cemetery, Plot 2, Row I, Grave 8.

Born   Donegal
Lived
Enlisted   Hamilton, Lanarkshire

It is thought that Peter was born in County Donegal and that the family moved to the Ballymoney district a few years later. Peter's brother was a policeman in Ballymoney in the early years of this century.

The 2nd battalion of the Irish Guards was formed at Warley Barracks in July 1915. Peter had enlisted before this and was immediately drafted into this battalion. On the 16th of August they left Brentwood station for Southampton and that evening were put aboard the "Anglo-Canadian" and the "Viper". Escorted by destroyers they were in Le Havre by midnight.

They entrained for Lumbres on the 18th of August and next day marched to Acquin, close to St.Omer. After a few weeks spent training they moved to the area around Vermelles. This was to be their first taste of battle.

The battle of Loos was about to begin and they were to attack Chalk-Pit Wood just to the north of Loos. There is no need to go into details of the battle as it has already been described in another story. After a rest at Bethune the men were moved to Laventie in a full blizzard. Conditions here were awful, mud everywhere, the German front 300 yards away, not a hedge or stump to guide men out or back from patrol, and German snipers waiting everywhere for a man to show himself. After this they were moved north to Poperinghe in the Ypres Salient. Here they were to stay until July when they moved again, this time to the Somme. The battles here for Ginchy and Guillemont have already been described and as Peter survived these there isn't much need to dwell on the circumstances. The battalion then took part in the battle for Bourlon Wood. By the middle of March they were in St.Pierre Vaast Wood and it was here that Peter was killed. Patrols were being sent out to try to find out how many of the enemy were still in the wood. Snipers were hiding everywhere that cover could be found and there were still a few machine-gun nests operating. Patrolling in the wood was dangerous work which had to be done, crawling in the mud from tree trunk to tree trunk, and it was probably doing this that Peter was killed. He is buried in Sailly-Saillisel British Cemetery a short distance away.

A.I.F. Cemetery at the Somme

49714 PRIVATE ALFRED JOHN SMYTH
14th Bn Durham Light Infantry
K.I.A. 6-3-17
Aged 36
Interred in Philosophe British Cemetery, Mazingarbe. Plot 1, Row M, Grave 36.

Born   Rasharkin.
Lived   Streatham.
Enlisted Kingston-upon-Thames.
Son of Thomas and Margretta Smyth, of Rasharkin.
Husband of Edith Negus of Bognor, Sussex.
Commemorated in Finvoy Presbyterian Church.

The 14th battalion of the Durham Light Infantry was formed at Newcastle in September 1914 and began their training at Aylesbury. They then moved to Halton Park in October, and were in billets at High Wycombe from then until April, when they returned to Halton Park. In July 1915 they moved to Witley and landed at Boulogne on 11th September of that year. Alfred is buried in Philosophe British Cemetery, close to the town of Mazingarbe, that infamous place where so many innocent, young British soldiers were shot for desertion by their own side. They were ordered to be executed as an example to others by men to whom a human life meant nothing. Alfred John Smyth was born in Rasharkin, about five miles south of Ballymoney, the son of Thomas and Margretta Smyth. He had been living in England for some considerable time and was married to Edith Negus of Bognor, Sussex. The 14th battalion were taken to the region around Ypres and by December were at Wieltje. At this particular point No Man's Land was about 300 yards wide and on Sunday morning, the 19th of December 1915, the enemy started a gas attack. The British replied with shell-fire and this succeeded in keeping the enemy in his trenches. The gas drifted across but by the time it reached the British trenches it had dissipated and did not cause any casualties. There were many attacks of this type over the next few months but Alfred came through it all. His battalion were then moved south, to the area around Vermelles and the other small villages north of Lens. It was here that Alfred was killed close to Mazingarbe on the 6th of March 1917. The family worshipped in Finvoy Presbyterian Church and it is there that Alfred is commemorated. The Roll of Honour is just inside the door of the church.

Front Centre, Philosophe British Cemetery

1511 RIFLEMAN ALEXANDER McCLEAN
7th Bn Royal Irish Rifles.
K.I.A. 8-3-17
Interred in Kemmel Chateau Cemetery. Row N, Grave 59.

Born   Ballymoney.
Lived   Castle St, Ballymoney.
Enlisted Belfast.
Commemorated in Ballymoney Parish Church.

Alex had been born in Ballymoney and the family lived in Castle Street. They worshipped in St. Patrick's Parish Church in Ballymoney and it is there that Alex is commemorated. He attended the Church school. The building still stands in the Church grounds and was used until just lately as the local library.

He was employed in the shop of Mr Thomas Henderson of High St, Ballymoney. The shop was close to where the Gift Shop or Kerr's Drapery is in High St today. After enlisting and some very intensive training in England as a sniper, he was moved across to France. In March 1917 they were close to Elverdinge, just north of Ypres and Alex had gone out into No Man's Land

in his usual role as a sniper. He had worked his way to a shell hole and was lying in wait when a night attack started and he was shot. By the time he was killed he had shot about twenty Germans. He is buried in Kemmel Chateau Cemetery on the edge of the village of Kemmel.

This is the same cemetery where William Bradshaw of Charlotte St is buried and where James McClean of Bushmills is also buried. This Cemetery was used on two occasions to bury men who had been on a charge of desertion, were found guilty by court martial and were shot at dawn. Stanley Stewart was shot at Kemmel on 29th August 1917 and is buried in Row G, Grave 66. James Smith on 5th September 1917 in Row M, Grave 25.

Kemmel Chateau Cemetery. Grave of Alex McClean to right of tree

907063 PRIVATE JOHN WILLIAM CLYDE JACK
16th Coy Canadian Machine Gun Corps
K.I.A. 12-3-17
Aged 24
Interred in Villers Station Cemetery. Plot 7, Row E, Grave 22.

Born Coleraine
Lived
Enlisted Canada.
Son of the late David Jack, formerly headmaster of the Model school.
Before emigrating he had held a position in Farrows Bank, in Belfast.

John William Clyde Jack was born in Coleraine on 16th April 1892. After leaving school he trained as a Bank Clerk. He was five feet seven and a half inches tall with a dark complexion, grey eyes and dark brown hair.

His father had been head master of the Model School, but by the time John William enlisted, both his parents were dead. After he emigrated to Canada he settled in Regina, Saskatchewan, and worked in the Broad St. branch of the Bank of Ottawa. He had a brother and sister. His brother, David Alexander, lived on the Antrim Road in Belfast, and his sister, Marion, was married to R.P.Mann, and lived in Cheshire. He enlisted in Regina on 16th February 1916 and embarked from Halifax on the 1st of November and arrived at Liverpool on the 11th. Later that day he was taken on strength of the 32nd battalion, C.E.F. and on the 27th moved to East Sandling. On the next day they landed in France and reported to his unit for duty on the 16th of December. On 1st January 1917 he transferred to the 16th Canadian Machine-Gun Coy. He was killed in action on the 12th of March 1917 and is buried in Villers Station Cemetery, near the village of Villers-au-Bois, north-west of Arras, and a short distance from Vimy Ridge.

Villers Station Cemetery

43495 PRIVATE PATRICK MOONEY
2nd Bn Gordon Highlanders formerly 20644 Cameron Highlanders
K.I.A. 28-3-17
Interred in H.A.C. Cemetery, Ecoust-St-Mein. France. Plot 3, Row C, Grave 26.

Born   Dunloy
Lived   Glasgow
Enlisted Inverness

Patrick Mooney was born in Dunloy but had been living in Glasgow. As was common practice at the time, he had probably gone to Scotland in search of work. This happened on a regular basis, particularly at harvest time, when the larger farms in Scotland needed extra help. When this dried up there was always the coal mines or the huge ship-building yards in Glasgow. Patrick enlisted in Inverness into the Cameron Highlanders. This would suggest that he was working in Inverness at the time as it would have been a very simple business to enlist in Glasgow. Some time after this he transferred to the Gordon Highlanders. The 2nd battalion were at Bucquoy with the 7th Division on the 14th of March 1917. A fortnight later, on the 28th they were fiercely engaged at Longatte, and it was here that Patrick was killed.

These actions were part of the general pattern of the fighting on the Western Front, and cannot be described as of great significance against the overall war campaigns along the full length of the front. This does not diminish the tragic losses suffered or the sacrifice of these young lives which were so typical of the period. He was buried in H.A.C. Cemetery, Ecoust-St-Mein, close to where he was killed. Another Ballymoney man is buried very close to where Patrick lies. John Boyd is buried in the same plot as Patrick, in the row in front, also grave 26.

This cemetery was used for the burial of John Woodhouse, a soldier who faced the firing squad on a charge of desertion and was executed on 4th October 1917. He is buried in Plot 8, Row C, Grave 23.

Ecoust-St-Mein is a vilage in the department of the Pas-de-Calais, between Arras, Cambrai and Bapaume. HAC Cemetery is about 800 metres south of the village on the west side of the D956 road to Beugenatre.

CAPT JAMES MAITLAND STUART
59th Sqdn, Royal Flying Corps
K.I.A. 13-4-17
Aged 20
No Known Grave. Commemorated on the Arras Flying Services Memorial.

Born   Queensland, Australia. in 1896
Lived
Enlisted
Commemorated in Derrykeighan Parish Church. Son of Annie M Stuart, of Somerset, Coleraine, and the late James Stuart, Stranocum,

James Stuart's father, the late James Stuart, had large station properties in Queensland, Australia, and it was here that James was born. The family came from Ballydivity, Dervock. James was the eldest son of the family. He was born in 1896 in Queensland, and was educated at King's School, Paramatta, New South Wales, Cheltenham College and the Royal Military College, Sandhurst. Having obtained a commission in the Royal Inniskilling Fusiliers, he was attached to the Royal Flying Corps in September 1915, going to France with his squadron as a second Lieutenant in December 1915. He was on active service on the Western Front until the following September, when he was posted to home establishment for four months.

Early in February 1917 he again went on active service as Captain and Flight Commander. He was a nephew of the late Admiral Stuart, R.N. of Ballyhivistock, Dervock. It was while on duty flying behind enemy lines in the area around Vimy Ridge that he was shot down and killed. He has no known grave and is commemorated on the Arras Flying Memorial.

148821 PRIVATE JOSEPH DEMPSEY
78th Bn Canadian Inf (Manitoba Regt)
K.I.A. 19-4-17
Aged 35

Born   Aghadowey
Lived
Enlisted   Winnipeg, Canada.

Joseph Dempsey was born at Drumail, Aghadowey, on 7th May 1881, the son of William and Sara Dempsey. Although on first sight this appears to be outside the scope of the Ballymoney Borough Council he is related to both the present Chief Executive and to Alderman Harry Connolly. It was Alderman Connolly who first brought to my attention the fact that his mother had lost two uncles during the First World War, men that he, sadly, knew nothing about. This was where the Chief Executive, John Dempsey, came into the picture with his Family Tree, which clearly showed the family connection and the link to Harry Connolly.

Joseph Dempsey had as a young man emigrated to Canada and settled close to Winnipeg, where he worked as a carpenter. He was not married.

He enlisted on the 2nd of July 1915 at Winnipeg and is described as being five feet seven and a half inches tall, with a dark complexion, hazel eyes and black hair. He named his brother, James, as being his next of kin. Joseph embarked at Halifax on the 20th of May 1916 and arrived at Liverpool ten days later. On the 12th of August 1916 they left Southampton for Le Havre, arriving the next day. Nothing appears on his record until he is reported wounded on 13th April 1917 and admitted to hospital at Boulogne. Three days later he is reported as being dangerously ill but died of his wounds another three days afterwards on the 19th. He is buried in Boulogne Eastern Cemetery outside the town.

The other uncle of Harry's mother, this one named McKillop, has been more difficult to identify, and sadly I have been unable to find him. Until more information becomes available nothing more can be done and this one may never be found.

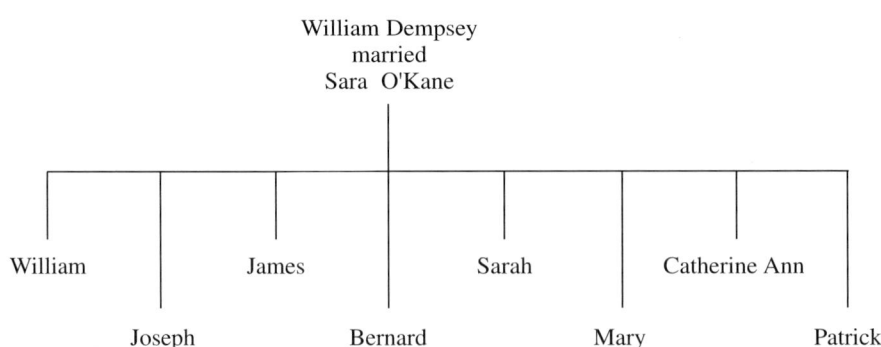

17849 PRIVATE THOMAS ROBINSON
9th Bn Royal Inniskilling Fusiliers
K.I.A. 19-4-17
Aged 24
Interred in Dranoutre Military Cemetery, Belgium. Plot 2, Row H, Grave 2.

Born   Connswater.
Lived   Ballymoney.
Enlisted   Belfast.
Commemorated in Trinity Presbyterian Church.

Thomas Robinson was brought up by Mrs Getty of the Roddenfoot, and after leaving school in Ballymoney, was employed by Mr Todd, of Main Street. He enlisted in Belfast and did his training at Finner Camp in Co.Donegal. When this was completed he was taken to England to finish his training there, and then across to France in time for the Battle of the Somme. This battle was planned to take pressure off the French Armies at Verdun and to divert German troops further north. The area behind the British front lines was crowded with troops preparing for an attack. The weather had turned wet and the battle had to be postponed for two days but the date was set for 1st July. As the battalion moved forward, they were shielded at first by a dip in the ground but as they emerged from this shelter they were mowed down by machine-guns trained on the gaps in the German wire. Thomas was injured as he made his way across No Man's Land. He was hit in the jaw by a bullet, which passed through his tongue and emerged from his neck. He was taken to a dressing station behind the lines and from there he went to a hospital for treatment. By the time he had recovered from this the Battle of the Somme was over. He was home on leave shortly after Christmas of 1916 and during his time on leave he got married. He had only returned to the front about a month when he was killed. The 9th battalion were involved in trench

repair work on the morning of 19th April at Harlettes. It was during this work that Thomas was killed, probably by a sniper. His wife continued to live in Belfast.

Dranoutre Cemetery was used for the burial of a man who faced the firing squad here. Fred Broadrick was found guilty on a charge of desertion and shot on 1st August 1917. He is buried in Plot 2, Row J, Grave 24.

Cemetery location information.

Dranoutre Military Cemetery is 11.5 kilometres south of Ypres town centre, on a road leading from the N 375

On passing through the village of Dikkebus, the road continues for 6 kilometres to Loker. Continue through Loker for 2 kilometres to Dranoutre. 50 metres before Dranoutre, turn right into a semi residential area. The Cemetery is another 50 metres on the left.

Norfolk Cemetery

400738 PRIVATE HUGH HAMILL
4th Bn Canadian Mounted Rifles.
D.O.W. 22-4-17
Aged 24
Interred in Quatre-Vents Military Cemetery. Plot 1, Row C, Grave 11.

Born   Belfast.
Lived   Ballinagarvey.
Enlisted Canada.
Son of Mrs. Mary Ann Hamill
Commemorated in Drumreagh Presbyterian Church.

According to his records Hugh Hamill was born in Belfast on 26th August 1892 but the family lived at Ballinagarvey, Bendooragh. His father was William J. Hamill and his mother Mary Ann. A few years after he left school he emigrated to Canada where he settled in London, Ontario, and it was here that he enlisted on 5th March 1915. He was a tall young man at six feet one with a medium complexion, blue eyes and brown hair. After a lengthy training period in Canada he sailed for England on S.S.Lapland, arriving on 26th March 1916. He was based at West Sandling where he went absent without leave and forfeited eight days pay for his trouble. On 5th June he was transferred to the 4th Canadian Mounted Rifles and sailed for France the following day. On 21st September 1916 he was admitted to hospital at Wimereux where he stayed for a week. He was then moved to the convalescent hospital at Boulogne, where he spent another month, being discharged on 25th October. Then on 15th March 1917 he again reported sick to No13 Canadian Field Ambulance and was discharged after treatment a week later. Exactly a month later he was again admitted to No13 C.F.A. This time it was more serious. He was very badly wounded and later that day, in spite of all that could be done for him, he died of his wounds. He had been involved in the very heavy fighting for Vimy Ridge.

Vimy is where the Canadian National Monument now stands in memory of the thousands of Canadian soldiers who lost their lives in the First World War. He is buried in Quatre Vents Military Cemetery and it is in this same cemetery that four men, all held on charges of desertion, faced the firing squad, between June and December 1916, are buried.

Estree-Cauchy is a village and commune 16 kilometres north west of Arras on the old Roman road to Therouanne, now part of the main road from Arras through Therouanne to Boulogne.

Les Quatre-Vents is a hamlet about 2 kilometres south east of Estre-Cauchy. The cemetery is found just north of the junction of the main road (D341) and the road from Aubigny-en-Artoisto Servins (D57).

Quatre-Vents Military Cemetery

18194 PRIVATE THOMAS CONAGHY
1st Bn Royal Inniskilling Fusiliers
K.I.A. 23-4-17
Aged 32
No Known Grave. Commemorated on the Arras Memorial. Bay 6.

Born
Lived
Enlisted   Ballymoney.

Judging by Thomas's age he was probably a regular soldier at the time war was declared. At any rate he sailed with his battalion for Gallipoli and after an extremely difficult landing, when they were fired upon from all angles, he eventually managed to get to comparative safety under a cliff at the upper edge of the beach. Here they were forced to stay until darkness fell. When they did manage to get to a safer place and get dug in it was almost daylight again. After the campaign in Gallipoli was over they were evacuated and brought back to Marseilles and the long train journey up to the Western Front. They were then stationed at Mailly-Maillet, close to the area of the Battle of the Somme. The 29th Division were to attack Beaumont Hamel on the 1st of July and Thomas was again very lucky to survive this day of high casualties. After this they were moved south to the area around Guillemont and desperate fighting in flat, open country, with no cover whatever.

By April 1917 the 1st battalion had been moved from Guillemont to Arras. They were still with the 29th Division. On the 23rd they were involved in a battalion advance and it was in this advance that Thomas was killed. He has no known grave and is commemorated on the Arras Memorial.

Cemetery location information.

The Arras Memorial is in the Faubourg-d'Amiens Cemetery, which is in the Boulevard du General de Gaulle in the western part of the town of Arras, near the Citadel, approximately two kilometres due west of the railway station.

The memorial commemorates over 35,000 casualties of the British, New Zealand and South African forces who died between Spring 1916 and 7th August 1918, excluding casualties of the battle of Cambrai in 1917, and who have no known grave.

640382 FARRIER SGT JOHN RANKIN
152nd Bde Royal Field Artillery
D.O.W. 25-4-17
Aged 43
Interred in Haute-Avesnes British Cemetery. Row D, Grave 8.

Born   Dervock
Lived   Port Glasgow
Enlisted
Son of James and Mary Rankin of Dervock. Husband of Mrs Rankin of 11, Argylle St, Port Glasgow.

John Rankin was born in Dervock, a village a few miles north east of the town of Ballymoney in 1874. After leaving school he went to work in Scotland where work was more plentiful and eventually settled there.

At the time he enlisted he was living with his wife in Port Glasgow. At 43 years of age he was a lot older than the average soldier but had a great deal of experience of working with horses on the large farms in North Aryshire and Lanarkshire and this was to be his job in the army. No-one that I have spoken to now remembers anything about the Rankin family living in Dervock and an advertisement placed in the Greenock Telegraph in an effort to find the Scottish connection has not produced anything either. It would appear that the family has died out.

John was injured in the fierce fighting that took place for the capture of Vimy Ridge just a short distance north of Arras. He was removed to a Dressing Station a few miles to the west of Arras close to Haute-Avesnes but in spite of all that could be done, died later that day. He is buried in the nearby cemetery.

Haute-Avesnes is a village 9 kilometres west of Arras on the south side of the Arras-St.Pol road. The cemetery is north of the village on the road leading to Habarcq.

5444 SAPPER JOHN WALLACE
1st Australian Tunnelling Coy
K.I.A. 25-4-17
Aged 45
Interred in Railway Dugouts Burial Ground, Belgium. Plot 4, Row C, Grave 15.

Born   Leitrim, Ballymoney.
Australian Infantry.
Lived   Charleville, Queensland.
Enlisted Charleville, Queensland
Third son of the late James Wallace, of Leitrim, Ballymoney.
Commemorated in Bushvale Presbyterian Church.

The Wallace family lived at the Leitrim, close to Stranocum. They worshipped in Bushvale Presbyterian Church where John is commemorated on the Roll of Honour.

John Wallace, as a young man, had worked on the railways and had been a railway tunneller. He was five feet nine inches tall, with a florid complexion, grey eyes and sandy hair, and enlisted on 20th March 1916 at almost forty-four years of age.

He had emigrated to Australia and lived in Charleville, Queensland. He was single. His eldest brother, Richard, had also emigrated to Australia and lived at West Guildford, Western Australia. Another brother, Thomas, remained at home. The troops embarked at Melbourne on 30th September 1916 on "A23 Suffolk" and landed at Plymouth on 2nd December. On New Years Day they left Folkestone for France, arriving at Etaples the next day. They were attached to the 1st Anzac Entrenching battalion in the field on 12th January and joined the 1st Tunnelling Co on the 27th. They were taken to Ypres, and it was here, just south of Ypres, that John Wallace was killed on 25th April 1917.

Railway Dugouts Burial Ground, Belgium

624781 PRIVATE JAMES ALEXANDER BLEAKLEY
10th Bn Canadian Infantry
K.I.A. 28-4-17
Aged 35
No Known Grave. Commemorated on the Vimy Memorial

Born   Seacon.
Lived
Enlisted   Vegreville, Alberta, Canada.
5th son of R.J. and Mrs. Bleakley.

James Bleakley was the fifth son of Robert John and Mrs Bleakly of Seacon, Ballymoney. He was born at Seacon on 22nd March 1882. After leaving the local school he attended college and became a teacher and was principal of Cushybracken and Tardree national schools near Ballymena. A few years later he emigrated to Canada where he was appointed principal of a school there under the Government and held the position of Secretary and Treasurer of Two Hills school. He was five feet eight inches tall with a dark complexion, brown eyes and black hair. He had been married and at some stage prior to enlisting his wife had died. James enlisted on 11th February 1916, at Vegreville, Alberta, and is described on his attestation papers as a merchant. After intensive training he embarked at Halifax on the 3rd of October 1916 on the S.S. California and disembarked at Liverpool on the 13th.

He was then transferred from the 151st Overseas Bn to the 9th Reserve battalion and then in November was transferred again to the 10th Overseas Bn. Three days later, on the 15th November 1916 he arrived in France. On 17th February 1917 he was attached to a Canadian Pioneer Company, the 1st Canadian Entrenching Battalion and joined them in the field on 13th April 1917. The battle for Vimy Ridge was at it's height and on the 28th of April, James was killed in action. He has no known grave and is commemorated on the Vimy Memorial.

422453 PRIVATE DAVID CARSON FERRIS
8th Bn Manitoba Regt originally 44th Bn C.E.F.
K.I.A. 28-4-17
Aged 26
Interred in Orchard Dump Military Cemetery. Plot 9, Row J, Grave 2.

Born   Dirraw, Finvoy.
Lived   Winnipeg, Canada.
Enlisted Winnipeg, Canada.
Commemorated in Finvoy Presbyterian Church.

David Carson Ferris was born at Dirraw, Finvoy, on 7th April 1891. As a young man he emigrated to Canada, settling in Winnipeg. On 17th December when he was 23 years of age, he enlisted in the 44th Battalion Canadian Expeditionary Force. He was a barber in civilian life. At five feet four inches he wasn't tall but had a fresh complexion with blue eyes and dark brown hair. By June 1915 he was back in England and left Shorncliffe for France on 11th June 1915. Just five weeks later, on 16th July he was transferred to the 8th Battalion Manitoba Regiment and by 22nd July he was serving with them. The following year, on 30th May, he was granted seven days leave. Then on 16th June 1916 he was admitted to Southern General Hospital, Bristol, and immediately transferred to the Canadian Casualty Assembly Centre at Folkestone. He was seriously injured with bullet wounds to the left shoulder and head. He was a patient in the Canadian Command Hospital in Wokingham for five weeks and then on 27th July he was transferred to the Canadian Convalescent Hospital at Woodcote Park, Epsom.

By the middle of August 1916 he was well enough to be discharged from hospital but it was November before he was able to be returned to his unit. He joined them on 21st November and was killed in action on 28th April 1917 aged 26.

He had a twin brother, William. These two were identical twins and even their teacher at Carrowreagh, where they went to school could

Orchard Dump Military Cemetery

not tell them apart. She suggested that their mother should tie different coloured ribbons on them so that she would know which was which. It didn't work either as the boys often swapped ribbons on the way to school. On many occasions they signed each others homework and this caused more confusion. Eventually, after leaving school, both boys emigrated to Canada, where David enlisted. He was killed in the fierce fighting around Vimy Ridge and is buried in Orchard Dump Cemetery close to where he fell. As a young man, before he emigrated to Canada, he had a great interest in horse ploughing, and competed regularly in the matches around Ballymoney.

D.C. Ferris twin brother William

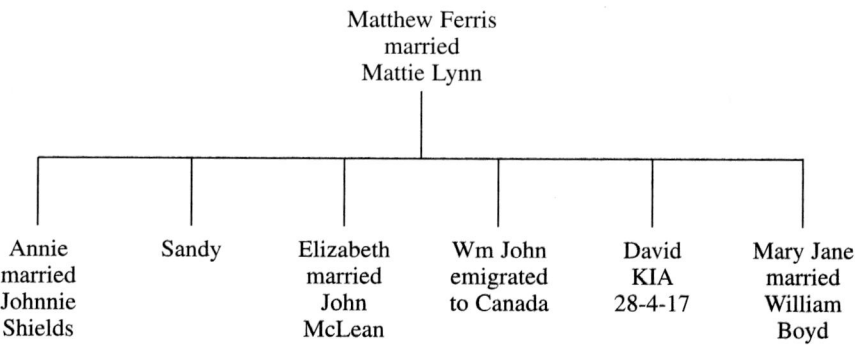

Matthew Ferris married Mattie Lynn

- Annie married Johnnie Shields
- Sandy
- Elizabeth married John McLean
- Wm John emigrated to Canada
- David KIA 28-4-17
- Mary Jane married William Boyd

40615 PRIVATE JOHN HAYES
6th Bn. King's Own Scottish Borderers. Formerly 4122 H.L.I.
K.I.A. 3-5-17
No Known Grave. Commemorated on the Arras Memorial, Bay 6.

Born   Finvoy.
Lived   Glasgow.
Enlisted   Glasgow.

John Hayes was born at Finvoy and spent much of his early life there. As a young man he moved to Scotland in search of work and when war was declared he enlisted into the Highland Light Infantry. Some time later he transferred to the 6th battalion of the King's Own Scottish Borderers, and went with them to France. In April 1917 the 6th battalion were training at Hermaville, west of Arras, but better conditions were found to be at Penin, so they were moved there. Towards the end of April they were moved forward again to relieve the 13th K.R.R. in the trenches east of Arras, and near to the village of Gavrelle. This was on the 29th of April.

On the 3rd of May they were hurriedly ordered to attack at 3.45am. They were hustled into this night attack (for it was dark, though dry) on the unreconnoitred slopes of Greenland hill.

When dawn came there was no trace of three companies of the K.O.S.B. The enemy had not been taken by surprise. What seems to have happened is that the 6th K.O.S.B. according to instructions, penetrated further and further into German territory, until the Germans, coming in from both flanks, got between them and the British lines. In spite of valiant attempts by the British to recover the situation with a desperate barrage laid down on the interposing Germans and a gallant effort by 150 men of the 12th R.S. only about fifty men of the 6th ever returned through the zone of fire under cover of darkness. It was during this attack that John Hayes was killed. He has no known grave and is commemorated on the Arras Memorial.

Arras Cemetery and Memorial Wall

117034 GUNNER ROBERT O'BRIEN
Royal Garrison Artillery 261st Siege Battery
K.I.A. 3-5-17
Interred in Tilloy British Cemetery, Plot 1, Row F, Grave 15.

Born   Dervock.
Lived   Dervock
Enlisted
Son of Thomas and Sarah Ann O'Brien, of Church St, Dervock.
Commemorated in Derrykeighan Parish Church.

Robert O'Brien was born in Dervock, a village about four miles from Ballymoney. Thomas and Sarah Ann O'Brien lived in Church Street and there was four of a family, three boys and one girl. Two of the boys, William and Robert, enlisted into the armed forces soon after war was declared and both of them were killed. William in September 1915 and Robert in May 1917. Robert was in the Royal Artillery and as such was not as much involved in the front line, being most of the time a bit further back with the big guns. It was still very dangerous work as the German artillery could reach them with ease. The weather had been very warm for the time of the year and much water was needed for both men and horses. In a letter to Robert's wife, 2nd Lieutenant Hugo M. Harvey tells of Robert being killed. He wrote, "Robert had been at the gun all morning, and walked over to the water cart to get some water, when a heavy shell unexpectedly hit the water cart, and Robert was killed instantly." This happened in the region just to the south of Arras and it is here that Robert is buried in Tilloy British Cemetery, Plot 1, Row F, Grave 15.

Cemetery location information.

Tilloy-les-Mofflaines is a village 3 kilometres south-east of Arras, on the south side of the main road to Cambrai. Tilloy British Cemetery is south-east of the village on the north-east side of the road to Wancourt, the D 37.

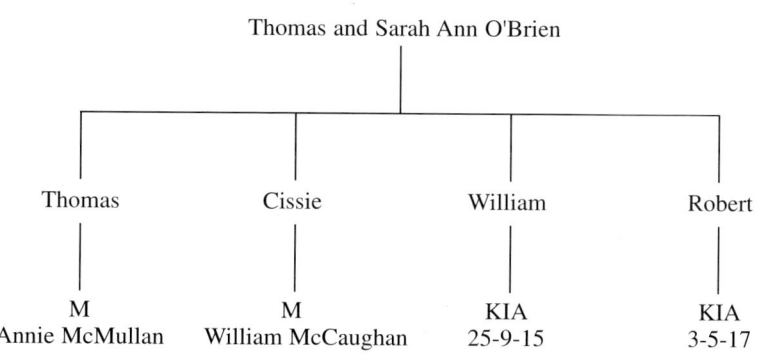

2842 PRIVATE ROBERT SHANNON
4th Bn Australian Infantry
K.I.A. 6-5-17
Aged 36
No Known Grave. Commemorated on the Villers-Bretonneux Memorial.

Lived   Narrabri, New South Wales.
Enlisted   Narrabri, New South Wales.
Commemorated in Killagan Parish Church, Cloughmills.
Son of Samuel and Agnes Shannon, of Montalto, Newtown Crommelin.

The family worshipped in Killagan Parish Church at Cloughmills and it is there that Robert is commemorated on the Roll of Honour. Robert Shannon had been a shop assistant in Turner's of Cloughmills for five years before he emigrated to Australia.

I wonder if it is a co-incidence that one of the Turner boys also emigrated to Australia or did they go together. He was five feet six inches tall, with a dark complexion, blue eyes and dark brown hair. His sister, Sarah, was also living in Australia at this time. He enlisted at Narrabri on 4th August 1915, and embarked at Sydney on Transport A14 "Euripides" on 2nd November. On arrival at Tel-el-Kabir, Robert was taken to hospital suffering from mumps. After recovering from this he embarked at Alexandria on H.T. "Simla" on 23rd March, arriving at Marseilles on the 30th. On 24th July 1916, Robert was very seriously wounded with bullet wounds to the head and left foot. He was taken to 1st Australian Field Ambulance.

Then on to 44th Casualty Clearing Station and immediately transferred to No 19 Ambulance Train. By the 26th of July he had arrived at hospital at Rouen. After three days here he was moved to Le Havre and taken on board the H.S. "Marami" and to hospital in Newport, Monmouthshire. He arrived there on the 30th of July and was there until the 17th October, when he was moved to Wandsworth where he spent another week before being granted two weeks leave. On 13th December he embarked on S.S. "Arundel" at Folkestone and landed next day at Etaples and on 20th December re-joined the 4th battalion.

He was killed in action on 6th May 1917 and a report states that he was buried in the vicinity of Bullecourt. There is now no known grave and he is commemorated on the Villers-Brettoneux Memorial. Bullecourt is a village between Arras and Bapaume, and is on the D 956 from Bapaume.

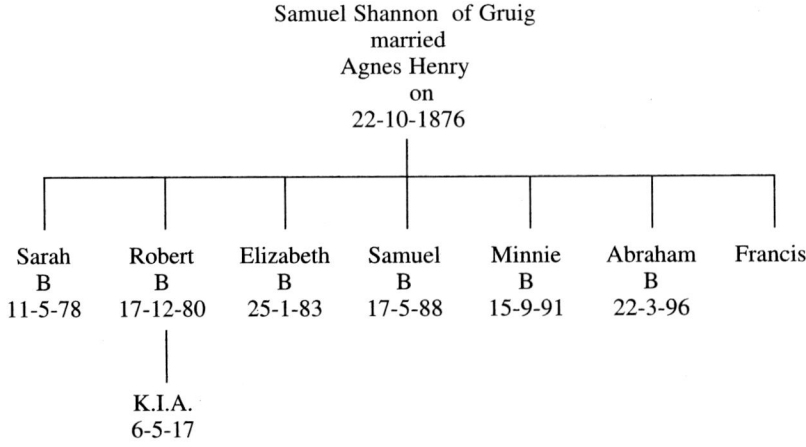

Samuel Shannon of Gruig
married
Agnes Henry
on
22-10-1876

Sarah	Robert	Elizabeth	Samuel	Minnie	Abraham	Francis
B	B	B	B	B	B	
11-5-78	17-12-80	25-1-83	17-5-88	15-9-91	22-3-96	
	K.I.A. 6-5-17					

5925 SERGEANT PETER KANE
12th Bn Royal Irish Rifles
K.I.A. 18-5-17
Aged 28
Interred in Bailleul Communal Cemetery, France. Plot 3, Row B, Grave 151.

Born   Lisnagunagh.
Lived   Stranocum.
Enlisted Ballymoney
Son of Peter Kane.
Husband of Caroline Kane of Stranocum
Commemorated in Dunseverick Parish Church
Commemorated in Drumtullagh Parish Church.

Peter Kane was born at Lisnagunagh on 24th February 1890. We don't know much about his early life but he had attended school in Lisnagunagh. He married Caroline Hutchinson and moved to the Stranocum area to live and is commemorated on the Stranocum War Memorial. His son, Walter, had the garage in Mosside for many years. On the outbreak of war with Germany, Peter enlisted at Ballymoney into the 12th battalion, Royal Irish Rifles. His early training took place at Newtownards and it was there that he was promoted Sergeant. He was then moved to Seaford on the south coast of England for further training and by May of 1916 the battalion was considered ready to go to France. When they arrived in France they were taken to the small French village of Martinsart. Planning for the Battle of the Somme was at an advanced stage and Martinsart was very close to the front line. They were housed in tents. The battle was planned for 28th June, but a change in the weather from lovely warm sunshine to an absolute downpour changed all that and the date was set for 1st July.

At 7.30am on the 1st of July the Battalion went over the top at Hamel on the north bank of the River Ancre. The high ground on both sides of the river provided a perfect line of sight for the German machine-gun crews and the Ulstermen were just mowed down. Peter somehow got safely through this day and next morning the battalion was taken out of the line. They were taken back for rest and reinforcements to Eperlecques and a few days later moved to Kortepyp Camp, south of the village of Neuve Eglise. They were to stay in this general area for over a year. They were moved into position just to the north of here to take over the front line whenever they were needed and were mostly in the Messines -- Wytchaete area. This was a quieter time and they were mostly just in the line for short periods. It was during one of these turns in the line on 18th May that Peter was killed. He is buried along with four other Ballymoney men in Bailleul Cemetery. A story told to me by Brian McKay that Peter was killed at night while on sentry duty is probably the correct one. Peter had asked another soldier to stand in for him while he went to a nearby toilet and it was while he was there that a shell burst in the vicinity and he was killed.

8854 L. CPL. SAMUEL PATTON
1st Bn Royal Inniskilling Fusiliers.
K.I.A. 19-5-17
No Known Grave. Commemorated on the Arras Memorial, Arras, France. Bay 6.

Born   Loughguile
Lived   Ballyweaney
Enlisted Ballymoney.
Commemorated in Kilraughts Presbyterian Church.

The Patton family worshipped in Kilraughts Presbyterian Church and it is here that he is commemorated although a search of the adjoining graveyard has not turned up any information concerning the family.

Kilraughts Church lies a few miles south east of Ballymoney, in a very prosperous farming district and has a very large congregation.

The 1st battalion were at Trimulgherry, in India, when war was declared and sailed for England in early December, arriving at Avonmouth on 10th January. They went immediately to Rugby to join the 29th Division. In March 1915 they set sail for the Mediterranean, arriving at Mudros in early April. On 25th April they took part in the landing on Gallipoli and fought many gallant battles in this wild region. They were eventually evacuated from this area in January 1916 and taken to Egypt. They arrived at Marseilles in March. Samuel Patton tried to enlist on two different occasions and was turned away both times. He was determined not to be beaten and eventually managed it at the third attempt. He was a very good friend of Alex and James Huey, of Ballycraigagh, Stranocum, who were both killed in action. James in September 1915, and Alex in August 1917.

A letter still exists, written by Alex, and asking about Samuel and what has happened to him. The 1st battalion were at Arras on 19th May 1917, with the 29th Division. It was here that Samuel Patton was killed when their position was obliterated during an unsuccessful advance. He has no known grave and is commemorated on the Arras Memorial. Of the three friends mentioned above not one of them has a known grave.

48865 GUNNER JOHN BOYD
"D" Bty, 312th Bde, Royal Field Artillery
K.I.A. 26-5-17
Aged 29
Interred in H.A.C. Cemetery, France. Plot 3, Row B, Grave 26.

Born   Mosside
Lived   Knockmore, Mosside
Enlisted
Son of Patrick and Mrs. Ellen Boyd, Knockmore, Mosside.
Commemorated in Mosside Presbyterian Church.

Jack Boyd was killed when a fire started in the gun pit followed by a horrendous explosion. Fourteen men and two officers were either killed or wounded in the inferno. Jack Boyd was later buried behind the lines.

He had been home on leave for Christmas of 1916, and soon after this, in March 1917, after a very severe winter, was in hospital in France suffering from frostbite. When he had fully recovered from this, he rejoined his unit a few miles north of Bapaume and it was here that he was killed on the 26th of May. He is buried in H.A.C. Cemetery, Ecoust-St.Mein. France. His brother, Robert, served throughout the war and was demobilised in February 1919.

Another Ballymoney man, Patrick Mooney, who had been born at Dunloy, is buried in the same plot as John Boyd, in the next row back.

H.A.C. Cemetery, France

893 RIFLEMAN JOHN HANNA
12th Bn Royal Irish Rifles
K.I.A. 2-6-17
Aged 18
Interred in Pond Farm Cemetery, Belgium. Row P, Grave 18.

Born
Lived   Drumaheglis
Enlisted Ballymoney
Eldest son of the late Robert Hanna, stationmaster, and Mrs. Margaret Hanna. Hanna, of Drumaheglis, Ballymoney. Commemorated in St. James's Presbyterian Church.

John Hanna lived at Drumaheglis, a townland about five miles from Ballymoney and close to the River Bann. John appears to have been a very early recruit to the 12th Battalion. Not much is now known about the family and I have been unable to find anyone who remembers them at Drumaheglis. John enlisted into the 12th battalion at Ballymoney and did his training at Clandeboye and Newtownards.

Then in July of 1915 they were taken across to England for final training at Seaford.

John had been through the horrendous fighting on the first day of the Somme and had survived. The battalion was then taken out of the line and brought to St. Omer to be brought back up to strength. They were then sent to the area around Wulverghem in Belgium. Here they were in and out of the line on a regular basis for almost a year. By early summer plans were being made for an attack at Messines and it was in the preparations for this attack that John was killed. He was in a trench at Wulverghem with two of his mates, both Ballymoney boys, when a shell exploded beside them. They were killed instantly. Another young Ballymoney man, George Wales, was

injured in the blast, but was sufficiently shielded from it to survive. He was killed later at Cambrai. These three are buried side by side in Pond Farm Cemetery at Wulverghem, a Cemetery that I have visited on two different occasions. There is a certain amount of doubt as to whether the shell that killed them was a German shell well aimed or a British shell falling short. British shells had a habit of falling short and even not going off at all. Many unexploded shells to this day are ploughed from the French and Belgian soil and it is a common sight to see a pile of them lying at the roadside waiting to be destroyed by the French or Belgian army.

Cemetery location information.

Pond Farm Cemetery is located 9.5 kilometres south-west of Ypres on a road leading from the Kemmelseweg N331. Leave Ypres through the Lille Gate and straight on towards Armentieres (N365). 900 metres after the crossroads is the right hand turning on to the Kemmelseweg. (Made prominent by a railway level crossing). One kilometre after passing the village of Kemmel lies the left turn on to the Gremmerslinde. One kilometre along this turn right on to Vrooilandstraat. 800 metres along the cemetery is on the right. Visitors should note the 400 metres grassed access path is not suitable for vehicles.

903 L. CPL. JAMES McCOUBREY
12th Bn Royal Irish Rifles
K.I.A. 2-6-17
Aged 29
Interred in Pond Farm Cemetery, Belgium. Row P, Grave 19.

Born   Ballymoney
Lived   Ballymoney.
Enlisted   Belfast.
Husband of Mrs. Frances McCoubrey, of Market St, Ballymoney.
Commemorated in Ballymoney Parish Church.

James McCoubrey was killed along with two other Ballymoney men, John Hanna, and William Wade, on the morning of 2nd June 1917. All three were standing close together when the shell burst among them.

It has never been established whether it was a German shell perfectly aimed or a British shell falling short. George Wales was injured by the blast but was sufficiently shielded from it to survive although he too was killed later in the year. Hanna, McCoubrey and Wade are all buried together in Pond Farm Cemetery in Belgium.

From a newspaper report at the time it would appear that James was a son of John McCoubrey, and a nephew of James, who owned the Manor Hotel, in Ballymoney. He was a member of L.O.L. 930.

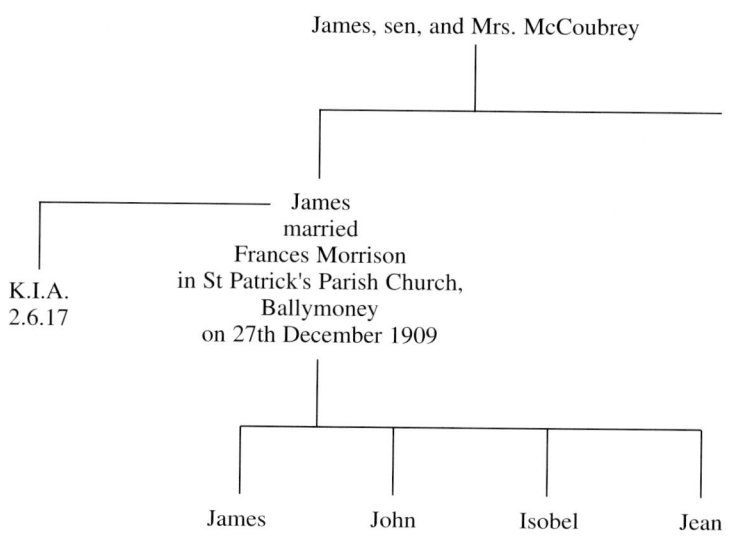

Mill Road Cemetery

1067 RIFLEMAN WILLIAM WADE
12th Bn Royal Irish Rifles
K.I.A. 2-6-17
Aged 20
Interred in Pond Farm Cemetery, Belgium. Row P, Grave 20.

Born   Edward St, Ballymoney.
Lived   Coleraine
Enlisted   Ballymoney.
Son of William and Margaret Wade of Edward St. Ballymoney.
Commemorated in Ballymoney Parish Church.

William enlisted at Ballymoney and went almost straight away to train at Clandeboye. The family lived at Edward St in the town and worshipped in St.Patrick's Parish Church where William is commemorated. As soon as his training was complete he moved to Seaford on the south coast of England. This was in July of 1915 and by the following October they had landed in France. After more training, this time in trenches which more or less resembled the trenches at the Somme, they were moved to the small French village of Martinsart. This was close to what we now know as the area of the Battle of the Somme. Plans were that the British would make an attack to draw the German armies away from Verdun and it was to be at the Somme. The 12th battalion were to attack on the north bank of the River Ancre from the little village of Hamel. The ground here is low lying and is overlooked by the high ground south of the river at St.Pierre-Divion. On the morning of the 1st of July the village of St.Pierre-Divion was not directly attacked and the machine guns at this village had a clear line of sight on the men as they advanced across the river. Many of the men were killed or badly wounded and the battalion was withdrawn next day. William survived this tragic day. They were moved back to the training grounds at St.Omer for a few days where they were brought back up to strength and then moved to Belgium. The Wulverghem area was to be their base for the next year and they were in and out of the line on numerous occasions.

By early summer plans were being finalised for an attack on the Messines Ridge. It was in the final days before the start of the Battle of Messines that William Wade was killed at Wulverghem by an exploding shell. There is doubt as to whether it was a well placed German shell or a British shell falling short. Anyhow, William and two of his pals, James McCoubrey, and John Hanna were killed instantly. Another Ballymoney man, George Wales was injured in the blast, but had been sufficiently shielded from it to survive. George was killed at the Battle of Cambrai the following November.

The build-up to the Battle of Messines was in full swing and the shelling was continuous. There were to be five days of preliminary bombardment on the German lines aimed at disorganising his defences rather than the destruction of his trench systems and it was at the beginning of this bombardment that William was killed. All three are buried side by side in Pond Farm Cemetery at Wulverghem.

Pond Farm Cemetery

4854 RIFLEMAN ROBERT COLVIN
12th Bn Royal Irish Rifles
K.I.A. 7-6-17
Aged 18
Interred in Lone Tree Cemetery, Belgium. Plot 1, Row D, Grave 12.

Born   Ballymoney
Lived   Ballymoney
Enlisted   Newtownards
Commemorated in Drumreagh Presbyterian Church.
Son of Robert and Jeannie Colvin (nee Douglas).

Robert Colvin must have been one of the youngest of the Ballymoney men to be killed. At only 18 years of age when he was killed in 1917 he would surely not have been allowed to enlist at the very beginning. He must have been a later volunteer.

Most of the graves in Lone Tree Cemetery are of men who fell on the first day of the Battle of Messines. Two Ballymoney men are buried here, Robert Colvin and Thomas Logan. These two would have known each other very well although Thomas was a good bit older than Robert, they had lived close to each other, one at Ballybrakes, the other near Drumreagh. Robert's Father and Mother were married in Drumreagh Presbyterian Church on 18th February 1898.

There appears to be no connection of Robert Colvin left in the Drumreagh district. Many enquiries made in the area have yielded nothing and it appears that the family have died out.

It was in this area that John Meeke, of Benvarden, was responsible for seeing that the mines were properly blown.

Cemetery location information

Lone Tree Cemetery (Spanbroekmolen) is located 8.5 kilometres south of Ypres town centre on a road leading from the Rijselseweg N 365, which connects Ypres to Wijtschaete and on to Armentieres. From Ypres town centre the Rijselsestraat runs from the market square, through the Lille Gate and directly over the cross roads with the Ypres ring road. The road name then changes to the Rijselseweg.

On reaching the village of Wijtschaete the first right hand turning leads on to Hospicestraat which leads on to the village square. The Kemmelstraat leads from the village square towards the cemetery. Two kilometres along the Kemmelstraat lies the left hand turning on to Kruisstraat.

The cemetery lies one kilometre along the Kruisstraat on the right hand side of the road.

Visitors to this site should note a 100 metre grassed access path leading to this cemetery.

Lone Tree Cemetery was begun in June 1917, after the explosions, and holds 88 graves, 60 of which are of men of the 36th Ulster Div. Two Ballymoney men are buried here.

Robert Colvin and Thomas Logan, whilst Hugh Rock is buried in nearby Spanbroekmolen Cemetery. Many of the Ulstermen were killed by falling debris as they waited in No Man's Land for the mines to explode and this is probably what happened to Robert and Thomas. Hugh Rock was killed the following day.

I visited Lone Tree Cemetery in July 1990 although at that time I did not know about the two Ballymoney men buried there.

1231 L. CPL. THOMAS LOGAN
9th Bn Royal Irish Rifles
K.I.A. 7-6-17
Interred in Lone Tree Cemetery, Belgium. Plot 2, Row C, Grave 9.

Born   Ballymoney
Lived   Ballybrakes
Enlisted Ballymoney
Commemorated in Trinity Presbyterian Church.
Left a wife and eight children.

As a young man after leaving school in Ballymoney, Thomas worked in Baxter's shop. The Logan family worshipped in Trinity Presbyterian Church in Ballymoney and it is there that Thomas is commemorated. When he enlisted and went to war he left behind a wife and eight young children. No contact has been made with the family and it is unusual that a family of that size would have died out. They lived on the outskirts of Ballymoney, in the townland of Ballybrakes. Thomas enlisted at Ballymoney very early in the war and did much of his training at Ballykinlar. When he had completed his training there he was moved to Seaford on the south coast of England and then went to France in October of 1915. Later when plans were being made for the Battle of the Somme he was transferred to the area around Martinsart. Here more training took place in trenches similar to those they would use at the Somme. Thomas came through the first day on the Somme safely and was then taken out of the battle area and sent to St Omer and from there to the area around Wulverghem in Belgium. He spent the last eleven months of his life in this region being regularly in and out of the front line. In the early summer of 1917 plans were being made for an offensive at Messines in order to have the high ground at Messines as a vantage point. Much planning had gone into this and a number of mines had been dug and filled with high explosive. A local man, John Meeke, of Benvarden, was one of those in charge of the mines, and had responsibility for seeing that they were blown as planned. It was during this day that John Meeke won the Military Medal for his fearless attention to the injured Major Redmond. The attack started at 3.10am and it was during this early attack that Thomas was killed. He is buried in Lone Tree Cemetery beside the Pool of Peace at Spanbroekmolen. Nearly all of the graves in this cemetery are of men who fell on the first day of the Battle of Messines, 7th June 1917. The cemetery lies in what was formerly, No Man's Land, next to the German line that ran through the farm and along the edge of the Pool of Peace.

Lone Tree Cemetery, Belgium

Some of the men buried here were killed by fall-out from the Spanbroekmolen mine which exploded fifteen seconds late, by which time the 8th Royal Irish Rifles were already in No Man's Land. Of the 88 British burials in the cemetery, sixty are Royal Irish Rifles. The 36th (Ulster) Division had been rebuilt from it's near annihilation on the first day of the Battle of the Somme nearly twelve months before and now contained nine battalions of Royal Irish Rifles who attacked in an easterly direction through the site of this cemetery, making rapid progress and taking the Wijtschaete- Messines road. Another young Ballymoney man, Robert Colvin, was killed in this same attack and is buried here too. Hugh Rock, of Cloughmills, was killed the next day and is buried in Spanbroekmolen Cemetery a short distance away.

Cemetery location information.

Lone Tree Cemetery, (Spanbroekmolen) is 8.5 kilometres south of Ypres. On reaching Wijtschaete the first right hand turning leads on to Hospicestraat which leads on to the village square. Take the Kemmelstraat for 2 kilometres and turn left into Kruistraat. The cemetery lies 1 kilometre along on the right. There is a 100 metre grassed access path to the cemetery.

1647 RIFLEMAN SAMUEL WALLACE ANDERSON
9th Bn Royal Irish Rifles
D.O.W. 8-6-17
Aged 20
Interred in Bailleul Communal Cemetery Extension. Plot 3, Row R, Grave 266.

Born   Drumdollagh.
Lived   Drumdollagh
Enlisted Ballymoney.
Commemorated in Kilraughts Presbyterian Church.
Son of James and Rachael Anderson

Samuel Anderson was born at Drumdollagh, the son of James and Rachael Anderson. By the time he was a young man, war had been declared against Germany and an opportunity to see the world had presented itself. Samuel enlisted into the 9th battalion of the Royal Irish Rifles. Much of his early training took place at Ballykinlar and it was from here that he eventually left for England. After finishing his training at Seaford, on the south coast of England, he was taken to France and the small villages of Martinsart and Mesnil. Here much work still had to be done and they were kept busy doing all sorts of things. Their first big attack, the Battle of the Somme, was only a few days away. Samuel attacked from Thiepval wood across towards where the Ulster Tower now stands. German machine guns were used to great effect and the Ulster boys were just mowed down.

Samuel survived this attack and his battalion was taken out of the line next day. They were moved to the vast training area at St. Omer for rest and re-organisation. After a time spent training new troops, the battalion was moved to Belgium and the area around Wulverghem. They were in and out of the line on numerous occasions during the next year and this gained valuable experience for the attack at Messines. Samuel's battalion was in the front line at Messines and as far as can be

ascertained it was here that Samuel was wounded. He was taken back to the dressing station at Bailleul but the doctors were unable to save him and he died next day. He is buried in Bailleul Cemetery. Four other Ballymoney men are buried here. Peter Kane of Stranocum, John Magill, John Caldwell of Rasharkin and John Porteus of Ballymoney.

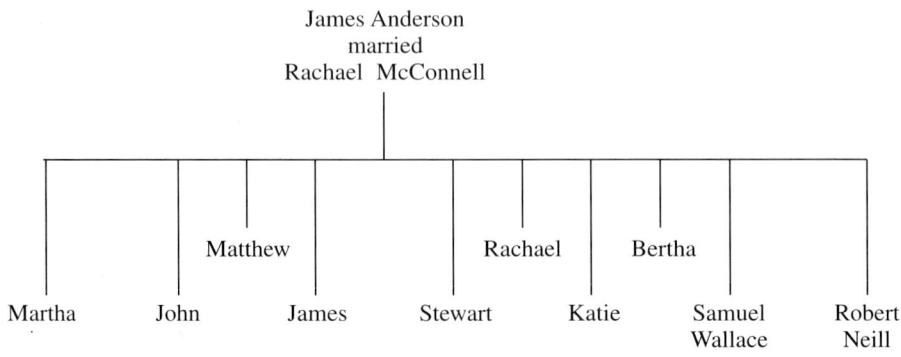

1289 RIFLEMAN HUGH ROCK
11th Bn Royal Irish Rifles
K.I.A. 8-6-17
Aged 22
Interred in Spanbroekmolen British Cemetery, Belgium. Row A, Grave 9.

Born   Carabeg, Cloughmills.
Lived   Carabeg, Cloughmills.
Enlisted Ballymoney.
Son of George and Agnes Rock, of Ballylig.
Commemorated in Ballyweaney Presbyterian Church.

Soon after Hugh left school he got a job in Cloughmills as a postman. But like many of the young men of the time the lure of seeing a bit of the World was too much, and the chance to go to war in France or Belgium was too good to miss. So he went to Ballymoney to enlist. We do not know his Mother's reaction but we can be pretty sure she was distressed. His sister's reaction was that when Hugh came home again he would need a job, and so she took on the job of postman until Hugh would be able to return. In those days the postman wasn't even allowed a bicycle and the mail had to be delivered in all weathers and on foot. It was a tough job for a young girl not long left school and many a time she came home soaked to the skin.

But she stuck to her task. As time went on news began to filter home and eventually Hugh was to get leave. Hugh's mate, John Finlay, was coming home on leave and Hugh sent his watch, which had broken, home with him so that his Mother could have it repaired and he would get it the following week when it was his turn to be on leave.

Spanbroekmolen Cemetery, Belgium

Spanbroekmolen Cemetery, Belgium

IN LOVING MEMORY

OF OUR DEAR SON,

1289 RFM HUGH MORRISON ROCK,

R.I.R.,

CARAREG, CLOUGHMILLS,

Killed in Action on the 8th June, 1917.

AGED 22 YEARS.

For King and Country well he stood,
   Unknown to cowards' fears,
At Messines he shed his blood
   With the Ulster Volunteers.

May the heavenly winds blow softly
   O'er that sweet and hallowed spot;
Though the seas divide his grave from us,
   He will never be forgot.

Hard, hard was the blow, the shock severe,
   To part with one we loved so dear.
We loved him in life; He is dear to us still,
   But in grief we must bow to God's holy will

During the week that John Finlay was home the telegram arrived to say that Hugh had been killed. A short time later a letter arrived to break the news of what had happened, to his parents. Hugh was a brave young man and he had been given the job of carrying dispatches for his Officers. It was while he was carrying a dispatch from one trench to another that he was killed by a German sniper. This had been Hugh's job the previous day, when the Battle of Messines Ridge had been at it's height, and messages just had to be got backwards and forwards and very often a runner was the only way. Hugh had carried on as usual. It was a dangerous task and eventually it cost him his life. He is buried close to where he fell, in Spanbroekmolen Cemetery. Two other Ballymoney men, Robert Colvin and Thomas Logan, had been killed as the Battle of Messines began the previous day and are buried close to here in Lone Tree Cemetery.

Cemetery location information

Spanbroekmolen Cemetery is 8 kilometres south of Ypres. On reaching Wijtschaete, turn right on to Hospicestraat which leads on to the village square. Take the Kemmelstraat for 1.5 kilometres, turn left on to Scheerstraat. The Cemetery lies 500 metres along the Scheerstraat on the left. There is a 200 metres grassed access path to the Cemetery.

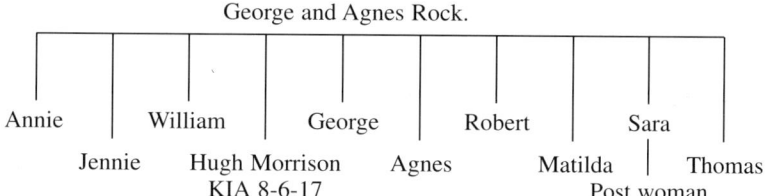

953 RIFLEMAN ROBERT CAMPBELL
12th Bn Royal Irish Rifles
K.I.A. 7-6-17
Aged 22
No known grave. Commemorated on the Menin Gate Memorial. Ypres. Panel 40.

Born   Ballymoney
Lived   Drumaheagles
Enlisted Ballymoney
Son of Samuel and Elizabeth Campbell of Ballywindeland

Robert enlisted at Ballymoney on the outbreak of hostilities when he was just nineteen years of age. After a short time spent at home he was told to report for training at Clandeboye. This lasted into the early summer months when he was transferred across the water to England. He was based at Seaford on the south coast and much of their training took place there. When the time came for them to be moved to France, it was to the small village of Martinsart that they were taken. The French Military Commanders were clamouring for a move by the British to take the pressure off the French Army at Verdun. And so plans were made for the Battle of the Somme. It was hoped that this would force the Germans to move men to the north and away from Verdun. There is no need to go into details here about the battle of the Somme. Enough to say that Robert survived the battle and was relieved the next day and taken to the vast military training area at St. Omer for the battalion to be rested and reorganised. Soon after this they were sent to Belgium to the area around Wulverghem. They were to be in this area for the next year. Here they gained vast experience through being in the front line on numerous occasions. Although no major battles were fought at this time there was always plenty of smaller skirmishes. By the summer of 1917 the British Commanders were beginning to think of an attack to try to take Messines Ridge from the enemy.

This would make a good vantage point and would be very useful in British hands. Much mining had taken place in the area and as June approached these mines were packed with explosives. Everything was ready by the 7th of June, the date set for the battle. It was a Ballymoney man who was in charge of exploding some of the mines in the Messines area. John Meeke of Benvarden, was the man detailed to the job. John survived the war, but died a short time after the war ended and is buried in an unmarked grave in Derrykeighan Old Cemetery. He had won the Military Medal. It was this attack on Messines Ridge in which Robert Campbell was killed. He has no known grave and is commemorated on the Menin Gate Memorial. His brother, David, lived at Coolderry.

Cemetery location information.

Ypres is a town in the province of West Flanders. The memorial is situated at the eastern side of the town on the road to Menin and Courtrai, and bears the names of 55,000 men who were lost without trace during the defence of the Ypres Salient in the First World War.

9470 RIFLEMAN THOMAS JOHN GAULT
2nd Bn Royal Irish Rifles
K.I.A. 18-6-17
Aged 36
No Known Grave. Commemorated on the Menin Gate Memorial, Ypres. Addenda Panel 58.

Born   Market St.
Lived   Market St.
Enlisted
Commemorated in Ballymoney Parish Church.
Son of Mrs. Nancy Gault, of Market St.

His Mother and brother were also living in Market St. in June 1917. Thomas was employed by Mr. John Kirkpatrick, of Union St, Ballymoney.

The 2nd battalion were at Tidworth when war was declared and ten days later landed at Rouen. Then in October 1915 they joined the 25th Division. Lieut Tirrell, writing to his Mother at the time stated that

> "Rifleman Gault was by my side when he was killed instantly by a piece of shell. The battalion was proceeding to the trenches at the time and German artillery caught them at the cross-roads. He was buried near Messines Ridge and his grave marked."

Heavy shelling and later fighting over the same ground probably destroyed the grave as he now has no known grave and is commemorated on the Menin Gate.

RIFLEMAN	
ARONOW H.	POST OFFICE RIFLES
CARPENTER R.	ROYAL IRISH RIFLES
EARLEY J.	THE RIFLE BRIGADE
FOLEY W. J.	11TH BN. LONDON REGIMENT
GALLERY H.F.	ROYAL IRISH RIFLES
GAULT T. J.	ROYAL IRISH RIFLES
GHEM C.E.	QUEEN VICTORIA'S RIFLES
JENNETT J.	ROYAL IRISH RIFLES
MCKISSICK T.	ROYAL IRISH RIFLES
MOLDOFSKY S.	THE RIFLE BRIGADE
PARFECT G.J.	KING'S ROYAL RIFLE CORPS
ROSE W. A.	ROYAL IRISH RIFLES
SCOTT W. J.	THE RIFLE BRIGADE
SHAW J.	ROYAL IRISH RIFLES
SMART W.J.E.	QUEEN'S WESTMINSTERS
THOMPSON E.	ROYAL IRISH RIFLES
THOMPSON T. J.	ROYAL IRISH RIFLES

PRIVATE GEORGE McNOCHER
9th Bn Scottish Rifles
D.O.W. 17-5-17
Aged 20

Born   Ballybogey
Lived
Enlisted

Official intimation has been received by Mr and Mrs George McNocher, 42, Main St, Plantation, Glasgow, and formerly of Ballybogey, that their son, Private George McNocher, died on the 17th, from wounds received in action in France. On the 7th, Mrs McNocher received a letter from an army Chaplain at a casualty clearing station stating that her son was badly wounded, and having been lying out for five days before assistance could be rendered to him, had naturally lost much strength from that cause as well as from his wounds. On the 19th May, she received a further letter from a Chaplain at the base showing that Private McNocher had been dangerously wounded in the back, stomach and legs. Everything possible had been done but in vain, by the doctors and nurses to save the gallant young life. Deceased was previously wounded on the 14th July 1916, at the Somme. He was aged 20 years and 11 months. His elder and only brother, William, has been wounded three times. Both enlisted on the outbreak of war.

Hermies Hill

7188 RIFLEMAN THOMAS TURNER
8th Bn Royal Irish Rifles
D.O.W. 20-6-17
Aged 21
Interred in Cabin Hill Cemetery, Belgium. Row A, Grave 2.

Born   Cloughmills.
Lived   Cloughmills.
Enlisted Belfast.
Son of Alexander and Rose Turner of Cloughmills.
Commemorated in Ballyweaney Presbyterian Church.

Alex and Rose Turner had a family of five, three boys and two girls. Two of the boys, Thomas and Robert were killed in the 1st World War. Herbert, the other son, died as a young man. One of the sisters married but had no family and the other never married. So the family just died out. This is a classic example of just what can happen to a family and in a number of cases did.

The family worshipped in Ballyweaney Presbyterian Church where Thomas and his brother, Robert, are commemorated on the Roll of Honour. Thomas for some reason enlisted in Belfast, joining the 8th battalion Royal Irish Rifles and did his training at Ballykinlar. They moved to Seaford on the south coast of England and then went to France in October 1915. Thomas was through the Battle of the Somme and was then moved to Belgium. Here they were close to the village of Wulverghem and were regularly in and out of the line for most of the next year.

The family owned the shop in Cloughmills which still bears their name in the middle of the main street. Thomas and Robert died within three months of each other and are buried less than five miles apart. Thomas was injured in the desperate fighting which followed the taking of Messines Ridge in June 1917. He was brought back by stretcher bearers to the dressing station beside the cemetery where he is buried but died of his injuries a short time later. Another young Cloughmills man, Robert Shannon, worked in Turner's shop for five years before emigrating to Australia. He later enlisted and was killed in action on 6th May 1917, just a few weeks before the first of the Turner boys. Robert Turner also emigrated to Australia. It would be interesting to know if they emigrated together.

Cabin Hill Cemetery is 8.5 kilometres south of Ypres. Leave Ypres through the Lille Gate and directly over the crossroads on to N 336. After 4 kilometres the road forks with N 365 towards Witschaete.

On passing through Wijtschaete, turn left on to Groenestraat towards Torreken Farm Cemetery and beyond, reaching a crossroads after 1.5 kilometres. Turn left and the Cemetery is 100 metres. There is a grassed access path to the Cemetery.

Cabin Hill Cemetery and the grave of Thomas Turner on the front row, centre.

12-586   SERGEANT JAMES ADAMS
9th Bn Royal Irish Rifles
K.I.A. 21-6-17
Aged 24
Interred in Derry House Cemetery, Wytschaete. Belgium. Plot 1. Row B, Grave 13.

Born   Mullin Hill, Co. Antrim.
Lived   Carncullagh,
Enlisted Belfast
Son of James C. and Agnes Adams, of Carncullagh.
Commemorated in Carncullagh Presbyterian Church.
Mentioned in Despatches.

The 9th battalion were raised in Belfast in September 1914 from the Belfast Volunteers and trained at Ballykinlar. In July 1915 they went to Seaford on the south coast of England where they completed their training and landed at Boulogne in October. They served with the 4th Division from November 1915 to February 1916. James Adams's father had been a blacksmith at Carncullagh and made farm implements. Before he enlisted James had worked along with his father in the business. The family worshipped in Carncullagh Presbyterian Church and it is here that James is commemorated.

In the attack at the Somme on the 1st of July, James was on the south bank of the River Ancre attacking towards the small French village of St.Pierre-Divion, a hamlet on the high ground beside the river. This attack was across a very steep hillside with no cover and machine-guns

Derry House Cemetery

positioned at St. Pierre-Divion just mowed them down like so much corn. He survived this day of tragedy and was evacuated with his battalion and moved north to Belgium where they were to stay for a long time. Much of this time was spent in and out of the line, but then in June of 1917 the Battle of Messines took place. This was a success but as the troops followed up their success two weeks later, James was killed close to Wytschaete. He is buried in Derry House Cemetery close to where he fell.

Derry House Cemetery

James Adams grave to left of tree

10695 CORPORAL JOHN McCONNELL
5th Bn Connaught Rangers
K.I.A. 21-6-17
Interred in Lahana Military Cemetery, Greece. Plot 3, Row E, Grave 2.

Born   Ballymoney
Lived   Rasharkin.
Enlisted   Glasgow.

The 5th battalion was formed in Dublin in August 1914 and trained at Kilworth with the 10th Div. By January 1915 they were training at the Curragh. In May they went to England, to Hackwood Park, Basingstoke. On 9th July they embarked at Devonport and arrived at Mudros on 25th July and on 5th August landed at Anzac Cove, Gallipoli.

By the end of September they were back at Mudros and on 5th October embarked for Salonika. John McConnell saw action with the 5th Battalion in Gallipoli in August and September of 1915. This was difficult fighting in a country of steep cliffs and rugged hills and the Connaught Rangers suffered many casualties.

Weather conditions were also against them, the heat was almost unbearable, which meant that water had to be constantly available in a country where water was not always plentiful. Flies were everywhere and dysentry was a constant problem. After the battles here they were moved to Salonika and again John saw a lot of action in this area. Conditions here were very much different in that they were now facing winter in the hills north of Salonika. It was intensely cold at night with constant snow and frost and the troops were mostly in the open with only the very minimum of cover. These conditions lasted throughout the winter but the Rangers were not always in the front line and so they had some respite from the cold. They were in this region for over a year. John was killed close to the town of Lahana, about thirty miles north-east of Salonika and is buried in the cemetery there.

9469 RIFLEMAN JOSEPH CRENAN
7th Bn Depot formerly 7th Bn R. Irish Rifles
DIED HOME 28-6-17
Interred in St. Helier, (Almorah), Cemetery, Channel Islands. 8.11.Y.

Born   Ballymoney
Lived   St.Helier, Jersey.
Enlisted   Jersey, C.I.
Son of Mrs. Jane Crenan, of Mill House, Trinity Rd, St. Helier. Jersey.

It appears that Joseph Crenan was born in Ballymoney. It hasn't become clear whether the family originally came from the Channel Islands or if they originated in Ballymoney, but Mrs Crenan, Joseph's mother, had an address in Jersey. It was there that he died, but repeated attempts at finding out information have drawn a blank. We know that he enlisted on the island of Jersey and joined the 7th battalion of the Royal Irish Rifles. At some later stage he transferred to the Depot, probably because of poor health or a recurring illness which kept him from performing his duties competently in the trenches. We know that he was not killed in action nor did he die of wounds. It states simply in "Soldiers Died" that he died at home. We can take this to mean that he died of an illness at some location on the island of Jersey and he is buried in the local Cemetery. It was most likely an illness brought on by the harsh environment that he had to contend with in the trenches and probably the result of a gas attack.

Serre Road

6958 RIFLEMAN JOHN CALDWELL
16th Bn Royal Irish Rifles - This was the Pioneer battalion at the Somme.
D.O.W. 29-6-17
Interred in Bailleul Communal Cemetery Extension, France. Plot 3, Row D, Grave 132.

Born   Rasharkin
Lived   Rasharkin
Enlisted Belfast

John Caldwell was born in Rasharkin, a village now enlarged by new housing projects seven miles south of Ballymoney. He attended school in the village and after leaving there, worked for the local farmers until he enlisted in Belfast after the outbreak of hostilities. He joined the 16th battalion of the Rifles. This was mostly raised in Co. Down and in Lurgan in September 1914. In January 1915 they became the Pioneer battalion for the 36th Ulster Division. This involved much digging of trenches and the laying of miles of belts of barbed wire among other duties. John served his battalion well and survived the battle of the Somme. They were then moved to Belgium and the area around Wulverghem. This was a different type of country, the soil was of clay, much changed from the chalk of the Somme, and breastworks had to be built up in front of the trenches to give the troops some cover. There was little or no cover from shells bursting behind the soldiers and this caused very many casualties. After the battle of Messines the troops of the 36th Div were again moved north to prepare for Passchendaele and it was during these preparations that John was seriously wounded. He was taken to the field hospital at Bailleul but died there of his injuries a short time later. He is buried in the Cemetery nearby. This cemetery is a large one and four other Ballymoney men are buried here. This Cemetery was also used for the burial of three men found guilty of deserting their post and shot at dawn by their own side. They were Pte John Rogers, Pte William Roberts and L Cpl William Moon.

Cemetery location information.

Bailleul is a large town in France, near the Belgian border, 14.5 kilometres south - west of Ypres and on the main road from St. Omer to Lille. The communal cemetery is on the eastern outskirts of the town.

From the Grand Place, take the Ypres road and 400 metres along this road is a sign indicating the direction of the cemetery. Turn down the right into a small road and follow for 400 metres. The cemetery is on the right and the Communal Cemetery is at the bottom end.

Bailleul Cemetery and the grave of John Caldwell

STOKER JOHN DEVINE
Royal Navy.
KILLED 9-7-17
No Known Grave. Commemorated on the Portsmouth Naval Memorial.

Born   Townhead St.
Lived
Enlisted

The second seaman from Ballymoney to make the supreme sacrifice was John Devine, R.N. son of the late Hugh Devine. He was lost with H.M.S. Vanguard. Stoker Devine had a most eventful career. Joining the Royal Inniskillings, he completed his time with the colours, when he joined the Royal Navy. His time was up in the Navy some time before war broke out and as he was on reserve for both Army and Navy he awaited the first call. The Navy was first in and he became a unit in the Grand Fleet. Twice he was transferred from ships which were afterwards mined. Prior to being called up he was at sea with the Merchant Service. He was home on leave in November 1916 when he got married. His wife lived at 21, Artillery St, Belfast. The blast which destroyed H.M.S. Vanguard also killed a number of Coleraine men who were serving on the ship, one of them being Jack Adams.

© *R.N. Museum 1997 HMS Vanguard (1909) 200097 A. Neg. 4876*

H.M.S. Vanguard was a St. Vincent class battleship. She was built by Vickers in Barrow and launched on 22-2-1909 and completed in February 1910. Her dimensions were 536' by 84' by 28' with a displacement of 19560 tons. Her top speed was 21 knots. She carried the following armaments. 10 twelve inch guns, and 20 four inch guns. Her complement was 718. She was commissioned into the 1st Division Home Fleet in March 1910 and joined 1st Battle Squadron in 1912 and then the Grand Fleet in August 1914. She saw action at Jutland with no casualties. She blew up while at anchor in Scapa Flow on 9th July due to faulty ammunition, and 804 men were killed. Lying in shallow water, and a danger to shipping, she was raised and broken up in 1927 on Tyneside.

London Cemetery

6151 PRIVATE JOSEPH PATRICK McMULLEN
1st Bn Connaught Rangers
K.I.A. 11-7-17
No Known Grave. Commemorated on the Basra Memorial, Iraq.

Born   Rasharkin.
Lived   Kilrea.
Enlisted Londonderry.

The family lived at Glenbuck, close to the village of Dunloy and as a young boy Joseph attended the school at Slatt.

On the outbreak of hostilities the 1st battalion were stationed at Ferozepore, with the 3rd Lahore Division. On the 28th of August they embarked at Karachi and after spending five days in Egypt arrived at Marseilles on 26th September. Then on 5th December 1914 the 1st and 2nd battalions amalgamated at Le Touret. A year later they sailed again from Marseilles, for Mesopotamia, arriving at Basra on 10th January 1916. They were to be in this area for most of the remainder of the war. Joseph Patrick McMullen was born in the townland of Glenbuck but the family later moved to Kilrea and Joseph spent much of his early life there. He was a member of the Ancient Order of Hibernians and belonged to the Rasharkin branch with the number 153.

Joseph was killed in heavy fighting on the 11th of July 1917. According to the family he was attached to an elite force belonging to Lawrence of Arabia and was on a special job attempting to blow up a railway when the unit he was a part of was attacked and overwhelmed. He has no known grave and is commemorated on the Basra Memorial.

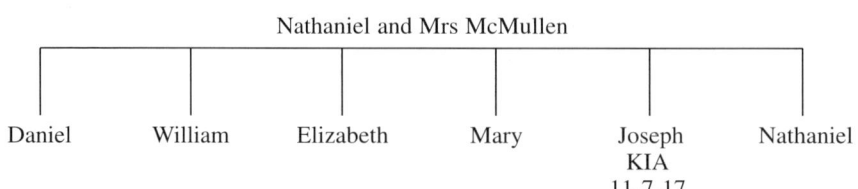

Nathaniel and Mrs McMullen: Daniel, William, Elizabeth, Mary, Joseph KIA 11-7-17, Nathaniel

79354 GUNNER ALEXANDER SIMPSON
9th Siege Battery, Royal Garrison Artillery.
K.I.A. 21-7-17
Interred in Dikkebus New Military Cemetery Ext. Belgium. Plot 3, Row E, Grave 10.

Born   Ballymaconnelly, Rasharkin.
Lived   Kilbride, Scotland.
Enlisted
Elder son of Mr. James Simpson, of Firview farm, Ballymaconnelly.
Commemorated in Rasharkin Presbyterian Church.

Before the outbreak of hostilities, Alexander had been studying Art at the Page Davis School in London. He had just completed a course in Art and Advertisement writing and was a student of Mr Eugene Sandow. A strong young man, he had a great interest in athletics and was a good footballer. He was the elder son of Mr. James Simpson, of Ballymaconnelly, Rasharkin, and had been living in Kilbride, in Scotland, for a short time. He was a member of St.Andrew's Masonic Lodge, No, 524, Kilbride.

Alex was killed in the fierce fighting which took

place around Ypres. The Battle of Messines, in which the British had taken Messines Ridge, had just finished and preparations were in hand for what was to become known as the Battle of Passchendaele.

It was between these two battles that Alex was killed, close to the village of Dikkebus. His Mother never recovered from the shock and died two years later.

Dikkebus New Military Cemetery

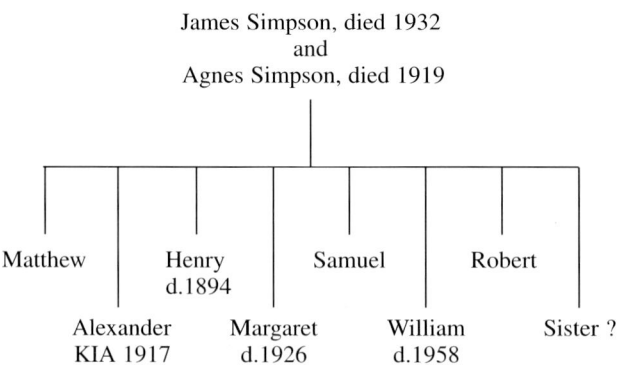

29115 DRIVER WILLIAM CLEMENTS
48th Div Signals. S.M.R.E.
K.I.A. 23-7-17
Aged 25
Interred in Mendinghem British Cemetery. Plot 2, Row F, Grave 22.

Born   Ballymoney
Lived
Enlisted
Foster son of Patrick Laverty
Commemorated in Trinity Presbyterian Church.

Very little is known about William Clements. He was born in Ballymoney in about 1892 and it would appear that some unfortunate incident robbed him of his parents because a report in the papers tells of him being fostered by Patrick Laverty. He is commemorated in Trinity Presbyterian Church in Ballymoney where we can assume Patrick worshipped. Not a great deal of information has come to light about the unit William served with but he was killed in action on 23rd July 1917. He is buried in Mendinghem British Cemetery at Proven, between Poperinge and the coast. A Bushmills man, James McGrattan, is buried a little further along the same row as William, Plot 2, Row F, Grave 53. He died of wounds three days after William, on 26-7-17.

Mendinghem British Cemetery.

2ND LIEUT THOMAS LONG CARSON
4th Squadron, Royal Flying Corps.
K.I.A. 31-7-17
Aged 22
No Known Grave. Commemorated on the Arras Flying Services Memorial.

Born   America
Lived   Colorado Cottage, Bellisle, Dervock
Enlisted
Commemorated in Carnaff Reformed Presbyterian Church.
Son of Daniel Long Carson, Bellisle, Dervock.

An article in the Chronicle for 1-9-17 states.

An official telegram has been recieved by Mr Daniel L. Carson, Bellisle, that his eldest son second Lieut Thomas Long Carson, R.F.C. has been missing since 31st July. Born in America, he came over with his parents at an early age and settled in Ireland. He was educated at Ballymoney

Faubourg-d'Amiens Cemetery in Arras showing the position of the Memorial Bay

Intermediate school, and was about to enter on his college career when war broke out and he enlisted in the Royal Engineers and was stationed for some time at the Victoria Barracks in Belfast. After serving a year with the Royal Engineers, he applied for a commission in the Royal Flying Corps, which he obtained, being recommended by his commanding officer. He was on active service in France since May 1916.

The Arras Flying Services Memorial is in the Faubourg-d'Amiens Cemetery, which is in the Boulevard du General de Gaulle in the western part of the town of Arras, near the Citadel, approximately 2 kilometres due west of the railway station.

The Arras Memorial

S 40544 PTE WILLIAM McAULEY
8th/10th Bn   Gordon Highlanders
K.I.A. 31-7-17
Aged 20
No known grave. Commemorated on the Menin Gate Memorial, Ypres. Panel 38.

Born   Urble, Dervock.
Lived
Enlisted
Son of Margaret McAuley of Urble, Dervock.

William McAuley was born at the Urble, a townland a short distance from the village of Dervock, on the road to Ballycastle. He appears to have been another of these young men who went to Scotland to find work.

This was mostly a harvest time occupation when extra hands were needed on the large farms of North Ayrshire, Lanarkshire and the district around Edinburgh. At any rate he enlisted into the Gordon Highlanders. Not much is known about his early life at the Urble but the Gordon Highlanders Museum has been a big help in telling part of his military story. The battle in which he was killed was known as Third Ypres. The 8th/10th battalion went over the top at 3.50am, as part of the 46th Brigade, with the Black Watch on the left. Fighting continued throughout the day, and into the next, with hand to hand contact with the bayonet. The battalion was relieved in the front line by the 7th Camerons on the 2nd of August, having suffered heavy losses, and making a major contribution to what was regarded as a success overall by the British command. The weather on the morning of the 31st was overcast, which meant that when the troops left their trenches it was still very dark. Finding their way in these conditions was difficult with almost no available landmarks and only the light of exploding shells to guide them. The Germans were taken by surprise and it was four minutes before they managed to bring down their barrage, by which time the Gordons were clear. They attacked on a frontage of 350 yards with two companies, each with two platoons in line and two in support. The third company moved in similar formation in rear of the two foremost. The fourth brought up the rear in artillery formation, and with it moved two machine-guns and a Stokes mortar. This attack ran across what is now known as the Frezenberg Ridge, a rise of only a few feet on what is generally very flat countryside, and by 4.25am they had captured their first objective. The weather had been unsettled for some time and when it did start to rain, it came down in sheets. The soil, spongy by nature, with a surface on which the shell-holes were already full to the lip, could take no more. This was a disaster to the already stressed British troops, but to their credit they hung on to what they had and advanced to their next objective. Here they met very stiff opposition and were forced to retire for about 300 yards, but a company of the 6th Camerons came to their aid and they managed to hold on and take their objective. It was during this day of heavy fighting that William was killed. He was only twenty years of age. There is no known grave and he is commemorated on the Menin Gate Memorial. During this action the battalion had 36 killed, 227 wounded and 59 missing.

8555 PRIVATE HENRY ADAMS
1st Bn Irish Guards.
K.I.A. 2-8-17
No Known Grave. Commemorated on the Menin Gate Memorial. Panel 11.

Born   Ballymoney.
Lived   Newbuildings North.
Enlisted   Ballymoney in May 1915.
Commemorated in St. James's Presbyterian Church, Ballymoney.

In May of 1915 the family were thinning turnips at Newbuildings and Henry was helping with the work. Some of his mates were going past the field on their way to Ballymoney to enlist and Henry dropped everything and went with them. He enlisted into the Irish Guards and almost immediately his training began. Towards the end of October he was allowed home on a few days leave and then after more intensive training he went to France in February 1916. In May of that year and before the new troops were allowed into the line he was home on ten days leave.

This was to be the last time he would see his family. When he returned to the Front he joined the 1st Battalion which had been badly mauled in the retreat from Mons and first approached the Somme in early August. The Battle of the Somme had been raging for over a month and the battalion were to occupy trenches at Englebelmer, well within range of the big guns.

However a change of plans meant them being moved again, this time further south, to the region of Delville Wood.

By early September Henry was involved in his first heavy fighting to the south of Delville Wood and the area around Guillemont. On 15th September a major attack was to take place and Henry and his mates had to lie out all night to be ready for zero hour at 6.20am. In this attack Lieut J.K.M.Greer of Ballymoney,who was in command of No 1 Company, was severely injured and was later to die of his wounds. Sergeant Hugh Carton, also of Ballymoney and serving in No 1 Coy along with Greer was killed a short time after Greer was injured. Henry took part in the fierce fighting between Delville Wood and Ginchy and in spite of heavy odds achieved their objective. This was followed by a quieter time and the battalion had time to rest. By 1st February 1917 they were still close by at Carnoy but the easy time was now over and they were moved by train to the area around St. Omer.

From here they moved into camp at Cassel in preparation for the attacks in the Boesinghe area north of Ypres. By early July they were in the front line at Boesinghe and on 5th July were attacked by gas.

This was a difficult time, the heat was oppressive and the wearing of gas masks made it worse but it was soon to change. The weather gradually became cooler and rain began to take over from sunshine.

By the 1st of August the rain had become a continual downpour and to make it worse the Germans had stepped up their campaign and were heavily shelling the British lines. It was during the shelling on the next day, the 2nd of August, that Henry was killed at Boesinghe. He has no known grave and is commemorated on the Menin Gate. On the following day, the 3rd of August, the battalion was withdrawn and taken to Poll Hill Camp near Bandaghem for training.

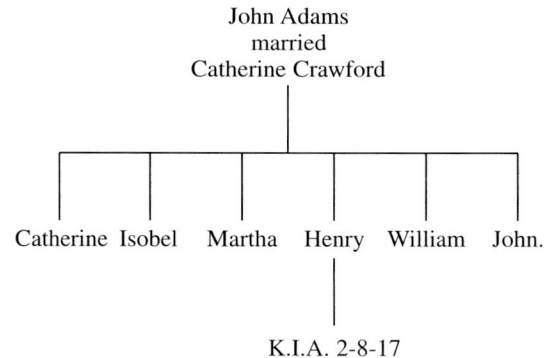

The Last Post Ceremony at The Menin Gate at 8.00 p.m.

27322 PRIVATE SAMUEL McMILLAN
9th Bn Royal Inniskilling Fusiliers.
K.I.A. 7-8-17
Aged 22.
No Known Grave. Commemorated on the Menin Gate Memorial, Ypres. Panel 22.

Born   Ballymoney.
Lived   Currysisken, Ballymoney.
Enlisted Belfast.
Eldest son of William John, and Annie McMillan, of Taughey, Ballymoney. Commemorated in Drumreagh Presbyterian Church.

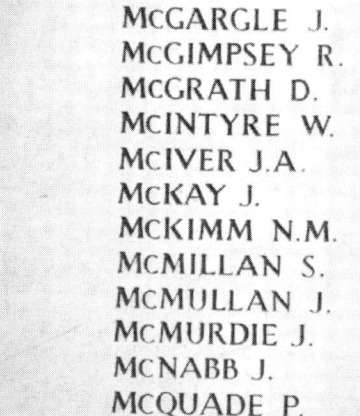

McGARGLE J.
McGIMPSEY R.
McGRATH D.
McINTYRE W.
McIVER J.A.
McKAY J.
McKIMM N.M.
McMILLAN S.
McMULLAN J.
McMURDIE J.
McNABB J.
McQUADE P.

In May 1916 Samuel crossed to France and after thirteen months was killed by shell-fire in the defence of Ypres.

The 9th Inniskillings were raised at Omagh in September 1914 from the Tyrone Volunteers. They were taken almost immediately to Finner Camp for training. In January 1915 they were moved to Randalstown and then in July to Ballycastle.

From here in September 1915 they were taken over to England and the training area at Bordon. The following month, October, saw them off to France in preparation for the Battle of the Somme. Samuel was one of the later recruits and went to France in May 1916. They were stationed at the small French villages of Mesnil and Martinsart and went from their trenches on the morning of the first of July into a withering hail of flying metal. Samuel was lucky to escape uninjured on this drastic day and the battalion were evacuated and taken back for rest and the training of new recruits. They then moved north into Belgium and the area around Wulverghem. Here they would stay for over a year. The 109th Brigade were south west of Dranoutre in the build up to the Battle of Messines. During the battle the 9th Inniskillings were attacking the village of Wytschaete with "mopping up" to do. This they accomplished successfully. When the battle was finished the troops were moved north to prepare for Langemarck. Shelling by the Germans was going on all the time and was causing a steady stream of casualties. It was during one of these periods of heavy shelling that Samuel was killed. He was probably just blown to pieces. There is no known grave and he is commemorated on the Menin Gate.

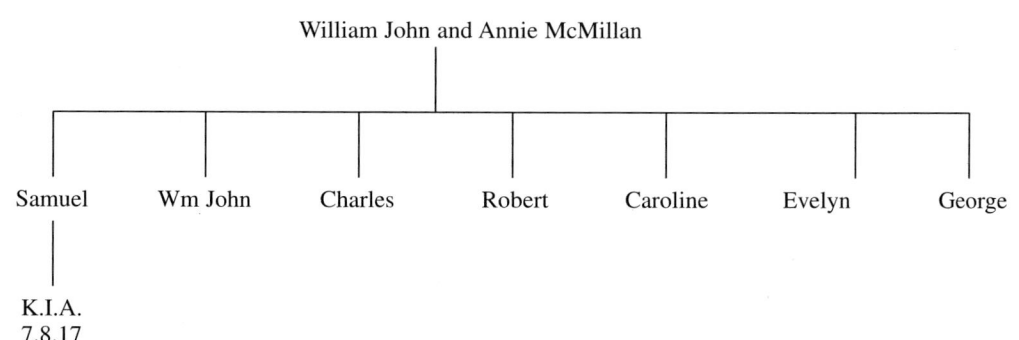

762386 L.CPL JAMES DICKSON
28th Bn London Regt
D.O.W. 8-8-17
Interred in Bailleul Road East Cemetery, St Laurent- Blangy. Plot 1, Row O, Grave 2.

Born   Ballymoney
Lived   Main St.
Enlisted
Son of Mr William Dickson, Main St,

St Laurent-Blangy is a village adjoining the north east side of Arras. Leave St Laurent- Blangy on the D919 towards Bailleul-sire-Berthoult for about two and a half kilometres. Bailleul Road East Cemetery is about two kilometres north east of the village on the right hand side of the road.

Mr William Dickson was a publican in Main St, thought to have been near the bottom of the street. Two brothers, William and John served.

The 28th City of London battalion (Artists Rifles) was formed in London in August 1914. Later they went to Richmond Park and then in July 1915 to High Beech in Epping Forest. In November 1915 the 1/28th battalion in France was recognised as an Officers Training Corps and absorbed the 2/28th battalion.

The 3rd line now became the 2/28th battalion and by March 1916 was at Hare Hall, Romford. It now became No 15 Officer Cadet battalion, and remained at Romford.

During the war 10,256 officers were commissioned after training with the Artists Rifles. They went to the Foot Guards, every infantry regiment and most of the other arms. The Royal Field Artillery alone took 953 officers and the London Regiment 783 officers from the Artists Rifles. The battalion left G.H.Q. and joined the 63rd Division on 28th June 1917.

James Dickson had been in the trenches for a week for a course of instruction prior to coming home on leave and to receive his commission, and on his last night on duty, when in the act of mending some barbed wire, he was shot, being wounded in five places and he was buried on his birthday.

His Commanding Officer wrote that "He was a splendid young man, and had done fine work in the trenches, while as a bayonet instructor, he was priceless."

At this time his father was living in London with his two daughters. One of his brothers had been serving in France, the other in Salonika.

Bailleul Cemetery

681087 PRIVATE EDWARD CAMPBELL
170th Bn Canadian Exp Force
K.I.A. 9-8-17
Aged 41
No Known Grave. Commemorated on the Vimy Ridge Memorial.

Born   Ballywillan, Portrush.
Lived   Toronto, Canada.
Enlisted   Toronto, Canada
Commemorated in 1st Ballymoney Presbyterian Church.

Edward Campbell has been one of the soldiers that I have been at last able to identify. A report in one of the newspapers stated that he had been in the Canadian Forces and the National Archives of Canada have found him after an exhaustive search of their files.

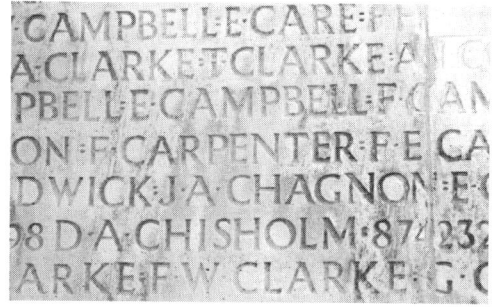

He was born at Ballywillan, Portrush, on 26th April 1876. He had emigrated to Canada some time before the outbreak of hostilities and was living in Toronto. It would appear that by the time he enlisted at Toronto his father was dead as his mother is given as his next of kin. He was over six feet tall with a fair complexion, blue eyes and fair hair and enlisted at Toronto on 31st January 1916. At almost forty years of age he was much older than most of the young men who were enlisting at the time. After a few months training he embarked at Halifax on the 15th of October 1916 and arrived at Liverpool on the 31st. He was taken to the huge Military training camp at Bramshott after being made Acting Quartermaster Sergeant on 25th October. In May of 1917 he reverted to Private at his own request and was reported missing, believed killed on the 9th of August only a few weeks after going into action. He has no known grave and is commemorated on the huge Canadian Memorial at Vimy Ridge.

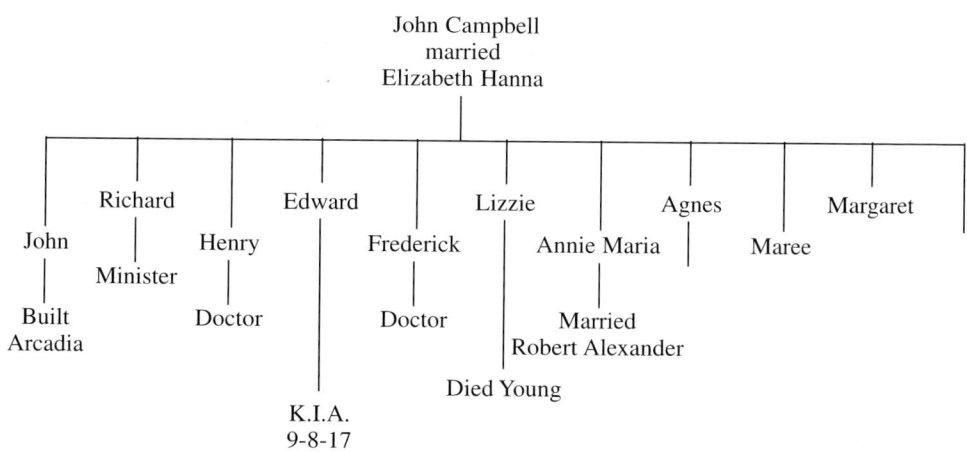

19048 PRIVATE JAMES CASSIDY
"A" Coy, 10th Bn Royal Inniskilling Fusiliers
K.I.A. 9-8-17
Aged 28
No Known Grave. Commemorated on the Menin Gate, Panel 22.

Born   Londonderry
Lived   Castle St, Ballymoney.
Enlisted   Coleraine
Son of William and Margret Cassidy, of Upperlands.

The 10th battalion were raised at Omagh in September 1914 from the Derry Volunteers and trained at Finner Camp in the 3rd Brigade, Ulster Division. On 2nd November the formation became the 109th Brigade.

In May 1915 they moved to Randalstown and then in July they moved again, this time to Seaford, on the south coast of England. After intensive training here they moved again, this time to Bordon Camp in early September.

Then in October 1915 they moved to France. After this move to France they were introduced to trenches for the first time and drilled in the art of trench warfare. These trenches were a close replica of what the soldiers could expect when they eventually went into the front lines and as the Battle of the Somme was by now at the planning stages this was where it was intended that they should go. James survived the battle and moved with the Division to Belgium.

In May 1917, he was awarded a parchment certificate for gallantry in battle. It was about this same time that he was wounded, and was home on ten days leave. This was just before the Battle of Messines. On the 9th of August 1917 the 10th battalion were in the front line at Ypres. Heavy shelling was going on and it was during this heavy bombardment that James was killed.

21242 PRIVATE ROBERT SHIELDS (BERTIE)
10th Bn Royal Inniskilling Fusiliers
K.I.A. 9-8-17
Interred in Wieltje Farm Cemetery Special Memorial, B, 7.

Born   Templemore
Lived   Dervock
Enlisted   Londonderry

Bertie Shields was born at Templemore in the late 1890's. Very little information has come to light concerning him. The family seems to have moved into the Dervock area around the beginning of the century and that Bertie attended school there. Bertie enlisted at Londonderry into the 10th battalion of the Royal Inniskilling Fusiliers and did much of his training at Ballykinlar. He is commemorated on the War Memorial in the centre of Dervock village.

At the time Bertie was killed, in August 1917, he was in action in the defence of Ypres and was buried behind the British lines close to where he fell. After the Armistice he was re-interred in Wieltje Farm Cemetery but due to some mix up there is a doubt as to just where in the cemetery he is actually buried and therefore the headstone is a memorial one.

Canadian Memorial at Vimy Ridge

1632 RIFLEMAN DAVID JOHN TAYLOR
12th Bn Royal Irish Rifles
K.I.A. 10-8-17
Aged 20
Interred in White House Cemetery, Belgium. Plot 3, Row A, Grave 17.

Born   Meetinghouse St, Ballymoney 9th May 1896.
Lived   Castle St, Ballymoney.
Enlisted Ballymoney.
Son of David John and Jane Taylor, of Castle St, Ballymoney.
Commemorated in 1st Ballymoney Presbyterian Church.

David John and Samuel Taylor, two brothers from Castle St in Ballymoney, enlisted at Ballymoney in August 1914. When Mrs Taylor found out what had been done behind her back she went to the recruiting officer and got Samuel released as he was too young. This was alright for a time, but as soon as Samuel got the chance, he re-enlisted, and by now Mrs Taylor realised that she could not hold him back and so she allowed him to go.

Training took place at Clandeboye and then Seaford on the south coast of England. When training was complete the battalion moved to France in time for the start of the Battle of the Somme. They were based at Martinsart.

Bright sunshine greeted them on the morning of the 1st of July as they prepared for the attack. At 7.30am the whistles sounded and the men moved out of their trenches and started to cross No Man's Land.

Machine-guns at St.Pierre Divion had a clear line of sight on them, as had those at Thiepval, and they were mowed down. It was at this time that Samuel was killed as he tried to attack the German trenches. David was wounded in this same attack, although not seriously. By the end of the day the battalion was decimated and had to be withdrawn for a rest and re-organisation. David was taken to hospital for treatment and a few weeks later was well enough to be allowed

White House Cemetery, Belgium

home on leave. He arrived in Ballymoney at the beginning of August 1916 and spent a week with his parents, benefitting from a well earned rest.

Afterwards the battalion was moved to Belgium and the area around Wulverghem and it was to here that David returned. They were to be in this area, Wulverghem and Ypres, for over a year.

From the beginning of August 1917, the weather had been wet. It rained almost continuously and there was mud everywhere in places eighteen inches deep.

The mines at Wieltje provided some cover from the downpour but water ran down the passages and seeped down the walls and everywhere was damp and cold. Preparations were being made for the Battle of Langemarck, and troops were being moved forward. Ammunition had to be

brought up through the mud and men and horses laboured day and night. Heavy shelling was going on all the time and German planes kept up a steady bombing routine.

German machine-guns were firing continuously and snipers shot at anything that moved. It was during this build-up to the Battle of Langemarck that David John was killed at Wieltje. He is buried in White House Cemetery a short distance away.

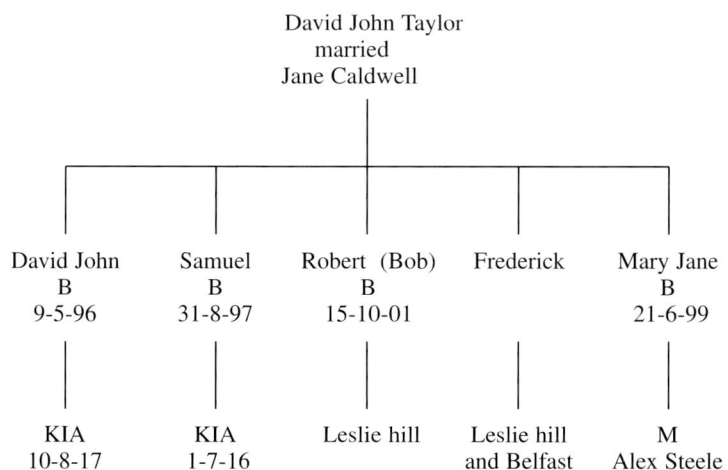

David John Taylor married Jane Caldwell

David John	Samuel	Robert (Bob)	Frederick	Mary Jane
B	B	B		B
9-5-96	31-8-97	15-10-01		21-6-99
KIA	KIA	Leslie hill	Leslie hill and Belfast	M Alex Steele
10-8-17	1-7-16			

40841 RIFLEMAN NEASON HENRY HALE
1st Bn Royal Irish Rifles
K.I.A. 11-8-17
Aged 22
No Known Grave. Commemorated on the Tyne Cot Memorial, Belgium. Panels 138-140 and 162 to162A and 163A

Born   Finvoy,
Lived   Finvoy Lodge.
Enlisted Ballymoney.
Commemorated in Finvoy Parish Church.

After leaving school Neason joined the staff of the Ulster Bank. His close neighbour at Finvoy, John Gray, was already on the staff of the Ulster Bank, so it is reasonable to assume that John might have had a hand in getting Neason a job there. In any case Neason started work with the bank on 25th March 1912 and left to join HM Forces in March 1916, the same month as John Gray left to enlist. He is mentioned in the Ulster Bank staff magazine, "Passing Events", the issue dated Christmas 1918, when the editor referred to him as being still on the "missing" list and expressed hope that he (and several others who were still missing) would turn up. He didn't turn up. In fact the family were never officially informed that he had been killed, and until her dying day his mother always believed that one day he would come home. He is commemorated, along with John Gray, on a plaque in the entrance hall of the Ulster Bank buildings in Waring St, in Belfast.

He was the eldest son of William and Annie Rose Hale, of Finvoy Lodge, and had been in hospital suffering from illness in May 1917. When the family headstone was erected in the grounds of Finvoy Parish Church, Neason's mother would not allow his name to be inscribed on it and it was only put there after her death, so strong was her conviction that he would turn up. For over thirty years every knock at her door was answered with a glow of hope that it would be her long lost son.

Cemetery location information.

The Tyne Cot memorial to the Missing forms the north-eastern boundary of Tyne Cot cemetery, 9 kilometres north-east of Ypres town centre.

William Hale
married
Annie Rose Speers
in Finvoy Prsbyterian Church
on 1st June 1894.

Neeson Henry   John Edward William J.P.

Annie Rose's two sisters, Letitia and Nancy, lived with her at Finvoy Lodge.

Bernafay Wood Cemetery

1733 RIFLEMAN ROBERT STEWART
12th Bn Royal Irish Rifles
D.O.W. 11-8-17
Aged 24
Interred in Brandhoek New Military Cemetery, Belgium. Plot 6, Row B, Grave 6.

Born   Ballymoney
Lived   Bootown.
Enlisted Ballymoney
Son of Mr John Stewart, of Druckendult, Ballymoney.
Commemorated in St. James's Presbyterian Church.

A report in the Chronicle in August 1917 says — Robert Stewart enlisted very soon after war was declared and was allowed home on leave to marry Anna Hamill in St James's Pres Church, Ballymoney, on 14th May 1915. He was at that time a serving soldier and was still in training at Newtownards. Anna's Father, William Hamill, was a blacksmith at Seacon. The best man was David J.Taylor, most likely to have been the same David J.Taylor as was killed on 10 August 1917, the same day as Robert was so seriously injured. When training was complete Robert was taken across to England and the training grounds at Seaford, on the south coast. From here he went to France and to the area of the battle of the Somme where a huge build up of troops was taking place. The French Commanders had been clamouring for the British to commence a major offensive to draw German forces away from Verdun and this was to take place at the Somme. Robert was lucky on the 1st of July and came through the battle unscathed. The battalion were withdrawn next day to the huge training area at St. Omer for reorganisation and after a rest were sent to Belgium. Here in the battlefields around Wulverghem they would stay for almost a year. Skirmishes were taking place all the time and the battalion were kept busy between stints in the line and constant work and training when out of it. The next big offensive would be the Battle of Messines in June of 1917 and again he came through safely. By early August the weather had deteriorated and rain fell, day after day. The ground underfoot became a sodden mass and was continuously ploughed up by shell-fire. This was the beginning of one of the worst periods of the war with gas shelling and bombing from aeroplanes being a major threat.

On the 10th of August Robert was very seriously injured and was taken back to a dressing station at Brandhoek. In spite of all the attention and care he died here next day and is buried in the nearby cemetery. On 22nd November 1922 Anna married John Taggart in St.James's Presbyterian Church, Ballymoney.

Brandhoek New Military Cemetery, Belgium

A report in the Chronicle in August 1917 says---

"Much sympathy is extended to Mrs. Anna Stewart, of Bootown. Her Father-in-law, Mr John Stewart, of Druckendult, died on Wednesday and next day as she was proceeding to his residence she was handed an official message that her husband, Pte. Robert Stewart, who was wounded on the 10th, had died the following day." His brother Wilson, also served.

Cemetery Location Information:

Brandhoek New Military Cemetery is 6.5 Kilometres west of Ypres on the N 308 from Ypres to Poperinge. From Ypres town centre the N 308 is reached via Elverdingestraat, then directly over two small roundabouts and a railway level crossing. Pass the village of Vlamertinge and just beyond the church in Brandhoek turn left on to Grote Branderstraat.

After crossing the N 38 dual carriageway turn right and in 300 metres the cemetery is on the right.

The Lancashire Dump Cemetery in Aveluy Wood at the Somme

18626 L. CPL. ROBERT PAULL
12th Bn Royal Irish Rifles
K.I.A. 13-8-17
Aged 25
No Known Grave. Commemorated on the Menin Gate Memorial, Ypres. Panel 40.

Born   Drumnagee, Bushmills
Lived   Mosside
Enlisted Ballymoney
Son of John and Isabella Paull, of Islandranny.
Commemorated in Drumtullagh Parish Church.

John and Isabella Paull lived for a time at Drumnagee, Bushmils, and it was there that their third son, Robert was born. There were three sons, James, John and Robert. After the birth of Robert the family moved to live at Islandranny where they remained for a number of years.

After leaving school he worked as a farm labourer to Robert Cunningham, of Ederone, Mosside and remained there until he joined the army.

Robert enlisted soon after the outbreak of hostilities and trained at Clandeboye. From there he went to Seaford on the south coast of England to complete his training and from there to France.

He joined the 12th battalion at St. Omer and after more training was taken to the Wulverghem area of Belgium where the battalion were to stay for almost a year. In this time they were regularly in and out of the line and were involved in a great deal of fighting. However their next big battle would be the battle of Messines in June of 1917. This was a well planned attack and the battle was over very quickly.

This was the start of one of the worst periods of the war with gas being used on a regular basis by the enemy. Heavy fighting was taking place all around Ypres at this time and plans were made to try to take the Passchendaele Ridge. It was in these preparations that Robert Paull was killed. He has no known grave and is commemorated on the Menin Gate Memorial.

WHELAN J. P.
WILLIAMS C. B.

LIEUTENANT
DIGGES La TOUCHE A.
GAVIN R. F.
HILL W. C. M. C.
La NAUZE W.
McKEE W. D.
MORTON W.
RAYMOND A. A.

SECOND LIEUT.
AMY A. B.
BROWN H.
YRNE V. C.
URNISS J.
ENDERSON T.
OY F. C. P.
cINTOSH J. M.
cKEE P. J.
R W. L.

McCARRON P.
McCARTNEY A.
M'CLURG W.
McDONAGH J.
NELSON G.
O'CONNER A.
PARKER J. A.
PARKINSON S.
PAULL R.
RIDDELL J.
TATAM J. W.
VOKES B.
WALSH T.
WARD K.
WHITE H.
WHITWORTH R.

RIFLEMAN
ADAIR R. H.
ADAIR R. J.
ADAIR R. M.

CRAINEY W. J.
CREGAN P.
CRIGHTON W.
CULL D.
CURRAN S.
CUTLER J.
DALEY D.
DALTON J.
DALY F.
DARRAGH W
DELANEY L.
DEMPSTER
DICKER C. W
DINES T.
DOGGART
DONOHOE
DORAN B.
DORAN H
DORBER
DOUGLAS
DOWD J.
DOYLE P

29324 PRIVATE WILLIAM JOHN ANDERSON
10th Bn Royal Inniskilling Fus.
K.I.A. 16-8-17
No Known Grave Commemorated on the Tyne Cot Memorial, Belgium. Panels 70-72.

Born.   Ballymoney
Lived   Roddenfoot.
Enlisted. Omagh, Co. Tyrone.

William John Anderson was born in Ballymoney and attended school there.

The family lived at the Roddenfoot, probably in the row of houses now sadly demolished, where the old peoples home now stands, at the bottom of Queen Street. William John enlisted in Omagh, and the reason for this is not clear, but he was probably working in the Omagh district at the time, and just followed the example set by everyone else and signed on. The 10th battalion did their training at Finner Camp in County Donegal before going to England to finish their training at Seaford. They arrived in France in October 1915. From then on preparations were being made for the Battle of the Somme and the 10th battalion were eventually moved into the area of Martinsart. They were to attack from the edge of Thiepval Wood across the ground where the Ulster Tower now stands to their memory. On the morning of the 1st of July the battalion suffered heavy losses as they attacked the Schwaben Redoubt.

They were under intense fire from machine-gun positions at Thiepval village and from positions in front of them, one of which still remains in the field, down the lane beside the Ulster Tower. The battalion was later withdrawn from this part of the line and taken back for reinforcements. At the Battle of Passchendaele on 16th August 1917 the 10th battalion were in Brigade Reserve at Wieltje, a short distance north-east of Ypres.

Wieltje had been taken by the British on the 31st of July, but wet weather and mud slowed their advance, and desperate defending by the Germans almost stopped it altogether. By the 16th the front was less than a mile away. It was on this day that William John was killed. The 10th were in Wieltje Dugouts and heavy German shelling was reaching them with ease.

Of the nine Ballymoney men killed on this day, not one of them has a known grave. Thunder storms and incessantly heavy rain over the previous two days had left everywhere in a sea of glutinous mud. You were just as liable to be drowned as shot. Every shell hole was full to the lip with water. Little wonder then that so few bodies could be recovered. They just sank into the soft mud or were buried or blown apart by the next shell. One of the worst disasters of this day was the fact that the infantry could not keep up with the barrage because of the ground conditions. Communication, for the most part, was by runner, and much of this had to be done in the open and under heavy shell and machine-gun fire. The heavy artillery was in the back areas where ammunition was easier to get up and the runners often had a distance of two or three miles to go to deliver their messages.

The timing of the barrage could not be changed as it had been worked out in advance and both the gunners and the infantry knew what the timings were and any change under the circumstances could have had the barrage falling on the advancing British troops.

1420 RIFLEMAN JOHN BIGGART
14th Bn Royal Irish Rifles
K.I.A. 16-8-17
Aged 19
No known grave. Commemorated on Tyne Cot Memorial Panels 138-140

Born   Bendooragh   1898
Lived   Bendooragh
Enlisted Ballymoney
Commemorated in Ballymoney Parish Church

John Biggart was born in 1898, three years after his brother William. After leaving school he was employed up until the commencement of hostilities, at Leslie's of Leslie Hill. In 1914 he enlisted in the 14th battalion Royal Irish Rifles, from his home at Bendooragh, his regimental number being 1420. This unit was raised from the young citizens volunteers (Y.C.V.). They were formed after the outbreak of war and after completing training in Bramshott, were sent overseas in October, 1915. The battalion landed at Le Havre on 6th October and proceeded to Amiens. Most of it"s early service was spent in the Auchonviellers and Thiepval areas.

After the fighting of the Somme the battalion was transferred to Flanders. They remained in the Ploegsteert area until the end of 1916.During the early part of 1917 the battalion was still in the northern area, being opposite the Messines Ridge when on duty in the trenches. In May it made two raids, one on the 22nd being very successful, and in the great attack of 7th June it was conspiciously successful, reaching and securing the German third line-- the objective assigned to it. It was in the attack of 16th August, near Fortuin (North - East of Ypres) the battalion made considerable progress at first but was compelled to fall back by meeting much uncut wire, it was in this sector that 19 year old John Biggart lost his life. He has no known grave and is commemorated on the Tyne Cot Memorial.

There were a number of big problems at Passchendaele. First, the weather had been very wet and everywhere was a sea of mud. Nothing could move. Second, communications were poor, telephone lines could not be kept open, and so communication was by runner for the most part. The creeping barrage got too far ahead of the infantry and the infantry could not catch up with the result that the Germans came out of their well camouflaged bunkers which had hardly been touched and just mowed them down. Runners had no hope of getting back two or three miles to warn the gunners and anyhow the timing had all been pre-set and could not be changed.

This was a brother of Dan Biggart who had the Jewellers shop in Main Street, Ballymoney in the 1940's and 50's.

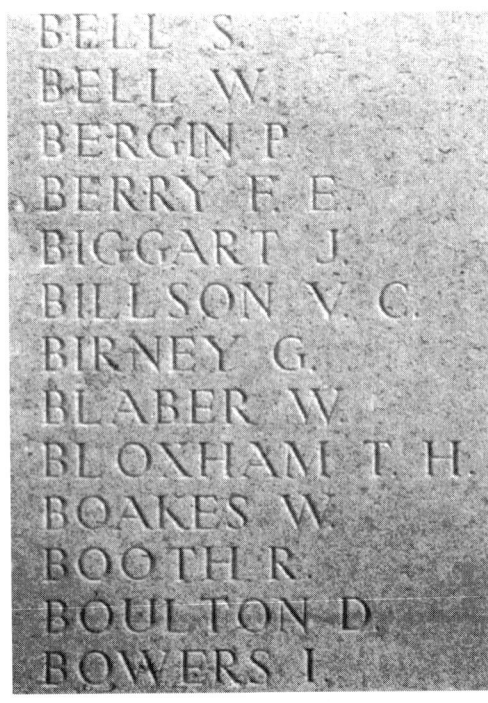

This week's Memory Lane picture

IS Dunaghy Protestant Flute Band in 1908. Back row (from left)— William Patterson, David M'Alister, Robert M'Alister, Sam Martin, Tom Grey, William Stirling, Tom M'Conaghie, Clarke Stirling, John Culbertson, Charles M'Kitterick, William Workman. Third row — Sam Grey, John M'Conaghie, Alex. M'Conaghie, James M'Conaghie, Hugh Cameron, James Grey, James M'Queston, Robert M'Ateer, Sam Torrens. **Second** row — William Martin, Ernie **Wales**, Tom M'Conaghie, Sam Grey. In front—John Biggart, Bertie Stinson.

Photograph submitted and names supplied by Mr. James M'Conaghie, Portballintrae.

John Biggart Born 1869, Died 1952
married Mary Ann McNeill Born 1869.
on 11th Jan 1889

| William | John | Neil | Robert | Jeannie | Martha | Mary | Daniel |

17390 RIFLEMAN ALEXANDER CAIRNS
12th Bn Royal Irish Rifles
K.I.A. 16-8-17
Aged 21

Born   Ballymoney
Lived   Balnamore
Enlisted Ballymoney
Son of Samuel and Mary Cairns of Balnamore. Commemorated in Drumreagh Presbyterian Church.

PRIVATE ALEX. CAIRNS,

A member of the "Chronicle" staff whose fall in action is recorded in our Ballymoney Notes. His fellow-workers put on record that no cheerier or more loyal lad ever came to learn a trade in any establishment—apt, keen, obliging, and courteous, he was loyal to employer and comrades alike. Thus there was sadness in the place he used to be, and which shall know him no more, when word came that he had laid down his young life in the country's service; and, with such memories, dim eyes and "lumpy" throats were nothing to be ashamed of. To quote the words of a comrade, "there was no call for him to go" —his youth and slight stature might have excused him in his appearance before the recruiting sergeant, even as it had almost led to his undoing when scanned by the benevolent eye of a factory inspector! But "Alick" wanted to be there, and gained his point— he got to France, where his bones will mingle with those of the gallant boys who showed no fear—because they didn't know any! When he enlisted they must have "weighed his heart." and, finding it beat true, passed him on. He was one of the many brave youths we would fain have seen "come back," but instead he has "gone west," and left sad yet pleasant memories behind.

Samuel and Mary both came from Balnamore. Samuel the son of Robert Cairns and Mary, the daughter of Alex McDonald.

Alex Cairns was a lightly built young man. He had been working for some time in the Chronicle office in Coleraine and was very popular with the staff there. He was well liked and to quote the words of a comrade "there was no call for him to go "but he enlisted at Ballymoney. When his training was complete he was transferred to Seaford on the south coast of England and then a few months later was taken across to France. Housed under tents at Martinsart, a short distance from the front lines wasn't a pleasant experience for young men away from home for the first time. The weather had turned wet and there was mud everywhere. They were set to work immediately, either repairing trenchs, or digging new ones or training. There is no need to go into details about the preparations for the start of the Battle of the Somme. The low lying ground on the north bank of the River Ancre was ploughed up with shellfire and very wet from the recent bad weather and it was across this that the young men of the 12th battalion had to go on the opening day of the battle carrying a load of equipment that their superiors said they would need. Many of them

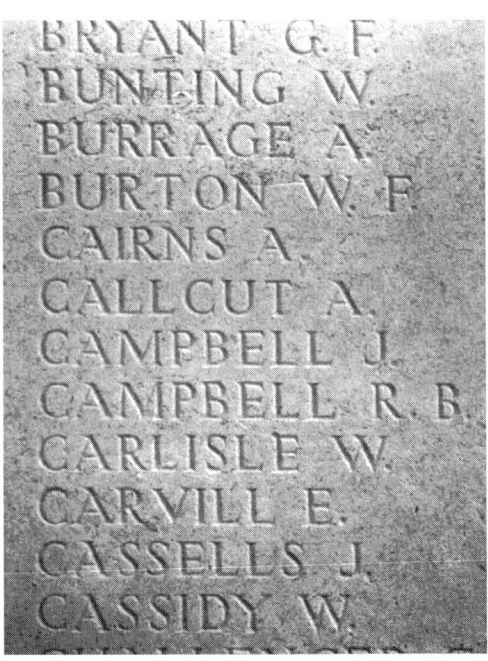

didn't even get the chance to fire a shot. Machine-gun fire from the area around St. Pierre Divion hit them as soon as they started to cross No Man's Land. Alex was slightly wounded on the 1st of July but recovered after treatment at a dressing station behind the lines. The battalion were taken out of the line, brought back up to strength with new recruits, and sent to Belgium. After spending six months in Belgium, Alex was sent home on leave in February of 1917. This was to be the last time he would see Balnamore. February was a quiet time in the trenches with only the usual sniping going on, but this was not to last. As the year wore on plans were made for the battle of Messines and Alex saw much action here. This was followed by the battle for Passchendaele Ridge in August. The weather had again turned wet, with each day wetter than the one before. The ground was again ploughed up by shell-fire, with every shell-hole full to the brim with water. Deep trenches could not be dug here so sand bags had to be filled with mud and placed in front. This was very unpleasant work and nobody liked it but it had to be done. Early on the morning of the 16th of August the attack started close to Fortuin, to the north-east of Ypres. It was here that Alex was killed. He was one of nine young Ballymoney men killed on this day, not one of them with a known grave. This shows to some extent the atrocious conditions under which they had to fight when not one of them was ever seen again. The only other son of the family, James, died five months later, on 5th January 1918, aged 26.

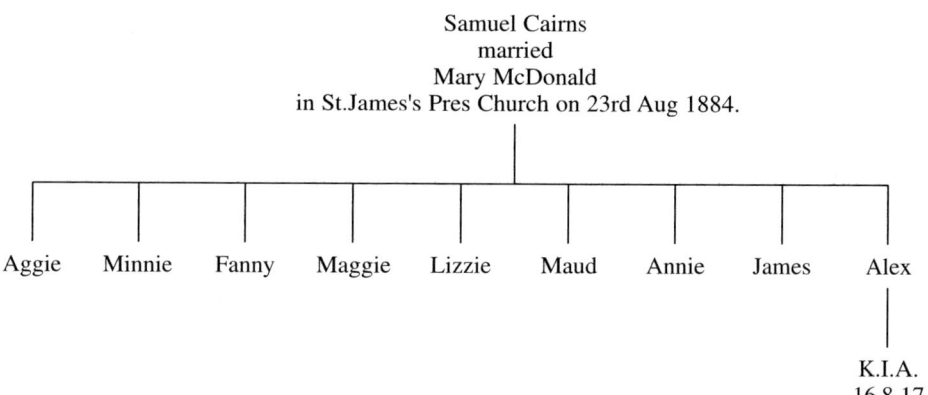

16448 PRIVATE ALEXANDER HILL
8th Bn Royal Inniskilling Fusiliers
K.I.A. 16-8-17
Aged 23
No Known Grave. Commemorated on the Tyne Cot Memorial, Belgium. Panels 70

Born   Ballymoney
Enlisted   Ballymoney
Son of Samuel and Catherine Hill, of Dunaverney.
Commemorated in Roseyards Presbyterian Church.

Alex Hill was born at Dunaverney, about three miles from Ballymoney, the son of Samuel and Catherine Hill. He spent most of his life in the Roseyards district, but enlisted soon after war was declared. The family worshipped in Roseyards Presbyterian Church and it is there that Alex is commemorated on the Roll of Honour. His early training took place at Ballykinlar, but when this was complete he was moved to England and then in October 1915, went to France. The 107th Brigade was sent to the area around Martinsart in preparation for the Battle of the Somme. Alex was lucky to come through this day without injury and was taken out of the line and eventually sent north to the Ypres area. Over the next year he saw a great deal of action but the worst was to be the Battle of Langemarck in August 1917.

The 8th battalion were involved in a Brigade attack in the area around Vlamertinghe on the 16th of August 1917. Two Ballymoney men were killed with them on this day.

Alex Hill and James McCann. This was a period of intense fighting mixed with wet weather. The ground had been churned into mud with the continual exploding of shells and each day wetter than the one before. Men could just as fast be drowned in shell holes as shot by the enemy. Conditions were atrocious and stretcher bearers were often up to their knees in mud when carrying out casualties. In these conditions an injured man, unless quickly found, would die of exposure or just sink in the mud. Alex Hill has no known grave and is commemorated on the Tyne Cot Memorial.

Cemetery location information.

The Tyne Cot Memorial to the Missing forms the north-eastern boundary of Tyne Cot Cemetery, which is 9 kilometres north-east of Ypres town centre.

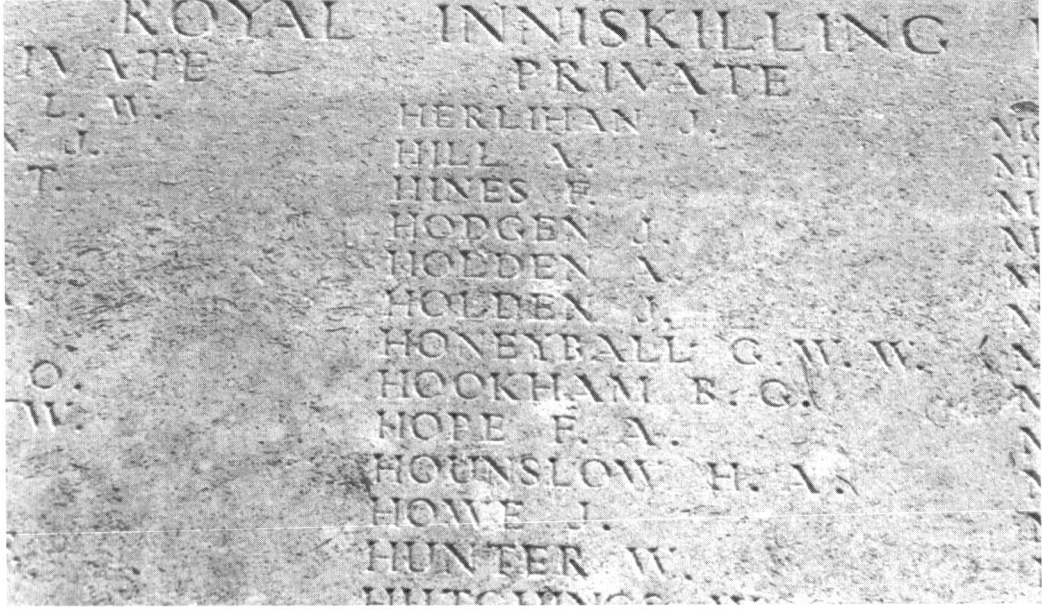

801 RIFLEMAN ALEXANDER HUEY
802 12th Bn Royal Irish Rifles
K.I.A. 16-8-17
Aged 22
No Known Grave. Commemorated on the Tyne Cot Memorial, Belgium.
Panels. 138-140 and 162 to 162A and 163A.

Born   Ballynagashel
Lived   Ballycraigagh, Stranocum.
Enlisted   Ballymoney.
Son of William and Rose Huey, of Ballycraigagh.
Commemorated in Bushvale Presbyterian Church.

According to the family headstone in Bushvale Presbyterian Churchyard, William Huey died in 1911. This was to be the beginning of a very tough time for Mrs. Huey, with the death of two of her sons and a neighbour's lad that she had also brought up. Most of the family were born at Ballynagashel and later moved to Ballycraigagh.

Alex enlisted as soon as war was declared and there are letters from Newtownards in February and March 1915, where he was training. There are many letters from Alex at this period and during training at Seaford in August 1915. In November there is an anxious letter from Alex saying that he has not heard from his brother James for seven weeks and wondering if he has been killed. Mrs Huey had reared William Laverty, and there is a letter from Alex on 12th August 1916 telling of William being killed at the Battle of the Somme on 1st July. Mrs.Huey already knew that something was wrong with

William as she had written twice to the records office asking for news of him and being put off with an evasive answer. In November there is another letter from Alex telling of Samuel Patton trying to enlist and being turned away twice. He eventually managed it and was killed on 19th May 1917.

After the start of the Battle of the Somme, the 12th Battalion were withdrawn and brought up to strength again with new recruits and moved to Ypres in Belgium. They were to be in this region for well over a year. In June 1917 Alex took part in the battle for Messines Ridge and was killed on 16th August at Passchendaele. In early August there was torrential rain in the Ypres Salient and everywhere was a sea of glutinous mud. Every shell-hole was full to the lip with water. Conditions were unbelievable and it was just as easy to drown in a shell hole as be killed by the enemy. Stretcher bearers struggled knee deep in this quagmire to get injured soldiers away to relative safety. Little wonder that not one of the nine Ballymoney men killed on this day has a known grave.

The Tyne Cot Memorial forms the north-eastern boundary of Tyne Cot Cemetery and is 9 kilometres north-east of Ypres town centre.

F. McClarty and A. Huey

25083 PRIVATE JAMES McCANN
8th Bn Royal Inniskilling Fusiliers
K.I.A. 16-8-17
Aged 29
No Known Grave. Commemorated on the Tyne Cot Memorial. Panels 70-72.

Born   Ballymoney
Lived   Coleraine
Enlisted Portrush
Son of Joseph and Elizabeth McCann, of Long Commons, Coleraine.
Husband of Minnie McCann, of Long Commons, Coleraine.

James McCann was one of two Ballymoney men killed with the 8th battalion on this day, the other being Alex Hill. Neither of them was ever found.

The 8th battalion was with the 16th Division at Vlamertinghe and were involved in a battalion attack when James was killed. The weather for the previous two days had been continuous heavy rain which left every shell hole full to the lip and men and horses had to struggle through this up to their knees. Guns became bogged down when they had to be moved and we can only imagine the difficulty of getting rations up at night to men who were cold, wet through and hungry. In most cases it was only possible to move at night because the enemy had everything that moved during daylight under observation and fired at anything they could see. Of the nine men from Ballymoney killed on this day not one of them has a known grave. They are all commemorated by Regiment on the Tyne Cot Memorial. To a great extent this shows the conditions under which they had to fight. Conditions where water and mud, shortage of ammunition and uncut wire, fresh German troops and a scarcity of reserves all contributed to a situation where the British troops were pushed to the limit.

Cemetery location information.

The Tyne Cot Memorial to the Missing forms the north-east boundary of Tyne Cot Cemetery, which is located 9 kilometres north east of Ypres town centre.

6313 PRIVATE JOHN PATTISON
9th Bn Royal Irish Fusiliers
K.I.A. 16-8-17
No Known Grave. Commemorated on the Tyne Cot Memorial, Belgium. Panel 140 to 141.

Born   Ballymoney
Lived
Enlisted Greenock.

The 9th Royal Irish Fusiliers were raised in September 1914 from the Armagh, Monaghan and Cavan volunteers. In November they were stationed in Belfast but moved to Newtownards in February 1915. In July they moved to Seaford on the south coast of England and in October 1915 landed at Boulogne.

4.45am on the 16th of August 1917 marked the beginning of the second Battle of Langemarck. It is an indication of the ferocity of the fighting and of the ground conditions at the time, that not one of the local men killed on this day has a known grave. The weather at the Front had been very wet and every shell-hole was full to the lip with water. It was just as easy to drown in a shell-hole as be killed by rifle fire.

John Pattison was born in Ballymoney but had been working in Scotland when he enlisted at Greenock soon after war was declared. Training was a long drawn out affair with an awful lot of route marches in all weathers. By the time they arrived in France, in October of 1915, much of the early fighting had been done. The Battle of the Somme, in the summer of 1916, was John's first major battle and he came through this uninjured. A number of moves followed this but eventually he arrived in Belgium for the battles around Ypres. It was here that he was killed on the morning of the 16th of August 1917 as he went forward to the attack at the start of the Battle of Langemarck.

Ground conditions meant that the troops could not keep up close to the creeping barrage which gradually got farther and farther ahead of them. Timings could not be changed and soldiers struggled through mud up to their knees. Many of them fell from utter exhaustion in those awful conditions and were never seen again. John has no known grave and is commemorated on the Tyne Cot Memorial.

18623 RIFLEMAN HUGH PATTON
12th Bn Royal Irish Rifles.
K.I.A. 16-8-17
Aged 21
No Known Grave. Commemorated on the Tyne Cot Memorial, Belgium. Panels 138-140

Born   Ballymoney
Lived   Bushmills
Enlisted Ballymoney.
Son of Samuel and Eliza Patton

Although Hugh had been born in Ballymoney, he was living in Bushmills at the time he enlisted. His early training took place at Clandeboye, just outside Newtownards and when this was considered complete he was transferred to Seaford on the south coast of England, for final training.

After this the move across to France and the march to the Front at Martinsart in time for the Battle of the Somme. Having survived the Somme without a scratch he was then transferred with his battalion to Belgium, where they remained for over a year. During his time in Belgium he took part in many of the actions there. At the Battle of Messines, in June 1917, he again came through safely. By the beginning of August plans were being made for what was to become known as the Battle of Passchendaele. This was to be one of the major battles of the war. The weather had been changable and long, wet periods had left the ground sodden. Continuous shelling kept the ground muddy and soft. The Battle of Langemark was about to begin, but thunder storms and very heavy rain meant that it

had to be postponed for two days. The rain left the ground in an utter morrass, with every shell hole full to the lip and everywhere knee deep in mud. It was impossible to keep dry. Zero hour was to be 4.45am on the 16th of August. There had been very heavy shelling of the assembly trenches and the roads in the rear on the night of the 15th.

At zero hour, as the troops went out there was again very heavy shelling of the assembly trenches but this had little effect on the leading waves. But then enemy machine-guns opened up all along the line and heavy casualties were caused among the troops. It was during this early morning attack that Hugh Patton was killed as they attacked Langemark village. He has no known grave and is commemorated on the Tyne Cot Memorial.

1030 RIFLEMAN WILLIAM WHITE
12th Bn Royal Irish Rifles
K.I.A. 16-8-17
Aged 25
No Known Grave. Commemorated on the Tyne Cot Memorial.

Born   Fernalizery, Ballymoney.
Lived   Fernalizary, Ballymoney.
Enlisted   Ballymoney.
Son of William and Matilda White of Fernalizary.
Commemorated in Roseyards Presbyterian Church.

Wm White, (sen) was a member of Dunaghy L.O.L. 791 and had five sons in the lodge. William (KIA), David, Bob, John and Tom. At one time there were seven Whites altogether in this lodge.

William White was born at Fernalizary, about three miles from Ballymoney, and as a young boy attended Roseyards Presbyterian Church. When he enlisted into the 12th battalion of the Royal Irish Rifles in September 1914, he was sent for training almost immediately. This training took place at Clandeboye, in County Down. When this part of his training was complete he was moved to Seaford, on the south coast of England, and then in October 1915 they were taken across to France. Already plans were being made for the Battle of the Somme and it was to this area that William was taken. They were housed in tents at Martinsart, a village just behind the front lines. The date for the battle had been set for 28th June 1916, but heavy rain had turned the chalky ground to glutinous mud and the battle had to be postponed. The new date, 1st July 1916, dawned bright and sunny and at 7.30am the attack began. A change of plans meant that St Pierre-Divion, a small village in German hands, was not directly attacked, and the machine-guns here had a clear line of sight on the 12th battalion as they attacked across the river. The ground here rises fairly steeply from the River Ancre and gives a very good view north of the river. The 12th battalion were almost annihilated and were taken out of the line next day and sent to St Omer to be rested and brought back up to strength. William was lucky to escape injury on this day and a short time later was moved to Belgium and the area around Wulverghem. They would be here for over a year. Sporadic fighting was taking place all along the line and they saw a great deal of action here over the next few months. By the following summer plans were well advanced for the battle of Messines and mines strategically placed and filled with explosives gave the British a quick victory. Here, one of the men in charge of setting off the mines, was John Meeke of Benvarden.

When they were exploded he was then to revert to his normal job of stretcher bearer. It was during this later work that he saw Willie Redmond, the Irish nationalist, fall wounded. He made his way to Redmond's side under heavy shell and machine-gun fire and dressed Redmond's wounds, being injured himself in the process. He then got Redmond away to a dressing station before allowing his own wounds to be dressed. These actions won John Meeke the Military Medal. Redmond later died of his injuries. John Meeke died at home at Benvarden in 1923 and is buried in an unmarked grave in Derrykeighan Old Cemetery. After the success at the Battle of Messines William White was moved with the 12th Rifles to the north-east of Ypres for the Battle of Passchendaele. Here, wet weather again set in and shell holes were full to the lip with water. Conditions were atrocious, with continuous rain. Guns couldn't be moved, food could only be brought up at night, and darkness made that even more difficult, ammunition was another problem, with roads almost blown apart

and awash with mud and in places blocked with broken down waggons and dead horses. William was killed on the 16th of August, the first day of the Battle of Langemarck.

Of the nine Ballymoney men killed on this day, not one has a known grave. It gives some indication of the conditions under which these men had to fight and die when you consider that not one of them was ever seen again. They were just swallowed up by the mud where they fell. William has no known grave and is comemorated on the Tyne Cot Memorial, the huge wall at the back of Tyne Cot Cemetery.

LIEUT GEORGE LYONS GRAHAM
6th Bn Royal Dublin Fusiliers
K.I.A. 17-8-17
Aged 24
No Known Grave. Commemorated on the Tyne Cot Memorial, Belgium. Panels 144-145.

Born   Ballymacfin
Lived
Enlisted
Son of Mr S. Graham of Dervock.
Commemorated in Carncullagh Presbyterian Church.
Husband of Margaret Graham, of 42, Channing St, Castlereagh, Belfast.and the father of two children.

George Graham lived at Ballymacfin, very close to where Robert John McMullan lived. He was married and was living with his wife in Belfast and there were two children. He obtained his commission in October 1915, through Queen's University Officer Training Corps.

No other information has turned up concerning him although I would be surprised if there are not some family members still alive.

George was killed during the very difficult fighting at Passchendaele.

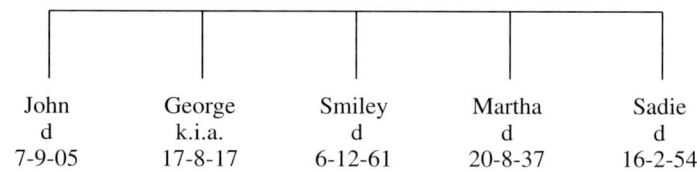

John	George	Smiley	Martha	Sadie
d	k.i.a.	d	d	d
7-9-05	17-8-17	6-12-61	20-8-37	16-2-54

LIEUT HUGH STEWART LATIMER JORDAN
Royal Flying Corps.
K.I.A. 20-8-17
Interred in Heroes Corner, in Wembley Parish Church burying ground

Born
Lived   Castle St, Ballymoney.
Enlisted

Chronicle 1-9-17

Lieut H.S.L.Jordan, Royal Flying Corps, who with Sgt E. Handley, R.F.C. was killed on the 20th August, was a son of Mr. H.S.Jordan, of Napier Rd, Wembley, and grandson of Mrs. Jordan and the late Mr. James Jordan, Castle St, Ballymoney.

In 1911 Catherine Jordan was still living in Castle Street. Stewart Jordan is commemorated on a lovely Roll of Honour inside Wembley Parish Church. He joined the H.A.C. in January 1915, and went to Egypt in the following May, returning to England last year. He was then given a commission in the reserve of officers in the Field Artillery. After serving in France for seven months, he returned to England, and was being trained as an observer when he was killed. Sgt Handley had flown in France, and had received a medal from the French Government for bravery. Lieut Jordan was educated at the Tower School of John Lyon, Harrow, and was a member of the staff of the Anglo-Egyptian Bank. At an inquest at Addlestone by the West Surrey Coroner, a gardener, John Hoare, of Woodham Grange, said that about ten o'clock on Monday morning he saw two machines in the air, one above the other. Suddenly there were two explosions, and the lower machine came straight down for some distance, when it straightened out and the right wing folded back on to the body of the machine. It next took a horizontal course for some distance with one plane, which also suddenly folded back. The machine then pitched over some trees into a field. Witness ran across and found Lieut Jordan and Sgt Handley, under the engine, dead. Evidence was given that the machine was in perfect order when it went up from Brooklands

Heroes Corner in Wembley Parish Church Burying Ground. Grave of H.S.L. Jordan

Aerodrome. Flight Commander Cecil Faber said that Sgt. Handley was acting as pilot, and was instructing Lieut Jordan as an observer. An Officer said he saw the machine come down with a spinning dive from 3,000 feet. A verdict was returned in each case of "death from misadventure". Another brother of Lieut Jordan's (Private Henry Jordan) was serving in Palestine.

The Memorial inside Wembley Parish Church

Grave of H.S.L. Jordan

41344 RIFLEMAN WILLIAM McCAUGHERN
4th Bn, 3rd New Zealand R.B.
K.I.A. 21-8-17
Aged 36
Interred in La Plus Douve Cemetery, Belgium. Plot 3, Row C, Grave 24.

Born   Cusheybracken, Rasharkin. on 27th Dec 1881.
Lived   Porangahau, North Island, New Zealand.
Enlisted At Napier on 18th November 1916
Son of Andrew and Hanna McCaughern, of Kells, formerly Rasharkin Presbyterian.

William John McCaughern emigrated to New Zealand in 1913 and owned a large sheep farm at Porangahau, on the Porangahau River on the east coast of the North Island about sixty miles south of Napier. He was examined at Waipukurau on the 7th of November 1916 and passed, and enlisted at Napier on the 18th of November. He was then thirty-five years of age. He was six feet tall with a dark complexion, hazel eyes and black hair. He was posted to his company on 1st January 1917 and after some preliminary training, embarked at Wellington on 14th March. After a long and tedious journey they arrived at Devenport on 21st May and joined the New Zealand reserve group for further training. On the 6th of July 1917 they left for France, arriving at the New Zealand Infantry and General Base Depot at Etaples on the 10th. Here they were given more training before being sent to their Division on the 8th of August. Next day they joined their battalion in the field.

After being brought up to strength the 4th battalion was moved to Belgium and to the area close to Ration Farm, so called by the troops because this was as close to the front lines as battalion transport could get at night with rations. Very heavy fighting took place here and on 21st August William John was killed in action. He was buried in La Plus Douve Cemetery close to where he fell and altogether there are sixty-one New Zealanders buried here. Another of the Ballymoney men, Robert Ramsey, is buried in this cemetery, and Alex Taylor, of Bushmills, is also here. Altogether, William John had seen less than three weeks of actual fighting and as can be seen by the letter, his Mother was to receive the sum of £54-15-0 after a wait of three and a half years. He had been home on leave at Cushybracken about a month before he was killed.

Grave of William John McCaughern middle of back row

982 RIFLEMAN ANDREW McGAHEY
11th Bn Royal Irish Rifles
D.O.W. 22-8-17
Aged 20
Interred in Etaples Military Cemetery, Plot 22, Row G, Grave 15a.

Born   Balnamore
Lived   Bushmills
Enlisted Bushmills
Son of Henry and Nancy McGahey of Balnamore.

Andrew McGahey was born at Balnamore in 1897. Some time after this the family moved to Bushmills where he eventually enlisted. Very little is known of his early life as the family died out many years ago. They lived in Market Square and another brother, Henry, travelled the Bushmills district every day selling pins and needles and other small household goods. He was very well recieved everywhere he went and was liked by everyone for his honesty and integrity. Andrew did his training at Clandeboye and was home a few times on leave. When this initial training was complete he was taken across to Seaford on the south coast of England to finish his training and then moved to France. The French Commanders were clamouring for the British to make a move to draw German forces away from Verdun and so the Battle of the Somme was planned. Andrew survived this and next day his unit was taken back for rest and re-organisation. From St Omer they were moved north to Kortepyp Camp, south of the village of Neuve Eglise. They were in the front line again at Mont Noir on the night of the 23rd of July in relief of two battalions of the 20th Division. In September they were moved to the area around Wulverghem and here they would stay for over a year. Continually there was fighting going on and men were being killed but their next major battle was the Battle of Messines in June 1917. Again Andrew survived but in August at Passchendaele he was severely injured. He was evacuated to Etaples to await a hospital ship to England for treatment for his injuries. He died there and is buried in the nearby cemetery. Sergeant John McGahey, killed in the Second World War, and named on the Bushmills War Memorial was probably another brother.

Connaught Cemetery at the Somme

26495 RFN SAMUEL ALEXANDER BUICK
10th Bn Scottish Rifles
K.I.A. 25-8-17
Aged 30
No Known Grave. Commemorated on the Tyne Cot Memorial, Belgium. Panels 68-70 & 162 & 162A.

Born   Culbane, Stranocum.
Lived   Drumdollagh
Enlisted
4th Son of James Buick, Rate Collector, Drumdollagh.
Commemorated in Kilraughts Presbyterian Church.

The 10th battalion was formed at Hamilton in September 1914 and trained at Bordon. By February 1915 they were at Winchester. They moved in April to Salisbury Plain and on 10th July landed at Boulogne.

Samuel Alexander Buick and Lily McCaughan went to Scotland and got married there. Samuel was twenty-four and Lily seventeen.

Their first child was a girl, Margaret, born in 1913. The second was a boy, born 21st April 1915. Lily, unknown to her parents, was very sick and had contracted T.B. When this became known to her family, her mother travelled to Scotland and fetched her and the two children home to the family farm at the Drones, where she died ten weeks later, on 14th July 1915, aged twenty-one years. Samuel had enlisted some time previously while Lily was still in good health and was probably completely unaware of her condition and by the time he found out he would have been at the front. She died just four days after he landed at Boulogne. In January 1916 the battalion were in action in the Rambert area and then they were moved up to the trenches at Hulluch for six days which passed fairly quietly. Over the next few weeks they were in the area around Loos and withstood some very heavy shelling from the enemy. Later on they were again moved, this time to the area around Ypres. Samuel was home on leave in July of 1916 and it was just after returning to his unit in Belgium that he was killed. On the 18th and 19th of August the battalion were improving their trenches and salvaging material. They were then taken back to Bivouac Camp, West of Ypres, where they were involved on the 21st in cleaning up and preparation for active operations. At 4.45am next morning the battalion moved up to the O.B. lines and were attached to the 44th Infantry Brigade and an attack was made on the modified green lines. On the evening of the 23rd, at 9.00pm they relieved the Gordon Highlanders in the front line. Next day, the 24th, was quiet, with some hostile artillery active on the support area. On the 25th the 44th Brigade attacked Gallipoli Farm, while the battalion attacked positions known as Iberian and Beck House with Lewis gun and rifle fire.

Patrols sent out by "C" and "D" coy's found Iberian strongly held. They were unable to take the position and were forced to dig in 100 yards west of Gallipoli. It was during this attack that Samuel Buick was killed. His death left the two children at home, orphans. He has no known grave and is commemorated on the Tyne Cot Memorial.

234835 PRIVATE DANIEL COULTER HILL
52nd Bn Canadian Infantry
K.I.A. 27-8-17
Aged 37
Interred in Aix-Noulette Communal Cemetery Extension. Plot 1, Row K, Grave 17.

Born   Killans, Finvoy on 9th May 1879.
Lived   Macdowall, Sask,Canada.
Enlisted Prince Albert, Sask.Canada.
Son of John Clarke Hill and Mary Hill, of Killans, Finvoy.
Husband of Jane Hill, of McDowall, Saskachewan.

Daniel served throughout the Boer War in the Imperial Yeomanry. When that war finished he emigrated to Canada where he worked as a railroad foreman. On 25th April 1916 he enlisted at Prince Albert. He was five feet eleven inches tall, with a fresh complexion, blue eyes and brown hair. He sailed from Halifax on S.S.Grampian on the 26th of October 1916 and arrived in England on the 4th of November, disembarking at Liverpool. They were immediately taken to Seaford for training and it was while he was there that he got leave and was home at the Post Office at Killans in February 1917. After he returned from leave intense training took place and he was transferred to the 18th reserve battalion. On 3rd May he was drafted to the 52nd battalion at Dibgate and the following day landed in France. He joined his unit for duty in the field on 28th May and just three months later, in August, he was killed in action. He is buried in Aix-Noulette Cemetery to the north of Vimy Ridge and the huge Canadian Memorial. On the 10th of April 1919 his sister Martha, died at Yellow Grass, Saskatchewan.

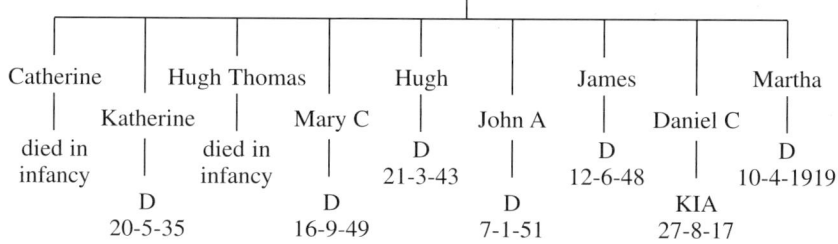

Aix-Noulette Communal Cemetery

7536 RIFLEMAN ROBERT W. McILHAGGA
12th Bn Royal Irish Rifles
D.O.W. 4-9-17
Interred in Rocquigny-Equancourt Road British Cemetery. Plot 1, Row B, Grave 20.

Born   Ballyportery.
Lived
Enlisted   Ballymoney.
Eldest son of Daniel and Mrs. McIlhagga, of 104 Main St. Livingston.
Commemorated in Ballyweaney Presbyterian Church.

The Cemetery is thirteen kilometres north of Peronne and twelve kilometres south-east of Bapaume. This was the site of a Casualty

4th from left

Clearing Station in September 1917 and a huge number of injured soldiers were treated here.

The 36th Division had been moved south in preparation for the Battle of Cambrai and there was much sporadic fighting going on. They were based close to the main Bapaume-Cambrai road and when Robert was injured he was moved to No 48 C.C.S. south of Ytres.

Between the 28th and 30th of August the 12th battalion were in the line at Havrincourt and it is most likely this was the time when Robert was injured.

A Memorial card in the possession of Mrs. Crawford, Finvoy road, reads,

In fond and loving memory of
Rifleman Robert W McIlhagga,
D coy, 12th Bn, Royal Irish Rifles
who died from wounds recieved in action
in France,
On Tuesday, 4th September, 1917.

" *Until the day break, and the shadows flee away.*"

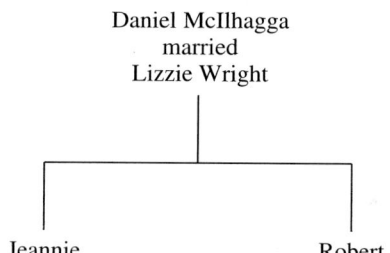

Daniel McIlhagga
married
Lizzie Wright

Jeannie   Robert

6489 L. CPL WILLIAM J. WRIGHT
2nd Bn Irish Guards
K.I.A. 4-9-17
Aged 36
Interred in Duhallow A.D.S. Cemetery, Ypres. Plot 7, Row B, Grave 5.

Born   Ballyrattahan, Dervock.
Lived   Dervock.
Enlisted Dublin.
Son of James and Eliza Wright, of Dervock.
Commemorated in Carncullagh Presbyterian Church.

William was born at Ballyrattahan, Dervock, about four miles from Ballymoney. He was the son of James Wright and a brother of R. Wright of 32. Spencer St, Belfast. He had been in the Royal Irish Constabulary for ten years before enlisting. He was stationed for a long time in Donegal before being moved to Henry St Barracks, in Belfast. He was a member of the police at the front and was just about to come off duty when a shell dropped in his dug-out, killing him and four of his pals instantly. The police had a cross made and erected on his grave and many of his comrades deeply grieved at his death.

Dunhallow A.D.S. Cemetery, Belgium

According to a report in the newspapers William was through the Battle of Mons and had been severely wounded in one arm. He had been removed to a hospital in Devon for treatment and was progressing satisfactorily. When he was considered well enough a few weeks later, he rejoined his unit.

The family lived at Ballyratahan, Dervock. The 2nd battalion had just moved to Elverdinghe, to the north-west of Ypres, and into Abbingley Camp, when this incident occurred. They were not in the front line at this stage, but near enough to be within range of the big guns. The weather had turned cold for September and driving rain kept everywhere in a sea of mud. Most of the men were housed in tents at the camp and the stormy weather and flapping canvas kept all but the soundest sleepers awake. But at least they had cover in the tents, something they were not used to in the trenches. William is buried in Duhallow A.D.S.Cemetery just to the north of Ypres.

The grave of Wm Wright in Dunallon A.D.S. Cemetery

LIEUT WILLIAM SHIELDS
14th Bn Manchester Regt & Royal Flying Corps
K.I.A. 5-9-17
Aged 28
Interred in Voormezeele Enclosures No 1, and No 2. Plot 1, Row H, Grave 41.

Born
Lived   Stranocum.
Enlisted
Son of Samuel and Sarah Shields, of 33, Upper Frank St, Belfast.

The 14th battalion were formed at Lichfield in October 1914. In April 1915 they became a 2nd reserve battalion in the 3rd reserve brigade, remaining at Lichfield. In January 1916 they moved to Brockton, Cannock Chase. This did not suit William and he transferred to the Royal Flying Corps. He served in the 45th Squadron of the R.F.C. and was killed in air combat over Voormezeele on 5th September 1917. His brother, Samuel, had already been killed at the Somme.

It would appear that the family had earlier moved to Belfast before the two brothers enlisted and that William was working in England. This would partly explain enlisting into the Manchester Regiment. His subsequent move into the Royal Flying Corps fulfilled a long standing ambition and he very quickly gained his Pilot's wings.

By the time he was killed in September 1917 he had become very experienced and was an outstanding pilot. His death was a heavy blow to a family who had already lost one son. He is buried in the village of Voormezeele, just four

kilometres south-west of Ypres town centre. This cemetery is very close to where his plane came down on the outskirts of the village.

Voormezeele Enclosures No 1, and No 2, are 4 kilometres south-west of Ypres town centre, on the Voormezeele Dorp, a street in the village of Voormezeele.

The grave of Wm. Shields at Voormezeele Enclosures

1842 CORPORAL ROBERT TURNER
54th Bn Australian Infantry
K.I.A. 25-9-17
Aged 26
Interred in Menin Road South Military Cemetery, Belgium. Plot 2, Row G, Grave 12.

Born   Cloughmills.
Lived   Liverpool, New South Wales
Enlisted Liverpool, New South Wales
Son of Alexander and Rose Turner, of Cloughmills.
Commemorated in Ballyweaney Presbyterian Church.

Robert Turner had only been in Australia for a few years when war was declared. He was five feet eight inches tall with a light complexion, grey eyes and red hair. A lightly built young man, he weighed eleven stone. He enlisted on 28th December 1914 at Liverpool, New South Wales and began training immediately.

It was while he was training that he overstayed leave from midnight on 8-3-15 to 9pm on 9-3-15. For this he was fined 10 shillings and one day's pay (5 shillings). He was promoted Corporal on 10th April 1915, the same day as he embarked at Sydney on H.M.A.T. "Argyllshire" for Gallipoli. On 25th June he complained of stomach pains and was operated on for Appendicitis. The wound didn't heal properly and it was decided to send him back to Australia to recuperate. At the same time he reverted to the ranks with effect from 26th June. He sailed from Cairo on the "Horarato" on 28th July 1915, and returned to Egypt on 21st February 1916.

He then embarked on the "Transylvania" at Alexandria on the 29th of March and landed at Marseilles on 4th April.

Four days later he reported sick and was sent to hospital at Etaples. A skin disease was diagnosed and he spent 37 days in hospital. On 10th June he was granted ten days leave and it is believed that he visited Cloughmills at this time. He then returned through Etaples and in July joined the 2nd battalion

In August, while doing ration fatigue at night, a wheel ran over his foot, injuring a toe very badly. He was taken to 4th Casualty Clearing Station and moved on to No 22 General Hospital at Camiers. By mid September he had recovered and was allotted to the 54th battalion, joining them on the 11th of October. Then on 31st January 1917 he was again promoted Corporal, this time for good. He was killed at Ypres on 25th September 1917, and is buried in Menin Rd South Military Cemetery in Ypres.

Menin Road South Military Cemetery, Ypres.

Alex and Rose Turner had a family of five, three boys and two girls. Thomas and Robert were both killed in the 1st World War, and Herbert died as a young man. One of the girls married but had no family and the other never married. So the family just died out. It is interesting to note that another Cloughmills man, Robert Shannon, as a young man, worked in Turner's shop. He emigrated to Australia after having served in the shop for five years. Robert Turner also emigrated to Australia and it would be interesting to know if they emigrated together. Robert Shannon was killed in action on 6th May 1917, just a few weeks before Robert Turner.

The shop which bears their name still stands in the main street in Cloughmills. The family worshipped in Ballyweaney Presbyterian Church and it is there that Robert and his brother Thomas are commemorated on the Roll of Honour.

Menin Road South Military Cemetery at Ypres

1003 PRIVATE ARCHIBALD JOHNSON KENNEDY
Canadian 1st Div.Supply Column
DIED 28-9-17
Aged 33
Interred in Shorncliffe Military Cemetery, Kent.

Born   Ballyboyland
Lived
Enlisted   Valcartier Camp, Canada.
Commemorated in Kilraughts Presbyterian Church.

Archie Kennedy was born at Ballyboyland, a short distance outside Ballymoney on 25th September 1883. He had at least one brother, Robert, and a sister Mary. As a young man he spent five years in the Royal Navy before he emigrated to Canada and settled near Quebec where he worked as an engineer. He enlisted at Valcartier Camp, a huge military camp on the outskirts of Quebec on 8th September 1914. He was five feet eight and a half inches tall with a dark complexion, brown eyes and brown hair. He eventually arrived in France on 10th February 1915. In July of that year he spent a week in hospital suffering from a bowel complaint, followed by another spell in hospital with a severe toothache. Then in January of 1916 he was granted a weeks leave to help him recover from these complaints. Following this in April he was transferred to the Canadian Supply Column and here he was to remain. He was again granted leave in October 1916 and was home for ten days. On 22nd January 1917 he was awarded the Good Conduct Badge although his records do not state the reasons for this award. Then in April he reported sick and was removed to the hospital ship "Lanfranc" and transferred to England. Reports by the doctors there mention a heart problem and of him being fat and very much over weight. Reports tell of a very gradual, slow recovery, but always mention the seriousness of the situation and the fact that he is over weight. He died from heart failure on the 28th of September 1917. He is buried in Shorncliffe Military Cemetery, Kent. In April 1917 Archie Kennedy was in hospital suffering from shell shock.

Beaumont Hamel Cemetery at the Somme

28359 PRIVATE GILMOUR PATTERSON
1st/5th Bn King's Own Scottish Borderers
DIED 12-10-17
Interred in Hadra War Memorial Cemetery, Alexandria. Plot A, Grave 71.

Born   Ballymoney.
Lived   High St, Ballymoney.
Enlisted   Lanark.
Son of Mrs. Patterson, High St.

The 1st/5th battalion were stationed in Dumfries at the time war was declared on 4th August 1914. They were a Dumfries and Galloway battalion. A week later they went for training at Bannockburn and in May 1915 joined the 52nd Div. On the 21st of May they sailed from Liverpool for Mudros, arriving on the 29th. Then on 6th June they were in the Dardanelles where a great deal of fighting took place. By early January 1916 they were back at Mudros and sailed for Alexandria on 4th February. They would remain here for over two years.

Gilmour was the eldest son of the family. He was educated at the Model School in Ballymoney and for a few years afterwards served in his mother's grocer's shop in the town. He then emigrated to Canada where he remained for two or three years before coming home to get married. Afterwards he obtained a position in a large firm, Cooper & Co, in Glasgow, and remained there until he enlisted. He was home on leave in early April 1917 but after returning to his unit in Egypt he contracted Dysentry and died in hospital on the 12th of October. It was probably a sister of Gilmour's who had earlier married Rev J.G. Paton M.C. It is believed that the grocers shop belonging to his mother is where the newsagents is now in High St.

If one looks closely at the shop, the floor is on two levels, suggesting that the higher area at the back of the shop was at one time the part used as a living area by the family. Gilmour is interred in Hadra War Memorial Cemetery, Alexandria. Plot A, Grave 71.

Ploegsteert Cemetery

18/1626 RIFLEMAN ANDREW KINNAIRD
10th Bn, Royal Irish Rifles
K.I.A. 3-11-17
Interred in Metz-en-Couture Communal Cemetery British Extn. Plot 2, Row C, Grave 5.

Born   Tullaghgore.
Lived   Tullaghgore.
Enlisted
Commemorated in 1st Ballymoney Presbyterian Church.

Andrew Kinnaird was born at Tullaghgore, a townland two miles to the north of Ballymoney. The family all attended the old school at Seacon just outside Ballymoney. Many of the families in this district were in the habit of going to Scotland in search of the seasonal work on the large farms of North Ayrshire and Lanarkshire and the Semples, who lived close to Kinnairds went every year. It is believed that Andrew went with them to Scotland and that he married Sarah Semple while they were both working in Scotland. The Semple family worshipped in 1st Ballymoney Presbyterian Church and if Sarah had followed family tradition she would have been married there, but there is no record of the marriage in their books and therefore we have to assume that she married somewhere else. The only other place where it was likely to happen was in Scotland and the family believe that this is what happened.

Soon after the outbreak of hostilities Andrew enlisted in Scotland and we can reasonably assume that this was just after the completion of the harvest work, most likely September 1914.

The 10th battalion were raised in Belfast in September 1914 from the Belfast Volunteers. They trained at Newcastle and moved to Ballykinlar in January 1915. Then in July they crossed to Seaford on the south coast of England

KINNIARD—In sad and loving memory of our dearly-beloved son Rifleman Andrew Kinniard, Royal Irish Rifles, B Company, killed in action 3rd November, 1917.
He sleeps in death, far, far from home,
　He owns a soldier's grave;
He nobly laid his young life down
　That others he might save.
We little thought when he left home
　That he would ne'er return;
That he so soon in death would sleep,
　And leave us here to mourn.
Ever remembered by his loving Father and Mother, also Sister and Brothers and Cousins (two brothers with the colours, one in France and the other in hospital).

Front row right

and in October of that year they landed at Boulogne. They were with the 4th Division from November 1915 to February 1916. At some stage after Andrew was killed on 3rd November 1917, Sarah and her little daughter returned to Tullaghgore. Sarah later married Robert Thomas Graham, an engineer from Glasgow, in 1st Ballymoney Presbyterian Church on 27th August 1920. Up until the very last years of her life Sarah returned almost every summer to visit her friends at Tullaghgore and her daughter, Annie, kept the friendship up until her death just a few years ago.

Metz-en-Couture is a village between Bertincourt and Gouzeaucourt From Metz-en-Couture take the D 29 B in the direction of Gouzeaucourt and in 2 kilometres the cemetery is on the road side, next to the Communal Cemetery.

Andrew went to Scotland in search of work and probably enlisted there.

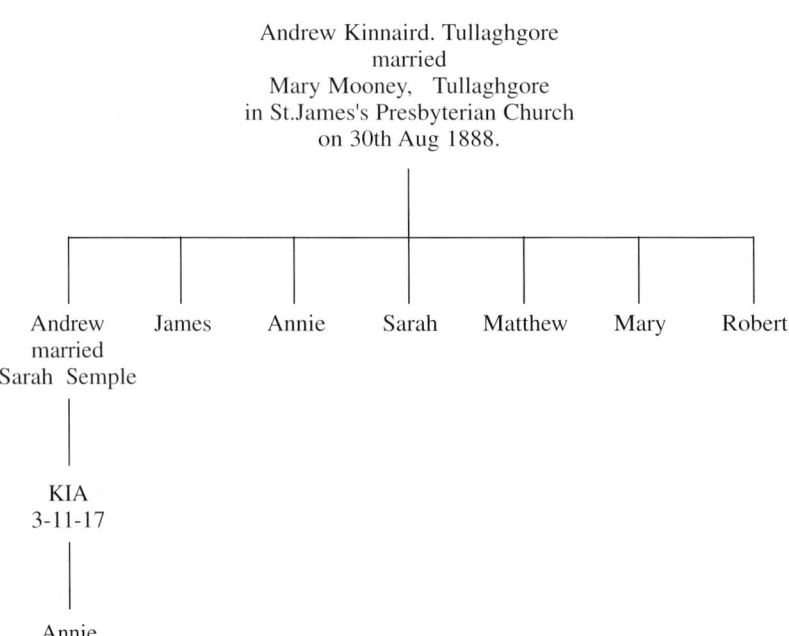

Andrew Kinnaird. Tullaghgore
married
Mary Mooney, Tullaghgore
in St.James's Presbyterian Church
on 30th Aug 1888.

Andrew married Sarah Semple — James — Annie — Sarah — Matthew — Mary — Robert

KIA 3-11-17

Annie

203051 A.CPL SAMUEL KERR
5th Bn Highland Light Infantry
K.I.A. 8-11-17
Aged 34
Interred in Gaza War Cemetery, Israel. Plot 10, Row A, Grave 6.

Born
Lived
Enlisted Kilmarnock, Ayrshire.
Commemorated in 1st Ballymoney Presbyterian Church.
Son of the late John and Mrs Kerr, of Baillieborough, Co.Cavan.
Husband of Annie E. Kerr, of Rossnegad, Maryborough.
Brother of Mrs. Ferguson, Queen St.

Samuel Kerr, a brother of the late Mrs Ferguson of Queen Street, enlisted at Kilmarnock, in Ayrshire. Probably like many other men from the district, he had gone to Scotland in search of work, and on the outbreak of hostilities enlisted at the nearest depot. He was obviously well known in Ballymoney.

The 5th Battalion HLI, were serving in Palestine in early November 1917, as part of the 52nd Lowland Division. On 7th November Gaza had been captured and the troops now moved into open country to the north, into what we now call the Gaza strip. Fierce fighting took place in this mountainous region north of the Wadi el Hesi, which lies about seven miles north of Gaza. The Wadi el Hesi rises in the Judaean Hills and flows in a succession of pools in a westerly direction to the Mediterranean Sea. On either side of it's mouth sand dunes run from three to four miles inland. Behind these sand dunes there is a strip of fairly good land with several small villages and then a wild mountainous region to the north. It was here that the advance took place but did not start until after darkness had fallen. By 8.20pm they had taken their objective. It was in this attack that Samuel Kerr was killed. He is buried in Gaza War Cemetery.

Gaza War Cemetery

20431 PRIVATE THOMAS BLACK
1st Bn Royal Inniskilling Fusiliers
K.I.A. 20-11-17
Aged 28
No known grave. Commemorated on the Cambrai Memorial, Louverval. Panels 5 and 6.

Lived   Greenock, Lanarkshire.
Enlisted   Greenock, Lanarkshire.
Son of Thomas and Ellen Black of 12 Mill St, Greenock.

Thomas and Ellen Black, who had lived in Meetinghouse St for many years, had gone to Greenock to live, taking the family with them. Work in the Ballymoney district was scarse and with better prospects in southern Scotland, the family had moved there. This was common practice at the time and a number of Ballymoney families moved to Scotland. It was in Greenock that his son, Thomas, eventually enlisted.

The battalion saw a great deal of action in Gallipoli during the summer of 1915 and suffered very heavy casualties in the fighting there. Then in January they were evacuated from Gallipoli and eventually arrived in the south of France to prepare for a very long and tiring journey by train up to the Western Front. Towards the end of the Battle of the Somme the 1st battalion were in the area close to Guillemont and Thomas saw much heavy fighting in this region. The area around Guillemont is reasonably flat with very little cover for attacking troops and when an attack was launched it had to be under a smoke screen or during the hours of darkness. The battalion saw many moves to different locations but by November of 1917 they were at Masnieres on the Cambrai to St. Quentin road and it was here on the 20th of November that Thomas was killed. The Battle of Cambrai had just begun and a very determined attack had been launched by the 1st battalion. At this time they were still with the 29th Division and for a while the attack was successful. But they were eventually driven back, almost to their starting point. It was at this critical time at the point where they were being turned back, that Thomas was killed. News of this was slow in coming to the Black home. They had to wait until July of the following year before being informed that Thomas was dead. He has no known grave and is commemorated on the Cambrai Memorial. An advertisement placed in the Greenock Telegraph in April 1999 asking the family to get in touch has failed to produce any response and so it must be assumed that the family has probably died out.

Cemetery location information.

The small village of Louverval is on the north side of the N30 Bapaume to Cambrai road, 13 kilometres north east of Bapaume and 16 kilometres south - west of Cambrai. The memorial stands on a terrace in Louverval Military Cemetery which is on the north side of the N30, south of Louverval village. The names of the dead are carved on a semi - circular wall behind a colonade.

The inscription reads,

> To the glory of God and to the enduring memory of 7048 officers and men of the forces of the British Empire who fell at the battle of Cambrai between the 20th November and the 3rd December 1917, whose names are here recorded but to whom the fortunes of war denied the known and honoured burial given to their comrades in death.

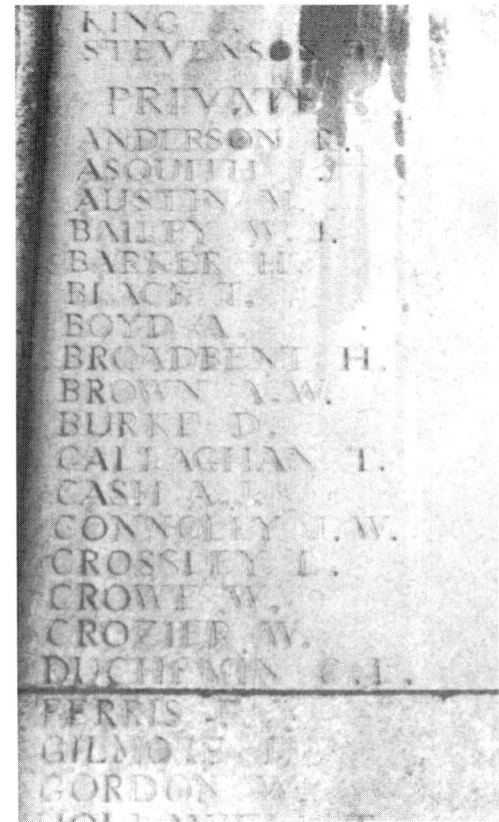

13210 C.S.M. SAMUEL CRAIG
7/8th Bn Royal Irish Fusiliers
K.I.A. 20-11-17
Aged 27
Interred in Croisilles British Cemetery, France. Plot 2, Row C, Grave 15.

Born   Dervock
Lived   Clones, Co. Monaghan
Enlisted   Armagh.
Husband of Sarah Craig of 12 Gosford Place, McClure St, Belfast.

Samuel Craig was born at Dervock in about 1890. His grandfather and grandmother, Samuel and Nancy lived at the "Corner House", still known as Craig's Corner.

It was here that Samuel worked as a shoemaker, whilst his two daughters, Jane and Sarah, were dressmakers upstairs. His son, Thomas, was the father of two boys, Thomas and Samuel, and it is this Samuel who was killed in the First World War. Samuel and Nancy are buried in Carncullagh along with their son Thomas, and Thomas's son, Thomas is buried in Singapore. Samuel had married and had been living in Clones in County Monaghan for a time. He enlisted in Armagh. Soon after this his wife appears to have moved to live in Belfast.

Her new home in McClure St was just off the Ormeau Road. It seems that Samuel enlisted early in the war and had been involved in a lot of heavy fighting. He was through the Battle of Messines in June of 1917 and was then moved

Croisilles British Cemetery, France

south into the area around Arras. The Battle of Cambrai was about to start and the battalion was in trenches a short distance in front of the village of Croisilles. Fighting was intense and in some parts of the line the troops were being pushed back and their positions anhiliated whilst in others small advances were being made.

Samuel was killed in the heavy fighting between Arras and Cambrai and is buried in Croisilles British Cemetery. For some obscure reason he is not mentioned on Dervock War Memorial but then there are a number of very obvious ommissions there.

Cemetery location information.

Croisilles is a village about 13 kilometres south-east of Arras. Croisilles British Cemetery lies off a track, approximately 300 metres long, to the south-east of the village on the road to Ecoust-St-Mein (D 9).

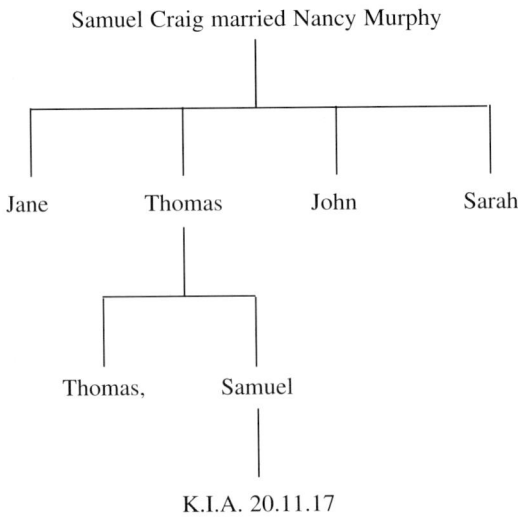

21495 L. CPL JOHN LAVERTY M.M.
7/8th Bn Royal Irish Fusiliers
K.I.A. 20-11-17
No Known Grave. Commemorated on the Arras Memorial.

Born   Ballymoney
Lived   Townhead St.
Enlisted Ballycastle

In June 1916 John Laverty was suffering from bullet wounds in both legs. He was taken to No. I. Base hospital for immediate treatment. His wife, living at Townhead St, had trouble of her own. Their young son, called John, after his

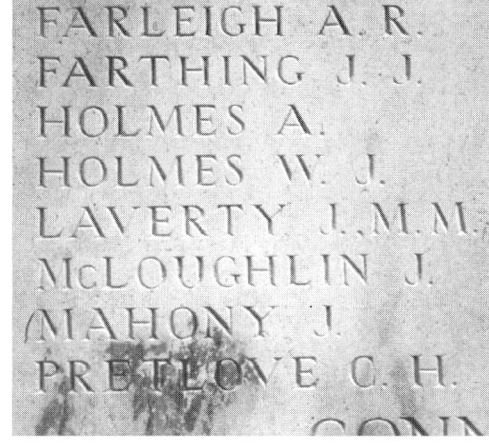

father, had been ill and died the same morning as the news of his father's injuries arrived. A few days later John was invalided back home to a hospital in Dublin. It was at this time that friends in Ballycastle, Ballymoney and Garvagh decided to buy him a wrist watch and it was presented to him at Portobello Barracks in Dublin in September 1916.

Before enlisting John had been employed by Alex McCormick, of Linenhall St. John Laverty and Patrick McKee were both Ballymoney boys. They were very good friends and were actually related. They eventually ended up in the same gun crew and spent most of their time in the Army together. In August 1917 they were together and for their bravery both were awarded the Military Medal. Again on 20th November they were still together and their unit was under severe attack. Their Commanding Officer told them to stay on their machine-gun as long as they could to allow their comrades the chance to escape. The Germans were creeping up on them from all directions and the fire being poured onto them was intense, but they stayed at their post. They were both killed in this very brave act but they had allowed their comrades to escape. Neither has a known grave and they are both commemorated on the Arras Memorial.

20912 PRIVATE PATRICK McKEE M.M.
7/8th Bn Royal Irish Fusiliers
K.I.A. 20-11-17
No Known Grave. Commemorated on the Arras Memorial, France.

Born   Ballymoney
Lived   Newbuildings
Enlisted Randalstown

The Military Medal won by Patrick McKee

Patrick was born and reared at Newbuildings and after leaving school worked as a farm labourer to Mr Henry Stuart of Newbuildings.

Patrick McKee enlisted just after the outbreak of hostilities along with his good friend John Laverty. They were related by marriage, and their lives were to run in a remarkably parallel course from now on. They were serving in the same Battalion and on the same gun team. They were together when both of them were awarded the Military Medal in August 1917. The Parchment certificate won by Patrick and presented to his Mother after Patrick was killed, still survives. On the morning of 20th November 1917, Patrick's unit were being very heavily attacked and were remorselessly being driven back.

The situation was desperate and Patrick's Commanding Officer told him and John Laverty to stay on the machine-gun as long as possible to allow their comrades to escape. He knew he had the right men for the job and that they would not flinch. They stayed to the end, both being killed

M'Kee—Killed in action in France on 20th November, 1917, Private Patrick M'Kee, Royal Irish Fusiliers.
  "Sweet Jesus, have mercy on him."
No mother there did him attend,
Nor o'er him did a father bend;
No sister' near to shed a tear,
No brother his last word to hear.
But—I seem to see his dear face
Through a mist of anguished tears;
Ah! the mother's part is a broken heart,
And the burden of lonely years.
Ever remembered by his sorrowing father and mother.
            Frances and Mary M'Kee.
Newbuildings, Ballymoney.

together and this allowed their comrades to get back to a stronger position and get dug in.

In the severe winter weather of January 1917, Patrick was taken from the trenches suffering from frost-bite in both feet. He was brought back to hospital in England for treatment and afterwards sent home on leave. After a period on leave he returned to his unit but sustained bullet wounds to both legs which proved serious and he was again in hospital. By October of that year he was again well enough to come home on leave and it was just a few weeks after returning to his unit that he was killed. He has no known grave and is commemorated on the Arras Memorial.

Both Military Medals still survive in the Ballymoney area, and are lovingly cared for by both families. They were on display, side by side in Ballymoney Heritage Centre in September 1997.

Patrick's brother, Archibald, served with the Canadian Forces and was also killed.

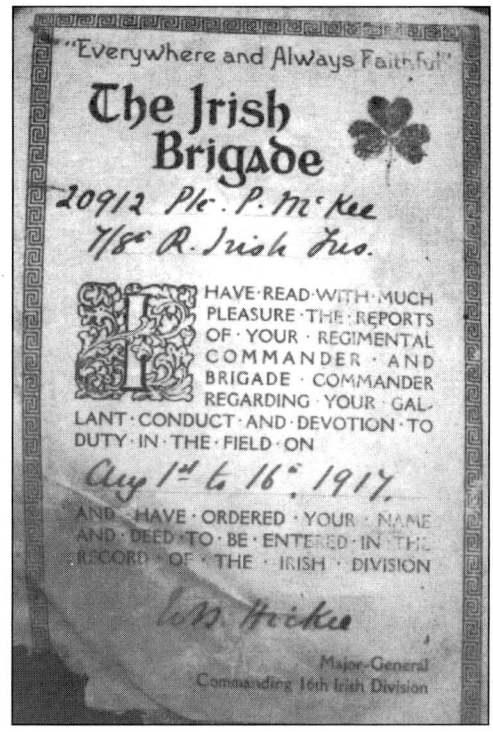

The certificate presented to Mrs McKee after Patrick won the Military Medal in 1917

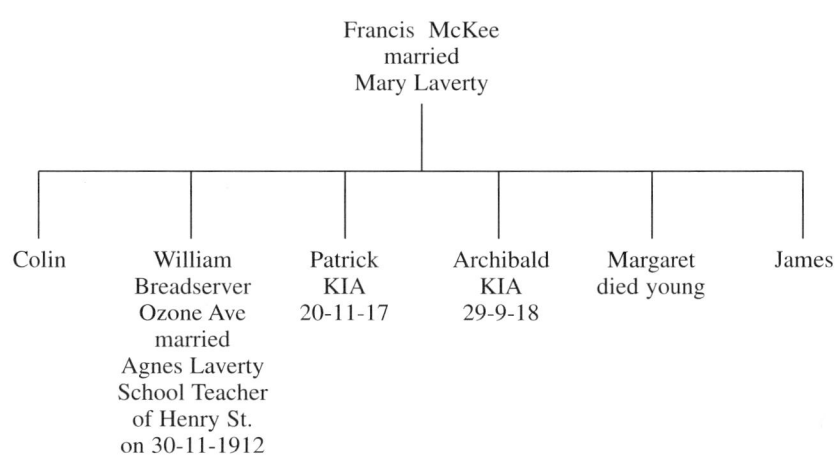

CAPTAIN WILLIAM BRUCE GEORGE STUART M.C.
12th Bn R. Irish Rifles.
K.I.A. 22-11-17
Aged 24
No Known Grave. Commemorated on the Cambrai Memorial, France. Panel 10.

Born
Lived   Mount Earl, Ballymena.
Enlisted
Son of William and Barbara Frances Stuart. of Mountearl, Ballymena.
Commemorated with a cross in Derrykeighan Parish Churchyard.

Killed in action at Moeuvres. The citation in the London Gazette of 17th September 1917 to the award of the Military Cross reads as follows.

"For conspicious gallantry and devotion to duty in commanding his company during an attack. He led them with great dash and personal gallantry, capturing many prisoners, and later on doing excellent work in consolidating captured positions. Throughout the action his fine example of determination and enthusiam kept his men going at a time when they were dead beat."

12971 RIFLEMAN JAMES THOMPSON
15th Bn Royal Irish Rifles
K.I.A. 22-11-17
Aged 21
Interred and commemorated at Special Memorial B5, Moeuvres Communal Cemetery, France.

Born   Ballymoney.
Lived
Enlisted   Belfast.
Son of Andrew and Catherine Thompson, of 33 Limestone Rd, Belfast, his last known address. He was killed at Moeuvres.

James Thompson was born at Ballymoney in about 1896 and was the son of Andrew and Catherine Thompson, of 33. Limestone Road, Belfast, his last known address. Most of his training took place at Ballykinlar. He was in action very early in the war and  was seriously wounded at the Battle of the Aisne in June 1915. He was invalided home for a few weeks, but then returned to his unit. He was home again on leave in September 1915. The battalion was then withdrawn for re-organisation and moved to Belgium and Kortepyp camp at Neuve Eglise. From here they moved at intervals

Moeuvres Communal Cemetery, France.

either north or south as they were needed and were in Belgium for over a year. In June 1917 at the Battle of Messines he was fighting close to the village of Wytschaete and again survived. He was also through the Battle of Langemarck and from here was ordered south to the area close to Cambrai.

The 15th Rifles were to clear the first and second lines of the Hindenburg Support System up to the Canal north-west of Moeuvres. It was this action which was to cost James his life. He is known to be buried in Moeuvres Cemetery, although the position of his grave is now, not known. The headstone is just a commemorative one.

Moeuvres Communal Cemetery

1161 RIFLEMAN GEORGE WALES
12th Bn Royal Irish Rifles.
K.I.A. 22-11-17
No Known Grave. Commemorated on the Cambrai Memorial, Louverval.

Born   Ballymoney
Lived   Queen St, Ballymoney.
Enlisted Ballymoney.
Commemorated in Trinity Presbyterian Church.

The small village of Louverval is on the north side of the N30, Bapaume to Cambrai road, 13 kilometres north-east of Bapaume, 16 kilometres south-west of Cambrai. The memorial stands on a terrace in Louverval Military Cemetery on the north side of the N30, south of Louverval village.

George was born in Queen St, in Ballymoney and the family worshipped in Trinity Presbyterian Church, at the bottom of the street. He did much of his early training at Clandeboye and Newtownards, later moving to Seaford and then to France in October 1915. George was through the Battle of the Somme but survived the tragic 1st of July, when so many of his friends were killed. He was then moved to Belgium and to the area around Wulverghem, where they stayed for over a year.

George Wales had been injured at the time that John Hanna, James McCoubrey and William Wade had been killed at Wulverghem. The four of them were pals and George had been lucky on that occassion to escape with his life. William Wade lived just round the corner from George in Edward Street. This was in early June 1917 during preparations for the Battle of Messines. He was not to be so lucky here. The 12th Battalion had been brought south for the Battle of Cambrai and were at the village of Moeuvres. The Germans produced a very heavy attack between Inchy and Moeuvres and were threatening to break through the British defences. It was here that George Wales was killed.

He has no known grave and is commemorated on the Cambrai Memorial.

1396 RIFLEMAN ROBERT MARSHALL
15th Bn Royal Irish Rifles
K.I.A. 23-11-17
Aged 26
No Known Grave. Commemorated on the Thiepval Memorial.

Born   Finvoy
Lived   Finvoy
Enlisted Coleraine
Son of Robert and Sophia Marshall, of Finvoy.
Commemorated in Finvoy Parish Church.

Robert was the eldest of a family of seven, three boys and four girls.

The 15th battalion was part of the 107th Infantry Brigade of the 36th Ulster Division and did much of their training at Ballykinlar. During this early training he was home on leave on a number of occasions. Later they were moved across to Seaford on the south coast of England and then to Bordon and Bramshott for final training. When they arrived in France they were taken to the area around Mesnil and Martinsart, a short distance from what was to become the front lines at the Battle of the Somme. The French Commanders had been clamouring for the British to do something to draw the German armies away from Verdun and the Battle of the Somme was the result. The date of the start of the battle had to be postponed due to the very wet weather, but the new date, 1st July 1916, dawned bright and sunny.

As the men left their trenches they were met with a withering hail of machine-gun and rifle fire. The 15th battalion were in support to the south of the River Ancre and were attacking across a steep hill, on top of which now stands the Ulster Tower. The machine-guns at St. Pierre-Divion had not

been silenced and they took a heavy toll of the men coming up the hill. These same guns had, moments before, been trained on the men of the 12th battalion as they crossed the valley of the Ancre, a few hundred yards to the north. Robert was lucky to escape with his life on a day when so many lost theirs. Next day the battalion was taken out of the line and moved to St.Omer for a rest and to be brought up to strength again. When this was completed they were moved to Belgium and the area around Wulverghem. They were to be in this area for over a year. Much of the time sporadic fighting was taking place but as the year wore on plans were made for the battle of Messines. This was followed by the battles for Passchendaele and Langemarck in August 1917 before being moved south for the battle of Cambrai. He was killed on 23rd November as he went forward to the attack between Moeuvres and Bourlon Wood.

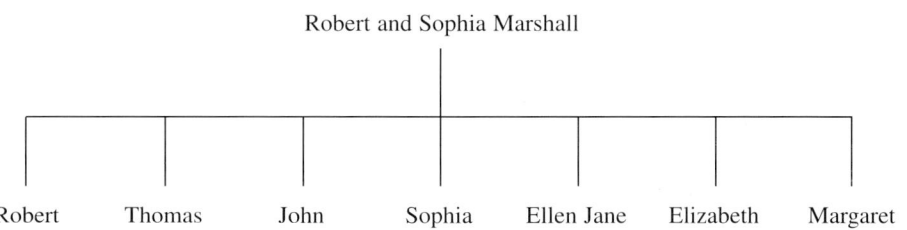

The Arras Memorial

14557   PRIVATE GEORGE MOORE
8/9th Bn Royal Irish Rifles
K.I.A. 23-11-17
No Known Grave. Commemorated on the Cambrai Memorial, Louverval. Panel 10.

Born   Coleraine
Lived   Balnamore
Enlisted   Ballymoney
Son of Mr William Moore, of Balnamore.

In March 1915 George had been in the trenches for two days when he got frost-bite in both feet and had to be taken to hospital. He soon recovered from this and arrived back with his unit a few weeks later. In July he was injured in the knee and also had a bullet through the shoulder. This took longer to heal and another stay in hospital was necessary. By the time he had recovered from these injuries winter had set in and again the cold was intense. In early 1917 he was again in the trenches and was in the trenches almost continuously until September, when he was sent home on leave. This was to be the last time he would see his family. In the heavy fighting which took place in the Battle of Cambrai, George was killed. He was reported by Private Rooney to be lying in a shell hole at Cambrai, on 23rd November 1917, badly wounded. He was officially reported missing in January 1918. There is no known grave and he is commemorated on the Cambrai Memorial at Louverval. Soon after being notified of George's death, his father, Mr. William H. Moore, of Balnamore, underwent an opeation and failed to recover.

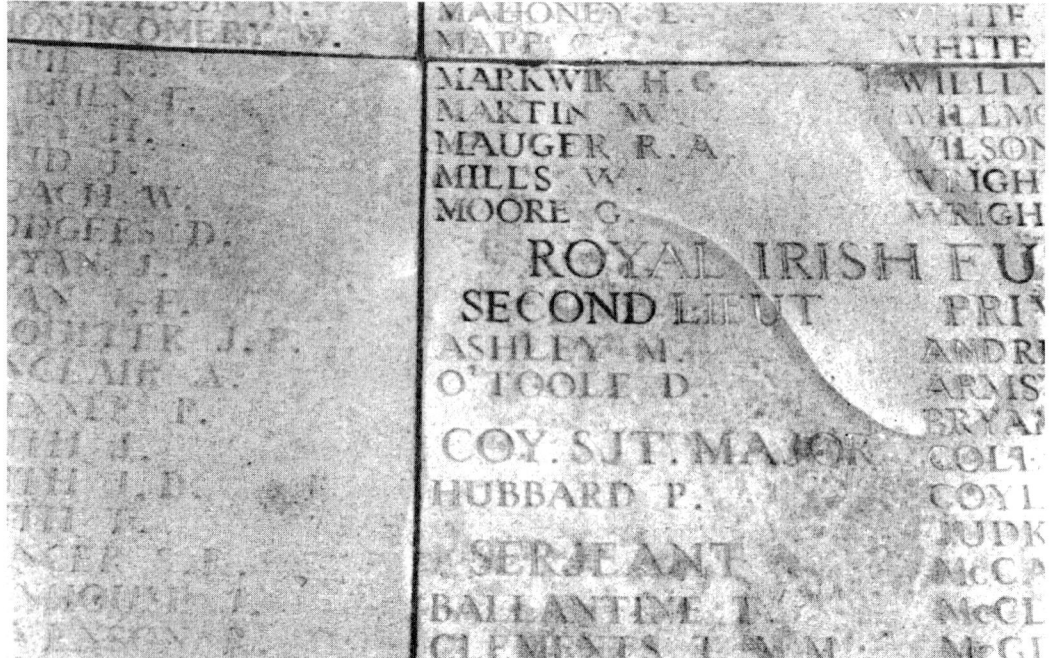

1596 RIFLEMAN BRYCE CAMPBELL
8th Bn Royal Irish Rifles
D.O.W. 26-11-17
Aged 17
Interred in Achiet-Le-Grand Communal Cemetery extension. France. Plot 1, Row Q, Grave 8.

Born   Ballymoney
Lived   Killymaddy
Enlisted Ballymoney
Son of Mr & Mrs Thomas Campbell of Tates Fort, Bendooragh.
Another son, Thomas, won the Military Medal. Commemorated in Drumreagh Presbyterian Church.

Bryce was named after his father's twin brother who also lived at Tates Fort.

The 8th battalion did most of their early training at Ballykinlar and in July of 1915 moved across the Channel to Seaford on the south coast.

Here they were quickly accepted by the residents of the district and many friendships were made. These were East Belfast Volunteers and it is more likely that Bryce was a later recruit to the battalion and joined them probably after the Battle of the Somme, where the battalion had been decimated even before they reached their jumping off point on the edge of Thiepval Wood. The battalion were quickly taken out of the line and moved to St.Omer and it was probably here that Bryce joined them. At any rate they moved to Belgium and the area around Wulverghem. They were regularly in and out of the line here.

In February 1917, Bryce Campbell was gassed in Belgium. It took time to get over this and he was

home on ten days leave at Bendooragh in March. The battle of Messines was to be the next major battle and Bryce came safely through this. They then moved north again to Wieltje to prepare for the battle of Passchendaele. When this was over they were moved again, this time south in

preparation for the battle of Cambrai in November. Here they were on both sides of the Cambrai, Bapaume road and it was in this region that Bryce was so seriously injured. He was taken to a dressing station at Achiet-le-Grand but little could be done to help him and he died there of his injuries. He is buried in the Cemetery near by.

Cemetery location information

Achiet-le-Grand is a large village in the department of the Pas de Calais 19 kilometres south of Arras. The Military Cemetery is situated at the north-west side of the village alongside the Communal Cemetery.

One should take the main road from Arras to Bapaume (N17). At Ervillers turn right on to the D9 towards Achiet. At the first junction in the village a CWGC signpost indicates the way towards the right.

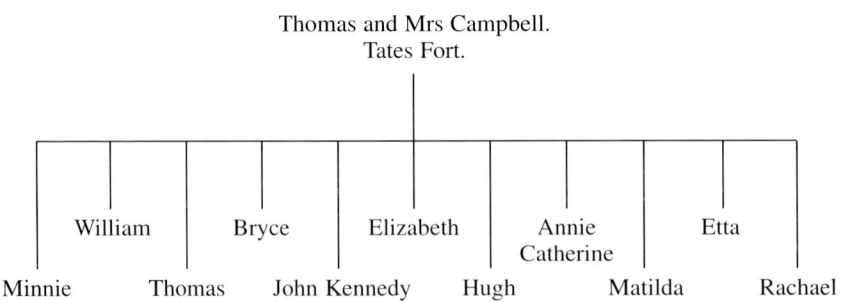

4/29314 PRIVATE HENRY BROLLY
5th Bn Royal Inniskilling Fusiliers
D.O.W. 29-11-17
Aged 28
Interred in Ramleh War Cemetery, Israel. Row P, Grave 13.

Born   Ballymoney
Lived   Balnamore
Enlisted Omagh
Son of Michael Brolly of Londonderry.

Although there is a report that Henry died in Alexandria this would appear to be untrue as he is buried many miles away close to the town of Ramla, in Israel.

The fact that Henry died of wounds, coupled with a scarcity of information on these battles, makes it very difficult to define which battle he was injured in. There is nothing to indicate how long he spent in hospital or what his injuries were but they were obviously very serious.

The 5th battalion was formed at Omagh in August 1914 and it was there that Henry enlisted soon afterwards. They then joined the 31st Brigade, 10th Division at Dublin. Early in 1915 they moved to Kildare and then in April, to Basingstoke. In July they crossed to the Mediteranean landing at Mudros. On 7th August 1915 they landed at Gallipoli. In September 1917 they arrived in Egypt.

Cemetery location information.

From Tel-Aviv, proceed along Route One (Ayalon) towards Jerusalem. Pass the exit to Ben Gurion airport and take the next exit signposted Petah Tiqwa, Ramla, Lod Route 40. Proceed along Route 40 to the T junction with Route 44, signposted Bet Shemesh, Lod. Turn right and follow Route 44 towards Lod until the first set of traffic lights. Turn right towards Ramleh prison. Before you reach the prison, Ramleh War Cemetery is signposted right along a minor road. Turn right and follow the minor road through the industrial area to the Commonwealth War Graves Comm cemetery. Parking is available at the cemetery which is open from 6.30 to 14.00 daily.

Ramleh War Cemetery, Israel

41407 PRIVATE WILLIAM THOMPSON
9th Bn Royal Irish Fusiliers. Formerly 2037 N.I.H.
D.O.W. 6-12-17
Aged 28
Interred in Rocquigny-Equancourt Road British Cemetery, France. Plot 6, Row D, Grave 13.

Born   Conagher, Ballymoney.
Lived   Conagher, Ballymoney.
Enlisted Ballymoney.
Son of James and Martha Thompson of Conagher.
Commemorated in Trinity Presbyterian Church.

William enlisted at Ballymoney into the North Irish Horse but later transferred to the Royal Irish Fusiliers and did most of his training at Clandeboye. From there he was sent to Seaford on the south coast of England to complete his training. He was home on leave in August of 1917 In September 1917, the 9th battalion Royal Irish Fusiliers absorbed dismounted squadrons of the North Irish Horse. It was at this stage that William joined the 9th battalion. He was seriously wounded on the 4th of December close to Equancourt and died from his wounds two days later. He is buried in the nearby cemetery.

William was seriously wounded on the 4th of December and died two days later in hospital. He was home on leave in August 1917.

Rocquigny-Equancourt Road British Cemetery

799804 PRIVATE WILLIAM JAMES YOUNG
19th Bn Canadian Highlanders
D.O.W. 18-1-18
Aged 38
Interred in Etaples Military Cemetery, France. Plot 31, Row F, Grave 22

Born   Pharis, on 29-3-1879.
Enlisted   Toronto, Canada.
Son of William Young, of Pharis, Ballymoney.
Husband of Margaret D. Young, of 99, Essex Ave, Toronto.
Commemorated in Kilraughts Presbyterian Church.

William James Young was born at Pharis and as a youth, emigrated to Canada, settling in Toronto. Around this time his sisters moved to Westbrooke Terrace, in Coleraine. On the 28th of January 1916, when William James had only been in Canada for a short time, he enlisted in the Canadian Highlanders. With his training completed, he arrived in France and spent the whole of the war there.

In Canada, William worked as a telephone linesman. He was five feet, nine inches tall with a fresh complexion, grey eyes and fair hair. He embarked at Halifax on SS. Scotian on the 8th of August and disembarked at Liverpool on the 19th.

No other entry appears on his record until 25th May 1917 when he left his base in France to join his unit in the field. He was seriously wounded on 9th November 1917 with gun shot wounds to the face, left leg, right thigh and right foot. There was also a fracture of the left leg. This necessitated his immediate removal to a casualty clearing station, and then to Field Ambulance. He was transferred to St John's Hospital, Etaples, on 21st November. The wound to the thigh seemed to be the most serious one and a report on 29th December describes him as "still a patient". It would appear that, in an attempt to save his life, the doctors amputated his right leg, and on 14th January he was described as seriously ill. He died

of his wounds at 7.35am on 18th January 1918 and is buried in Etaples Military Cemetery.

He was the only boy in the family and he had married. His wife was living in Toronto but we don't know if there was any family. His sister, Lizzie, the principal of Ballynagashel National School, died the following year in Dublin. She had been staying with her sister when she died on 15th February 1919.

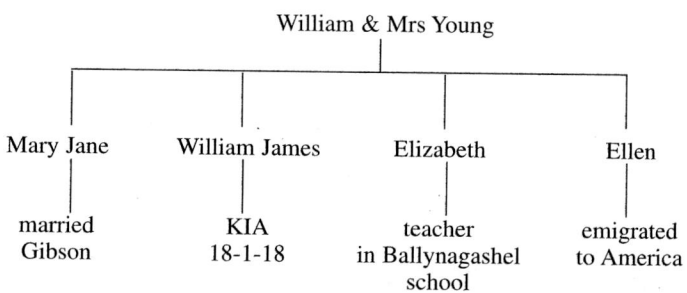

Etaples was one of the main embarkation points for wounded soldiers being sent to hospitals in England. There was a hospital here where the wounded were cared for until a place could be found for them . Many of them never made it and as a result the nearby cemetery is a very large one. Three other Ballymoney men are buried here, Dan McMullan of Rasharkin, who died on 29th September 1916 from injuries received at the Battle of the Somme, Joseph Allen, who died of wounds on 20th April 1918 and Andrew McGahey, who died of wounds on 22nd August 1917.

The huge Etaples Military Cemetery

954 RIFLEMAN WILLIAM WORKMAN M.M.
12th Bn Royal Irish Rifles
K.I.A. 21-3-18
No Known Grave. Commemorated on the Pozieres Memorial. Panels 30 & 31

Born   Kilraughts
Lived   Lisboy, Kilraughts.
Enlisted   Ballymoney
Commemorated in Kilraughts Presbyterian Church.

William Workman had married Elizabeth Bellingham in Bushvale Presbyterian Church on 26th February 1913. Both of them lived in the Kilraughts district. She was a sister of John Bellingham whose story is told elsewhere in the book.

William enlisted at Ballymoney and did his early training at Clandeboye and at Seaford on the south coast of England. His brother Andrew also served.

Towards the end of May 1917, the 12th Battalion was in the Messines area. The unit in which William served was ordered to attack the German trenches opposite them. They found the German wire intact and the Germans in great strength so they had to retire. That night it was William's turn to be on sentry duty and as it grew lighter during the early hours he saw something move. It was a German raiding party and suddenly they were going for the British Lewis gun. William got there first and opened fire killing the burly German leading the attack. The others were only a few yards away and attacked William, but he held on, killing five and wounding eight.

This was too much for them and they fled. Afterwards it was discovered that the German leader that William had killed had won the Iron Cross among other honours and William was presented with his trench dagger. This was the action for which William won the Military Medal. He then got home on leave for a few days at Kilraughts but was back with his unit in time for the Battle of Messines in which he was wounded but recovered.

In August the Battle of Langemarck was fought and a number of Ballymoney men were killed. This was a period of fighting in many different

The Military Medal of Rfn Wm. Workman

areas but soon the battalion was moved south again to Cambrai and the heavy fighting around Moeuvres in November 1917. From here they were moved south, this time to St. Quentin. It was here, near the village of Urvillers, that William was killed on the morning of the 21st of March 1918. His daughter, Mrs Eaton, now lives in Ballymena. In 1998 she willingly loaned us William's Military Medal so that we could put it on display in the exhibition held in the Heritage Centre in Ballymoney.

LIEUT THOMAS PATRICK CRAIG
7th Bn Leinster Regiment
K.I.A. 22-3-18
Aged 27
No Known Grave. Commemorated on the Pozieres Memorial. Panel 78.

Born   Liscolman in 1891.
Lived   Liscolman
Enlisted
Son of Samuel and Ann Craig (nee Murphy).
Commemorated in Billy Parish Church.

Samuel Craig, Thomas's Father, was the owner of the mill in Liscolman. After the death of his first wife Samuel had married again and Thomas was the second family. The second Mrs Craig had been of Scottish decent and when Samuel died she returned to live with her relatives in Scotland. Thomas had been studying at Dublin University on the outbreak of hostilities and obtained his commission through Dublin University Officer Training Corps, gaining the rank of Temporary Lieutenant on 26th September 1914. He was promoted to Lieut on 1st July 1917.

He was killed at the start of the German Spring Offensive of March 1918 as his men were being pushed steadily backwards by a horde of fresh German troops.

The position which they held on the morning of 22nd March was over-run by the opposing

enemy and they were just simply annihilated. Thomas has no known grave and is commemorated on the Pozieres Memorial.

Posieres British Cemetery and Memorial

15903 PRIVATE DANIEL PATRICK NEVIN
1st Bn Royal Inniskilling Fusiliers
K.I.A. 22-3-18
Aged 18
No Known Grave. Commemorated on the Pozieres Memorial, France. Panels 38-40.

Born   Paisley
Lived   Ballygan, Ballymoney.
Enlisted   Finner Camp.
Commemorated in St. James's Presbyterian Church.
Son of James M. and Catherine Nevin, of Church St, Ballymoney.

James Mallet Nevin married Catherine Sinclair. They had nine children, two girls and seven boys. The first, Daniel, born in Paisley, in 1899, enlisted at the outbreak of war. According to the family he enlisted under a false age, as he was only fifteen, but looked older. He joined the Royal Inniskilling Fusiliers. He was wounded at the Somme on 1st July 1916 and was taken to hospital where he made a speedy recovery and returned to his unit.

He was still with them at the time of Ludendorff's spring offensive in March 1918. He was reported missing, believed killed, when the position his platoon occupied was obliterated during the pre-assault bombardment and subsequently overwhelmed. He has no known grave and is commemorated on the Pozieres Memorial. His platoon was at the small French village of Hamel, at the Somme, and it was here that Daniel was killed.

His father served in the same unit throughout the war, but survived.

He was suffering from the results of gas and shell shock in March 1918 and was demobilised in November of that year. On returning to Ballymoney he purchased a farm at Coldagh and remained there the rest of his life.

In April 1917 Daniel's brother, Thomas, 43rd Cameron Highlanders (Canadians) was wounded by shell-fire and spent some time in a hospital in England. On showing good improvement, he was allowed home to the farm at Ballygan on ten days leave. This was just the treatment that he needed and he was lucky enough to survive the war.

Pozieres is a village some 6 kilometres north-east of Albert. The Memorial encloses Pozieres British Cemetery which is a little south-west of the village on the north side of the main road, D 929, from Albert to Pozieres.

Daniel and his sister Ethel

The Memorial relates to the period of crisis in March and April 1918 when the Fifth Army was driven back by overwhelming numbers across the former Somme battlefields, and to the succeeding period of four months during which there was built up, behind the new front, the army which on the 8th August 1918, began the advance to victory.

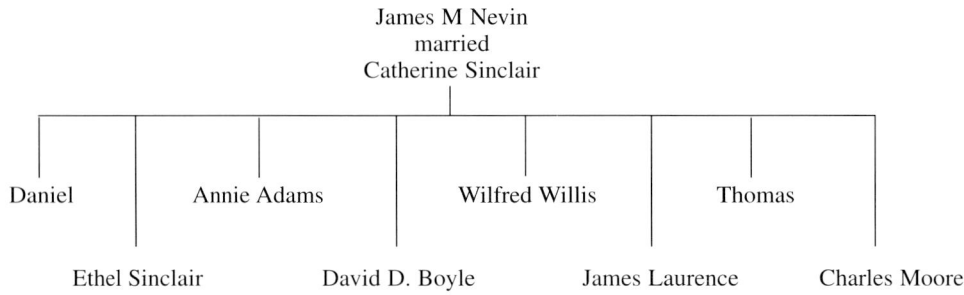

Pozieres Cemetery

CAPTAIN HOMER NEVIN TEAZ MC.
9th Bn King's Own Yorkshire Light Inf.
K.I.A. 23-3-18
Aged 23
Interred in Peronne Communal Cemetery Extension. Radegonde. Plot 3, Row H, Grave 29.

Born   Dervock
Lived   Dervock
Son of Ezekiel and Janet S. Teaz

From Bapaume, take the N 17 to Peronne. On entering Peronne, turn right towards the hospital. On reaching the hospital, which is on the right, take the small road opposite and the communal cemetery is at the end of this road on the left. The extension is on the south-west side of the cemetery.

The 9th battalion was formed at Pontefract in September 1914 joining the 21st Div. In October they moved to Halton Park, Tring, but by November had moved into billets at Maidenhead. By April 1915 they were back at Halton Park, but then by August had moved to Witley. They landed in France in September 1915. Homer was born in the Manse in Dervock in about 1895, the year in which the family appears to have left the district. His father, Rev Ezekiel Teaz, was minister in Dervock Reformed Presbyterian Church from 1886 to 1895.

While he was still an infant the family moved to Liverpool, his father having been called to the pastorate of a congregation in that city. Here, after a time, he was placed in a private school, and this was the beginning of a period of very intensive learning. He was also very interested in music and took easily to playing many different instruments. This was to stand him in good stead after he enlisted and went to France where he was much in demand in the various Y.M.C.A. huts in France and Belgium. After attending public school, he obtained a place in Liverpool University, where he studied for the Ministry.

On the occasion of his leaving Liverpool to take up his Theological studies in Glasgow, the Sabbath School teachers presented him with a very handsome Bible, as a token of their appreciation. It bears the following inscription,

> "Presented to Mr Homer N. Teaz by the teachers of the Hall Lane Sabbath School, as a small token of their esteem and regard. 4th July 1915."

In early 1915 the death of his mother had a demoralising effect on him but it also removed the greatest barrier which stood in the way of his joining the Army.

Later that year when he enlisted into the King's Own Yorkshire Light Infantry, and the training grounds at Rugeley, he realised one of his greatest ambitions, that of serving his country. He sailed for France in September 1915. His first major confrontation with the enemy was at the Battle of the Somme. Here he intimated his intention of trying to find his cousin, John Teaz, serving with the New Zealanders, and camped nearby. He found and made himself known to his New Zealand cousin. Although the two cousins had often corresponded, this was their first meeting, and it also proved to be their last as both were killed on the battlefield before they could meet again.

At Passchendaele in 1917 he was given the very dangerous task of bringing supplies up to the front line at night. This was over ground which had been continuously ploughed up by shell-fire over the previous three years and which was a sea of glutinous mud. The weather had turned wet and every shell-hole was full to the brim with muddy water. Supplies had in many cases to be carried over duck boards which very often just floated around on the water. It was almost impossible to move without being fired on by the enemy and extremely difficult to find one's way night after night in darkness. The flashes of bursting shells and Verey lights illuminated everything that moved and machine-gunners and snipers lay in wait for every opportunity. It was in these conditions that Homer had to bring up his supplies to the front lines and it was in recognition of the efforts made by him to get them up that he was awarded the Military Cross.

The Citation, announced in the London Gazette of 6th April 1918 reads as follows,

> "For conspicious gallantry and devotion to duty when in command of a carrying party. For five days he never failed to bring up ammunition, rations and water to the front line, though his party was continually under heavy shell-fire. He rendered very valuable service in getting up supplies immediately before the attack at a time when they were greatly needed"

In March 1918 his battalion was in action north east of Peronne when the Germans began their great spring offensive. Thousands of fresh troops had been brought from the collapsed Russian front in an attempt to take Paris and the Channel ports.

It was in this region, at Templeux-la-Fosse, that Homer was killed. He was buried, with three other Officers, in a garden beside the ruins of the village church. Later these bodies were removed and buried where they rest to-day.

A Memorial Sermon was preached by the Rev A.C.Gregg, of Loanhead Reformed Presbyterian Church, Edinburgh, in the Reformed Presbyterian Church, Hall Lane, Liverpool, on Sunday 12th May 1918. This was the Church where his father had gone to preach many years before. The text for the sermon that day was "I shall go to him, but he shall not return to me".

London Cemetery

S. 4875 PRIVATE WILLIAM GRAHAM
9th Bn Seaforth Highlanders
K.I.A. 24-3-18
No Known Grave. Commemorated on the Pozieres Memorial. Panels 72 and 73

Born   Ballymoney
Enlisted   Hamilton, Lanarkshire.

The 9th battalion were formed at Fort George in October 1914 and went immediately to train at Aldershot. On 3rd December they were attached to the 9th Div and early in 1915 became the Pioneer battalion for the Div.

In February 1915 they were training at Rowledge, near Farnham, and on 10th May of that year they landed in France.

William had been working in Southern Scotland during the Summer of 1914 and enlisted at Hamilton, in Lanarkshire. Going to Scotland to find work was common practice in those days and many of the large farms in Ayrshire and Lanarkshire employed the same men summer after summer. The shipbuilding yards of the Clyde also employed many young men from Northern, and Southern Ireland. William appears to have been through most of the battles of the 1st World War in France and Belgium but it is not until the beginning of 1918 that anything definite can be found of him.

The German Spring Offensive of March 1918 was in full swing and the 9th battalion were being forced back at an alarming rate. They were now in the Combles area trying desperately to staunch a very strong German attack.

Next day was the 24th and they were ordered to retreat to Bray. During the morning they passed through St Pierre Vaast Wood to positions at Rancourt and coming out of the wood were subjected to very heavy machine-gunfire. They then fought a rearguard action back to Hardicourt and manned positions on the river bank and finally were forced back to Maricourt, where they took up positions for the night. It was during the retreat through St Pierre Vaast Wood that William was killed. Amazingly he was one of only four casualties to be killed on this day although forty-five were missing.

As is usually the case with a retreating army there is no time to bury the dead and as a result there is no known grave. William is commemorated on the Pozieres Memorial.

5848 CORPORAL JAMES McALEESE
2nd Bn Royal Irish Rifles
K.I.A. 24-3-18
Aged 31
Interred in Grand-Seracourt British Cemetery. Plot 1, Row F, Grave 5

Born   Rasharkin.
Lived   Rasharkin.
Enlisted   Glasgow.
Son of Peter and Catherine McAleese of Rasharkin.

Peter McAleese of Dreen, Rasharkin, married Catherine McMullen, of Ballydonnelly, Rasharkin on 24th August 1884. Peter was a stonemason and Catherine, a dressmaker.

Peter's father, James McAleese, had also been a stonemason. Catherine's father, Daniel McMullen had been a farmer at Ballydonnelly.

At the time James was killed the Germans had just started their great spring offensive and were beginning to push the British forces back at an alarming rate. There was confusion everywhere and the 2nd Rifles were trying to maintain their position near Cugny on the morning of the 24th March. For a short time everything was quiet, but then at about 2.00pm a violent artillery barrage started, followed by machine-gun fire, and supported by an attack by low flying aircraft. The Germans came in from the left in overwhelming numbers and the 2nd Rifles were overrun. After a desperate hand to hand fight, it was estimated that of the one hundred and fifty men on their feet at the beginning, over a hundred were killed or wounded. It is thought that this was the attack in which James McAleese was killed. He had been home at Rasharkin on leave just six months

Grand-Seracourt British Cemetery, France

earlier, in February 1918. His cousin, Daniel McMullen, of Rasharkin, had died of wounds in a military hospital at Etaples on 29th September 1916, from injuries recieved in an accident at the Battle of the Somme.

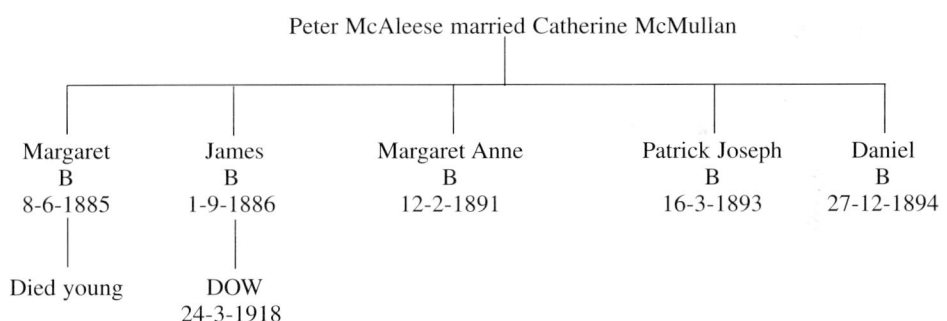

Peter McAleese married Catherine McMullan

Margaret	James	Margaret Anne	Patrick Joseph	Daniel
B	B	B	B	B
8-6-1885	1-9-1886	12-2-1891	16-3-1893	27-12-1894
Died young	DOW 24-3-1918			

1105 RIFLEMAN HUGH REID
1st Bn Royal Irish Rifles
K.I.A. 24-3-18
Aged 19
No Known Grave. Commemorated on the Pozieres Memorial, France.

Born   Glasgow.
Lived   Taughey, Ballymoney.
Enlisted   Ballymoney.
Commemorated in St. James's Presbyterian Church.

On the outbreak of hostilities on 4th August 1914 the 1st battalion were in Aden. They embarked for the U.K. on 27th September and arrived at Liverpool on 22nd October. They were then taken to Hursley Park, Winchester, joining the 8th Div. On 6th November 1914 they landed at Le Havre.

Hugh Reid was one of the youngest of the Ballymoney men to be killed in the 1914-18 war. At the time of his death in March 1918 he was only nineteen years of age. This was a time of great confusion in the British forces. The Germans had just started their great spring offensive and were pushing the British Armies back at an alarming rate. The 1st and 2nd Rifles had reached the village of Cugny and had managed to dig in to some extent. The 1st Rifles were close to Montalimont Farm with the 2nd closer to Cugny. They were very short of ammunition and were told to fire only at the best targets and to make each shot count. When the Germans attacked behind their barrage at 2.00pm, Hugh Reid and his mates were over-run. He has no known grave and is commemorated on the Pozieres Memorial.

869 RIFLEMAN SAMUEL YOUNG MM
2nd Bn Royal Irish Rifles
K.I.A. 24-3-18
No Known Grave. Commemorated on the Pozieres Memorial. Panels 74-76

Born   Ballymoney.
Enlisted Belfast.

Samuel Young had been working in Belfast and enlisted there. By the time he was killed he had seen an enormous amount of action in both France and Belgium. On the morning of the 24th of March 1918 the 2nd battalion were at Cugny. This was at the start of the great German spring offensive and the Germans were pushing everything in front of them and there was confusion everywhere in the British lines. At Cugny the 2nd battalion held on as best they could but they were short of ammunition and being fiercely attacked and at 2.00pm the German barrage opened, followed by machine-gun fire and supported by low flying aircraft. When the barrage lifted a little the Germans attacked and simply swarmed into the British position where fierce hand to hand fighting took place. Of the one hundred and fifty men left on their feet at the beginning, over one hundred were killed or injured. Samuel Young was one of those killed in this attack. He has no known grave and is commemorated on the Pozieres Memorial.

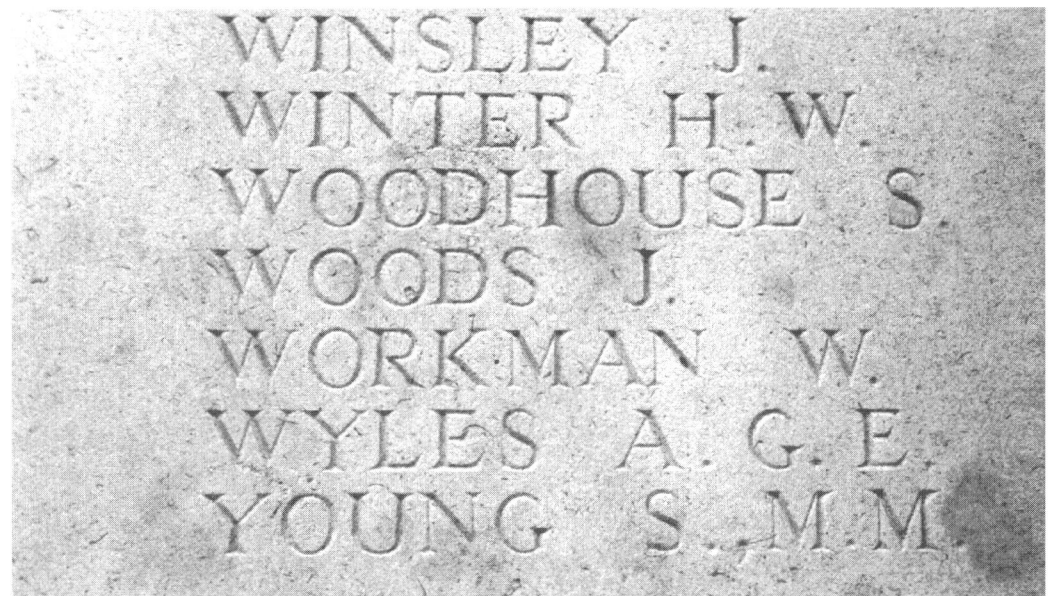

4403 RIFLEMAN ALEXANDER GIBSON
12th Bn Royal Irish Rifles
K.I.A. 26-3-18
Aged 21
No Known Grave. Commemorated on the Pozieres Memorial, France.

Born   Mullaghduff, Armoy.
Lived   Mullaghduff, Armoy.
Enlisted Ballymoney.
Commemorated in Armoy Presbyterian Church.

Cemetery location information
Pozieres is a village some 6 kilometres north-east of Albert. The Memorial encloses Pozieres British Cemetery which is a little south-west of the village on the north side of the main road, D 929, from Albert to Pozieres.

Alex Gibson enlisted at Ballymoney soon after hostilities was declared and trained at Clandeboye. In July 1915 the battalion moved to Seaford, on the south coast of England, and three months later, in October 1915, they landed at Boulogne. This was the start of the serious stuff. They were taken to the small French village of Martinsart, close to the front line trenches at the Somme. Here the noise was deafening, with shelling going on all of the time. The weather turned wet just when the troops needed a dry period and the date of the battle was postponed. The new date, set for the first of July 1916, dawned bright and sunny and at 7.30am as the whistles blew and the troops climbed out of their tenches, they were immediately caught in a maelstrom of flying lead and steel. Alex Gibson was very lucky to survive this day and the 12th battalion were withdrawn next day and moved to St Omer for re-organisation. They had been decimated. From here they moved to Belgium and the area around Wulverghem. They would be here for over a year. Much of their time now was spent in and out of the line, with sporadic fighting now being the order of the day. Then in June 1917 they took part in the Battle of Messines. After that, the bitter fighting at Passchendaele in August, and then they were moved south for the battle of Cambrai in November. They then moved south again, to St Quentin, and the German Spring Offensive of March 1918. At 8am on the morning of the 26th of March the battalion was on the Amiens - Roye road, north of Andechy, and it was in this region that Alex was killed. He has no known grave and is commemorated on the Pozieres Memorial.

10017 PRIVATE JAMES McERLEAN
1st Bn Irish Guards
K.I.A. 27-3-18
Aged 42
Interred in Douchy-Les-Ayette British Cemetery, France. Plot 4, Row J, Grave 5.

Born Armoy.
Lived
Enlisted Belfast
Son of John and Catherine McErlean, of Armoy. Husband of Mary Kate McErlean, of 10 Vicinage Park, Belfast.

An intense barrage on the morning of the 27th March heralded the crisis, but luckily went wide of all the battalion except No2 Company on the left.

The attack followed, and all down the line from Ayette to Boisleux-St.Marc the brigade answered with unbroken musketry and Lewis guns.

The 1st battalion were in trenches between Ayette and Boisleux-St Marc on the 27th and it was here that James was killed. This was just after the start of the great German offensive of March 1918 and the British forces were being pushed steadily backwards. They were being attacked with everything the German armies could throw at them and it was a case of getting back safely and trying to re-group in an attempt to withstand the next attack.

Ayette is a village some 13 kilometres south of Arras on the road to Amiens.

Douchy-les-Ayette is a village one kilometre west of Ayette.

The British Cemetery is opposite the Communal Cemetery on the north side of the road, half way between the two villages next to a barn.

Another Ballymoney man, Wm John Thompson, of Ballymaconnolly, killed on the same day,is buried close by, in Plot 4, Row F, Grave 4.

Douchy-Les-Ayette British Cemetery, France

2537 GUARDSMAN WILLIAM JOHN THOMPSON
2nd Bn Irish Guards
K.I.A. 27-3-18
Interred in Douchy-les-Ayette British Cemetery, France. Plot 4, Row F, Grave 4

Born   Ballymaconnelly.
Lived
Enlisted

The 2nd battalion of the Irish Guards was formed on 15th July 1915. They were in France in time for the Battle of Loos in September 1915. From here they went to the Ypres Salient and the area around Potijze. Next it was south to Hooge and then north again to Wieltje. By this time they were needed at the Somme and here they excelled themselves.

Much of the bitter fighting at the Somme in which the Guards were involved took place around the villages of Ginchy and Guillemont.

From here it was back to the Salient and Boesinghe in June and July of 1917. Then in August the Battle of Pilckem Ridge and the Battle of Passchendaele. They then moved to the south of Arras and were in action at Ayette on the 27th of March.

This was just a few days after the start of the great German offensive on the Somme and the 2nd battalion were in action at Ayette. Losses were heavy on both sides but the British were having to give way and try to re-group further back to stem the German advance. It was during this heavy fighting at Ayette that William John was killed.

Another Ballymoney man, James McErlean, killed on the same day as William John, is buried close by, in Plot 4, Row J, Grave 5. Of the same Cemetery.

19423 L. CPL WILLIAM SAMUEL CAMPBELL
11/13TH Bn R. Irish Rifles
DIED 28-3-18
Aged 22
No known grave. Commemorated on Pozieres Memorial.

Born   Ballymoney
Lived   Muckamore
Enlisted Antrim
Son of William Campbell and the late Elizabeth Campbell.

Cemetery location information
Pozieres is a village some 6 kilometres north-east of the town of Albert. The memorial encloses Pozieres British Cemetery which is a little south-west of the village on the north side of the main road D 929, from Albert to Pozieres.

It appears that although William was born at Ballymoney the family had moved and by the time he enlisted they were living at Muckamore. He enlisted at Antrim.

Very little information has turned up concerning William but the date of his death is during the Great German Spring Offensive of March 1918 when the British troops were being pushed quickly backwards. During this period the German troops were advancing at such a rate that British positions were being over-run and there was no time to bury the dead, with the result that most of the soldiers killed at this time have no known grave. This is the case with William, but it would appear that he died from natural causes and was not neccessarily killed in action. His details are recorded in "Soldiers Died" and these are usually very accurate and the fact that he is recorded as "died" rather than "killed in action" or "died of wounds" would probably refer to an illness and time spent in hospital. The fact that there is no known grave probably means that the area was over-run by the advancing German forces and any new graves would simply be destroyed by the accompanying shell-fire.

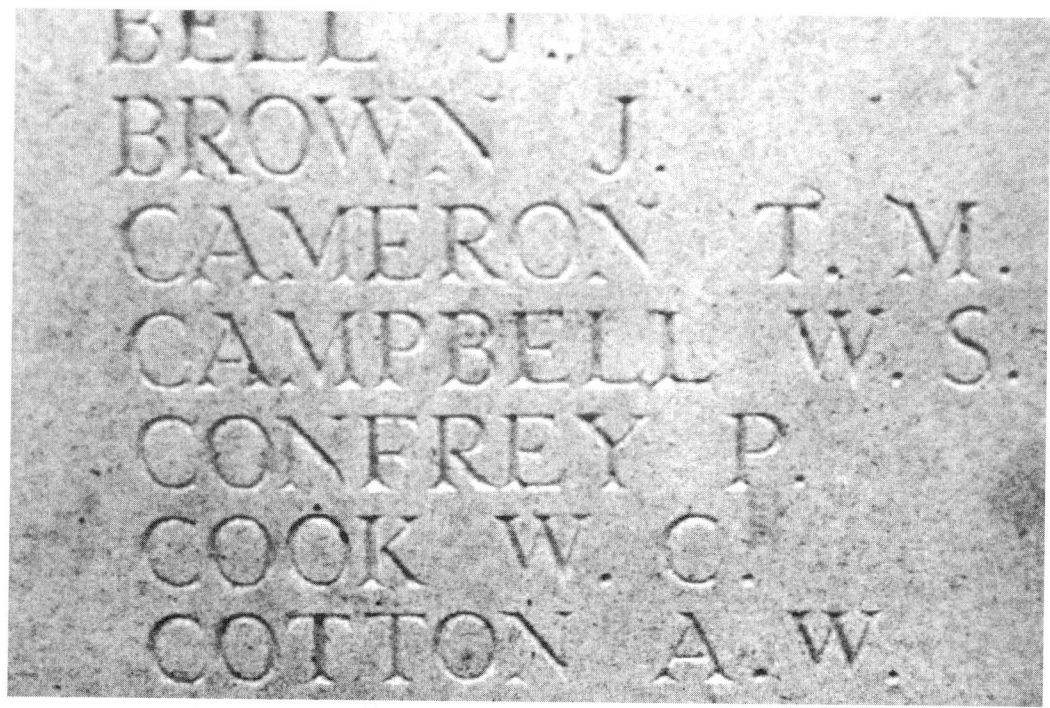

15351 SERGEANT JOHN BRANGAM M.M.
9th Bn Royal Inniskilling Fusiliers
K.I.A. 29-3-18
Aged 28
No known grave. Commemorated on Pozieres Memorial, panels 38-40.

Born   Coleraine
Lived   Londonderry
Enlisted Finner Camp, Co. Donegal.
Son of David and Ann Jane Brangam.
Commemorated in Ballymoney Parish Church.

The 9th battalion were raised at Omagh in September 1914, from the Tyrone Volunteers and included two companies of Volunteers who had already joined the 5th and 6th battalions. They went immediately to Finner Camp. On 2nd November 1914 the formation became 109th Brigade, 36th Division. In January 1915 they moved to Randalstown and then in July to Ballycastle. When their training here was finished they went across to Bordon Camp in England. This was in September. After a short period there they moved to France during October in preparation for the Battle of the Somme. Chronicle, March 16th 1918.

Sergeant John Brangam, of Castle St, has been awarded the Military Medal. The act for which the decoration was awarded took place on 20th November 1917 at the battle of Cambrai.

His battalion reached the front line trenches without much opposition, but on going over to the second line met with fierce resistance from the Germans, who were securely entrenched with machine guns . For a time his company was held up with the severe machine gun fire, but creeping round on the right flank, Sgt Brangam got within distance of a machine-gun, which he bombed, killing two of the gunners and taking two German prisoners. As a result of this action his company was enabled to advance and hold the German second line trench. On the third day of the battle the Germans began a severe counter attack. The officers of his battalion were all casualties when he assumed command of his men, and beat back the German attack. For this act he was recommended for the D.C.M. Before the war Sergeant Brangam was in the employment of the Midland Railway Co, and the station at Ballymoney was a virtual hive of activity with a vast amount of goods being moved by rail, and many of the young Ballymoney men found employment there. He was home on leave in March 1918 and was killed just after rejoining his men.

The great German attack which began on 23rd March was well under way and the British were being pushed back at an alarming rate. The British armies were doing everything possible to hold back the enemy and in a battalion advance at Bovillancourt John Brangam was killed. There is no known grave and he is commemorated on the Pozieres Memorial.

There is a report in the Chronicle of July 20th 1918 that John Brangham had been awarded the D.C.M. but so far I have been unable to confim this.

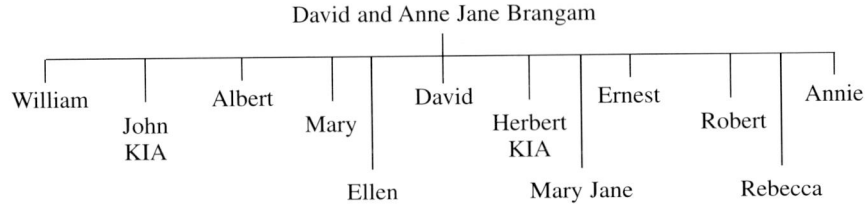

29096 PRIVATE THOMAS KANE
9th Bn Royal Inniskilling Fusiliers
K.I.A. 29-3-18
Interred in Grand-Seracourt British Cemetery. Plot 2, Row A, Grave 4.

Born   Dervock
Lived   Dervock
Enlisted Coleraine

The 9th battalion was raised in Omagh in September 1914 from the Derry Volunteers. They did their early training at Finner Camp and then in January 1915 they moved to Randalstown. They then moved to Ballycastle in July and eventually went to England in early September. This was to Bordon Camp. In October 1915 they landed in France. It would appear that Thomas was not present at the Battle of the Somme but that he joined the battalion as a recruit after the disaster of the 1st of July. He went with the 36th Division to Belgium and the area around Wulverghem. Thomas took part in many of the battles in the Ypres Salient over the next year. At first it was minor skirmishes in and out of the line but then the serious stuff began with an attack at Messines.

The Battle of Messines was a success right from the beginning with the 9th Inniskillings in the southern half of Wytchaete village. Thomas came through this without injury and then took part in the Battle of Langemarck in August. From here it was south to Cambrai in November of 1917 and then south again to the region around St Quentin. Here the Germans attacked with fresh troops in March of 1918 and the British were driven back across the old Somme battlefields. Seraucourt-le-Grand is to the south-west of St. Quentin and it was close to here that

Thomas was killed during the Great German Spring Offensive of March 1918. He is buried in Grand-Seracourt Cemetery nearby.

Grand-Seracourt British Cemetery, France

41388 TROOPER WILLIAM BIGGART
9th Bn Royal Irish Fusiliers formerly 1932 North Irish Horse
D.O.W. 3-4-18
No known grave. Commemorated on Pozieres Memorial. Panels 76 - 77.

Born   Inchinagh Lane. Bendooragh.
Lived   Bendooragh
Enlisted Ballymoney
Died of wounds as prisoner of war
Commemorated in Ballymoney Parish Church.

William Biggart was born in a house up Inchinagh Lane in 1895, the son of John and Mary Ann Biggart. After leaving school he was employed on the local estate at Leslie Hill, as a farm labourer. When war broke out in 1914, William enlisted at Ballymoney in the North Irish Horse. He served with this regiment until 1917 when the N.I.H. was dismounted and the army at that time amalgamated it's battalions and reconstructed it's brigades. Along with 300 or so of his comrades from the N.I.H. William transferred to the 9th battalion Royal Irish Fusiliers. This was a service battalion raised from the units of the Armagh, Monaghan and Cavan U.V.F.

In January 1918 the 36th Ulster Division took over the line again in the Somme sector, relieving the French from Sphinx Wood to the St. Quinten / Roisel Railway. Once again the British Army was being restructured, with smaller brigades of three battalions being the new format. The 108th Infantry brigade consisted of the 12th Bn, Royal Irish Rifles, (a great number of the Ballymoney men served in this unit), the 1st Royal Irish Fusiliers and the battalion William now served with, the 9th Royal Irish Fusiliers. He was home on leave in August 1917.

By March 23rd 1918 the German armies had broken through the British defences, a brave attempt was put up by the 108th brigade to curb the swiftly advancing German armies, this advance was to prove devastating for the 108th brigade.

Between 21st March and the end of the month the 36th Ulster Div in which William now served suffered 7,252 casualties. The brigade in which he served was now reduced to 300 men. It was during this fierce fighting that William was injured. He is listed in military records as having died of wounds on 3rd April 1918. His burial place is unknown but his name is commemorated on the Pozieres Memorial, panels 76 - 77. The panels are on the wall enclosing the Cemetery.

This cemetery and memorial is named after a village on the North side of the straight main road from Albert to Bapaume. It contains the original burials from 1916, 1917, and 1918, plus graves concentrated there after the armistice with 2754 burials.

John Biggart B 1869, D 1952. married Mary Ann McNeill B 1869
on 11th Jan 1889

William	John	Neil	Robert	Jeannie	Martha	Mary	Daniel
KIA	KIA						Watchmaker in Main St., Ballymoney

793 RIFLEMAN WILLIAM McCURDY
12th Bn Royal Irish Rifles
D.O.W. 3-4-18
Aged 23
Interred in St. Souplet British Cemetery, France. Plot 2, Row B, Grave 21.

Born   Artnagross, Finvoy.
Lived   Kilrea.
Enlisted Ballymena.
Son of Alexander and the late Anna McCurdy, of Kilrea.
Commemorated in Finvoy Presbyterian Church.
Died of wounds as a prisoner of war.
Previously wounded in 1917.

William McCurdy was a very early volunteer and enlisted at Ballymena at the first opportunity. He was a son of Alexander and the late Anna McCurdy, of Artnagross, a townland close to Kilrea. As far as I can find out no photograph of William now exists. The family have died out and are gone for ever. William did his early training at Clandeboye and in July 1915 was moved across to Seaford to complete that training.

He then went to France in the following October and eventually to the huge training area at St.Omer. It was in this region that he was introduced to the trenches for the first time and when they had practised their drill here they moved up to near the front line at Martinsart. This was in preparation for the Battle of the Somme. William came through this attack safely on the 1st of July and was moved a short time later to Belgium and the area around Wulverghem. There were a number of major battles in 1917, Messines in June, Passchendaele in August, and Cambrai in November. These were all battles in which Ballymoney men lost their lives. William was through all of these battles and was injured although it is not clear which one he was injured in. He then came south again to St. Quentin early in 1918. He was involved in the retreat from the German armies in the Spring Offensive of March 1918 and was taken prisoner. He died as a prisoner of war on the 3rd of April 1918 close to St. Souplet. He is now buried in St. Souplet Cemetery, the only Ballymoney man to be buried here although James Connor of Bushmills lies in this same cemetery.

St. Souplet British Cemetery, France.

50887 L.CPL. HUGH CRAWFORD M.M.
6th Dragoon Guards 1st Machine-gun Squadron
K.I.A. 4-4-18
Aged 24
Interred in Villers-Bretonneux Military Cemetery, France. Plot 4, Row A, Grave 1.

Born   Enagh, Ballymoney.
Lived   Ballybrakes
Enlisted   Scotland in December 1914
Son of William and Ellen Crawford of Ballymoney.

Hugh went to Scotland in early 1912 and stayed with James and Jessie Crowe, at Livingston Station, Mid Calder, near Bathgate.

He worked at Dean's Wines in Bathgate from March 1912 to August 1914.

In her book, "The Way Bridge", Maureen Mc.Gauran, Hugh's niece describes him.

"He was the most likeable and unbiddable of the whole family. All his life he was in danger of being shot instead of the crows or drowned in the layde or the Bann for that matter. He had many friends, both Catholic and Protestant. He played football Finding sitting on an office stool in Boyle's office training to be a Solicitor's clerk was far too frustrating he took off to Scotland to join Jamie and from there he enlisted in the First World War. He died in France on 4th April 1918, aged 24.

My Mother never really recovered from the shock and it marked all our lives." Hugh was killed at the little village of Corbie and buried on the Battlefield.

It was after the war was over that his grave was moved to Villers-Brettoneux.

He was home on leave in May 1917. Hugh had been offered a Commission, which would have

Hugh Crawford killed WWI - his friends are, I think from about Bathgate (near Edinburgh)

taken him back to a safer position. He refused, preferring to stay with his men where they could be together. This was typical of a very brave young man.

In September 1918 the parents of the late Hugh Crawford, who resided at Ballybrakes, received the Military Medal awarded to their son who fell on 4th April. Captain Charles H. Reid, Commander of 1st Machine gun squadron, says in the letter that L.Cpl Crawford was doing fine work and died a gallant soldier. Men of his character can ill be spared.

One of the soldiers serving with Hugh, Jim Crowe, from Scotland, wrote to his father and mother telling them about his chum being killed. Hugh Crawford had almost certainly lodged with the Crowe family when he was working in Scotland before the war. The letter is as follows,

Dear father and mother," You will be pained to hear that I have lost my dear chum, Hugh, it happened on the night of the 4th April. He was killed by a shell falling right into the gun

emplacement, killing two and wounding three severely. I was only about twenty yards off him at the time having just left him about three minutes before to go to my own gun when this shell came. Being dark at the time, I crawled back to see who was hurt. I saw there was two dead but could not discern who they were. The wounded ones must have crawled away to some dressing station, one of them, I know, lost a hand. We had to wait until the daylight came before we could see who the two dead were and I got a shock I can tell you when I saw one was my old chum, Hugh. I asked leave of our officer to bury him for fear we would be forced to leave him lying where he fell but the officer said it would be too dangerous to go out as Fritz was making things hum with big guns and machine-gun fire. Several times I begged to be allowed to bury him and at last he consented in the afternoon. Another of Hugh's favourite chums and I took him out and laid him to his last long rest as best we could. We made a cross and went out when it was dark and placed it on his grave. This is the saddest task that has fallen to my lot since I came out here.

For three years him and I have chummed it together, sharing everything, sleeping together under the same blanket under all sorts of conditions, sometimes under cover, very often in the open, in sunshine and in storm and many a tight corner we've been in and now this is the end of our comradeship. Nothing but a memory now, but a sweet memory that shall live with me as long as life itself shall last. How long, God alone knows."

Hugh was promoted Sergeant just a few days before he was killed and was in charge of two machine-guns. It was at this same time that he was awarded the Military Medal.

Cemetery location information
Villers-Bretonneux is a village 16 kilometres east of Amiens on the straight main road to St. Quentin

The cemetery is about two kilometres north of the village on the east side of the road to Fouilloy.

For many years after the war Jim Crowe's family kept in touch with the Crawfords at Ballymoney. I suppose over the years as the older family members died, contact was eventually lost. A photograph of Hugh, along with an appeal for information, placed in the West Lothian Courier in October 1997 has once again found the Crowe family. It appears that Jim Crowe survived the war and emigrated to Canada where he died many years later. Hugh's niece, the author of "The Way Bridge", now has the chance to keep the friendship going. I know she will do that.

War Memorial Livingston Village Churchyard

William John Crawford
married
Ellen Dunlop

John	Hugh	Lizzie	Katie Ann	Andrew Gerard
B	B	B	B	B
15-1-90	14-5-1893	20-4-1897	28-12-1900	11-1-1905

James	Mary	Patrick	William	Joseph Columba
B	B	B	B	B
3-8-1891	12-7-1895	13-2-1899	10-9-1902	5-3-1908
	KIA			
	4-4-1918			

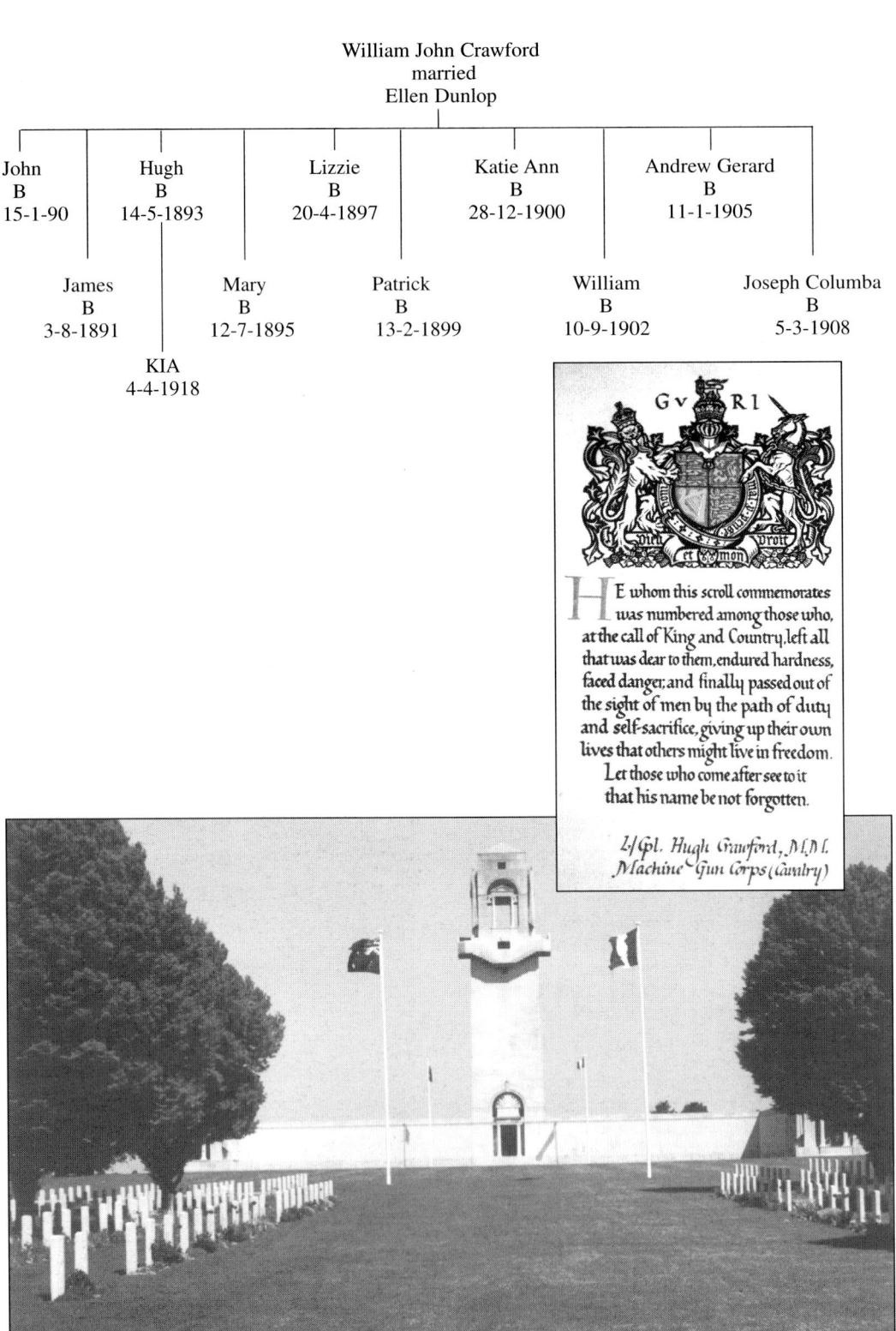

HE whom this scroll commemorates was numbered among those who, at the call of King and Country, left all that was dear to them, endured hardness, faced danger, and finally passed out of the sight of men by the path of duty and self-sacrifice, giving up their own lives that others might live in freedom. Let those who come after see to it that his name be not forgotten.

L/Cpl. Hugh Crawford, M.M.
Machine Gun Corps (Cavalry)

Australian Memorial Villers-Brettoneux

1997A SGT MICHAEL McFERRAN
Australian Field Artillery Brigade, 37th Bty
K.I.A. 5-4-18
Aged 25
Interred in Warloy Baillon Cemetery

Born   Rasharkin
Lived   Slatt.
Enlisted   in Australia
Son of Mrs. Doherty, Slatt,

Michael McFerran was born in the Rasharkin district but emigrated to Australia at an early age. He enlisted at Liverpool, New South Wales, on 20th January 1915, using his Mother's maiden name of McFerran. This caused a great deal of confusion and added considerably to the difficulties of tracing his military records and of finding the family. But thanks mainly to a massive good turn done for me by Saemus McFerran of Dunloy, I have been able to find the family. Not only that but Seamus introduced me to a Director of the War Graves Commission, home on holiday in Dunloy, and this has turned out to be a very, very useful link indeed. By the time Michael enlisted his mother was living at Cusheybracken, a townland between Rasharkin and Dunloy. His age, given as 24 on the enlistment form has been stroked out and then changed to 22, leaves some room for doubt, but 22 is probably the correct age. He was five feet ten and a half inches tall, with a dark complexion, grey eyes and dark brown hair. After a period spent in training he joined his unit at Gallipoli on the 13th of July 1915. On the 7th of August he sustained a bullet wound to the left hand which required hospital treatment, and he was sent to hospital in Alexandria and then moved to Heliopolis on the outskirts of Cairo. After three weeks treatment he was almost ready to re-join his unit when it was discovered that the wound was not healing as it should and he had to go back to hospital.

The wound was more serious than at first thought and it was October before he was able to re-join his unit. He then returned to Mudros and again sailed for Gallipoli where he re-joined his battalion on 21st of November 1915. On the 3rd of January he disembarked at Alexandria from the "Tunisian". He was suffering from nerves and the old injury to the hand was again giving trouble so he was returned to the hospital at Heliopolis. A month later he was discharged to duty at Ghezira.

In early March he re-joined his unit at Tel-el-Kebir and was then transferred to 4th Division Artillery. The next day he was taken on strength of the 10th Brigade and posted to 37th Battery. He was promoted to Temporary Rank of Bombardier on 23rd April 1916 at Serapeum and re-joined the B.E.F. at Alexandria in early June, sailing for Marseilles and action on the Western Front. On Boxing Day 1916 he was admitted to hospital suffering from sickness and was transferred to Rouen and then Etaples.

Two months later, in March 1917 he was well enough to return to his unit. Then on the 7th of April he was wounded with a bullet wound in his right buttock. He was again sent to Rouen, where the hospital ship, "Aberdonia" took him to England. By mid June he was fairly well recovered from this injury and left Folkestone for France on the 2nd of July, re-joining his unit in the field five days later. On the 29th of September he was wounded again, but remained on duty and was

promoted Corporal on the 12th of October, when Cpl Moseley was killed in action. Later that day promotion came again when he was made Temp Sgt after Sgt Hall was evacuated sick. He was made full Sergeant on the 12th of January 1918. Michael was killed in action on the 5th of April 1918 close to Warloy Baillon as the German Armies pushed their way across the old Somme Battlefields in their Spring Offensive of March and April of 1918. He was buried in Warloy Baillon Cemetery on the 7th of April by Rev R. Finnigan, attached to 4th Australian Division H.Q.

Warloy-Baillon Cemetery

877 CORPORAL ANDREW CURRY McBRIDE
42nd Bn Australian Imp Force
K.I.A. 5-4-18
Aged 28
Interred in Heilly Station Cemetery, France. Plot 2, Row I, Grave 16.

Born   Ballymoney
Lived   Newbuildings.
Enlisted   Brisbane
Only surviving son of David and Mary McBride, of Secon, Ballymoney. Commemorated in Ballyrashane Presbyterian Church.

After leaving school Andrew became apprenticed to the Drapery trade in a shop in Coleraine and was there for five years. After he had served his time he decided to emigrate to Australia. This was about 1912 and he eventually settled in Brisbane, Queensland.

He enlisted on 28th December 1915, at Brisbane, and joined "D" Company of the 42nd Battalion. He was five feet nine inches tall of a fresh complexion, with blue eyes and brown hair. He embarked at Sydney on the 5th of June 1916 on the "Borda", arriving at Southampton on the 23rd of July. After an intense training programme he left Southampton for France on 25th November.

On 31st December 1916 he was admitted to hospital in the field suffering from mumps. Next day he was transferred to 7th General hospital, St. Omer, where he spent the next three weeks, re-joining his unit on the 22nd of January. A few days later, on 28th January he was sent to 3rd Division school at Etaples and was promoted Corporal two months later, on 31st March 1917. On 6th July he returned to England as Cadre to the 11th Tng Battalion at Fovant in Wiltshire and was drill instructor there. On 6th November he was admitted to Hurdcott hospital, Fovant, with tonsilitis. Nine days later he was back with his unit and then in December he was moved to Tidworth. From here, in March 1918, he went via Southampton, to Rouelles in Belgium, and the journey south to the area around Corbie. It was here that he was killed near the village of Sailly-le-Sec on 5th April 1918 while the battalion was holding the line in that Sector. He was struck in the throat by a piece of shell which severed the jugular vein, and he died shortly after. He had only been in the firing line for about a month.

The original grave marker

Heilly Station Cemetery, 3rd from right, 2nd row

S7420 L/CPL SAMUEL BALMER
7th Bn Seaforth Highlanders
K.I.A. 11-4-18
No known grave. Commemorated on Tyne Cot Memorial.

Born   Finvoy
Enlisted   Hamilton, Lanarkshire.

The 7th Seaforth Highlanders were formed at Fort George in August 1914 and during that winter were training on Salisbury Plain. In May 1915 they landed at Boulogne and on 1st/2nd July took over the trenches at Festubert.

Their first major battle was the attack at Loos on 25th September where they attacked the strong German position of the Hohenzollern Redoubt. In a series of attacks over three days they took their objective at a cost of over 500 casualties. They spent October to December in the Salient at Ypres. Conditions in the trenches were miserable with rain, snow, sleet and mud and all the time defending desperately the positions they held.

From January to May 1916 they were at Ploegsteert where conditions were better. With preparation for the battle of the Somme under way, they were moved south to Longueval, in readiness for an attack on Delville Wood.

After this battle the 7th were seriously under strength and were withdrawn on the 23rd July 1916. They held positions at Vimy Ridge in August and September of that year but in October were moved again to the Somme and to attacks at the Butte de Warlencourt in mud and heavy rain. In December they were moved to Arras and on 9th April 1917 were fighting at Blangy, which they captured. By July they were at Cambrai and after intense fighting there they were moved again, this time to Ypres and on 12th October they were attacking Passchendaele Ridge. In wet, miserable conditions in deep mud, the battalion suffered over 230 casualties in one of the grimmest and most thankless battles of the war. When the Germans launched their last major offensive on 21st March 1918, the 7th were holding positions on the Somme and this sector bore the full brunt of the German attack. They were forced to withdraw, losing over 300 men in the process.

In April they were moved north to Flanders in readiness for an attack on Wytschaete, and during preparations for this Samuel Balmer was killed. On this one day the battalion lost about 130 men killed, wounded and mising. He has no known grave and is commemorated on the Tyne Cot Memorial.

Tyne Cot Memorial

864 RIFLEMAN HERBERT BRANGAM
12th Bn Royal Irish Rifles
K.I.A. 11-4-18
Aged 19
No known grave. Commemorated on Tyne Cot Memorial, panels 138 - 140

Born   Portrush
Lived   Ballymoney
Enlisted Clandeboye
Son of David and Ann Jane Brangam
Commemorated in Ballymoney Parish Church.

Bobby Brangam and Hugh Meehan

The Brangams lived at Gate End, Ballymoney, in the last house on the Chapel side of the street. Now, I think, no longer there.

Herbert helped to teach the younger children in St. Patrick's Church school at the corner of Queen St.

Another brother, William, was well known as a bus conductor, and another brother, David, was a train driver.

It is believed that the Brangams' lived for a time in Portrush in the late 1890's. Herbert appears to have been born there before the family moved to Ballymoney and the house at Gate End.

We don't know when Herbert enlisted but judging by his age when he was killed he would have surely been too young to have enlisted at the beginning. He was more likely to have been a later recruit. We know that he took part in the Battle of Messines and Passchendaele and that he was present at the Battle of Cambrai and the retreat of March 1918. When the battalion moved to the Kemmel area in April 1918, Herbert was there too. The 1st Irish Fusiliers were ordered to take up a line on the Messines-Wytschaete road, from 500 yards north of the village to Pick House. The 12th Rifles were on Spanbroek Ridge in support. There is a report that Herbert was accidentally killed and it was probably somewhere in this region that the accident happened. This was the second fatality in the family in a fortnight. His brother, John, had been killed in action on the 29th of March at Bovillancourt.

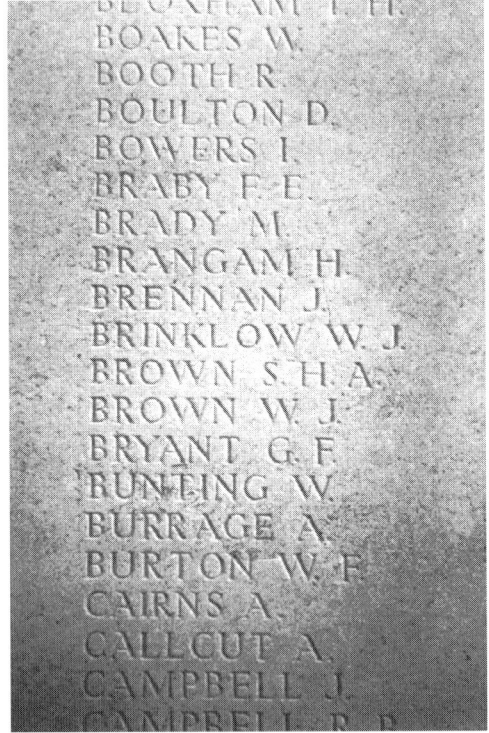

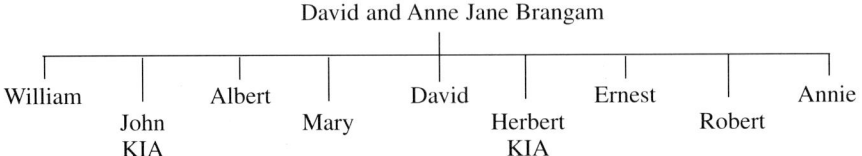

David and Anne Jane Brangam

William   John KIA   Albert   Mary   David   Herbert KIA   Ernest   Robert   Annie

68330 PRIVATE JOHN McARDLE
61st Bn Machine Gun Corps formerly 1st Bn Connaught Rangers
K.I.A. 12-4-18
Aged 19
Interred in St. Venant-Robecq Rd British Cemetery, Robecq. Plot 2, Row E, Grave 12

Born   Ballymoney
Lived
Enlisted
Son of John and Mary McArdle of 1, Bellevue Terrace, Port Glasgow.

John McArdle was born in the Ballymoney district in 1899. He attended school in Ballymoney but it would appear that the family moved to Scotland soon after this. The need to find steady work was a major factor in the life of many of the families at the time and Scotland was a popular place to find it. Many of the large farms in the North of Ayrshire and Lanarkshire took on extra labour for the harvest work and in this region there were also coal mines. So there were two sources of work to be had within a short distance. If this failed there was also the shipbuilding yards of the Clyde.

John enlisted into the Connaght Rangers but for some reason later transferred to the Machine Gun Corps. Very little information has come to light concerning him and an advertisement placed in the Greenock Telegraph asking any surviving family members to contact me has produced nothing and so it can only be surmised that the family has died out and are gone for ever. It is sad when something like this happens but it would appear to be the case with many of the families. By early 1918 John was in action a few miles north of Bethune and it was here that he was killed on the 12th of April 1918. He was only nineteen years of age.

John is buried in St. Venant-Robecq Road British Cemetery close to where he was killed.

St. Venant-Robecq Rd British Cemetery. Grave of John McArdle

1053 RIFLEMAN WILLIAM McCORMICK
12th Bn Royal Irish Rifles
K.I.A. 15-4-18
Aged 25
No Known Grave. Commemorated on the Tyne Cot Memorial, Belgium.
Panels 138 to 140 and 162 to 162a and 163a

Born   Belfast
Lived   Castle St, Ballymoney.
Enlisted Ballymoney.
Commemorated in Ballymoney Parish Church.
Son of the late Robert and Minnie McCormick.
Nephew of Mrs. Murphy, Castle St.

Although William McCormick was born in Belfast he lived in Ballymoney and enlisted there. The 12th battalion trained at Clandeboye before going to Seaford on the south coast of England for final training. From here they went to France and eventually to Martinsart for the battle of the Somme.

William survived this battle and was taken with the battalion to the area around Wulverghem in Belgium. They were to be here for over a year.

This was to be a time of sporadic fighting, in and out of the line. Then in June of 1917 they took part in the Battle of Messines. This was a very successful battle but worse was to come in August when they moved to Passchendaele. Here conditions were unbelievable, mud everywhere, shell-holes full to the lip with water, mud so slippery under foot that it was almost impossible to stand up, never mind walk. It was just as easy to drown in a shell-hole as be shot by the enemy. William managed to fight his way through this horror that was Passchendaele. When they had done all they could do at Passchendaele they were moved south for what was to be the battle of Cambrai in November 1917. It would be a long cold winter for the men of the 36th Ulster Division in this region.

After Cambrai, they moved south again to the area around St.Quentin, and it was here that they met the German Armies as they began their Spring Offensive of March 1918. They were pushed backwards very quickly before this huge onslaught. Again William survived and after it was over the battalions of the 36th Ulster Division were moved once again to the area to the south of Ypres. By the middle of the month they were at Wulverghem, in much the same place as they had fought in previously. By this time the enemy had captured Neuve Eglise and very heavy shelling was taking place all along the line. The 12th battalion were west of Wulverghem and were being forced back. At 10.30pm on the 14th orders were recieved to withdraw a short distance to a new position. This was carried out before dawn, the line pivoting back on the left of the 12th Rifles, which joined up with the 178th Brigade west of the village. With morning light the Germans opened an intense bombardment on the new position and it was during this bombardment that William was killed. He has no known grave and is commemorated on the Tyne Cot Memorial.

3428 PRIVATE PATRICK JOHN GLASS
9th Bn Royal Irish Fusiliers
K.I.A. 19-4-18
Aged 26
No Known Grave. Commemorated on the Tyne Cot Memorial, Belgium. Panels 140 & 141

Born   Castle St, Ballymoney.
Lived   Hordle, Hants.
Enlisted   Ballymoney
Son of Sarah and the late James Glass.
Husband of Annie May Glass, of 8, Council House, Hordle, Hants.

Patrick was born in Ballymoney in 1892. He went to school in Ballymoney, but after leaving it he went to work in England. Soon after the outbreak of hostilities he enlisted, but it would appear that he first of all served in some other unit and joined the Royal Irish Fusiliers at a later date. He is mentiond as having fought through Gallipoli and Serbia. In early 1917 he was invalided from Salonika suffering from dysentry and spent some time in hospital in England.

In May of that year he was home at Castle St on leave. There are conflicting reports of when he got married but it would seem more likely that he was married before he enlisted and had been living in England. When he returned to his unit in June of 1917 men were desperately needed and he would have taken part in the Battle of Messines. From there it was Passchendaele and Langemarck in August, before being sent south to Cambrai in November. Patrick was involved in the hurried retreat before the Germans in March of 1918 but was again back in the Ypres sector by mid April. It was in this region that he was killed in action attempting to push the German Armies back from Ypres.

He has no known grave and is commemorated on the Tyne Cot Memorial.

I doubt very much if any family members remain. In spite of many enquiries in the newspapers no-one from the family has got in touch and it would appear that the family has died out.

Cemetery location information
The Tyne Cot Memorial to the missing forms the north-eastern boundary of Tyne Cot cemetery, which is located 9 kilometres north-east of Ypres town centre.

73228 PRIVATE JOSEPH ALLEN
34th Bn. Machine Gun Corps.
D.O.W. 20-4-18
Aged 22
Interred in Etaples Military Cemetery, Plot 29, Row J, Grave 2a.

Born   Ballymoney
Lived
Enlisted
Son of Mrs. Mary Allen, 4 Strand Terrace, Coleraine.

Joseph Allen was born in the Ballymoney district in 1896. Some time after this the family appears to have moved to Coleraine as his mother has an address in Strand Terrace. Joseph enlisted early in the war and was a machine gunner.

I have been unable to contact the family and so very little news has come to light, but he was injured in April 1918 and removed to Etaples Military hospital where he died of his injuries on the 20th. He is buried in the nearby cemetery.

Joseph is not commemorated in any of the local churches in Ballymoney or the surrounding district so it can be fairly safely assumed that the family had left the district when he was still a very young boy.

Bouzincourt Ridge Cemetery, France

39127   PRIVATE SAMUEL BORELAND
11th Bn Royal West Yorks transferred to 479165 49th Co Labour Corps
DIED 25-5-18
Aged 27
Interred in Querrieu British Cemetery, Row A, Grave 36

Born
Lived
Enlisted   England
Son of Mrs E. Borland, of Ballymoney.
Commemorated in Ballymoney Parish Church

The 11th battalion was formed at York on 10th September 1914 and started their training at Frencham with the 23rd Division. On 1st December they moved to Oudenarde Barracks, Aldershot. In February 1915 they moved to Folkestone and Maidstone and then in May to Bramshott. They finished their training here and on 26th August landed at Le Havre.

Samuel Boreland tried repeatedly to enlist in N. Ireland. He was not tall enough and recruiting officers repeatedly turned him away. He then moved to Scotland to try his luck there but the result was the same. Being determined to get to France with his mates he then went to England in a desperate attempt to find his way into the army. This time he succeeded, enlisting into the Royal West Yorkshire Regiment. Later on he transferred into the Labour Corps probably because of his height. He would have been much better suited to digging trenches than trying to fire over the top of a trench designed for men close to six feet tall. Samuel's Father, Thomas, was also serving in the trenches. He was with the Royal Inniskillings.

His brother James had been honourably discharged from service suffering from wounds.

Samuel was killed when a shell exploded in the village where he was billetted and killed several others of the same battalion. This happened at Querrieu on the road between Amiens and Albert while the battalion were at rest. He died instantly and is buried in the nearby cemetery.

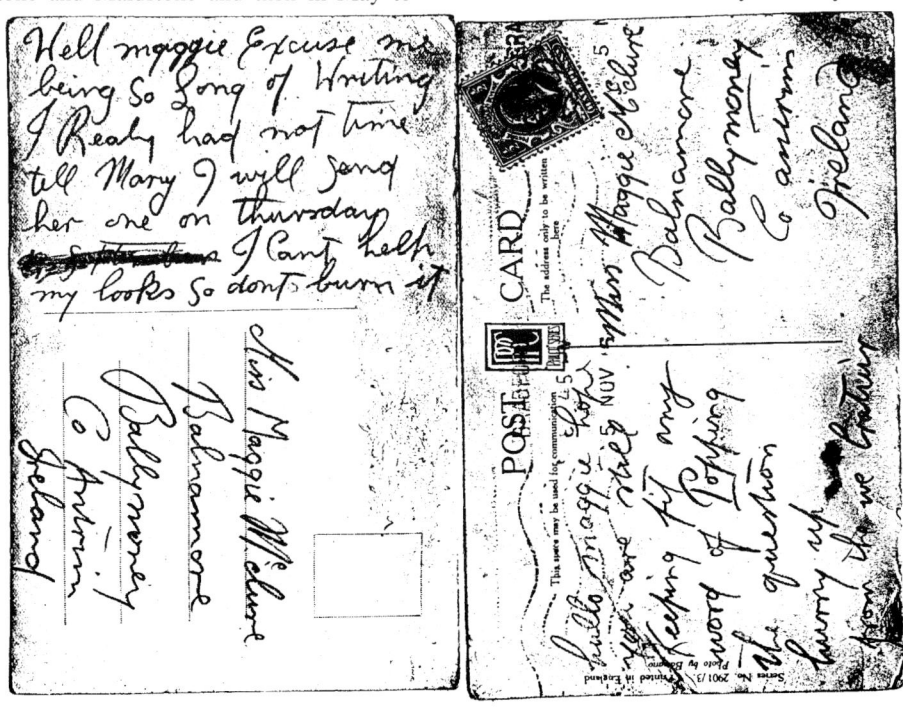

Querrieu British Cemetery. S. Boreland, back row

17461 L.CPL ROBERT COILS
15th Bn Royal Irish Rifles
K.I.A. 29-5-18
Aged 23
Interred in Canada Farm Cemetery, Belgium, Plot 4, Row A, Grave 6

Born   Dervock
Lived   Summerhill, Stranocum.
Enlisted Ballymoney
Son of Alexander and Annie Coils of Somerset Lodge, Coleraine.
Commemorated in Derrykeighan Parish Church.

Robert Coils was born at Summerhill, Stranocum, about five miles from Ballymoney.

The family worshipped in Derrykeighan Parish Church and it is there that Robert is commemorated. He enlisted at Ballymoney soon after war was declared into the 15th battalion of the Royal Irish Rifles. This battalion then formed part of the 107th Infantry Brigade and did their training at Ballykinlar. When this was finished they moved to Seaford on the south coast of England for final training and then to France in October 1915. After more training they were brought to the area around the French villages of Mesnil and Martinsart in preparation for the Battle of the Somme. The battalion attacked south of the River Ancre and across the steep hill leading up to the site where the Ulster Tower now stands. They attacked between the Tower and the river.

This area was guarded by a nest of machine-guns at St.Pierre-Divion and the attack eventually petered out. Casualties were horrific and the battalion was withdrawn next day. After a rest and re-organisation they were moved to the area around Wulverghem in Belgium and remained there for over a year. In June of 1917 plans were in place for the Battle of Messines and the 15th battalion were involved on the extreme right. As they approached the Messines-Wytschaete road they were held up by very heavy machine-gun fire. When they had overcome this the battalion went forward and captured Lumm Farm.

Robert was involved in this attack and the capture of Lumm Farm. He then took part in the Battle of Langemarck in August of 1917. Conditions here were attrocious with every shell-hole full to the lip with water and men sank up to the knees in mud at every step. Not one of the Ballymoney men killed at Langemarck was ever seen again. From here it was south to the area around Cambrai in November and then to St. Quentin to face the Germans in the Spring Offensive of March 1918. After being forced back across the old Somme battlefields, the 15th battalion was taken out of the line and sent again to Ypres. In May of 1918 they were in the back areas North West of Ypres. This was generally a quiet area but towards the end of the month the Germans started to carry out bombing raids and it was during one of these raids that Robert was killed. He is buried in Canada Farm Cemetery close by.

Canada Farm Cemetery is located 8.5 Kilometres north west of Ypres town centre, on the Elzenda-mmestraat, a road leading from the Veurnseweg N8, connecting Ypres to Elverdinghe and on to Veurne.

The grave of Robert Coils in Canada Farm Cemetery, front row centre.

8636 RIFLEMAN DANIEL McLERNON
2nd Bn Royal Irish Rifles
DIED HOME 30-5-15
Aged 21
Interred in Port Glasgow Cemetery, Renfrewshire. Row 05, Grave 83

Born   Mosside.
Lived   Port Glasgow,
Enlisted Ballymoney

On the outbreak of hostilities the battalion were based at Tidworth. Ten days later they landed at Rouen.

Daniel McLernon was born at Mosside, a village about seven miles from Ballymoney on the road to Ballycastle. His father was also Daniel, and he worked as a cooper. As a young man, Daniel went to Scotland in search of work and settled in Port Glasgow. It was in Port Glasgow that he found work as a mill labourer at Barr's Brae.

It was while working at the mill that he met and married Matilda Kitchen. Soon afterwards, on the outbreak of hostilities, he returned to Ballymoney to enlist and while under training was allowed home to Port Glasgow on leave. It was while he was on leave that tragedy struck. It appears he had gone over to the mill probably for a chat with some of his old mates, and was drowned.

He was found floating in the mill dam at Barr's Brae at 6.00pm on the 30th of May 1915. The cause of death was given as Asphyxiation by drowning. He was just 21 years of age and lived at 22 Bowrie St, Port Glasgow.

Port Glasgow Cemetery is on the east side of the town, and belongs to the Town Council. It contains 29 war graves.

Grave of Daniel McLernon in Port Glasgow Cemetery

17273 CPL HERBERT BLACKMORE M.M.
12th Bn Royal Irish Rifles
D.O.W. 7-6-18
Interred in Haringe Military Cemetery, Poperingue.

Born   Ballymacarret, Co. Down.
Lived   Chatham, Armoy.
Enlisted   Ballymoney
Commemorated in Armoy Parish Church.

Although he was born at Ballymacarret, County Down, the family seems have lived in the Armoy district ever since. Herbert enlisted at Ballymoney along with his brother, William, very soon after the outbreak of hostilities and soon both were taken to Clandeboye for initial training. This involved route marches in the hilly Co. Down countryside which was intended to bring the troops up to a high level of fitness and also make them aware of Army commands and procedures. When their training here was considered complete, they were sent to a training camp in the south of England. This was at Seaford, on the south coast. When they had completed their time here they were taken across to France to prepare for the Battle of the Somme.

The British High Command had been under pressure from the French to attack the Germans in the north in an attempt to draw German troops away from Verdun. This was to become known as the Battle of the Somme.

The 12th battalion were camped at the small French village of Martinsart, a very short distance from where they would eventually attack. Without going into details, because it has already been told in other stories, the 12th battalion attacked at Hamel on the 1st of July 1916. This was on the north bank of the River Ancre. The ground here close to the river, is marshy but quickly rises to drier ground. It was through this that the 12th battalion had to attack. William Blackmore was killed as he made his way across No Man's Land. His brother, Herbert, survived and went on to fight in other battles. Next day the 12th battalion were relieved and taken by train to St. Omer for a rest and to be brought back up to strength with new recruits.

They were then taken north to Belgium and the area around Wulverghem. They would be here for over a year. This was a difficult time for Herbert, knowing that his brother was dead and probably had seen him being killed.

Through the winter of 1916-17 they were engaged in relief work in the line and with rest and work out of it. Their next big battle would be the Battle of Messines in June 1917. A number of Ballymoney men were killed in this but again Herbert survived. He also survived the Battle of Passchendaele in August of 1917 where men were just as likely to drown in the mud as be killed by rifle fire. They remained in the area around Ypres and were in the fighting at Poperinge in May and June 1918. By the beginning of June they had moved back to near Proven for a rest when Herbert was seriously injured. He was taken to the Casualty Clearing Station at Haringe but died of his wounds on 7th June 1918. He is buried in the nearby cemetery.

1782 RIFLEMAN WILLIAM SMYTH
12th Bn Royal Irish Rifles
K.I.A. 9-6-18
Interred in Niederzwehren Cemetery, Germany. Plot 2, Row F, Grave 15

Born
Enlisted   Ballymoney.

William Smyth enlisted at Ballymoney on the outbreak of hostilities and did his early training at Clandeboye in Co. Down. When this part of his training was completed he was taken to Seaford on the south coast of England for final instruction. From here he was taken to France and the small village of Martinsart in preparation for the Battle of the Somme. He was lucky here, getting through this without serious injury. After this the 12th battalion were taken out of the line for re-organisation in the huge camp at St. Omer. From here, after they had done more training, they were sent to Belgium, to the area around Wulverghem. Here they would stay for over a year. In this time they saw much action in minor skirmiches which still took lives the same as major battles. The Battle of Messines was to be their next big undertaking and in this they were extremely successful. Some time around this period William was taken prisoner and was cooped up in very uncomfortable trains on the journey back to prison camp. They eventually arrived at the camp at Niederzwehren, in Germany. They were allowed to write home, but only to say that they were prisoners of war and were being well looked after. The conditions under which they had to live were attrocious and many of them died of disease or malnutrition. It was here that William died on the 9th of June 1918. He is buried in the adjoining cemetery with two other Ballymoney boys. In a grave in the row behind where William is buried lies Bushmills man Arthur Ross who died as a prisoner of war on 23rd August 1918. Plot 2, Row G, Grave 6.

Neiderzwehren Cemetery, Germany

18205 RIFLEMAN ROBERT McCAUGHAN
12th Bn Royal Irish Rifles
DIED 19-6-18
Aged 24
Interred in Niederzwehren Cemetery, Germany. Plot 2, Row G, Grave 14

Born   Armoy
Lived   Armoy
Enlisted Ballymoney.
Son of Mrs. Sarah McCaughan, of Railway St, Armoy.

Robert was a son of Mrs Sarah McCaughan of Railway Street, Armoy. After leaving school he worked on some of the local farms until at the outbreak of hostilities he enlisted at Ballymoney. He enlisted into the 12th battalion of the Royal Irish Rifles and did his training at Clandeboye and Newtownards. When this was complete he was taken to Seaford, on the south coast of England for final training and then in October of 1915 moved to France. It is thought that Robert did not take part in the Battle of the Somme, but joined the battalion in a later draft. He did, however, go with them to the Wulverghem area of Belgium.

They were here for over a year and Robert took part in the Battle of Messines in June of 1917 as well as the battles of Passchendaele and Langemarck in August of that year. They then moved south to Cambrai in November and then south again to meet the German Spring Offensive of March 1918 at Le Cateau.

It was in this region that Robert was taken prisoner and was eventually taken to the notorious camp at Niederzwehren in Germany. They had been packed like cattle into goods waggons and carted off to whatever prisoner of war camp could take them. The long train journeys were hazardous affairs. They had very little to eat or drink and had no room to sit down. Many of the men never made it to the camps. The cemetery beside the camp is evidence of just how many

died there. Three Ballymoney men died in this camp and this in itself must speak volumes for the number of men interned there. We have no real indication of what the conditions were like in this camp but they must have been awful.

When you consider that Robert died of heart failure at the age of twenty-four, when he should have been in the prime of life, you can really only guess at what conditions must have been like for the men interned there.

424724 PTE WALTER WM McGREGOR QUIN
217th Employment Co, Labour Corps. formerly 28652 R.Dublin Fus
D.O.W. 22-6-18
Aged 21
Interred in Terlincthun British Cemetery, Wimille, near Boulogne. Plot 1, Row B, Grave 4

Born   1897
Lived   Finvoy,
Enlisted
Son of Rev. William and Mary Emma Quin, of Finvoy Rectory.
Commemorated in Finvoy Parish Church.

Walter was at Trinity College, Dublin, and attempted to pass his Officer Training Corps exams there. Due to defective eyesight he failed to become an Officer and served in the Dublin Fusiliers as a private, later transferring to the Labour Corps.

In June 1917 he had seen action in the Battle of Messines.

George H. Frazer, Royal Army Medical Corps, won the Military Medal at Messines.

He survived the war. His father had been the Rev Frazer, rector of Finvoy Parish Church immediately before Mr. Quin The Reverend William Quin was rector of Loughguile from 1904 to 1914, when he moved to Finvoy, where he remained until 1924. He died on 3rd September 1928 and is buried in Loughguile graveyard.

His son, Walter, died in hospital on the outskirts of Boulogne on 22nd June 1918 and is buried in the cemetery close by.

Terlincthun British Cemetery

3378 PRIVATE ANDREW BOYLE
8th Bn Royal Irish Regiment formerly 7218 R. Irish Rifles
DIED 7-7-18
Interred in Longuenesse (St. Omer) Souvenir Cemetery. Plot 5, Row C, Grave 55

Born   Derrykeighan
Lived   Dervock
Enlisted Ballymoney
Commemorated in Derrykeighan Parish Church

St. Omer is a large town 45 kilometres south east of Calais. Longuenesse is a commune on the southern outskirts of St. Omer.

Andrew was born in Derrykeighan, in those times a small cluster of houses on a cross roads. Since then it has increased somewhat but is still only a small village.

Andrew enlisted early in the war and saw a great deal of action. He saw service with the Royal Irish Rifles at first but later transferred to the Royal Irish Regiment. There is no apparent reason for the change of Regiment but the 8th Battalion was a Garrison Guard battalion and were based at St. Omer. They joined the 59th Div.

It may have been that the illness he suffered from prevented him from taking an active part in the battles at the Front and he was allowed to help out at the Base where better conditions prevailed.

He was in France for about two years before being injured and eventually being invalided home. He was seriously ill, and after a long period of convalescence and care at home, he was allowed back to his unit. He had been back about two months when he contracted neuritis and passed away on the 7th. Andrew was married and there was one child. They lived at Main St, Dervock and worshipped in Derrykeighan Parish Church where Andrew is commemorated on the Roll of Honour.

A number of attempts at finding the family have failed to produce anything and it can only be assumed that the family have died out.

Grave of Andrew Boyle

SERGEANT JOHN JAMES CAMPBELL
American Exp Force. 165th Infantry, 42nd Div.
K.I.A. 28-7-18
Interred in Oise-Aisne American Cemetery, Fere-en-Tardenois, (Aisne), France.
Plot A, Row 6, Grave 16

Born   Craigs, Finvoy.
Lived   Finvoy.
Enlisted
Commemorated in Finvoy Presbyterian Church.

John Campbell had been living in America and enlisted into the American Army when America decided to join Britain in the fight against Germany.

By July of 1918 the American Forces were in position close to the Aisne-Marne Front and were ready for an attack which they knew was coming from the Germans. This was the period when the German Armies were pushing all in front of them in their Spring Offensive and trying to capture Paris. Gradually the Allies along with the American divisions halted the German armies and began to push them back. The bitter fighing which took place here cost many men their lives and Britain, France and America as well as Germany, suffered heavily. John Campbell was killed in this fighting and is buried in the Oise-Aisne American Cemetery close to where he fell.

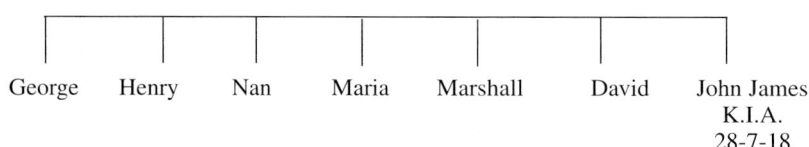

George   Henry   Nan   Maria   Marshall   David   John James
                                                  K.I.A.
                                                  28-7-18

27520 PRIVATE ISAAC DEMPSEY
9th Bn Royal Inniskilling Fusiliers
D.O.W. 29-7-18
Aged 31
Interred in Arneke British Cemetery, France. Plot 3, Row B, Grave 22

Born   Artiferral, Dunloy.
Lived   Artiferral, Dunloy
Enlisted Ballymoney
Commemorated in Garryduff Presbyterian Church.
Husband of M. Dempsey of Artiferral, Dunloy.

The Dempsey family had been farmers in Artiferral for many years and were very well known and respected in the district. When Isaac Dempsey was born around 1887 his Father, William, was running the farm. Isaac attended Galdanagh school, leaving there in 1901 when he was fourteen years of age. For a number of years he worked at home but as time wore on and headlines began to appear in the papers of unrest all over Europe, and of Germany's invasion of Belgium, and of England's declaration of war against Germany, a feeling of wanting to be part of it took hold. Soon after war was declared Isaac enlisted at Ballymoney into the Royal

Isaac with his wife Mary and son Isaac

Isaac's Wedding
Thought to be Isaac Dempsey, James Stevenson, Martha McKinley & Mary Beattie

Inniskilling Fusiliers. He was based at the Military Barracks in Enniskillen. It was here that much of his early training took place. In January 1916 he was allowed leave in order to get married. The wedding took place in Garryduff Presbyterian Church to Mary Beattie, the daughter of Samuel Beattie, of Artiferral. They were both twenty-nine years of age. Soon after this Isaac had to return to Enniskillen. Next it was overseas to France and the Battle of the Somme. The attack on 1st July from Thiepval Wood was a disaster. Although they reached their objective, a shortage of ammunition and food, forced them to fall back. Heavy machine-gun fire from Thiepval village took a desperate toll and the few remaining men of the battalion had to retire.

Next day they were relieved and sent back for re-organisation. Isaac was home on leave in the summer of 1917 to see his son Isaac for the first time. He survived into 1918 without any serious injury but on the 29th of July that year he was very badly injured while his battalion was in the front line at Bonnegues. He was taken to No 62 Casualty Clearing Station at Arneke, a long tiring journey from Bonnegues, but died there later that day. He is buried in the nearby cemetery at Arneke. Another Ballymoney man, Charles Ellison, died of wounds here three weeks later, and is buried in the same cemetery.

Cemetery Location Information

Arneke is about 50kilometres south-east of Calais and about 8 kilometres north-west of Cassel. Leave Arneke on the D11 heading north. After 1.3 kilometres turn right at the cross-roads. The cemetery is 800 metres on the right.

Arneke British Cemetery

Isaac Dempsey
married
Mary Beattie
in Garryduff Presbyterian Church on 25th January 1916

| Isaac | Rose | Hanah | Maud |

33483 PRIVATE WILLIAM WALLACE HUEY
1/7th Bn Royal Warwickshire Regt. formerly Royal Army Service Corps
K.I.A. 3-8-18
Aged 24
Interred in Barenthal Cemetery, Asiago, Italy. Plot 2, Row C, Grave 2

Born   Carncullagh, Dervock.
Lived   Carncullagh, Dervock.
Enlisted
Commemorated in Carncullagh Presbyterian Church.
Son of John and Mary Huey.

On the outbreak of hostilities the battalion was in Coventry and were sent to train in the Chelmsford area. On the 22nd of March 1915 they landed at Le Havre. On 13th May 1915 they joined the 48th Div, and in November 1917 they went to Italy.

Wallace was employed by Messrs. F. Kirkpatrick & Co, of Belfast, and was traveller for the firm. This involved visits to England

At the mid day service in Carncullagh Presbyterian Church on Sunday 18th August 1918, the Rev W.N.Maxwell made touching reference to the family and to the death of Wallace Huey in Italy. Through his work in Belfast he had been a member of the Y.M.C.A. Gymnastics club and had a keen interest in athletics. While in Italy he was one of twenty chosen by his battalion to give a demonstration of physical and bayonet exercises before His Majesty, the King of Italy.

He was killed by shell-fire on the 3rd of August near Asiago, the only Ballymoney man to be killed in Italy. Asiago is in the north of Italy, in mountainous country, close to the Austrian border.

Wytchaete Cemetery

5999 PRIVATE JOHN CRAIG
14th Bn Australian Infantry
D.O.W. 9-8-18
Aged 28
Interred in Vignacourt British Cemetery, France. Plot 5, Row B, Grave 3

Born   Cromachs, Armoy.
Lived   Prahran, Victoria.
Enlisted Prahran, Victoria.
Son of George and Jane Fulton Craig, of Cromachs, Armoy.
Commemorated in Armoy Presbyterian Church.

John Craig had been in Australia for some considerable time before war was declared. He enlisted at Prahran on 23rd Feb 1916. He was almost five feet nine inches tall, with a fresh complexion, blue eyes and fair hair. He embarked at Melbourne on 1st August on the Troop Ship "Miltiades" arriving at Plymouth on 25th September 1916. While in England he was awarded leave but overstayed it from Reveille on 9th Oct until Tattoo on 10th Oct. He was awarded seven days Confined to Barracks and forfeited two days pay. After intensive training he boarded the Princess Victoria at Folkestone on 4th December arriving at Etaples the next day. On Boxing Day the 14th battalion were brought up to strength at Etaples and on 11th April 1917 John was wounded in action. He was suffering from gun-shot wounds to the left arm and a fractured radius.

The arm was so badly damaged that he had to be brought back to hospital in Eastleigh for treatment. It took a long time to heal but by August he was fit enough to go back to France and sailed from Southampton on the 30th and re-joining his unit on the 10th of September. On 29th October 1917 he was promoted to L/Cpl in the field.

Then on 5th April he was wounded again but stayed on duty. He was admitted to hospital on 16th May with sickness but after ten days he rejoined his unit, only to be wounded again on 8th June. This turned out to be far more serious and he died of his wounds the next day.

Vignacourt is a village in the Department of the Somme on the west of the road from Amiens to Doullens, the D 933. From the D 933 take the D 113 from Flesselles and five kilometres along this road the Cemetery will be found at the entrance to the village.

The original grave marker

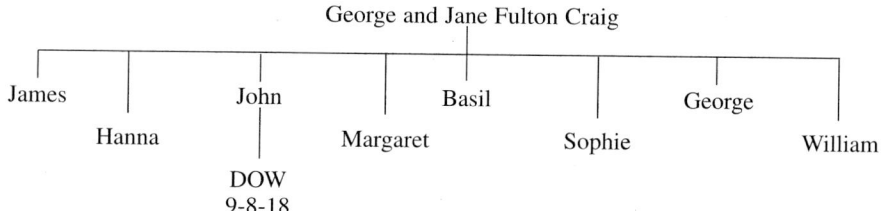

238211 PRIVATE WILLIAM McILVENNA
54th Bn Canadian Infantry 2nd Central Ontario Regt.
K.I.A. 9-8-18
Aged 38
Interred in Villers-Brettoneux Military Cemetery, Fouilloy. Plot 9, Row C, Grave 11

Born   Ballymena
Lived   New York.
Enlisted Toronto.
Son of William and Mary McIlvenna, of 27, Mount St, Ballymena.
Brother of Mrs. Thompson, Charlotte St, Ballymoney.

William McIlvenna was born on 10th January 1880. After leaving school he served his time as a mechanical engineer. His sister, Mrs Thompson, lived in Charlotte Street, in Ballymoney, and he spent a good bit of his time there. Later he emigrated to Canada, settling in New York and finding work there. He enlisted in Toronto on 21st February 1917 and arrived in England on board the SS, Saxonia on 7th April 1917. He wasn't that tall at five feet five and a half inches. He was of medium complexion with dark brown eyes and dark brown hair. He was transferred to 204th reserve battalion at Otterpool and then moved to East Sandling and then on 27th May to Witley. On 27th February 1918 he proceeded overseas for service with the 54th Battalion. On the 8th of August 1918 he was evacuated from the front line very severely wounded. He had gunshot wounds to the left thigh and left arm and was taken to the nearest field ambulance but the seriousness of the wounds meant that he had to be sent to hospital at once if his life was to be saved. He died of his wounds at No 48 C.C.S. next day.

247 PRIVATE HUGH DOHERTY
90th Winnipeg Rifles
D.O.W. 11-8-18
Aged 24
Interred in Mont Huon Military Cemetery, Le Treport. Plot 5, Row N, Grave 12b

Born   Bratwell, Articlave.
Lived   Dervock
Enlisted   Canada
Youngest son of Mrs. Doherty, Mosside Rd, Dervock.
(Patrick & Eliza Doherty of Ballyratahan, Dervock).

Hugh Doherty was born at Bratwell, Articlave, on 1st January 1894. There is no record of his early life, but after leaving school he worked as a labourer.

At about the time he left school the family moved to live in Dervock and soon after this Hugh emigrated to Canada. As far as can be ascertained the family consisted of Hugh and his sister and there may have been an older brother.

Hugh enlisted at Valcartier Camp, on the outskirts of Quebec, on 8th September 1914. He was five feet nine inches tall, with a light complexion, blue eyes and medium coloured hair. Having returned to England and completed his training he was sent to France in early 1915. Soon after arriving there he had to go to hospital for a Hernia operation. This was in March. On the 24th of April he was wounded and gassed at Ypres. A few days later he wrote to his sister at Dervock and asked her to go to Carnglass and tell the Lyons family about John Lyons being killed at his side by the same shell that wounded him. The story of John Lyons is told in "Bushmills Heroes". Hugh was sent to recuperate in hospital at Tunbridge Wells in Kent and was there for about a month. Immediately after re-joining his unit he was injured again, this time with a bullet in the left groin.

He crawled back to the nearest dressing station to have the wound attended to only to discover that the station had been shelled, and there were no ambulances available to take him to another one. So he had to make his own way back to another hospital, a distance of four miles, to have the wound dressed and the bullet extracted. In June 1915 he was allowed home on leave. This gave him time to recover but when he returned to England he was again admitted to hospital at Shorncliffe. The illness kept him there for about three weeks, and then he was transferred to Barnwell hospital, Cambridge, where he spent another month. After much hospital treatment over the next few months he eventually recovered well enough to go back to the Front. So in March 1916 he returned to the trenches. In May of that year he was ill again, this time with Measles, and was admitted to No7 General Hospital at St. Omer. He was moved to Wimereux and then back to hospital in England at Folkestone. By the time he got the proper treatment for his condition he was a very sick young man and it took a long time to recover. On the 25th of August 1916 he arrived back in France. Then on 3rd October he was injured, a shotgun wound to the left leg, and he was again in hospital, and again removed to England. By January 1917 he had recovered and was taken on strength at Seaford. In May he was promoted L/Cpl, but had to revert to the ranks again to go overseas. He was drafted to the 8th battalion on 27th August 1917 and taken once again to France. On 10th November he was wounded in the right thigh but it was a slight wound and he was treated at the depot. Early in 1918 he once again re-joined his unit. Then on the 3rd of May he suffered severe gunshot wounds and a compound fracture of the left femur and a dislocated right shoulder. After so many wounds and so much hospital treatment he was not in a condition to stand any more and he was declared seriously ill. In all he was wounded five times, the last injury necessitating amputation of the left leg on July 19th. He got gradually worse, so the doctors, in a vain attempt to save his life, cut off his right leg, but worn out by suffering, he passed away on the operating table at 1.00 pm. His only sister, the one who had taken the news of John Lyons's death over to Carnglass, had died just a few months earlier.

Le Treport is a small seaport 25 kilometres northeast of Dieppe. The cemetery is 1.5 kilometres south of the town. Go towards the centre of Le Treport and then follow the Littoral / Dieppe sign. The cemetery stands on the D 940.

> **18972 CORPORAL CHARLES ELLISON M M.**
> *12th Bn Royal Irish Rifles*
> **D.O.W. 21-8-18.**
> Interred in Arneke British Cemetery, Plot 3, Row C, Grave 17

Born   Ballymoney
Lived   Meetinghouse St,
Enlisted Belfast
Commemorated in Ballymoney Parish Church.

It would appear that the family lived in Meetinghouse Street in Ballymoney for a few years before moving to live in Mosside. Charles eventually enlisted in Belfast. He seems to have been a later recruit and probably joined the 12th battalion after the devastation of the Battle of the Somme. The battalion then moved to the Wulverghem area of Belgium and were to be in this general area for over a year. The first winter was spent in and out of the line in this region.

The following summer plans were made for the battle of Messines in June of 1917 and Charles was through this. He was home for ten days in June of 1917. After this he took part in the battles around Passchendaele and Langemarck. This was bitter fighting in atrocious conditions when men could just as easily drown in shell holes filled to the lip with mud and water. He was injured at the Battle of Langemarck but after a short time spent in hospital he returned to his unit. After this the battalion were moved south for the Battle of Cambrai in November 1917 and then south again to St. Quentin in March to try to stop the German Spring Offensive. This they failed to do and were rapidly pushed back across the old Somme battlefields. They were later withdrawn from this region and moved once again to Flanders. They were now close to the town of Bailleul and the German front line was less than a mile away at this time. In an attack on the German line Charles was very seriously injured and was removed to hospital at Arneke a few miles away. A telegram arrived at his home to say that he had schrapnel wounds to the head and that he was dangerously ill, and that permission to visit him could not be granted. He was taken back to the small village of Arneke for treatment but all to no avail and he died there on the 21st of August. He is buried in the cemetery nearby. Another Ballymoney man, Isaac Dempsey, is buried in the same cemetery.

Arneke British Cemetery, Nord, France

Chronicle, May 1918.

Referring to Charles Ellison winning the Military Medal. from his Commanding officer.

> " I have only just returned to the Divisional Wing and was very pleased indeed to see the Corps Commander had awarded you the Military Medal for good work done during recent fighting on the Somme. Will you please accept my heartiest congratulations as I know how well you did in the field. I hope you will live long to enjoy the distinction and also gain fresh laurels and so assist in maintaining the excellent name of the Royal Irish Rifles. My very best wishes for your future wellfare."

Three other brothers of Charles also served.

Sgt. W.J. Ellison served in the Royal Inniskilling Fusiliers and was a prisoner of war.

David served in Palestine, and Daniel was wounded and in hospital in England in April 1918.

4500 RIFLEMAN WILLIAM SPEERS
12th Bn Royal Irish Rifles
DIED 30-8-18
Interred in Niederzwehren Cemetery in Germany

Born   Ballymoney.
Lived   Castle St, Ballymoney.
Enlisted   Ballymoney.
Commemorated in St. James's Presbyterian Church

In December 1916 during an attack on the Germans, William got into their front line trench and captured a German machine-gun which he took back to his own trench under heavy enemy fire. Not content with this success he tried it again but had to make a hurried escape when the Germans saw him and opened fire. In the German Spring Offensive of 1918, William was taken prisoner but in June was allowed to send a post card to his wife in Ballymoney to let her know what had happened to him. From now on his health deteriorated and on 30th August 1918 he died of Dysentry as a prisoner of war. The Cemetery at Niederzwehren is quite a large one with three Ballymoney men buried within it's walls. It is well kept and a credit to those who look after it.

Died of Dysentry in Germany as a prisoner of war.

Cemetery location information
The Cemetery is located 10 kilometres south of Kassel and 2 kilometres from the main road from Kassel to Marburg. Approach Kassel on the A 49 motorway, leave at junction Kassel Niederzwehren, which forms the Frankfurterstrasse.

The first right turn leads into the Dittershauser Strasse. Continue on this road which becomes a

narrow road at the bend and follow the bend to the right. The cemetery is clearly signposted, leading to a small crossroads.

Turn left at the crossroads where Niederzwehren cemetery becomes visible from the roadside.

4552 PRIVATE GEORGE GRAHAM
2nd Bn Royal Inniskilling Fusiliers
K.I.A. 1-9-18
Aged 24
Interred in Wulverghem-Lindenhoek Road Military Cemetery, Belgium. Plot 2, Row F, Grave 18

Born   Ballymoney
Lived   Castle St, Ballymoney.
Enlisted Belfast
Son of George Graham

The old home in Castle Street, just before being demolished

George was one of a family of six, four girls and two boys. His mother died in child-birth when George was born. His father was left to bring up the children on his own. They all attended the St. Patrick's Church school together. The building still stands at the corner of Queen St although it is no longer used as a school. The school master in those days was Mr Norris. His father worked as a Tinsmith, as did his older brother, William James. George was a labourer and was not married. As a young man he joined the Orange Order and belonged to a local lodge, L.O.L. 96.

After a few years as a widower, his father re-married and there was another family, this time two girls and a boy. When George enlisted into the 2nd battalion of the Royal Inniskilling Fusiliers he was almost straight away sent for training. The family believe that once he got to France he never got home on leave again and that he spent four years in France and Belgium. He was the holder of the Mons Medal.

On the morning of the 1st of September 1918 the 2nd battalion were involved in a Brigade advance with the 36th Ulster Division at St. Jans Cappell. Enemy artillery fire had been very heavy and during a particularly vicious engagement a shell exploded very close to George, killing him instantly. He is buried in Wulverghem-Lindenhoek Road Military Cemetery, close to where he was killed.

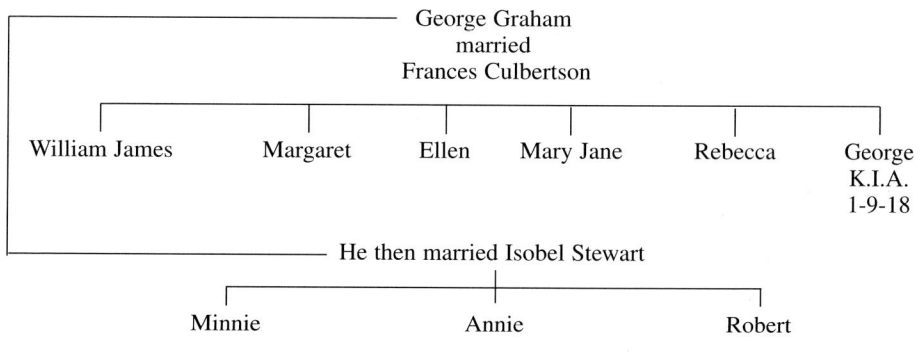

Cemetery location information

The cemetery is located 13 kilometres south of Ypres town centre on a road leading from the Kemmelseweg N331 connecting Ypres to Kemmel. From Ypres town centre the Kemmelseweg is reached via the Rijselsestraat, through the Lille Gate and straight on towards Armentieres (N365). 900 metres after the crossroads is the right hand turning on to the Kemmelseweg. 2 kilometres after passing the village of Kemmel lies the left hand turning on to the hooghofstraat. The cemetery lies 1.5 kilometres along the hooghofstraat on the right hand side of the road

Wulverghem-Lindenhoek Road Military Cemetery, Belgium

2507334 PRIVATE DANIEL CAMPBELL
54th Bn Canadian Infantry. Central Ontario Regiment
K.I.A. 2-9-18
Aged 26
Interred in Dury Hill British Cemetery, France. Plot 2, Row D, Grave 34.

Born   Cuppindale, Stranocum.
Lived   Canada
Enlisted Toronto, Canada.
Commemorated in Roseyards Presbyterian Church.
Son of David and Mary Murmis Campbell, of Cuppindale, Stranocum.

Daniel Campbell was born at Bushbank, Stranocum, on 17th April 1892 the son of David and Mary Campbell. The family worshipped in Roseyards Presbyterian Church where Daniel's name appears on the Roll of Honour. As a young man he emigrated to Canada, settling in the town of Rennselear, close to New York. He worked in Canada as a labourer and was not married. He was five feet six inches tall, with a medium complexion, grey eyes and brown hair. When he enlisted on 29th June 1917 at Toronto he was twenty-five years of age. The training period was short, because he embarked on the 20th of November 1917 and arrived at West Sandling on the 7th of December. The S.S.Scotian was one of the ships which regularly plied the North Atlantic bringing troops from Canada and it was this ship which brought Daniel back to England. He joined the Canadian forces in France on the 29th of March 1918 and was transferred to the Canadian Machine Gun Corps on the 30th of April. On 17th June he was up on a charge of losing a good clasp knife by neglect and forfeited a days pay as a result. Nothing more appears on his record until he is reported missing at the beginning of September. By this time he was fighting along the main road between Arras and Cambrai. They were in the vicinity of the small village of Dury. He was at first reported missing and then two days later reported killed in action. Obviously they had found his body. He is buried in the local cemetery at Dury.

The Cemetery is about half way between Arras and Cambrai and just north of the main road.

Peronne Road, Maricourt

1232 RIFLEMAN GEORGE HUNTER McLEAN
12th Bn Royal Irish Rifles
K.I.A. 2-9-18
Aged 20
Interred in Nieuwkerke (Neuve-Eglise) Churchyard, Belgium. Row W, Grave 1

Born   Armoy
Lived   Clintyfinnan, Armoy.
Enlisted Ballymoney.
Commemorated in Armoy Presbyterian Church.
Son of John and Maria McLean, of Clintyfinnan, Armoy.

George was one of a family of five boys and one girl and lived with his father and mother at Clintyfinnan. He attended school in the nearby village of Armoy. When he left school at the age of thirteen he immediately got a job in the drapery business of Adam McMullan in Armoy and it was here that he worked until he decided to enlist on the outbreak of hostilities. He enlisted at Ballymoney and was soon on his way to Clandeboye to start training. Much of this consisted of long route marches through the hilly Co Down countryside which soon brought the men up to peak fitness. When this had been completed they were moved to Seaford on the south coast of England where more training took place. By the time this was finished the French Commanders were clamouring for the British to attack in order to draw some of the German Armies away from Verdun. It was agreed to make an attack at the Somme.

The 12th battalion, of which George was now a part, was taken to the small French village of Martinsart. Here, close to the British front lines, they were housed in tents, there wasn't anywhere else to put them, every house and building in the area was crammed with soldiers. On the night of the 30th of June 1916, George and his mates were moved up to the front line trenches in readiness for the attack at 7.30am next morning. They were on the north bank of the River Ancre at Hamel. Somehow George survived the opening day of the Battle of the Somme in which so many of the Ballymoney boys died. The battalion, decimated by the machine-gun fire from the heights around St.Pierre Divion, was taken out of the line next day and sent to St Omer for re-organisation and a draft of new troops. After a rest they were moved to Belgium and the area around Wulverghem. They were to be here for

over a year. Sporadic fighting was taking place all of the time and they were continually in and out of the line but their next major battle would be the Battle of Messines in June 1917. This was an outstanding success and from here they moved north for the Battle of Passchendaele in August. Here the conditions were unbelieveable. Every shell-hole was full to the lip with water, guns couldn't be moved, food could only be brought so far, men could drown as fast as be shot.

By November the battalion had been moved south again for the Battle of Cambrai. From here they went south again to the area around St Quentin.

By now, in the spring of 1918, the German Armies were gathering for one massive push against the British in a last desperate attempt to gain victory.

After a hurried retreat the battalion once again moved north and attacked in the area of Neuve-Eglise.

Neuve-Eglise is a village and commune in the province of West Flanders, south west of Ypres, on the French border. It was in German hands from 14th April 1918 until it was recaptured by the 36th Ulster Division on the following 2nd September. The attack in which George was killed.

The family believe that he was killed by a sniper.

The Church, destroyed in the war, has been rebuilt. The churchyard was used by Field Ambulances or fighting units at intervals during the war.

The British graves are in short rows on the north side of the church, between it and the road. They comprise those of 76 soldiers from the United Kingdom, ten from Australia, five from New Zealand and one from Canada. One of these is unnamed.

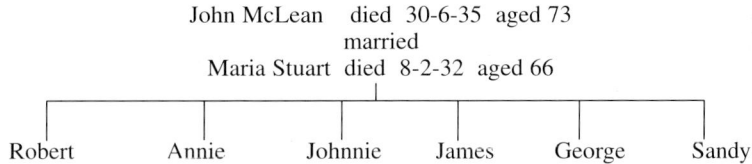

```
            John McLean   died 30-6-35 aged 73
                         married
            Maria Stuart  died 8-2-32 aged 66
   ┌──────────┬──────────┬──────────┬──────────┬──────────┐
 Robert    Annie     Johnnie    James     George     Sandy
```

16692 CORPORAL GEORGE McCAUGHAN. M.M.
1st Bn Royal Irish Rifles
K.I.A. 4-9-18
Aged 27
Interred in Wulverghem-Lindenhoek Road Military Cemetery. Plot 5, Row C, Grave 8.

Born   Philadelphia, U.S.A.
Lived   Drumdollagh, Stranocum.
Enlisted Ballymoney
Son of William and Lizzie McCaughan
Commemorated in Armoy Presbyterian Church.

George McCaughan had been on active service with the 1st battalion since 29th April 1915. He was home on leave in early June 1916 for a few days and had taken part in the Battle of Loos and of Armentieres.

He then joined a trench mortar battery in his regiment and was awarded a certificate for gallantry in March 1917.

Another Armoy man, Frank Heggarty, was serving in a machine-gun section in the same battalion as George until he was killed in October 1916.

"During operations at Moislin's Ridge on the 4th-5th March 1917 while in the German trench which was being attacked his section officer was wounded. He carried him back across No Man's Land under heavy fire, reported to his Officer Commanding, and returned to his gun. This Rifleman has always shown great courage and determination during the many months he has been in the field with this battery. After this he was promoted to Lance Corporal." He was awarded the Military Medal for gallantry and devotion to duty near Ypres on 15th-17th August 1917, and was again home on leave in September of that year.

His brother, John, also served, being in the 7th RIR, but survived the war.

Wulverghem-Lindenhoek Road Military Cemetery, Belgium

1009418 PRIVATE JOHN McKINNEY
46th Bn Canadian Infantry Saskatchewan Regt.
K.I.A. 4-9-18
Aged 32
Interred in Ligny-St.Flochel British Cemetery. Plot 4, Row A, Grave 21

Born Eden
Commemorated in Drumreagh Presbyterian Church.
Son of William and Jane McKinney, of Eden, Ballymoney.

John McKinney had emigrated to Canada and was living in Windthorst, Saskatchewan.

He was engaged in farming. At this time his father and mother, William and Jane McKinney, were still living at the Eden, Bendooragh. John was born at the Eden on 29th July 1888.

When he enlisted on 2nd March 1916 he was still single. He was five feet eight and a half inches tall, with a fair complexion, blue eyes and light coloured hair. In October 1915, through an accident at his work, he sustained a fracture of the right leg, but it healed well.

He enlisted at Windthorst, Saskatchewan, on 2nd March 1916. His training appears to have taken rather a long time as it is the 2nd of June 1917 before he embarks at Halifax on the "Olympic", arriving at Liverpool on the 9th. He arrived at the segregation camp at Bramshott next day and was immediately taken on strength of the 19th Reserve Bn.

On 14th October he was posted to the 15th Reserve battalion, which was absorbing the 19th Reserve battalion. Even now they were still at Bramshott. He proceeded overseas with the 46th Battalion on 8th November 1917 and joined them in the field on the 23rd.

A week later he forfeits three days pay for inadvertently wandering out of the line while on active service. He was absent from 9.00pm on the 18th of November to 1.00am on the 19th. A total of four hours. This was almost a Court Marshalling offence and he was lucky to escape with a fine. John was home on leave at the Eden in January 1918 for ten days. Nothing more appears on his record until the 2nd of September 1918, when he is reported seriously injured with gun-shot wounds to the head and a fractured leg. He was taken to No 7. Casualty Clearing Station at Ligny-St.Flochel, where he died of his wounds two days later.

Ligny-St.Flochel is a village about 6.5 kilometres east of St. Pol, off the main road to Arras, and about 24 kilometres from Arras. The cemetery is situated to the south of the village on the east side of the road to Averdoingt.

Ligny-St.Flochel British Cemetery.

PRIVATE JAMES KYLE
American Force 53rd Pioneer Infantry
K.I.A. 10-9-18
Interred in St. Mihiel American Cemetery, Thiaucourt, France. Plot D, Row 21, Grave 26

Born   Carrowcashel
Lived
Enlisted
Commemorated in Armoy Presbyterian Church.
Son of John Kyle of Carrowcashel.

It is thought that John Kyle was married twice and that the first family all emigrated to America, where James enlisted.

The Commander-in-Chief of the American forces in Europe, General John J. Pershing, arrived in France on 17th June 1917. (The United States entered the war on 6th April 1917). Since this date American forces had been concentrating in the area south of Verdun with the intention that when enough American forces were available, they would attack the St. Mihiel Salient. This was a prominent salient, twenty-five miles long at it's base and protruding sixteen miles into the allied lines, with it's apex pointing towards Paris, and had been a thorn in the side of the French forces for a long time. By early September it was felt that the Americans were ready and that the time was right for an attempt to straighten out the salient. Pershing had been anxious about depletion of his troops by having them help out in other regions as they were needed, and so the date was set for an attack at St. Mihiel. And so, on the 12th of September 1918, for the first time, the Americans went into action on the Western Front as an independent army. Just prior to this their pioneers had been out preparing the way for this attack. Much work had to be done and it was dangerous. The German army, well camouflaged and dug in on the heights around St. Mihiel, could see everything that was going on. Most of the preparation for the attack had to be done at night. It was during these preparations two days before the first attack that James Kyle was killed. He is buried in St. Mihiel American Cemetery at Thiaucourt.

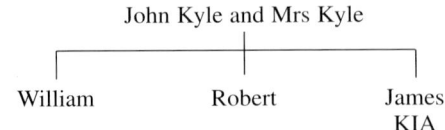

John Kyle and Mrs Kyle

William   Robert   James
                             KIA

2ND LIEUT WILLIAM BAIRD
1st Bn King's Regiment
K.I.A. 15-9-18
Interred in Hermies Hill British Cemetery, France. Plot 1, Row G, Grave 6.

Born   Dervock
Lived   Partick, Glasgow.
Enlisted
Recieved Commission on 1st May 1918.

The 1st battalion was in Talavera Barracks at Aldershot when war was declared.and landed at Le Havre nine days later but William was not with them at this stage.

William Baird was born in the Dervock area, but appears to have been living in the Partick district of Glasgow before he enlisted. We don't know when William enlisted but it was probably early 1915. At any rate he recieved his commission on 1st May 1918 and was attached to the King's Regiment. Very little is known about William Baird. Appeals in the local papers have produced nothing and it would appear that there are no living relatives left in this district. His name appears on the new War Memorial in Dervock but otherwise no information seems to be available. By September 1918 the King's Regiment was in the Hermies area and it was close to here that William was killed. The Cemetery is on a hillside at the end of a broad grass covered path and is in a beautiful location about a hundred yards back from the road.

Hermies is a town approximately 3.5 kilometres south of the road from Bapaume to Cambrai, the N 30. From the N 30 take the D 34 for 3.2 kilometres to it's junction with the D 5 E where the first CWGC sign is situated. The cemetery lies on the left, 150 metres from the junction.

Hermies Hill British Cemetery, Pais de Calais France

6444 C. S. M. WILLIAM WILSON
7th/8th Royal Inniskilling Fusiliers
D.O.W. 16-9-18
Aged 37
Interred in La Kreule Military Cemetery Hazebrouck. Plot 3, Row E, Grave 3

Born   Drumcon, Rasharkin.
Lived   Enniskillen.
Enlisted
Son of John Wilson, of Drumcon.
Husband of Jeannie Wilson of Enniskillen.
Commemorated in Rasharkin Presbyterian Church

The 7th and 8th battalions were both formed at Omagh and trained at Finner Camp.

In September 1915 they moved to Woking and in February 1916 landed in France.

On 23rd August 1917 the two battalions amalgamated to form the 7th/8th battalion. This was just three weeks before William died of wounds in hospital at Hazebrouck.

William Wilson was a lot older than most of the Ballymoney men serving at that time. He had more experience than most and had served in the Boer War. His battalion were in training at Westoutre on the day on which William died of wounds. He had been in hospital at Hazebrouck and is buried in nearby La Kreule Military Cemetery which I visited in 1993.

After the war his 2 sons emigrated to Canada. One of the sons was subsequently killed in the 2nd World War. Pte. Wm. Wilson (killed 4-9-44), amcona War Cemetery, Italy.

La Kruel

10/5667 L. CPL. WILLIAM McNAUL
72nd Bn, Canadian Infantry British Colombia Regiment
K.I.A. 27-9-18
Aged 31
Interred in Quarry Wood Cemetery. Plot 3, Row C, Grave 22

Born   Ballynafeigh, Stranocum.
Lived   Prince Rupert, British Colombia
Enlisted Prince Rupert, British Colombia.
Son of Hugh and Mary McNaul of Ballynafeigh

Born on 6th April 1888, William was the third son of Hugh and Mary McNaul, of Ballynafeigh, Stranocum. After leaving school, he emigrated to Canada, while the great gold rush was going on and for a number of years worked the gold mines.

When this began to dry up he turned his attention to the lumber camps, and for a time he worked these. By 1914, when war was declared, he was again looking for adventure and decided, when the chance came, to enlist. He enlisted in his home town, Prince Albert, on 27th June 1916, naming his brother, D.C.McNaul, as next-of-kin, and describing himself as a miner. He was five feet ten inches tall, with a fair complexion, blue eyes and light brown hair. He embarked at Halifax on 10th April 1917and arrived at Liverpool on the 22nd. Later that same day he reached his destination, Seaford, on the south coast, and was transferred to the 24th Reserve Battalion, for further training. A month later, he was transferred again, this time to the 1st Res Bn. Then, on 16th June 1917, he proceeded, on draft, to the 72nd Bn, and next day arrived in France. In mid July he joined his unit in the field and through the next few months took part in much heavy fighting. By mid December he was suffering from Varicose veins and was admitted to 13th Canadian Field Ambulance for treatment. This lasted for about five days, during which time he was evacuated sick, but returned to his unit on the 18th. Just before Christmas he was sent to 182nd Tunnelling Co where his experience as a miner was put to good use. Then after re-joining his unit on 19th January, he was involved in heavy fighting on and off for a month. On 22nd February 1918 he was granted fourteen days leave. This was spent visiting his mother and father at Stranocum, and when he re-joined he was used as a Lewis gunner. On 24th August he was appointed Lance Corporal. He was killed in action on 27th September 1918 at Cambrai.

The family headstone in the graveyard of Carncullagh Presbyterian Church in Dervock records the names of the other three sons, John died on 21st November 1900, aged 15.

Hugh died in March 1935. David died on 13th July 1981, aged 86.

The father, Hugh, died on 21st January 1937 and their mother Mary died on 31st July 1925 aged 68.

Sains les Marquion lies twelve kilometres north-west of Cambrai and two kilometres south of the Arras to Cambrai road (D939).

The cemetery lies at the end of an access path to the left of the D 15 road heading towards Havrincourt, about two kilometres from the village.

Ovillers

71699 TROOPER ALEXANDER BLAIR
North Irish Horse
K.I.A. 29-9-18
Aged 19
Interred in Varennes Military Cemetery, Plot 3, Row J, Grave 13.

Born   Bendooragh
Lived   Bendooragh
Enlisted Ballymoney

Varennes is a village in the department of the Somme, a little way south of the Doullens - Albert road. It is 11 kilometres from Albert and 18 kilometres from Amiens. The communal cemetery is on the north side of the road to Leavillers, less than one kilometre from Varennes church and the military cemetery is opposite it, across a side road.

When Alex first enlisted he was under the age limit and when his mother found out about it she got him released but he just waited his chance and enlisted again as soon as the opportunity arose. It was pointless and so she had to let him go.

Alex Blair's sister, Jeannie, the youngest of the family, still has vivid memories of her brother being home on leave. Another brother, Tommy, was a well known Lambeg drummer and after one particularly warm 12th of July, spent in Bushmills, he came home complaining of a

severe headache. His mother gave him whatever cure she had in the house and he went to bed. During the night he became worse. The doctor was sent for and some time in the early morning he arrived. There was nothing he could do and Tommy died early the next day, from meningitis.

Alex was allowed home from France on compassionate leave for the funeral, and one of her memories is of seeing the sun glinting on the buttons of Alex's uniform as the funeral moved up the hill away from the house.

Such were the conditions in France that Alex had to return to his unit immediately the funeral was over and he left for the last time that evening. Jeannie, or Mrs. Morrison, as she later became, can still remember Alex's last words to her as he left the house. Toys were few in those days and he promised to bring her a wee circus the next time he was home. He was not to come home again and was killed in action a short time later. A report in the Constitution of 5th October 1918 tells of him being in hospital suffering from shell-shock. It doesn't mention any wounds, but the timing would be right.

Alex Blair and Johnnie Biggart were great friends and lived close to each other at Bendooragh. They enlisted together on the same day and the war claimed both their lives. They were both aged nineteen.

Mrs. Morrison

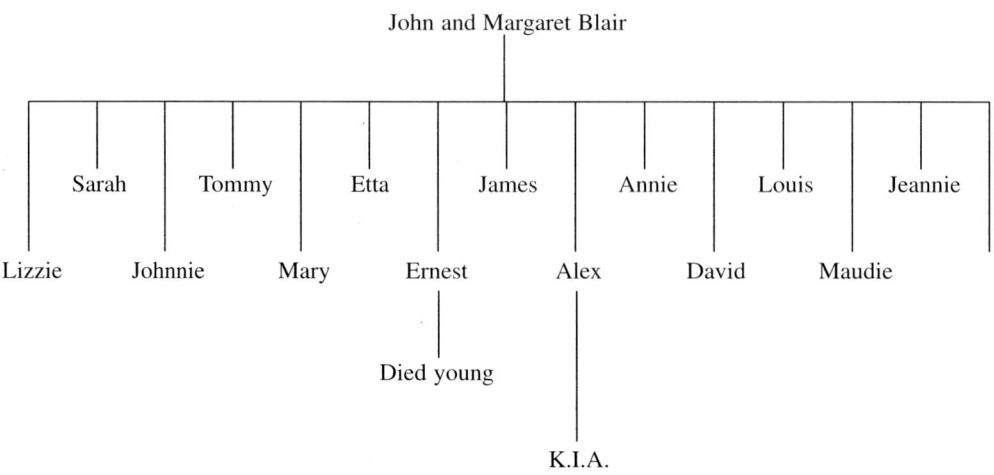

3106304 PRIVATE ARCHIBALD McKEE
116th Canadian Infantry
K.I.A. 29-9-18
Aged 23
Interred in St. Olle British Cemetery, Row B, Grave 25

Born   Newbuildings.on 8th Dec 1894
Lived   Sanford Ave, Totonto,
Enlisted   Toronto, Canada.
The Cemetery is on the western outskirts of Cambrai on the road to Arras.

I am directed, by the Honourable the Minister of Militia and Defence, to convey to you the enclosed medal for the deceased officer or soldier whose name is engraved thereon, and to express to you the regrets of the Militia Council that he did not live to wear this award.

Major-General,
Adjutant-General,
Canadian Militia.

The McKee family lived at Newbuildings South, and it was from here that Archie emigrated to Canada, and settled in Toronto. When he enlisted on 24th October 1917 he was twenty-three years of age and was working as a machinist. He had a dark complexion with blue eyes and black hair. He was fairly tall at almost five feet ten inches. His brother Patrick had already been in the War for some considerable time. Archie embarked on the S.S. Scandinavian at Halifax on 3rd February 1918 and arrived at Liverpool on the 16th February.

After six months of training he sailed for France on the 18th of August and two days later joined the 116th Bn Canadian Infantry.

By the 27th of August he had arrived with his unit and was in the front line pushing the Germans back towards Cambrai. It was in the heavy fighting for Cambrai that he was killed just a month after arriving in France. His brother Patrick had already been killed in a very brave attempt to save his friends as they were being overwhelmed in a heavy German attack.

Mrs McKee had now lost two sons in less than a year.

This photo shows Archie's brother Patrick, second from right, back row.

24019 PRIVATE THOMAS GEORGE DIXON
9th Bn Royal Irish Fusiliers
K.I.A. 30-9-18
Aged 20
Interred in Duhallow A. D. S. Cemetery, Belgium. Plot 9, Row E, Grave 9

Born   Ballymoney
Lived
Enlisted   Belfast
Son of William And Mary J. Dixon, of 67, Dehli St. Belfast

Thomas Dixon enlisted in Belfast into the 9th Bn Royal Irish Fusiliers and was sent to Clandeboye for training. They were mostly Armagh, Monaghan and Cavan Volunteers, and were with the 108th Brigade. In July 1915 they moved to Seaford on the south coast of England for final training and in October sailed for France. But it would appear that Thomas was a later recruit to the battalion and was not with them at this period. He probably joined them after the Battle of the Somme when the battalion was withdrawn for reinforcement after being torn to pieces in the fatal advance at Hamel on the 1st of July 1916.

He was then moved to Belgium and the area around Wulverghem and was regularly in and out of the front line for the next year. Their next major offensive was the Battle of Messines in June 1917 and Thomas came through this safely.

Passchendaele in the wet weather of August of that year was the worst he had so far faced. Conditions under foot were treacherous, mud everywhere, every shell-hole full to the lip with water, and continual heavy rain. Soaked through, there was nothing for it but to try to keep going, and ignore death all around you. The fighting dragged on but the Division was later moved south for the Battle of Cambrai in November. Thomas took part in the attack on Moeuvres and was again lucky enough to come through safely. After this battle the Division was again moved south, to the area of St. Quentin, and it was here that they met the full force of the German Spring Offensive in March 1918.

On the morning of the 21st of March the 9th battalion were in Divisional Reserve but it wasn't long until they were needed as the Germans attacked in great strength. There isn't any need to describe the actions here of the British armies being pushed back to the Somme. Suffice to say that the 36th

Division was again sent to the Ypres area as soon as they could be done without at the Somme. On the 30th of September the 9th Royal Irish Fus attacked and reached the Menin-Roulers road at Kezelberg. They attempted to work up this road to obtain touch with the 12th Rifles, who had got around Hill 41 on the north side, but were stopped by machine-gun fire. It was here that Thomas was killed in the attempt to surround Hill 41. He is buried in Duhallow A.D.S. Cemetery just to the north of Ypres.

Cemetery location information
From Ypres, Duhallow A.D.S. Cemetery is located on the Diksmuidseweg, N369 road, in the direction of Boezinge.

From Ypres station turn left into M. Fochlaan and go to the roundabout. Here turn left and drive to the next roundabout, where you should turn right into Oude Veurnestraat. Take the second turning on the left which is the Diksmuidseweg.

The cemetery is on the right hand side of the road just past the first turning on the right.

Duhallow A.D.S. Cemetery and the grave of T.G. Dixon

1421 RIFLEMAN THOMAS RAMSEY DOCHERTY
2nd Bn Royal Irish Rifles
K.I.A. 30-9-18
Aged 20
Interred in Dadizele New British Cemetery, Belgium. Plot 4, Row F Grave 6

Born   Ballymoney
Lived   Kirkhills, Ballymoney.
Enlisted   Ballymoney
Son of Thomas and Elizabeth Docherty, of Kirkhills, Ballymoney.

Before enlisting Thomas had worked for Mr. A. Wilson of Bendooragh. The family lived at Kirkhills and Thomas enlisted at Ballymoney. When the second Battalion was sent to France their first engagement was close to Festubert in October of 1914.

From here they moved north to the Hooge area, south of Ypres, for the fighting of July 1915, but by September had again moved, this time to the area around Loos.

They were then moved again to the north of Arras in April 1916. Following this they took a brief part in the Battle of the Somme before being sent to Vermelles in September.

They then went north again to the battlegrounds at Ypres and followed this with a move to the south to help against the German Spring Offensive of March 1918.

Eventually they moved north to Ypres again and by September of 1918 the British forces had broken through the German defences and were pushing a tired and demoralised army ahead of them. By the end of the month they had reached the village of Dadizeele and it was here that Thomas was killed in action. He is buried in Dadizeele New British Cemetery. Aged just twenty, he was one of the youngest of the Ballymoney boys to be killed and must have been either under age when he enlisted or was a later recruit. Two days later another Ballymoney man was killed in this same region and today lies in this same cemetery. Robert Murphy was the second son of Clarke Murphy to be killed in the war and is buried in Plot 1.

Cemetery location information
Dadizele New British Cemetery is located 16 kilometres east of Ypres town centre on a road leading from theN8 Meenseweg, connecting Ypres to Menin via Geluwe.

From Ypres town centre the Meenseweg is located via Torhoutstraat and then right on to Basculestraat. Basculestraat ends at a main crossroads, directly over which begins the Meenseweg. 12 km along the N8 lies the village of Geluwe and the left hand turning on to the Nieuwestraat towards Dadizele. 5 kilometres along this road lies the village of Dadizele.

The cemetery is located 100 metres after the left hand turning at the junction with Geluwestraat and Beselarestraat, in the village of Dadizele.

Dadizele New British Cemetery

2ND LIEUT JOHN PURVES GRAY
1st Bn Royal Inniskilling Fusiliers
K.I.A. 1-10-18
Interred in Pont-du-Achelles Military Cemetery, Nieppe, France. Plot 3, Row E, Grave 12

Born   Dirraw, Finvoy.
Lived   Dirraw, Finvoy.
Third son of the late Hugh Gray of Finvoy.
Commemorated in Finvoy Presbyterian Church.

John Gray was born at Dirraw, Finvoy, about six miles south of Ballymoney. He was the third son of the late Hugh Gray. The family worshipped in Finvoy Presbyterian Church and it is there that John is commemorated on the Roll of Honour.

After John Gray left school he joined the staff of the Ulster Bank. Following correspondence with the Bank in Belfast, they informed me that he had joined the bank on 18th March 1904 but left to join the Army in March 1916. They go on to say, "There is a reference to his being wounded in the leg in "Passing Events", a staff magazine produced for two years or so during the 1914-18 period, and a second reference in the issue of July 1918 which says that he was recently observed passing through Belfast on route for his depot. This goes on to say that he appeared to have recovered from his wound.

Shortly after re-joining his unit he was killed in action and his death was reported in the October 1918 issue of the magazine.

He was indeed injured. In November of 1917 he was in hospital with a fracture of the right leg. He was home on extended leave to allow the leg time to heal and was then killed a short time after returning to his unit.

He was educated at Ballymoney Intermediate School. His brother, James, served at a Military Hospital in India with the Royal Army Medical Corps and was home on leave in May 1917.

During his time at the bank, in October 1915, his Father died, aged 66, and was buried in the old Knockans burying ground.

The Cemetery where John is buried, Pont du Achelles, was used for the burial of one of the men shot at dawn. Ernest Worsley had enlisted in 1914. He had been sent out of the line to draw rations but had not returned and was arrested near Calais a few days later. He faced the firing squad on 22nd October 1917 and is buried in Plot 1, Row F, Grave 3.

Cemetery location information
The village of Nieppe is about 3.5 kilometres north-west of Armentieres on the road to Bailleul. Leave Nieppe on the D933 . 900 metres from the church turn right onto Rue-de-Sac. The cemetery is on the right 200 metres from the main road.

Back row, Hugh Isabella, John
Front row, James, Hugh sen. and Peter

Hugh Gray Married Annie Purves

| Isabella | Hugh married Tillie Henderson on 26th Dec 1913 | John Purves K.I.A 1-10-18 | James served in R.A.M.C in India | Peter married Ida Keers 15th Jan 1919 |

86799 PRIVATE LESLIE KIRKPATRICK
5th Canadian Field Artillery
DIED 1-10-18
Interred in Bourlon Wood Cemetery, Plot 1, Row D, Grave 7

Born   Rasharkin on 14th June 1894
Lived   Ballymaconnelly.
Enlisted
Son of Alex Kirkpatrick, of Ballymaconnelly.

Leslie emigrated to Canada in 1911 and worked as a clerk. He enlisted at Yorkton, Saskatchewan, on 8th March 1915. He was five feet six inches tall, with a dark complexion, grey eyes and dark brown hair. He landed in England at Plymouth on the 18th of August 1915 from the S.S.Metagama and after intensive training embarked for France on 15th January 1916, where he joined the 5th Brigade of the Canadian Field Artillery. On 17th October he reported to 12th Canadian Field Ambulance with Conjunctivitis. He was then sent to a rest station and then to 54th Field Ambulance and discharged the next day. In December he was appointed Acting Bombardier and this was confirmed. In February of 1917 he was home at Ballymaconnelly on two weeks leave. On the 4th of May 1917 he was taken to hospital with a slight wound to the head and gassed. Three days later he was moved to No 32 stationery hospital at Wimereux where he made a good recovery and on the 13th was moved to the convalescent depot at Boulogne and discharged on the 21st. Then on 17th June he was admitted to No 7 General Hospital at St. Omer, suffering from Erysipelas, and five days later was diagnosed dangerously ill. A report at the time states as follows.

> "He reported sick at Vimy Ridge on the 14th of June. He complained of sickness and swelling of the face. After two days the swelling increased and he was removed to a C.C.S.at Barlin. Next day he was sent to No 7 General Hospital at St. Omer. He became unconcious and remained in that condition for nearly seven days. He left St. Omer on the 10th of July for Boulogne, remaining there for five days during which time the swelling decreased, but he still felt very weak. On the 15th July he was transferred to England.

Admitted having recovered from Erysipelas of the face. Feels alright except for weakness. Patient was nearly bald when admitted,

was specially treated and now shows a good growth of hair. General condition much improved and is recommended for transfer to Canadian Hospital."

He was transferred to the Northumberland War Hospital in Newcastle, where he stayed for two months and on 19th September he was moved to Woodcote Park hospital in Epsom, and was discharged a week later. In October 1917 he was appointed Acting Corporal but two weeks later reverted to Bombardier at his own request in order to proceed overseas. On 23rd November he joined the C.F.A. in France and was posted to the 5th Brigade in January 1918. Then on 5th March he was sent on a mined dugout course and rejoined from this course on 21st March. He was killed in action on 1st October 1918 and is commemorated in Rasharkin Presbyterian Church.

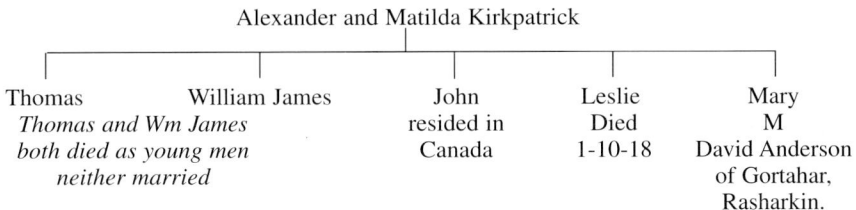

Bourlon Wood Cemetery

2ND LIEUT ROBERT MURPHY
1st Bn Royal Irish Rifles
K.I.A. 2-10-18
Aged 22
Interred in Dadizeele New British Cemetery, Belgium. Plot 1, Row E, Grave 4

Born   Ballymoney.
Lived   Main St, Ballymoney.
4th son of Clarke and Lizzie Murphy, of Main St, Ballymoney

Robert Murphy was born in Ballymoney, the fourth son of Clarke and Lizzie Murphy. The family lived about half way down Main St on the town clock side. Robert had probably enlisted at the beginning of the war and had been in France but obtained his commission in 1917 and was posted to the 1st battalion of the Royal Irish Rifles in October of that year.

Clarke had a coopering business at his house in Main St and was one of the practical jokers of the town. His sense of humour was well known and woe betide anyone who tried to pull a fast one on him. This sense of humour was to stand him in good stead over the years because as can be seen in the following few sentences life was not easy.

The family at home had had more than their fair share of grief. On 31st December 1876, their daughter, Martha, died, aged sixteen months. Fourteen years later, another daughter, Mary, died. This was on 6th September 1890, at the age of thirteen. On 12th October 1891 Clarke's wife, Lizzie, died, and then on 3rd April 1897, their son Clarke, died, aged 10. On the 12th of January 1915 Clarke married Matilda McMichael in St. James's Presbyterian Church, Ballymoney. He was very interested in the well-being of the town and was a member of the Urban District Council. On the 1st of July 1916, another son Johnston, was killed in action at Thiepval. The following year, in September 1917, Clarke became a J.P. and he adjudicated at the local Petty Sessions. Soon after this, on 3rd July 1918, he died at the age of 65. Their son Robert was home on leave for the funeral, and a short time after he went back, on 2nd October 1918 he was killed in action. He is buried in Dadizeele New British Cemetery in Belgium.

Dadizeele New British Cemetery

4276 PRIVATE JAMES BOYLE
6th Bn Royal Inniskilling Fusiliers
D.O.W. 3-10-18
Aged 23
Interred in Prospect Hill Cemetery, Aisne, France. Plot 1, Row D, Grave 5

Born   Balnamore
Lived   Balnamore
Enlisted   Coleraine
Son of Daniel and Mrs Boyle, of Balnamore.

James Boyle had enlisted right at the beginning of the war and had been involved in the fighting in many different regions. When his training was complete he was sent first of all to the Dardanelles. While there he was injured by a bullet striking his middle finger, which had to be amputated at the lower joint. He had been holding his rifle at the time and this saved him from serious injury. After he had recovered from this he returned to his unit and was then moved to Mesopotamia where he again saw action. The 6th Battalion remained in this theatre of war for much of 1917. James was allowed home on leave in August of 1918 while the battalion was being brought back up to strength. After he rejoined his unit they were taken to France where they were urgently needed as the British began to push the retreating German forces back across the old Somme battlefields. On 3rd October the 6th battalion were involved in a battalion attack with the 10th Division at Bony, a village on the St.Quentin Canal, just south of Le Catelet.The Germans were retreating across the canal using the bridge at Bony and trying desperately to hold the bridge long enough to let their men across. The battle in which James was injured so seriously was for this bridge. He was taken back to the nearest dressing station for attention but all that could be done couldn't save him and he died there later that day. He was the son of Daniel and Mrs Boyle of Balnamore. Two other brothers, Alexander and Daniel, also saw much service for their Country. Both survived the war, being honourably discharged as unfit for further service.

This was a severe blow to the Boyle family, one son killed and two more probably crippled and unable to earn a living.

James is buried in Prospect Hill Cemetery, Aisne, France, in Plot 1, Row D, Grave 5.

Prospect Hill Cemetery

> ### 42324 PRIVATE WILLIAM HANNA
> *1st Bn Royal Irish Fusiliers formerly 22198 3rd Bn R. Irish Rifles*
> **D.O.W. 3-10-18**
> No Known Grave. Commemorated on the Tyne Cot Memorial, Belgium. Panels 140-141

Born   Ballymoney
Lived   Mossend, Lanarkshire.
Enlisted Hamilton, Lanarkshire.
Commemorated in Finvoy Presbyterian Church.

William, like many of the young men at the time, was very keen to join the British Forces and get a chance to see a bit of the World. He ran away from home and enlisted in the Royal Irish Rifles while he was still under age. When his Mother discovered what he had done, she contacted the Army, to be told that William had given a false age to be able to enlist. His Mother then went and brought him home but when she got up next morning he was gone. He eventually enlisted at Hamilton, in Lanarkshire transferring to the Royal Irish Fusiliers. The 1st Battalion, which William joined became part of the 4th Division and were in action at Beaumont Hamel on 1st July 1916 at the Battle of the Somme. After the desperate fighting of the Somme, the troops were moved back for re-organisation to the well known training camp at St.Omer. From there it was North to the area of Messines.

They were to remain here for almost a year, and although fighting took place regularly they could not relax, their next big battle would be the battle of Messines Ridge in June 1917. This led on to the battle of Langemarck. By now the Division was under strength and new recruits had to be brought in. By early November they had been moved to Cambrai, and to a winter of snow and frost, much of it spent in the open.

To men already tired from months of heavy fighting, this was expecting too much and the collapse of the Russian front meant that the enemy could bring in thousands of relatively fresh troops for a counter-offensive. The British were pushed back to the Somme, but after desperate fighting the Germans began to fall back. By July 1918 the 1st Battalion were again in the Messines area and advancing against the enemy.

Fighting was extremely heavy and the advance slow but over the next few weeks they slowly pushed the Germans back. By the end of September they had reached Hill 41 and fighting for the hill itself was desperate. It was in this region that William was so seriously wounded. He died of his wounds on 3rd October 1918. In most cases a soldier who died of wounds usually has a grave but in William's case there is no known grave and he is commemorated on the Tyne Cot Memorial in Belgium.

163482 PRIVATE CUNNINGHAM FALCONER SHAW
3rd Bn Canadian Machine GunCorps
K.I.A. 3-10-18
Aged 24
Interred in Mill Switch Military Cemetery, Cambrai, France. Row A, Grave 9

Born   Tullaghans, Finvoy. 8-3-1894.
Lived   Toronto, Canada.
Enlisted Toronto, Canada.
Son of Robert John Shaw, of Tullaghans.
Commemorated in Finvoy Presbyterian Church.

Cunningham Shaw was born at Tullaghans, Finvoy, on 8th March 1894.

He grew up in the Finvoy district and as a young man, emigrated to Canada, with his brother James. He was a shipping clerk in Toronto.

He enlisted into the 84th Bn Canadian Expeditionary Force on 23rd August 1915 when he was 21 years of age. He set sail again for England on 18th June 1916 aboard the " Empress of Britain ", arriving on 28th June. On 11th August 1916 he sailed for France arriving at Le Havre next day when he was transferred to the 75th Bn , Canadian Infantry under Lt, Col. S. G. Beckett. In March 1917 he was sent on a signals course and obtained a certificate as a first class signaller with the Canadian Corps. Then in April he rejoined his unit.

At about this time he sent a set of German shoulder straps home to his Father. They had come from a Prussian Guard with whom he had an encounter.

In October 1917, he was given ten days leave but by mid November he was back fighting again. Then in January 1918 he reported sick to 42 casualty clearing station, and again in March 1918 was sick once more. After almost two years with this Battalion he was transferred to the 3rd Bn Canadian Machine Gun Corps, on 30th May 1918. He joined his unit for duty on 1st June 1918 and was killed in action on the 3rd of October 1918.

Mill Switch Military Cemetery with a new motorway in the background

10608 SERGEANT EDWARD ALEXANDER WEIR
1st Bn Royal Inniskilling Fus.
D.O.W. 14-10-18
Aged 22
Interred in Terlincthun British Cemetery, Wimille. Plot 5, Row E, Grave 16.

Born   Unchinagh
Lived
Enlisted   Paisley
Son of James and Mrs Weir of Unchinagh, Garryduff.
Husband of Agnes Weir, of 58, King St, Londonderry.

When war was declared the 1st battalion were serving at Trimulgherry, in India. In early December they sailed for England and arrived at Avonmouth on 10th January 1915. They were taken to Rugby where they joined the 29th Div and in March left for the Mediterranean, arriving at Mudros in April.

On 25th April they landed at Gallipoli and met very stiff opposition on the beaches. There was no cover whatsoever on the beaches but eventually they reached shelter below a cliff at the top of the beach and survived to night fall. As darkness decended they were able to find their way into the sand dunes behind the beach and to get dug in. They would be in Gallipoli until January. On the night of 8/9th January 1916 they were evacuated from Gallipoli and went to Egypt. They arrived at Marsielles on 5th February 1916 and eventually arrived at Mailley- Maillet where they joined the 29th Division. Preparations were being made for the Battle of the Somme at this stage and fresh troops were arriving every day. Every house and building in the district was being used for accomodation and still many thousands had to make do with tents. The battalion in which Edward was serving was to attack around the village of Beaumont Hamel to the north of the River Ancre. Here as was the case all along the line, casualties were extremely heavy, and new recruits had to be brought forward. Towards the end of the Battle of the Somme the 1st battalion were moved south to the area around Guillemont where fierce fighting took place over open ground where there was just no cover whatsoever. Edward survived the fighting here without serious injury and was then moved again, this time to the town of Arras. This was in January of 1917. There followed many moves but the one which concerns us here was the last one.

Edward had been advancing with his unit as they chased the German Armies back towards the German frontier. He was very seriously injured in this fighting and had to be sent back for treatment. He had got as far as the coast and was in hospital awaiting a ship to take him to England when he became too ill to travel and died there of his injuries. He is buried in the local cemetery. James and Mrs Weir of Unchinagh, Dunloy, had four sons engaged on active service. William, the eldest, was in the King's Own Scottish Borderers and had four years service in India to his credit. He was stationed in Gibralter for some time and in May 1915 was serving with his battalion at the Dardanelles. Private Robert Weir enlisted in 1913, joining the 2nd battalion of the Royal Inniskilling Fusiliers. On the 26th of August 1914 he went to France with the British Expeditionary Force and fought at the battles of Mons, Ligny, Ypres, Aisne and Armentierres. The third son, Edward, joined the Inniskillings with his brother Robert, and they were both serving together. He also fought through the same battles but at Armentierres he was injured by a piece of shrapnel in the shoulder and had to be invalided home. In May 1915 he had almost completely recovered and had rejoined his regiment.

A fourth son, Samuel, also served but so far no information has turned up concerning him.

Terlincthun British Cemetery is situated on the northern outskirts of Boulogne.

From Calais follow the A16 to Boulogne, come off at junction 3 and follow the D 96 E for Wimereux Sud. Continue on this road for approximately 1 kilometre when the cemetery will be found on the left hand side of the road.

44443 PRIVATE ALEXANDER McILREAVEY
1st Bn Royal Inniskilling Fusiliers formerly 21791 Royal Irish Rifles
K.I.A. 20-10-18
Aged 19
Interred in Harlebeke New British Cemetery. Belgium. Plot 8, Row A, Grave 19

Born   Greenville, Ballymoney.
Lived   39.Charlotte St, Ballymoney
Enlisted   Coleraine.
Son of Mr. Robert McIlreavey, 39.Charlotte St.

Alexander, or Sandy as he was generally known, was born at Greenville, Ballymoney, on 23rd April 1899 and two years later his sister Rose was born at Glenstall, on 20th April 1901. Very soon after this Sandy and Rose's mother died. Their father, Robert, later re-married and the family moved into Charlotte Street, where Sandy lived until he enlisted. After he left school he served his apprenticeship as a law clerk with Mr William Lewis, who was a solicitor and a leading Unionist. Mr Lewis was for a time, secretary of Ballymoney Unionist Club, and it is thought, was in partnership with Mr Greer where Mr Hugh Clarke is to-day in High Street. By the time Sandy was killed in 1918 Mr William Lewis had moved to Clonmel.

We don't know just when Sandy enlisted but it would appear that he was in one of the later drafts to join the Inniskillings. He had originally enlisted into the Royal Irish Rifles but for some reason transferred to the Inniskillings on 15th September 1918 and during the British Army's final advance to victory in that year was with the 29th Division near Harlebeke. It was here that he was killed on the 20th of October in the final few weeks of the war. He is buried in Harlebeke New British Cemetery in Belgium. The inscription at the bottom of the headstone, chosen by the family, reads, "Ever remembered by Father, Mother, Sisters and Brothers."

Two other local men, John Wisner, of Cloughmills, and Samuel Gray, of Culduff are buried in the same cemetery.

Robert McIlreavey maried Elizabeth Smiley. Alexander (Sandy) born 23rd April 1899, killed in action 20th Oct 1918. Rose (Cissi) born 20th April 1901, died of TB. date unknown. Elizabeth died of breast cancer soon after Rose was born.

Robert Mc Ilreavey married Margaret McNaul on 14th November 1903
Elizabeth born 18th December 1904 died in Australia on 1st May 1966.
Robert born 15th March 1906 killed in street accident 1910.
William James born 15th August 1907 died in Canada on 25th September 1971
John born 5th March 1909 died in infancy. (Pneumonia)
Matilda born 29th March 1911 lives in Lambeg.
George born 22nd April 1913 died in infancy (Measles)
Margaret born 11th May 1915 lives in Melbourne.
Daniel born 3rd June 1918 died 11th May 1947
Annie born 21st February 1920 died in infancy (Pneumonia).
Mary Jane born 12th October 1921 lives in Ballymoney
Joseph born 11th September 1923 died in Australia on 12th April 1996.
Martha born 20th January 1925 lives in Ballymoney.
Baby born dead in June 1929
Winifred born 13th February 1931 lives in Ballymoney

Robert McIlreavey was born on 6th May 1876 and died on 26th March 1958.

Margaret McIlreavey was born 27th May 1885 and died on 2nd December 1966.

Number 39 Charlotte St was one of three small houses where the entrance up to Eastermeade now runs. At one time they were stables with a hay loft over the top, but as time went on they were converted into living accomodation and were very comfortable little houses.

Harlebeke Cemetery

42380 PRIVATE JOHN WISNER
1st Bn Royal Irish Fusiliers
K.I.A. 23-10-18
Aged 36
Interred in Harlebeke New British Cemetery, Plot 6, Row B, Grave 17

Born   Cloughmills.
Lived   Cloughmills.
Enlisted
Commemorated in Killagan Parish Church.
Son of Daniel and Jane Wisner.
Husband of Annie Wisner of Cloughmills.

Harlebeke is a village in the province of West Flanders 5 kilometres north-east of Courtrai. The village was taken on the night of 19th-20th October 1918 by the 9th (Scottish) Division. The British were by this time advancing quickly and pushing back a tired and demoralised German army. John Wisner was killed in the sporadic and desperate fighting of the last few days of the war.

This was a remarkable family. Dan Wisner as well as three of his sons, Robert, John and Hugh all served in France and Belgium. Francis would have gone too, but for the fact that he was only twelve years of age at the time, being the youngest of the family. Many years later, Francis was to win the B.E.M. for lifting and carrying away a bomb at Cloughmills.

Another Ballymoney man is buried in the same plot, two rows behind where John lies. He is Samuel Gray, of Culduff, who was killed on the 25th of October.

Harlebeke New British Cemetery is on the north-east side of the village on the road to Deerlyck and was made after the Armistice by the concentration of graves from the surrounding battlefields and in 1924-25 by the addition of British graves from German cemeteries in Belgium. It contains the graves of 1,116 war dead.

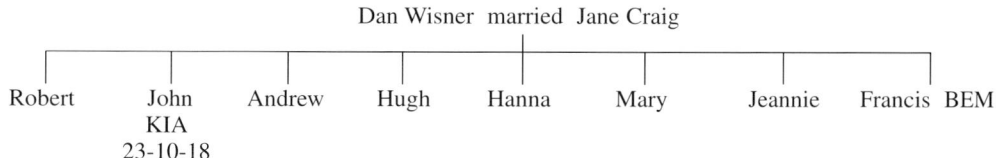

Dan Wisner married Jane Craig

Robert | John KIA 23-10-18 | Andrew | Hugh | Hanna | Mary | Jeannie | Francis BEM

20989 PRIVATE GEORGE KILLOUGH
1st Bn Royal Irish Regiment formerly 2363 North Irish Horse
DIED 24-10-18
Aged 27
Interred in Deir-el-Belah War Cemetery, Israel. Plot B, Grave 189

Born   Moneyleck, Rasharkin.
Lived   Rasharkin,
Enlisted   Ballymena
Son of Andrew and Mary Killough, of Moneyleck.
Husband of Annie L. Killough, of Granagh.
Commemorated in Rasharkin Presbyterian Church,

The 1st battalion was at Nasirabad, in India when war was declared and embarked at Bombay on 13th October arriving at Devonport on 18th November. They were immediately sent to Winchester where they joined the 27th Div. It was about this time that George transferred to the Royal Irish Regiment and they landed at Le Havre on the 20th of December 1914. After some action on the Western Front they were ordered south and sailed from Marseilles on 28th November 1915, bound for Salonika, arriving there on 5th December and were sent to join the 10th Div. They stayed in Salonika for over a year and a half and in late April of 1917 George was home on leave at Moneyleck.

On 2nd September 1917 the battalion sailed for Egypt, arriving on 6th September and a move into Palestine. The intense heat and humid atmosphere here did not suit George and he died of fever on active service. He is buried in the nearby cemetery.

A note on an old hand written Roll of Honour for Rasharkin, lent to me by Jennifer Bamford says that George died of Dysentry.

An interesting story appeared in the Constitution in June 1917. "A horse and cart belonging to Mr. Andrew Killough, Moneyleck, was being driven by his son and another young man. When at the Orange Hall, Lisnagaver, the animal bolted and the two young men were thrown out. The horse ran past McLaughlin's Corner towards the Bann Bridge. Bob McGoldrick got on a bicycle and followed and cleverly brought the animal to a stand-still near the bridge, preventing what could have been a nasty accident as on the County Derry side a motor car was coming from Kilrea."

HE whom this scroll commemorates was numbered among those who, at the call of King and Country, left all that was dear to them, endured hardness, faced danger, and finally passed out of the sight of men by the path of duty and self-sacrifice, giving up their own lives that others might live in freedom. Let those who come after see to it that his name be not forgotten.

Pte George Killough.
R. Irish Regt.

192 RIFLEMAN SAMUEL GRAY
12th Bn Royal Irish Rifles
K.I.A. 25-10-18
Interred in Harlebeke New British Cemetery, Belgium. Plot 6, Row D, Grave 4

Born   Ballymoney
Lived   Culduff, Ballymoney,
Enlisted Ballymoney.
Husband of Nancy Gray, of Culduff, Ballymoney.
Commemorated in St. James's Presbyterian Church.

Samuel Gray, described as living at Dunaghy, married Nancy McNeill of Culduff, in Trinity Presbyterian Church, on 14th February 1913. He was a son of Samuel Gray. Nancy was a daughter of Thomas McNeill.

Harlebeke is a village in the province of West Flanders 5 kilometres north-east of Courtrai. The village was taken on the night of 19th-20th October 1918 by the 9th (Scottish) Division. The war was drawing quickly to a close and the British were pushing back a tired and demoralised German army. Desperate fighting was taking place on rapidly changing new fronts as the Germans retreated and it was during this type of fighting that Samuel was killed.

He is buried close to where another Ballymoney man lies. John Wisner was killed two days earlier and is buried in the same plot as Samuel.

Harlebeke New British Cemetery is on the northeast side of the village on the road to Deerlyck and was made after the Armistice by the concentration of graves from the surrounding battlefields and in 1924-25 by the addition of British graves from German cemeteries in Belgium. It contains the graves of 1,116 war dead.

3925 RIFLEMAN ROBERT HARTE
12th Bn Royal Irish Rifles
K.I.A. 25-10-18
Interred in Ingoyghem Military Cemetery, Belgium. Row A, Grave 7

*Born
Glasgow
Lived
Mosside
Enlisted
Ballymoney*

Robert Harte was born in Glasgow and was an only son. As a very young boy he came with his mother to live at Mosside, a village on the road to Ballycastle.

He attended school in Mosside. When he grew up he married Mary McClenahan and there was a

family of four girls and one boy. They were all born at Mosside.

Robert and Mary both lived at Carrowreagh. He was a farm labourer. Mary was the daughter of William McClenaghan, also a farm labourer.

On the outbreak of hostilities he enlisted at Ballymoney because he could not find enough work at Mosside to support a family. He was sent immediately to Clandeboye to commence his training and remained there with his unit until the following July, when they moved across to England to finish their training at Seaford, on the Sussex Downs. In October 1915 they landed at Boulogne. From here they moved into the vast camp at St.Omer for final training and the introduction to trenches. French leaders were clamouring for the British to organise an attack to draw the German forces away from Verdun and it was agreed that this should be at the Somme. Plans were laid for an attack on a huge scale and was set for the 28th of June 1916. As the date approached men were rushed into the area. The 12th battalion were at Mesnil and Martinsart, two small villages close to what we now know as the Western Front.

They were housed mostly in tents. The weather had been warm and dry but towards the end of June it broke, and the rain came down in torrents. The French soil has a high chalk content and turns very quickly to mud. This would have been bad enough on it's own but the countryside had already been churned up by shell-fire and every-where was glutinous mud. The attack had to be postponed and was re-arranged for the 1st of July. The men had to stay in the trenches during the extra two days and make the best of it. On the morning of the 1st of July everywhere was bathed in bright sunshine, but a few minutes before zero hour a huge mine was exploded at Hawthorn Ridge by the British and every German for miles around knew that an attack was imminent. The 12th battalion were on the north bank of the River Ancre at Hamel and were to attack in the direction of Beaucourt. This was all very well, but south of the river the village of St Pierre-Divion had not been attacked and machine-guns there had a clear line of sight on

the 12th battalion as they left their trenches. They were just simply mowed down. Robert survived this attack and next day the battalion was relieved and taken back to St.Omer to be brought back up to strength with new reserves. A few days later they were moved to the Wulverghem area of Belgium. They were to be in this region for the next year. During this time they were regularly in and out of the line but it was to be June of the following year before they would have their next major battle. This was to be the Battle of Messines.

Huge mines were dug all along the Messines Ridge and filled with high explosive. These were blown at the start of the attack on the 7th of June and made a vast difference to the success of the attack. A Benvarden man, John Meeke, was in charge of seeing that the mines were properly blown. When this battle had been completed successfully plans were made to press on with the advantage and to take Passchendaele. But by early August the weather had changed, rain had set in and again everywhere was a sea of mud.

Conditions were atrocious and injured men just drowned in the mud. On the 16th of August the Battle of Langemarck began and on this day alone Ballymoney lost eight young men, all of them in this one battle, and not one of them with a known grave. When this was over the battalion was once again moved, this time south for the Battle of Cambrai in November. By March of 1918 they were at St.Quentin and Robert was allowed home on leave, the only time that the family can remember him being home. He told them then that he would not be back again as the Germans were advancing at an alarming rate. After he returned from leave and rejoined his unit they were moved back to Belgium for the final push against an almost defeated German Army. They had advanced through Courtrai and had reached the village of Ingoyghem when Robert was killed. At home the family were beginning to think that he would survive and be home soon. On the day on which the Armistice was signed word arrived to say that Robert had been killed. He is buried in the nearby cemetery.

Cemetery location information
Ingoyghem is a village and commune 14 kilometres east of Courtrai. The military cemetery is in the fields on the north-east side of the village, on a track which leaves the Renaix road near the church.

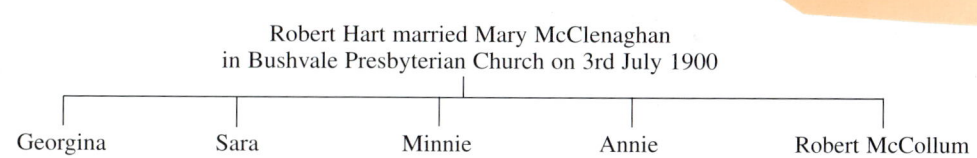

Robert Hart married Mary McClenaghan
in Bushvale Presbyterian Church on 3rd July 1900

| Georgina | Sara | Minnie | Annie | Robert McCollum |

Ingoyahem Cemetery

LIEUT JAMES HART M.C.
6th Bn West Riding Regiment
K.I.A. 1-11-18
Aged 26
Interred in Maing Communal Cemetery Extension, France. Row C, Grave 12

Born
Lived   Rosnashane, Finvoy.
Enlisted
Son of Thomas and Mary Hart of Oatlands, Myroe.

Cemetery location information
Maing is a village about 8 kilometres south of Valenciennes. The cemetery is on the southern side of the village on the north-eastern side of the road to Querenaing and two kilometres before Thiant.

The Citation for the Military Cross reads —-

Awarded the Military Cross.
T/ Lieut James Hart,
West Riding Regt.
For Conspicuous gallantry and devotion to duty south of Bailleul on 13th April 1918

This officer was in command of a company in the support line, and in spite of troops in the front line and on both flanks giving way, he held on to his position, inflicting heavy losses with rifle and Lewis gun fire at close range. Finally, when the company was withdrawn after dark, it was owing to his good leadership that it was not cut off. He carried away a wounded officer from the forward position, saving him from being made a prisoner.

Northern Constitution   5th Oct 1918.

The Military Cross has been awarded to Capt James Hart, West Riding Regt, son of Mr. Thomas Hart, of the Vow. Capt Hart was an engineering student at Queen's University, Belfast, where he took his B.Sc. and was for some time in the O.T.C. at the University from which he was appointed to the West Riding Regt on 20th July 1915.

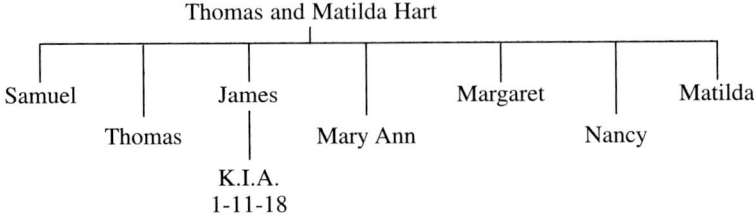

Medals of Lieut. James Hart M.C.

Maing Communal Cemetery Extension, Nord, France

44803 L. CPL. JOSEPH LYONS THOMPSON
3rd Bn New Zealand Rifle Brigade
K.I.A. 4-11-18
Aged 29
Interred in Romeries Communal Cemetery Ext. France. Plot 9, Row A, Grave 8

Born   Ballybogey.
Lived   Auckland, New Zealand.
Enlisted   Auckland, New Zealand.
Son of Robert and Martha Thompson of Ballylough, Bushmills.
Commemorated in Ballywatt Presbyterian Church.

Joseph Lyons Thompson was the second son of Robert Thompson of Ballybogey and his wife Martha Lyons of Benvarden. He left the family home in May 1913 to emigrate to New Zealand, where his elder brother James had gone five years before. Both settled in Auckland. Joseph had trained as a Chemist in Baxter's of Church St, Coleraine, and found a job in Auckland with Sharland & Co, Ltd of Lorne St, as a Chemist's Assistant. He was to be in this job for three and a half years. In October 1916 the family at home moved from Ballybogey to the farm at Ballylough, and it was about this time that William Thomas, another brother, decided to enlist, joining the Royal Air Force. On the twenty-fifth of November 1916, Joe enlisted at Auckland and volunteered for the 25th reinforcement draft. He was five feet four inches tall, with a fair complexion, blue eyes and brown hair. He was very lightly built and weighed less than nine and a half stone. He was posted to "A" Coy on 9th January 1917, but on 2nd February, transferred to "G" Coy of the 24th. He embarked at Wellington on the Troop Ship, Devon, on 5th April 1917, arriving at Devonport on 11th June. After very intensive training he sailed for France on the 6th of July and marched into camp at Etaples on the 10th. On 11th August he joined "A" Coy of the 3rd Battalion at Rouen and on 28th September

Romeries Communal Cemetery Ext, France

Photo of Auckland War Memorial, New Zealand

was detached to Brigade school, re-joining his unit on 5th October. On 1st May 1918 he was appointed L.Cpl and assigned to medical duties as his earlier training dictated.

Then on 3rd September 1918 he was granted leave. He was home for a little over two weeks and re-joined his unit on 21st September. By this time the British forces were moving forward quickly and Joe was working with the medical teams very close to the front lines. Advanced dressing stations had to be set up to deal with the injured and it was on the way to set up one of these that Joe was killed by machine-gun fire. Early morning mist obscured their view and they got too close to the German lines. A machine-gun opened fire and Joe was hit in the side. His mates were forced to take cover and by the time they got back to him Joe was dead.

He was buried in the field close to where he fell at the roadside and was later removed to Romeries Cemetery a few miles away.

It was here that I saw his grave for the first time in 1989 during a visit to the battlefields of the Somme. James had also enlisted at the same time as Joe and was in the R.A.M.C. but he survived the war although he never came home again, preferring to return to New Zealand. William Thomas did return home for a short time but emigrated to New Zealand in 1920 and settled in Dunedin.

He returned with his wife on holiday in 1959. I have visited Joe's grave on four different occasions and believe that I have also found the spot where he was killed on the road outside Le Quesnoy.

The cemetery at Romeries was used for the burial of one of the men who faced the firing squad. Ernest Jackson was already serving under a suspended sentence for a previous offence when he was found guilty and suffered the extreme penalty. He is buried in Plot 4, Row C, Grave 20.

The monument in Ballywatt grounds on which Joseph Thompson is commemorated

Ballywatt Presbyterian Church, circa 1908

CAPTAIN JAMES GASTON, M.C.
Royal Army Medical Corps. attached 4th Bn Suffolk Regiment
D.O.W. 5-11-18
Aged 36
Interred in Arras Road Cemetery, Roclincourt. Plot 2, Row N, Grave 38

Born.   Carabeg, Cloughmills.
Lived
Enlisted   Washington, England.
Eldest son of Andrew and Marian Gaston,
Carabeg, Cloughmills.

When James was just a young boy he attended Drumadoon Primary school. From there he went to Ballymena Academy and then to Queen's University where he graduated as a doctor. He practised in Washington, a small town to the west of Sunderland, in the north-east of England. When he enlisted at Washington he was 33 years of age. He is commemorated on the local War Memorial in his home town of Washington. After joining the Army he was attached to the 4th battalion of the Suffolk Regiment who were in Ipswich when war was declared. They landed at Le Havre on 9th November 1914.

James recieved his commission in January 1915 and joined his unit at Whitchurch, Hants. Soon afterwards he was posted to France where he was to see a great deal of action.

The family of James Gaston have been very helpful and did all they could to help with the story. They also loaned us a number of very interesting items for the exhibition in the Heritage Centre in Ballymoney, among them his Military Cross, the only one we have been able to put on display.

The Citation for the Military Cross, announced in the London Gazette on 26th July 1917, reads as follows.

Temp Capt James Gaston, M.B. R.A.M.C.

"For conspicious gallantry and devotion to duty. He attended the wounded of five other units besides his own throughout the day. The next day he led a party out in front and recovered twelve more wounded who were lying out. Throughout he set a splendid example to all."

Arras Road Cemetery is on the west side of the main N17 road from Arras to Lens, about 6 Kilometres north of Arras, and north of the village of Roclincourt.

Andrew Gaston married Marion Tate

James	Annie	Joseph	Andrew	John	Helena	Alfred
DOW			Capt	doctor		died
5-11-18			RAMC	in England		aged 5

7226 RIFLEMAN ROBERT JOHN McMULLAN
12th Bn Royal Irish Rifles
DIED HOME 17-11-18
Aged 26
Interred in Durrington Cemetery, Wiltshire. No. 352

Born
Lived   Ballymacfin
Enlisted   Ballymoney.
Commemorated in Carncullagh Presbyterian Church.

The 12th battalion was raised in County Antrim mostly in September 1914 from the Antrim Volunteers and by November were in training at Newtownards.

In July 1915 they moved to Seaford on the south coast of England to complete their training and in October, landed at Boulogne. From here they went to the area around Martinsart and Mesnil in time for the Battle of the Somme in July.

Robert survived this battle and went with the battalion to Belgium, where they were kept for over a year. Here they were regularly in and out of the line before their next major conflict, the Battle of Messines. Then in August 1917, the awful conditions of Passchendaele. This was one of the most difficult periods of the whole war. Water was everywhere and every shell-hole was full to the lip. Food and ammunition could only be got forward at night. We can only guess at the difficulties which faced the weary troops under these nightmarish conditions of mud and blood. When this was over the battalion was moved south for the battles around Cambrai and then the confused retreat in the German spring offensive of 1918. It was sometime in late 1918 that Robert became ill and was brought back to hospital in England. After what he had been through he was in no condition to withstand a serious illness and died a short time later. But the war by this time was over. He had lost his life just when his family would have been expecting him home.

Durrington Cemetery has been used by the Military from the beginning of the First World War. It is close to the Military training areas of Bulford and Larkhill. A number of soldiers lost their lives, not from action, but from the bad weather and flu when under training. Robert John died at Fargo Hospital, Durrington, from Tubercular Peritonitis and exhaustion. By this time the family were living at the Urble, Dervock. Ballymacfin and the Urble are adjacent townlands close to Dervock and another soldier who lost his life, George Graham, lived very close to Robert McMullan. The Authorities in Wiltshire also tell me that there was a flu epidemic at this time and it was at the height of this epidemic that Robert died. No mention is made as to why he was not brought home for burial but the reasons may yet become apparent.

Durrington Cemetery, Wilts. Grave of R.J. McMullan

19954 PRIVATE JOHN ARMOUR
5th Bn Royal Inniskilling Fus.
DIED 23-11-18
Aged 31
Interred in Busigny Communal Cemetery Extension, France. Plot 8, Row B, Grave 14.

Born   Ballymoney.
Lived
Enlisted   Glasgow.
Husband of Jane Armour, of 47, Coatbank St, Coatbridge.

John was born in Ballymoney in 1887 and attended school in the town. Soon after leaving school he went to Scotland to look for work and got into the habit of going there every year for seasonal work on the large farms of North Ayrshire and Lanarkshire. He eventually enlisted in Glasgow.

The 5th Battalion were in Gallipoli in 1915 and had disastrous losses there. We don't know for sure if John Armour was with them in Gallipoli. After the evacuation of Gallipoli the 5th Battalion were brought back to France to help with the war effort in that region. By the time of his death on 23rd November the war was already over. He is described as having died, so he had been taken ill, probably during the last few days of the war. There was a very serious Flu epidemic sweeping France at this time and it could well have been this that caused his death. Busigny is to the south-west of Le Cateau so the British Forces had advanced a great distance in pursuit of the German Armies and it was in this part of France that John became ill.

It is also possible that he had been a prisoner of war and had been released by the advancing armies.

Busigny Communal Cemetery

116525 GUNNER JOHN TAGGART
Royal Garrison Artillery
D.O.W. 23-11-18
Interred in Stockport (Willow Grove) Cemetery, Cheshire

Born   Friary, Armoy.
Lived   Friary, Armoy
Enlisted
Commemorated in Kilraughts Presbyterian Church.

The Taggart family worshipped in Kilraughts Presbyterian Church but a search of the nearby graveyard did not reveal a family headstone. It is possible that they used some other burying ground.

The death of John Taggart in a hospital in England almost a fortnight after the war finished was a cruel blow for those at home to take. His brother, Alfred had been killed just a few weeks after war was declared, on 27th October 1914. One brother lost at the very beginning, the other after the end of the war. This is one of the families that I have been unable to trace.

It appears that no-one from the Friary district can now remember the Taggart family living there. It is sad to think that a familly can disappear so completely and as easily as that. John Taggart is buried in Willow Grove Cemetery on the outskirts of Stockport. It has proved extremely difficult if not downright impossible to trace his movements across France and Belgium. Artillery

Willow Grove
Local (Reddish only) War Memorial on Reddish Road

units were not like battalions and were much less mobile. The larger guns were dug in and camouflaged and for long periods were more or less stationary. Very little information has come to light regarding John Taggart and it is unlikely that any more will turn up now.

Cemetery location information
The Cemetery is located at South Reddish, on the Stockport-Reddish road. There are graves from both World Wars in the cemetery.

A war cross is erected and there is also a Screen Wall bearing some of the names.

269045 GUNNER CHARLES MAITLAND STUART
2nd Bn, Reserve Brigade, Royal Field Artillery
DIED OF PNEUMONIA 5-12-18
Aged 18
Interred in Derrykeighan Parish Churchyard

Born
Lived
Enlisted
Son of Mr & Mrs. W.W.L.Stuart, of Glenmanus House, Portrush.
Commemorated in Derrykeighan Parish Church.

Charles Stuart served in the Royal Field Artillery but must have had very little experience of warfare at the front. He was only eighteen years of age when he died of pneumonia a few weeks after the end of the war. He is buried in Derrykeighan New Cemetery. He was probably a cousin of James Stuart who was killed flying behind enemy lines in the area of Vimy Ridge in April 1917.

Le Touret

759 L. CPL. JAMES McCRELLIS
12th Bn Royal Irish Rifles
DIED 4-1-19
Aged 27
Interred in St. Sever Cemetery Extension, Rouen. Plot S 4, Row J, Grave 14

Born
Lived   Stranocum
Enlisted   Ballymoney.
Commemorated in Derrykeighan Parish Church.
Commemorated in Drumtullagh Parish Church.
Son of James McCrellis.
Husband of Lizzie McCrellis, of Mosside.

James McCrellis lived in the Stranocum area, about four miles from Ballymoney.

The family worshipped in Derrykeighan Parish Church but when James got married and moved to live in the Mosside district he joined Drumtullagh Parish Church. He is commemorated in both churches. James enlisted right at the beginning of the war into the 12th battalion of the Royal Irish Rifles and did his training at Clandeboye and Newtownards. He then moved to Seaford, on the south coast of England where he completed his training. In October 1915 the battalion were sent across to France and to the vast training area at St. Omer.

Here they were introduced to trenches for the first time and when they had done their stint in these they moved to the area around Martinsart, close to the Somme.

In this area they dug trenches and did all sorts of military training in preparation for what was to become known as the Battle of the Somme. This has been described sufficiently in other stories to not have to repeat it here. At any rate James survived the first day on the Somme and was taken with his unit back to St Omer for a draft of new recruits. The battalion then moved to Belgium and Wulverghem became their new home. They were here for over a year. By the early summer of 1917 a major offensive was being planned for Messines. The Messines Ridge was being used by the Germans as an observation post and from it they could see everything that the British did for miles around. It had to be taken from them. The date set was to be the 7th of June 1917. Deep mines had been dug all along the ridge and packed with expolsives and on the morning of the attack these were blown. This was a major influence in the winning of that battle. A local man, John Meeke of Benvarden, was one of the men responsible for seeing that the mines were properly blown here.

John Meeke won the Military Medal for attending to the injured Major Redmond on this day. John died a few years after the end of the war and to this day lies in an unmarked grave in Derrykeighan Old Cemetery.

After this the battalion moved into the region north-east of Ypres for the Battle of Passchendaele and then Langemarck. They then moved south for the Battle of Cambrai in November of 1917. This was followed by a move south again to St. Quentin, where they had to try to stem the German Spring Offensive of March 1918. Here they were pushed back at an alarming rate as the enemy threw everything into a last desperate attack. It was during this attack that it is believed James was taken prisoner. He suffered immensely over the next few months in a prisoner of war camp in Germany. Eventually he was released back into British hands but by this time his physical condition was such that he could hardly walk. He was taken to a nearby hospital for treatment but had to be removed to the large hospital at Rouen in a last desperate attempt to save him, but by this time he was too ill and died there a few weeks later. He is buried in the nearby cemetery.

28917 PRIVATE SAMUEL MEEKE
2nd Bn Royal Inniskilling Fusiliers
DIED HOME 19-1-19
Aged 19
Interred in Derrykeighan Old Graveyard

*Born Dervock
Lived Benvarden
Enlisted Coleraine
Son of John Meeke, of Benvarden.*

Samuel was a prisoner in the most notorious of the German prison camps and was forced to work in the sulphur mines. He was released after the Armistice, but died a fortnight after arriving home. He was buried in Derrykeighan Old Graveyard and was the son of John Meeke, a gardener to Montgomery's of Benvarden. Another son, John, had a very interesting career in the Army. Private John Meeke, Royal Inniskilling Fusiliers, was the first man to render assistance to the late Major Willie Redmond, (Irish Brigade) and was severely wounded in the side, was home on leave in August 1917, having recovered from his injury. He enlisted on 14th March 1916, and went to France in July. It was at the Battle of Messines on the 7th of June 1917 that he won the Military Medal for gallant conduct and devotion to duty. The Irish Brigade was on the left of the Ulster Division, and the combined infantry of the Irish regiments had made a successful charge. The Germans threw up a heavy barrage to prevent our reserves coming up. With 2,400 British heavy guns hammering away at the German positions, not to mention the German barrage, the ground in front of the British front line trench across which our men had charged, was literally ploughed up with shells. Although it was daylight it was impossible to see more than a few yards ahead, so thick was the smoke of shells and fire. It was only when the flare lights lit up the scene that a portion of the battlefield could be seen. Private Meeke, who was a stretcher bearer, was in the front line trench waiting on the order to go over the top to assist the wounded when the bombardment lessened. He happened to see Major Redmond fall, and voluntarily went over the top, made to render assistance, taking shelter in shell holes and other cover on the way. He arrived at the Major's side without injury, and found him seriously wounded in the left knee and right arm at the elbow and weak from loss of blood. Major Redmond had hounded his superior officers until they relented and allowed him to go over the top with his men, but only to go to a certain point and then he had to return. He had almost reached this point when he was injured. Shells were dropping all around, and the rattle of machine-guns added to the danger of the task. He had one of the wounds dressed, and was working at the other, when a piece of shrapnel struck him on the left side, inflicting a serious wound. This did not deter him from his work, which he completed despite his injury. Soon there was a lull in the bombardment. Another "Tommy", with two German prisoners appeared, and Major Redmond being placed on a stretcher was carried to the dressing station by the German prisoners, accompanied by their two escorts.

Although the wound was bleeding freely, Private Meeke continued to render assistance to the wounded. Three times he was ordered back but manfully stuck to his task of mercy, until he became so weak from the loss of blood, that he had to be taken to the dressing station. Major Redmond, on reaching the dressing station, was attended to by Captain Boyd Campbell, R.A.M.C., nephew of Dr. Boyd, Ballymoney. He died later that day and is buried near Locre hospice. John Meeke survived the war but died at home in 1923 probably from the results of the hardships endured during 1914-18. He is buried near to his brother in an unmarked grave in Derrykeighan Old Graveyard.

Entry in the Chronicle in December 1923.

There was a large attendance on Sunday afternoon at the funeral of Mr John Meeke, Benvarden, who died at 28 years of age. He was a member of the U.V.F. and served with the Ulster Division in France where he was awarded the Military Medal for giving first aid under heavy fire to Captain Willie Redmond, though himself wounded. He stayed with the injured officer until some of the Division, escorting German prisoners, came to the rescue and who brought Captain Redmond in. Meeke was also one of the six men told to be with the Royal Engineers officer who exploded the mine at Messines on 7th June 1917. He was again wounded very severely in October 1918, by an explosive bullet, and underwent eight operations on his leg. He was a member of Benvarden L.O.L. 1001. His widow, now left with two infants, was injured in a projectile factory where she worked during the war and she had three brothers wounded during the war. The three were —— Fred Downes of Islandcarragh, serving in the Royal Inniskilling Fusiliers, was wounded at Messines and was home on leave in August 1917. Alex Downes, serving in the Royal Irish Rifles, was wounded twice, and in August 1917 was back in France for the third time. John Downes, serving in the Tank Section of the Inniskillings, was wounded once. Their Father, Joe Downes, lost two fingers while serving with the Royal Engineers.

Another brother, Patrick, died on 22nd March 1924, aged 16.

Entry in the Chronicle in January 1919.

There was widespread sorrow evidenced at the funeral on Tuesday afternoon of Private Samuel Meeke, Benvarden. The deceased lad, for he was only 19 years old joined up before he was of age, so anxious was he to serve his King and Country, and after seeing considerable service with his battalion, was taken prisoner in the great German push of March 1918. His captors were no more merciful to this boy than to thousands of men of more mature years. He was sent to the camp at Langansalza which has become notorious over the shooting of some French prisoners. He was here subjected to such ill-treatment and privation that on being re-patriated he was a physical wreck, and only two weeks ago arrived at his parents quiet country home at Benvarden, which he had fought and suffered to save, but only to linger for a few days. The remains were accorded full military honours on Tuesday, a firing party of thirteen men, under a Sergeant and Corporal, being sent from Belfast to pay a last tribute of respect to the memory of a gallant young comrade.

Samuel was taken prisoner on 21st March 1918, and his father received a letter from him in May 1918 with this news.

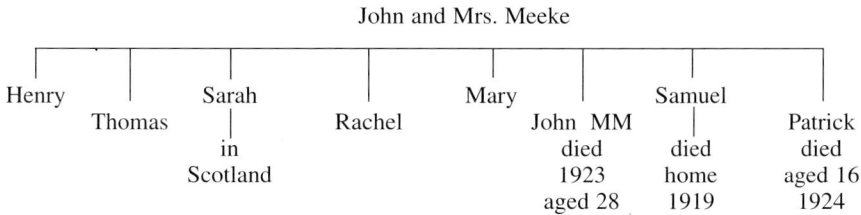

CORPORAL JAMES HANNA
American Forces
DIED 13-2-19
Aged 27
Interred in Oise-Aisne American Cemetery, Plot A, Row 21, Grave 4

Born   Bushside, Stranocum
Lived   Stranocum.
Enlisted America
Son of James and Jane Hanna of the Bushside.

James was the youngest of a family of six, three boys and three girls. At that time the family lived at the Bushside and all six of the children attended Clintyfinnan old school. As they grew up and became independent each of them in turn emigrated to America, all except the second son, John, who decided to stay at home and work the farm.

That part of the family still lives in the Stranocum area. James enlisted in America and arrived in France with his unit in April 1917. He survived the war itself but died in the very bad flu epidemic which swept France after the cessation of hostilities. A Memorial card in the posession of Norman Hanna reads as follows.

Died on 13th February 1919 at the base hospital, 101 St Nazaire, France and was laid to rest with full military honours in the American Base Cemetery at 21 St Nazaire, France, and the Guard of Honour was 346th Inf.

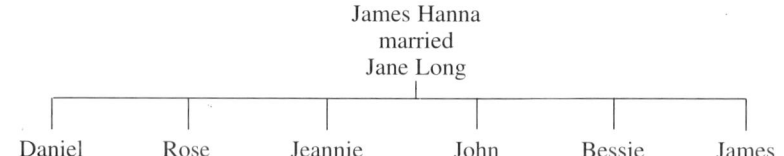

James Hanna married Jane Long

| Daniel | Rose | Jeannie | John | Bessie | James |

2ND LIEUT JAMES PATTISON
10th Bn Highland Light Infantry
DIED 27-2-19
Aged 28
Interred in Rutherglen Cemetery, Lanarkshire, Section 'J', Grave 77

Born   Ballymoney
Lived   Glasgow
Enlisted   Glasgow
Son of James and Jane Pattison of 21.
Polmaddie Road, Glasgow.

James Pattison was born in Ballymoney in about 1891. At some stage after this the family appears to have moved to Glasgow. Work in the Ballymoney district was scarce and prospects were better across the water, so in order to keep the family in better circumstances, they moved.

The shipyards in Glasgow in the period just prior to the First World War were a hive of activity and could well have provided the stability that the family craved. James enlisted at Glasgow and after obtaining his commission, was posted to the 10th battalion of the Highland Light Infantry. He served throughout the war but died in Glasgow just four months after the cessation of hostilities. He is buried in Rutherglen cemetery in Glasgow and was just twenty-eight years of age.

Pozieres

LT LESLIE ERNEST McNEILL
4th Royal Irish Dragoon Guards
DIED 25-3-19
Aged 32
Interred in Sanderstead (All Saints) Churchyard, Surrey

Born   Gardenvale, Stranocum.
Lived   Gardenvale, Stranocum.
Enlisted
Commemorated in Derrykeighan Parish Church.
Son of Adam and Janetta McNeill of Gardenvale, Stranocum.

Leslie Ernest McNeill enlisted at the beginning of the war and was promoted 2nd Lieut in February 1915, for services in the field, and gazzetted to the 4th Royal Irish Dragoon Guards He was one of the McNeills of Gardenvale, a son of Adam and Janetta McNeill. He died in South London, after a lengthy period of ill health, thought to have been the after effects of gas, and is buried in Sanderstead (All Saints) Churchyard, Surrey. Some years ago, vandals entered the Churchyard and about twenty memorial headstones were broken, including the one on Lt McNeill's grave. This has now been placed on the grave itself.

His brother, Sydney, a Lieutenant in the 18th R.I.R., also served, but survived he war, and came home to manage the family estate at Gardenvale.

It isn't yet clear just when the McNeills came to Gardenvale but believe that it was in the early 1920's, prompted, no doubt, by the deaths of Bobbie and Leslie. They originally came from Beckenham in Kent and this is probably the reason for the burials in London. Their youngest son, Bobbie Alexander Fulton McNeill, died on 26th July 1910, aged 21 and is buried in the same plot.

Janetta McNeill died at Gardenvale on 27th March 1921 followed three years later by Adam on 8th June 1924.

Sydney died on 11th November 1960, aged 78, at Gardenvale, and his sister Margaret, who was married and had spent most of her life in England, died on 12th February 1968. These last four are buried in Derrykeighan New Cemetery.

It would seem probable that Margaret had come to Gardenvale to tend her brother in his last years and had remained there.

304188 AIRCRAFTMAN 2ND CL. DAVID GETTY
Royal Air Force
DIED 5-1-20
Aged 18
Interred in Cologne Southern British Cemetery, Germany. Plot 6, Row A, Grave 16

Born   Ballywattick, Ballymoney.
Lived   Ballywattick, Ballymoney.
Enlisted

David Getty had been stationed at Cologne in Germany just after the cessation of hostilities. He was not yet eighteen. In September, on his way home on leave, he rendered valuable service during the railway strike in England, as a result of which his leave was extended by six weeks. He had been back in Germany about a month when the news of his death reached his parents at Ballywattick, the result of an accident while on duty. Another report describes it as a motoring accident in Cologne. His only surviving sister, Sadie, was training to be a nurse in North Staffordshire Infirmary, in England when she contracted pneumonia and died on 8th April 1920.

Sadie was brought home to be buried in Ballymoney.

This was a devastating blow to a family who had already lost their other daughter, Elizabeth, some time before, and then, their son David, in January.

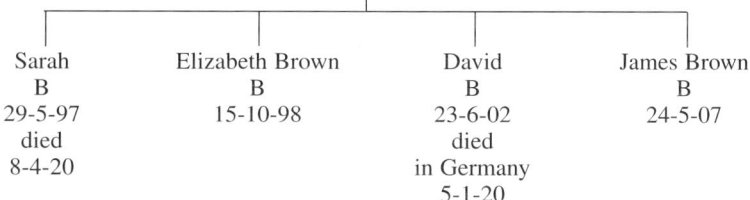

John Getty married Matilda Jane Brown
in St.James's Pres Church on 6th February 1895

Sarah	Elizabeth Brown	David	James Brown
B	B	B	B
29-5-97	15-10-98	23-6-02	24-5-07
died		died	
8-4-20		in Germany	
		5-1-20	

Cologne Southern British Cemetery in Germany. David's grave is 5th from right, back row.

20404 RIFLEMAN JAMES LAVERTY
Depot, Royal Irish Rifles
DIED 22-2-1920
Aged 22
Interred in Billy Parish Churchyard

Born   *Liscolman*
Lived
Enlisted
Son of Francis and Margaret Laverty, of Bouverie St, Port Glasgow.

James was born at Liscolman, the son of Francis and Margaret Laverty, in 1898.

It is believed that he saw a lot of action during the later stages of the war and was suffering from the after effects of gas. Later on, towards the end of the war, he was suffering from ill health and was allowed to serve at the Depot in Belfast.

This worked well for a time but his health did not improve and gradually he became worse until he had to go into hospital. He died of heart failure in the Military Barracks in Clifton Street, Belfast, late on the evening of 22nd February 1920 after suffering from Tuberculosis of the lungs for over a year and a half. His death was registered the following day and arrangements made for his funeral. He is buried in Billy Parish Churchyard, close to Bushmills. His parents appear to have moved to live in Port Glasgow, probably through the need to find steady work, and Billy would most likely have been the family burying ground. As James had not been married it is very unlikely that the family still survives. An appeal placed in the Greenock Telegraph in April 1999 produced nothing and the many people that I have spoken to in this district do not remember them.

The headstone in the grounds of Billy Parish Church has always intrigued me and it is nice to find out at last what was the cause of death. James was only twenty-two years of age when he died in 1920. This is the only instance in this publication of a soldier being buried in his own country apart from John Culbertson, who is buried in Dublin.

17974 RIFLEMAN WILLIAM J. JOHNSTON
13th Bn Royal Irish Rifles
DOW. 10-7-16
Aged 19
Interred in St. Sever Cemetery, Rouen. Plot A, Row 25, Grave 15.

Born   Hillsborough
Lived   Hillsborough
Enlisted   Lisburn
Commemorated in Ballymoney Parish Church

Son of William Johnston, of Hillsborough, Co. Down. William Johnston must have been a very young man when he enlisted and probably well under age like many of the rest of them. There are reasons why I am not content that this is the William Johnston that is commemorated in Ballymoney Parish Church. For a start he was born in Hillsborough and was living there. It is true that he may have been working in the Ballymoney area but his age would not have allowed him to have been any length of time there and certainly not long enough to have been established in the church and have his name commemorated there. The War Graves Commission have not been able to give me the name of any other soldier so I am stuck with this one. William enlisted at Lisburn but had he been working in Ballymoney surely he would have enlisted there. At any rate he was very severely wounded at the Somme and was evacuated to Rouen where he died of his wounds a few days later. He is buried in St. Sever Cemetery in that city.

PRIVATE JOHN CARSON
Canadians

Born
Lived
Enlisted

The name of John Carson appears on an old hand written Roll of Honour for Rasharkin district. Although I have been unable to find any other details to properly identify John Carson, there is no reason to doubt the validity of the hand written notes. They are correct in every other detail.

The notes do not give an address for any of the names mentioned but are very carefully written and came to me through Mrs Jennifer Bamford. The notes are a very careful record of those who lost their lives and of those who served.

It is sad that we cannot do the same for John Carson as we have done for the others, that is, record the date of death and where he is buried, but there are just not enough details.

He obviously came from the Rasharkin, Finvoy district but is not commemorated in any of the churches. Like the others, he is not forgotten.

PRIVATE PATRICK WILSON

Born   Bushside, Stranocum.
Lived   Bushside, Stranocum.
Enlisted
Son of Mary Ann Wilson, of the Bushside.

Patrick was the son of Mary Ann Wilson of the Bushside. Very little is known about him but the family tell me that he was brought up by Tillie McFarland of the Bushside and that Mary Ann later married a man named Burns from Balnamore. On the outbreak of hostilities Patrick enlisted but we don't know whether he enlisted under Wilson or McFarland, or used a false name. At any rate I have been unable to find any information which would lead to a positive identification.

The War Graves Commission have been unable to find any trace of him in their records which would suggest that he probably used a false name when he enlisted. So it would appear that nothing more will ever be known of Patrick Wilson. It is sad when a case like this turns up and no information is available, not even a date of death.

All we know is that he was killed in action during the 1st World War somewhere in France or Belgium.

JAMES McCLEAN
Royal Air Force

Born
Lived Cloughmills.
Enlisted
Commemorated in Killagan Parish Church.

GUNNER JOHN McKAY
Royal Field Artillery

Born Brevallen
Lived
Enlisted
Commemorated in 1st Ballymoney Presbyterian Church.

John McKay was born at Brevallen, a townland just a short distance to the south of Ballymoney. The family worshipped in 1st Ballymoney Presbyterian Church and it is there that John is commemorated. John enlisted into the Royal Field Artillery but a number of appeals in the newspapers have drawn a blank and it would appear that the family have died out.

William Thomson.

Can anyone identify the men in this picture.